P9-DHH-976

Social Problems in America

Social Problems

with illustrations by John Groth

NEW YORK, LONDON

in America

Costs and casualties in an acquisitive society

HARRY C. BREDEMEIER

Associate Professor of Sociology
Douglass College, Rutgers University
New Brunswick, New Jersey

JACKSON TOBY

Associate Professor of Sociology
Rutgers University
New Brunswick, New Jersey

JOHN WILEY & SONS, INC.

FOURTH PRINTING, FEBRUARY, 1963

Copyright © 1960 by John Wiley & Sons, Inc.

All rights reserved. This book or any part thereof
must not be reproduced in any form without the
written permission of the publisher.

Library of Congress Catalog Card Number: 60–5596
Printed in the United States of America

To Talcott Parsons, whose ideas we have borrowed freely

Foreword

Readers who go through this book are likely not to be quite the same afterwards.

Here is an analysis of American social problems which provides the combination of an orderly intellectual framework with a remarkable collection of vignettes of direct human experience. The reader is confronted with sound modern sociological thinking. But the concepts are not left dangling in a thin, cold upper atmosphere. They are brought directly into the heart as well as the mind, as one shares vicariously in the concrete frustrations, struggles, capitulations, or aggressive reaction formations of individuals and groups.

This book is the fruit of many years of experience in teaching undergraduates. A course in Social Problems, the authors believe, should be Education in the highest sense—not just imparting facts about social pathology, but challenging complacency and stretching the students' minds to think freshly and to feel deeply about things which they may have taken for granted.

The authors love America and American institutions. But as social scientists they know that in any society there are tensions, generated often by the very ideals which are most basic and most honored in that society. America is, of course, not an exception. And the authors pull no punches in showing in detail wherein this is so. The rewards for success are high—higher than perhaps anywhere in human history. But, correspondingly, the *relative* deprivation of failure is necessarily also high, even though *absolute* deprivation may be lower in America than in societies most of whose members can have only minimal aspirations.

In any society, the book says, there are group standards of adequacy, worthiness, gratification, and security which the individual is expected to meet. When he fails to achieve satisfactions through socially acceptable experiences, he may seek to obtain them through socially unacceptable experiences. Thus, individual frustrations are transformed into social problems.

The American pursuit of success, the authors show, can be conceptualized in terms of four major governing principles: materialism-secularism, self-reliance, competition, and negotiated exchange. These set standards and rules as to how we come in contact with what we want and as to which members of society have control over what scarce facilities.

Some members of our society accept defeat, and this passive behavior can take the forms of withdrawal or submission. Others, who refuse to accept defeat, can generate social problems in either of two directions, by the rejection of one of the principles governing the pursuit of success or by overaggressive and even ruthless adherence to these principles.

The case materials which often make vividly alive the ideas in this book come from an almost startling variety of sources. Some of it is autobiographical—for example, excerpts from Richard Wright or Whittaker Chambers. Some is from articles in the *New York Times, Harpers, The New Yorker* and other magazines. Some is from professional journals. Some—and this by no means dull either—is from court opinions. Some represents distillations of thinking about relevant topics in the American scene by a most diverse list of eminent commentators, several of them not academic. And some is straight fiction or drama, aptly chosen, for example, like the selections from *The Member of the Wedding* and *Picnic* in an early chapter.

Because this is a challenging book, not every teacher will agree with all of it. I, myself, would have hit harder at some points and not so hard at others. Others will feel likewise, and perhaps for different reasons. Some teachers may prefer an organization about problem areas—where crime, delinquency, alcoholism, etc., are taken up one by one and disposed of in turn—to an organization like that of Bredemeier and Toby which uses such problems all through the book, as *illustrative* of how strains and deviance are generated, given American goals and values. From their own teaching experience, the authors believe that their format "works" and is good. Good, that is, if a course's primary objectives transcend the communication of so-called facts and figures and aspire to the stimulation of an understanding of the deeper *whys*.

Samuel A. Stouffer
Professor of Sociology
Harvard University

Preface

The listing of names on the title page is a consequence of alphabetical accident; it does not signify inequality of participation. Our book is a joint product, and both of us accept full responsibility for every chapter.

In our teaching of "social problems," we have been impressed with the seeming lack of continuity between one topic and the next in many textbooks. A "social problems" course often provides a Cook's tour of personal and social pathologies rather than a systematic analysis of the significance of the symptoms held up to view. We wondered whether sociological theory could impart a coherent framework to the social problems field. We concluded that this was possible if sociologists were willing to chop conventional topics up and recombine them in new ways.

This we have done in the present book. The result is somewhat disconcerting—even to us, the authors. When we look at the table of contents, we see no familiar "Alcoholism" or "Family Disorganization" staring back. As a colleague, who saw the galley proofs, pointed out, he would not have known that ours is a social problems textbook were it not for the title. Truth to tell, however, most of the familiar problems *are* in the book. Look at the index if you are skeptical. We hope that the theoretical advantages of our framework will justify the far-reaching revisions we have made in the usual organization of social problems courses.

A second difficulty with many social problems textbooks is that they often seem dull to the student. Partly this is because of the telephone-directory organization just mentioned: the subject seems to change very rapidly. Partly it is because very few sociologists can write six hundred pages of scintillating exposition. Recognizing *our* literary shortcomings and yet wishing to present the material in as interesting a manner as possible, we decided to use illustrative readings. Do not be deceived, however. This is not just a collection of articles. We systematically defined for ourselves the characteristics of an illustration called for by our conceptual scheme and then scoured the literature to find an article that would meet our demands. Despite the small proportion of text which we have written ourselves, we consider ourselves authors rather than editors.

Now that we have differentiated our product positively, we must also concede its limitations. The focus of our book is almost entirely on the *genesis* of "problems." That is, we do not present statistics on the extent or seriousness of the social problems we discuss. By way of justification, we might point out that statistical data quickly become outdated. Second, we do not, except by implication (in the final chapter), proffer solutions. We feel that "solutions" can be most fruitfully considered after an understanding of the nature and sources of problems has been developed. We hope that these omissions will be taken care of by the instructor in his own ways through lectures and supplementary readings.

Third, and finally, we fear that the over-all impression of American society conveyed by our book is negative. In our effort to show the genesis of social problems in America, we emphasize those aspects of American society which (we believe) produce problems, and, necessarily, we ignore aspects of American society which (we believe) are achievements of human spirit. Specifically, we suggest that a competitive struggle for material possessions and social status produces a high rate of human casualties and certain inefficiencies in social organization. Nevertheless, we do not mean to imply that materialistic concerns are wholly destructive. The high standard of living which materialistic concerns help to bring about is more than gadgetry. It means longer life expectancy, less disease, less physical suffering and discomfort. A high standard of living means greater potential opportunity for widespread participation in the intellectual and artistic triumphs of society. Materialistic concerns also constitute a favorable climate for the development of science, technology, and rationality. Furthermore, it may be that a fairly high level of material welfare is a prerequisite for personal liberty and community self-government. In short, we *like* American society and our criticisms are not to be taken for over-all condemnation.

We believe that sociology should describe the functioning of social arrangements as accurately as possible, and the factors making for weakness and strife are just as important scientifically as those making for cohesiveness and strength. It so happens that the division of labor within sociology allocates to the social problems field a lugubrious enterprise: auditing casualties and costs. We, the authors, are not dismayed by our survey. Analysis of the forces generating casualties is a necessary step in reducing them.

We hopefully anticipate a more favorable balance sheet in the twenty-first century.

It would be indecent to end this preface without acknowledging the many ways in which we have been aided by Mrs. Marley O'Neil and Mrs. Barbara Reich Sivertson.

Harry C. Bredemeier

November 1959   *Jackson Toby*

Contents

xiv

PART ONE

Conceptual overview

CHAPTER ONE

Human needs and social problems

Benjamin Franklin's advice to the leaders of the American Revolution, "We must hang together or we shall certainly hang separately," could well serve as the slogan of the human race. Human beings cannot survive at all in isolation from one another, and they have abilities which enable them to profit handsomely from joint action. Both aspects of man—his extreme dependence and his augmented capacities when united with others—are based on a combination of biological and socio-cultural characteristics.

CONSPICUOUS CHARACTERISTICS OF HUMAN BEINGS

1. *Plasticity*. In an ant society the ant with the role of laying eggs is biologically forced to lay eggs. She can no more escape her egg-laying destiny than a fish can decide to walk instead of swim. With man it is different. No human being is biologically compelled to be a devoted mother or a conscientious worker or a brave soldier. This freedom from highly specific biological determination of behavior is what is meant by man's plasticity: Relatively few of his actions are genetically built-in. The range of possible responses to a stimulus on the part of a human being is very great. He can, for example, respond to a pain in his side by suspecting witchcraft and employing a sorcerer to charm it away, by thinking of appendicitis and summoning a surgeon, or by believing that it is "psychosomatic" and visiting his psychiatrist. In other words, human beings react to stimuli in terms of what they have learned. Moreover, they can learn from others' experiences as well as their own.

2. *Symbol Making and Symbol Using Capacity*. Basic to the human ability to learn is the capacity to make and use symbols.[1] Lower animals perceive what they perceive *directly*—that is, without the intervention of symbols. Man, on the other hand, is not the prisoner of his immediate experience. He can relate the tree he saw yesterday to the tree he sees today and to the idea of a tree. If man 1 could tell man 2 about a tree he had seen only if man 2 saw the same tree at the same time, communication would be a meager affair. Luckily, ideas which refer to classes of objects are able to convey meanings even though experience is not identical. That is why symbols are so useful. They vastly expand the range of communication which is possible and the range of stimuli which can elicit human response.

3. *Dependence*. Even on a purely physical level, man is extraordinarily dependent on his fellows. Human infants are helpless at birth, and for several years thereafter they cannot survive without nurturance. In adulthood, the dependence is no less pronounced, although, being less spectacular, it usually passes unnoticed until something happens to disrupt orderly cooperation, such as a nation-wide transportation strike. Then people begin to realize how dependent they are on the cooperation of others whom they may neither know nor care to know. One of

[1] A symbol is any observable entity—a sound, a gesture, a written mark—which arbitrarily stands for something else.

the critical problems of human society stems from the fact that cooperation is both essential and problematical. That is, in view of the relative freedom of man from biological determination, it cannot be taken for granted that the necessary cooperation will be forthcoming as it can in an ant or a termite society. (One writer has suggested that we can understand much about human behavior if we think of human beings as creatures with anthropoid equipment who are trying to live like termites.)

Man's plasticity and his capacity for making and using symbols heighten further the need for cooperation. They make it both possible and necessary for men to cooperate in the *assignment of meaning*. The meaning of a symbol is, by definition, arbitrary. Unlike the relationship between clouds and rain, the relationship between a symbol and the thing it stands for does not exist in nature. (For example, there is no biological reason why a feeling of hostility should result in the expression, "Go to hell!") Meaning is put there by the consensus of human beings. Without such consensus, communication is impossible. That is why, although one language is as good as another for purposes of interpersonal communication, it is very important that all members of the *same* community learn the *same* language. The necessity of maintaining a common symbol system is thus a basic form of mutual dependence.[2]

Symbols are to human beings what instincts are to other animals. Symbols are the glasses through which man looks at the world; an adult human being can scarcely perceive anything without the intervention of symbols. As an illustration of this principle, consider what happens when you are hungry. You do not simply crave food (anything at all that is nutritious). You crave beefsteak rather than horsemeat; and even starvation might not induce you to eat grubs, worms, mice, or another human being. These things are edible; human beings eat them in other parts of the world. But Americans are *symbolically* conditioned to regard certain nutritious objects as "food," and other equally nutritious objects as revolting. So, provided the symbols are clear—provided you know what the menu consists of—you are either gastronomically interested or you are nauseated. Similarly, symbols determine who is sexually attractive to Americans and on what occasions; it is never the sex drive alone. There is no biological reason why college students are more likely to

[2] Since the meaning of symbols is arbitrary, it is possible for human beings, under certain circumstances, to attach symbolic meanings to objects or events that are incomprehensible to other members of the community. We say that such persons are psychotic.

grow amorous in a parked car by moonlight than at 10:30 A.M. during a sociology lecture.

In short, symbols organize man's perceptions; they abstract aspects of reality for him to pay attention to. They tell him what to see or hear and how to respond to what he sees and hears. Determination by symbols is thus the distinctive character of human responses: It leads simultaneously to man's greatest triumphs and his most grievous errors. No animal but man could discover atomic energy because none but he can invent the symbol "atom." On the other hand, no animal but man has incinerated members of his own species because none but he can invent the symbols, "National Destiny" and "inferior races." On the one hand, symbolic development frees man to think and to love as lower animals cannot possibly do. On the other hand, it makes possible a special kind of slavery, enslavement to one's misperceptions of reality. The hallucinations and delusions of a psychotic person are dramatic examples of symbolic enslavement, but all human beings distort reality to some extent.

4. *Self-Evaluation.* Related to man's dependence on symbols is his self-consciousness. Unlike the horse or the cat, the human being is inescapably self-conscious; he perceives himself as an object.[3] He can be proud or ashamed of himself. He can treat himself as a tool to serve some "higher purpose," or he can elevate himself into a cause which everything else should serve. He often comes to love himself so much that he cannot conceive of the world without himself in it, but at the same time he is intellectually aware that all human beings die. The incompatibility between his intellectual awareness and his self-love may drive him to attempt to preserve his self from the threat of extinction by identifying it with some more permanent object: science, the United States, God, the human race, the Master Race.

Self-consciousness implies another dimension of man's dependence on his fellows: dependence on the attitudes of others. He is influenced in his self-evaluation by the evaluations that he learns others make of him. Human beings need more than food,

---

[3] "Perceiving the self as an object" should not be confused with "perceiving the self *objectively*." The human capacity for objectifying makes self-evaluations not only possible but inescapable. However, these self-evaluations are not necessarily objective. On the contrary, psychology has documented what political theory has long asserted, that no man can be trusted to be a fair judge in his own case. We often take a generous view of our own failings and an exaggerated view of our own virtues—although it is equally possible to err in the opposite direction by imputing all virtue and nobility to others and all sin and evil to ourselves. To be objective about oneself is extremely difficult.

shelter, and clothing; they crave praise, affection, esteem, and other symbolic rewards. Human beings develop an image of themselves which is a complex mixture of their perceptions of others' images of them and their reactions to those perceptions. When people communicate to you that they perceive you as bad, ugly, stupid, or awkward, you are psychologically wounded. You may respond to the wound by enduring it, by coming to perceive yourself as bad, ugly, stupid, or awkward; or you may respond to it by hotly asserting the opposite. But however you respond, you are influenced by the attitudes of others.

This process of evaluation by others leads to defensive maneuvering in order to minimize the pain of an unfavorable self-evaluation. Such maneuvering is of central concern here because the assumption of this book is that the individual's satisfactions or frustrations influence his relations with other people. He is constantly engaged in the process of evaluating himself in terms of the symbolic standards which he knows other people use in evaluating him. Just as human beings respond to pains in the side according to their interpretation of the *meaning* of a pain in the side, so they respond to themselves in terms of socio-cultural standards of evaluation which they have learned. They must adjust in one way or another to the self-images developed thereby. Under certain conditions these adjustments involve behavior which constitutes "social problems" and under other conditions these adjustments involve behavior which is considered socially desirable. What these conditions are will be discussed in a later section of the book. At this point more attention will be given to the standards by which people are evaluated by themselves and by others.

Four kinds of standards which nearly all human beings acquire can be distinguished. The first two, standards of adequacy and standards of worthiness, are symbolic yardsticks which assess the individual's conformity to impersonal rules. The other two, standards of gratification and standards of security, prescribe the kinds of satisfactions the individual learns to need, crave, demand, or expect.

THE STANDARDS OF SELF-EVALUATION

1. *Standards of Adequacy.* Every group or society has tasks for its members to perform—growing crops, hunting buffalo, building bridges, studying chemistry, and so on. The recognition of different degrees of skill or competence at those tasks is also found universally; and the ideas of how competent one should be are what we mean by "standards of adequacy." Whatever the

human individual is doing, shooting a bow and arrow or ordering wines to go with a dinner, his behavior is measured (by
himself and others) according to some cultural standard of competent performance. Measuring up to the standard gives the
individual a feeling of achievement and self-satisfaction; falling
below it produces a painful sense of failure, of self-devaluation,
of shame.

2. *Standards of Worthiness.* Not only are there, in all human
groups, standards of *how* people should do various things; there
are also cultural judgments of *what* things people should do and
be. It is never enough to be competent at anything at all. In
order to have a favorable self-image, one must be competent at
doing *what the culture regards as important.* The most proficient
taker-of-scalps in modern American society is not likely to sustain the favorable self-image that his counterpart in eighteenth
century Sioux Indian society could derive from the same accomplishment.

The cultural beliefs of *what* it is good to do and be are what
we mean by standards of worthiness. Which is better: to be a
warrior, or a priest, or a businessman? There is no scientifically
demonstrable way to answer this question, but every group
answers it nonetheless. The answers are contained in the culture's arbitrary symbolic definitions of worthiness. They influence importantly the individual's self-respect or self-contempt.
In American society it is generally considered "better" to be a
banker than to be a ditch-digger; to be white than to be Negro;
to be invited to dinner with the Van Astorbilts than to be invited
by the Smiths; to be religious than to be atheistic.

3. *Standards of Gratification.* So far the standards discussed
have been impersonal yardsticks, which people use to help them
answer the question, "Am I deserving?" Consider now the
standards people use to answer a different, though related, question: "What is it that I deserve?" The first of the latter sort of
standards, standards of gratification, are the cultural norms that
define fulfillment: what it is that gives life "point," makes it
worth living. In the United States, for example, boys may learn
that driving an automobile at high speeds is "fun"; girls may
learn that being taken to a nightclub where dancing, drinking,
and conspicuous waste of money occurs is important. If the individual fails to secure enough of the experiences which his
society defines as intrinsically worthwhile, he feels he is missing
out on something; he is dissatisfied.

4. *Standards of Security.* In addition to the symbolic definitions of fulfillment, the individual learns what constitute (in his

society) desirable emotional bonds with other people, and these become part of his expectations. In American society, where romantic love is so prominent, solidarities between adult males and adult females are emphasized. The ideal is one of great intensity and intimacy between a man and a woman. In other cultures other solidarities are emphasized: among siblings; between the generations of a family line; among adolescents of the same sex. But in all societies the individual learns to want to be accepted by other people. He learns his culture's conception of the feeling of "belonging." To the extent that he does not experience it, he feels rootless, lonely, insecure.

Societies differ with respect to the relative emphases placed on these four standards and with respect to the difficulties in the way of the individual's effort to live up to them. They differ also with respect to the interrelationships among the four standards. Individuals may learn, for example, that security and solidarity are theirs regardless of their adequacy; or they may learn that they can expect support and love from others only if they "earn" it by performing at a certain level of competence. In Part III of this book, four governing principles of American Society will be analyzed in order to assess the source of the difficulties Americans experience in trying to live up to socio-cultural standards of adequacy, worthiness, gratification, and security.

In Part Two, the emphasis will be, not upon causes of frustrations in attempting to meet such standards, but rather upon their initial effects. We shall try to convey an understanding of psychic suffering by giving the reader an opportunity to identify sympathetically with the victims. The justification for an extended treatment of the subjective side of frustration is this: The self-consciousness of human beings makes the *experiencing* of frustration an intervening variable between the unsatisfying situation and what the individual does about it. In Part IV, various problems of American society will be interpreted as efforts on the part of dissatisfied persons to make their life situations bearable.[4] As preparation for this discussion, it is necessary to understand first how much pain symbolic wounds can inflict.

[4] We are concentrating our attention on psychic pain, although it is certainly true that man, like other animals, can experience biological deprivation or injury such as hunger, thirst, sickness, fatigue, wounds. Such physical pain is probably incompatible with satisfaction; but we assume that physical pain is, at least for most Americans, less commonly experienced than psychic suffering; and the latter, therefore, is a more important motivating factor in American behavior. For an excellent discussion of this position by a psychologist, see A. H. Maslow, "Deprivation, Threat, and Frustration," *Psychological Review*, Vol. 48 (1941), pp. 364–366.

SUMMARY

Human beings need one another. One aspect of this dependence is the individual's adoption of group standards of adequacy, worthiness, gratification, and security. This means that he needs to feel that he can do competently the tasks his fellows think he ought to do; that what he is or does is a good thing to be or do; that he is getting a sense of fulfillment out of life; and that he "belongs," that there are others who care about him and about whom he cares, whose lives are closely interwoven with his. These feelings are necessary if the individual is not to be a conscious or unconscious rebel against the arrangements of his society. Moreover, they are interdependent. The individual cannot enjoy pleasures if he is anxious about his competence at his job, if he feels inferior because of a low I.Q. or a brown skin, or if he feels that no one cares whether he lives or dies. When these feelings of satisfaction are not available through socially acceptable experiences, one may seek to obtain them through socially unacceptable experiences. Thus, individual frustrations are transformed into social problems.

ANNOTATED BIBLIOGRAPHY

Boulding, Kenneth, *The Image* (Ann Arbor: University of Michigan Press, 1956). ⟨ Written by one of the foremost economists of the country. Boulding spent a year at the Institute for Advanced Study in the Behavioral Sciences at Stanford, California. This is a summary (a) of his enthusiastic discovery there of the power over behavior of peoples' images of themselves and others; and (b) of the communication processes by which such images are created, sustained, and modified.

Cassirer, Ernst, *An Essay on Man* (New Haven: Yale University Press, 1944. Reprinted by Doubleday Anchor Books.). ⟨ A book by an eminent philosopher for educated laymen. Cassirer here sets out in "popular" form his influential analysis of the nature of symbols and their relation to human behavior.

Frank, Lawrence K., *Society as the Patient* (New Brunswick, New Jersey: Rutgers University Press, 1948). ⟨ A collection of papers by the author. Nearly all of Frank's essays are relevant to the themes developed in this textbook, and all are wrtten in a literate and sensitive style.

Maslow, A. H., "A Dynamic Theory of Human Motivation," *Psychological Review*, Vol. 50 (1943), pp. 370–396. ⟨ A theory of human motivation based on the assumption of levels of priorities of needs: "higher" motives are claimed not to emerge and press for satisfaction until more "basic" needs are met.

Mead, George Herbert, *Mind, Self, and Society* (Chicago: University of Chicago Press, 1934). ⟨ A systematic presentation of the contributions to social psychology of an enormously influential teacher. Mead's analysis of the development of the "self" and the role of language and experience in shaping self-images is one of the foundations of the present text book.

Murray, Henry, *Explorations in Personality* (New York: Oxford University Press, 1938). ⟮ A famous and influential contribution to our understanding of human needs by an outstanding Harvard psychologist. The author here reports his theory of personality needs and describes his methods of discerning them, including use of the well-known Thematic Apperception Test.

Niebuhr, Reinhold, *The Nature and Destiny of Man* (New York: Scribner's, 1949). ⟮ The systematic exposition by a leading Protestant theologian of the nature and needs of man.

Sartre, Jean Paul, *Being and Nothingness* (New York: Philosophical Library, 1956). ⟮ A leading French existentialist's conception of the nature of man. Sartre derives human motivation from his analysis of the human situation and especially from the choices open to the individual.

Skinner, B. F., *Science and Human Behavior* (New York: The Macmillan Company, 1953). ⟮ A psychologist's thoroughgoing behavioristic analysis of human action. Skinner attempts to describe the development of human response patterns in terms of "conditioning." He goes on to present a reasoned defense, and suggestive application of the possibilities of scientifically controlling human behavior.

Thomas, William I., *The Unadjusted Girl* (Boston: Little, Brown & Company, 1931). ⟮ The first three chapters of this book present Thomas' exposition of his famous concept of the "four wishes" of human beings. Each is illustrated with extensive case histories.

PART TWO

Those who fail to meet standards:
The casualties

CHAPTER TWO

Frustration

Organized society is possible because people can usually be counted on to abide by rules in their contact with one another. The infant is not only younger than the adult, but he is also ignorant of social rules, and this makes his behavior distressingly unpredictable. We never know when he is going to take it into his head to break the prize china or to jump out the window. Like an animal the infant acts upon his impulses; he wants what he wants when he wants it. As he grows older, he finds that he cannot continue his self-centered ways. He learns that some activities get him into trouble with the Very Important People of his life (his parents). Since it is quite unpleasant not being on good terms with these VIP's, he begins to see himself through their eyes. He disciplines his behavior to conform with their standards of right or wrong. This is what we mean when we say that man is a moral animal. Human behavior—adult behavior, that is—is not a simple function of biological urges. It involves standards, values, norms, most of which have been learned from other people. It is this social dimension that makes human behavior so predictable. Biological urges drive us in every direction; but social rules provide channels which make it likely that only impulses for *approved* behavior will be acted upon.

We do not know, of course, *exactly* what people will do. But we know what they are likely to do and what they are not likely to do. If you come to a college class in economics, for instance, you expect the professor to arrive at the scheduled time—or thereabouts. You do not expect him to be dressed in a toga or bathing suit. You do not know whether the other students will pay attention to him, but you would not expect them to read newspapers or play chess while he is talking. You would be most disturbed if he spent the period singing the score of "The Barber of Seville" instead of talking about economics. You would be disturbed because your approach to the classroom situation involves standards which have been incorporated into your own personality. Thus, you might like "The Barber of Seville," and your professor might be a singer of Metropolitan caliber. Nevertheless, you will somehow feel that the world is not functioning properly if he bursts into song instead of delivering his customary dull lecture.

One would not dare to cross a city street unless one had faith that most people, most of the time, abide by the social rules. You do not expect a motorist to attempt to run you down deliberately any more than you expect an economics professor to sing arias during class. And this faith is justified. The relations between employer and employee, parents and children, high school boy and his date, motorist and pedestrian, friend and friend—in short, all of the thousands of possible social relationships—are governed by rules prescribing the essentials of expected behavior. Some of these rules are set forth in laws and codes; many are informal like the rules governing tipping. They are so numerous and so subtle that it takes all of childhood and most of adolescence to learn them. Most of them are *not* learned in school; hence this crucial education is sometimes overlooked in recounting what American children are taught.

From the point of view of the scientific understanding of human behavior, the transmission of institutional rules from one generation to the next is of the utmost importance. Even behavior on the physiological level is affected by social standards. For example, American men have learned not to cry even when they suffer great physical pain; American women, on the other hand, are expected to cry not only when they experience physical pain but also under the stress of any strong emotion. The explanation of the difference is not physiology but social training. Belching illustrates the same principle. An infant burps when gastric pressure reaches a certain point—but not an adult! Americans have learned not to belch in public because the sound is considered uncouth. Orientals, on the other hand, regard a belch as a sign that one has been well fed; therefore, a guest who wishes to compliment his host on an excellent meal will force up a belch, whether he feels gastric pressure or not. Since Americans stifle belches and Orientals produce them regardless of the gastric situation, the scientist who hopes to predict adult behavior should be as interested in cultural standards concerning belching as he is with the physiological state of the organism.

These socio-cultural standards in terms of which members of a society mutually evaluate one another make social life predictable and thereby possible. But the existence of standards also implies that some people are found wanting. They are rejected by the community for not being beautiful enough or for belching at the wrong time. And, since these social standards are internalized even by the persons who are regarded as failures in terms of them, social rejection and self-rejection go hand in hand. Consider the relationship between personal appearance and a favorable self-assessment. Of course, every society has its own standard of physical pulchritude. There is a tribe in Africa, for example, where a woman's beauty is reckoned in proportion to her bulk. A girl who wishes to make herself attractive to the young men goes to the fatting house and gorges herself for weeks. When she waddles out, the tribal equivalent of the American "wolf" gives the tribal equivalent of the American whistle of appreciation. Such a standard of beauty seems strange to us because we like our women thin. Americans encourage girls to keep themselves from gaining what they consider "too much weight." From the point of view of this African tribe, however, American women are emaciated; and the American concept of dieting sounds unbelievable. Why should women in their right minds, women in a country which is the richest in the world, voluntarily starve themselves?

In short, the ideals of physical attractiveness of a society, any society, are arbitrary. A man who would be handsome in one country might be considered homely in another. Nevertheless, the standards of a given society are stamped into the personalities of members of that society almost from birth. Americans, for instance, have definite notions of acceptable appearance: in terms of height, body build, profile, and skin condition. Hollywood did not invent these standards—although movies probably deserve credit (or blame) for narrowing the range of acceptable variation. Before Hollywood embodied our ideals and exhibited them to millions of people every week, homely women, short men, people with bad complexions or hooked noses had a better chance of escaping invidious comparisons. The reading which follows shows the consequences for those who are grossly unattractive by American standards.[1]

Mary Benchley, a 34-year-old housewife and the mother of a one-year-old girl, is a fourth-generation, Protestant American of Dutch and Scotch descent. She lives with her husband, 17 years her senior, to whom she has been married six years. Mr. Benchley is a mechanic who makes $130 a month working for a small firm. This is a second marriage for both of them.

Mrs. Benchley had come to the plastic surgery clinic to request correction for a marked deformity of the lip. A plain-looking woman, dressed poorly and without particular care, she was shy, but frank and responsive. She had been born with a harelip and cleft palate. Although the harelip had been operated on when she was one year old, her upper lip was noticeably short and retracted, and she was unable to bring her lips together. The nose was also deformed because of the extreme width and flatness of the right nostril. The teeth were poorly aligned and a front one was missing. In view of the fact that the patient had never had any formal speech training, she spoke remarkably well.

Mrs. Benchley stated that neither she nor her mother had

[1] From Frances Cooke Macgregor, et al., *Facial Deformities and Plastic Surgery*, 1953, pp. 30–36. Courtesy of Frances Cooke Macgregor and Charles C Thomas, publisher, Springfield, Illinois.

realized that further correction in her appearance could be made. Just recently, however, she had learned about the clinic from a neighbor who was interested in her plight. She had immediately come in search of help because she wanted to "look better" for the sake of her child: "She will want me to look more presentable when she grows up."

Mrs. Benchley was born in a small upstate town and was the youngest of four children. There were two boys and two girls. She described her father, a laborer, as "a man I never considered to be my father because of what he did to me." He was a poor provider and an alcoholic. He frequently lost his temper and became violent; once he threw a lamp at his wife and hit her in the stomach. At this time, she was pregnant with Mary and later attributed the child's deformity to this incident. Since the father seldom worked and could therefore not pay the rent, the family was forced to move from one town to another because of repeated evictions. The patient's mother was a hardworking, protective, and kindly woman who took the needs of her children seriously. Though she never blamed her husband for the deformity of the child, there were occasions later on when she told Mary that she had tried to interrupt the pregnancy and expressed guilt feelings about it.

When Mary was five and began to play with other children, she became aware that she was different from them. They taunted her because of her impaired speech and the way she looked. When she told her mother about the teasing, the mother tried to explain to her that she had been "born this way" and that it was not her fault. In grammar school, the children laughed and made fun of her, calling her "split lip" and "crooked talking." Often she was driven to tears and asked herself, "Why did this have to happen to me?" She hated school and played hooky a great deal because she was so ashamed. "I was afraid to recite because of the children's laughing." She had only one friend, a little girl who "invited me to her parties and knew how I felt in school. She used to stand up for me and fight back if the others teased me. She could understand my speech the most. She died when I was 12 and I was heartbroken." Most of the time Mary remained alone or played games with her closest sibling, a brother two years older than herself. When the other siblings were invited to parties from which she was excluded, the mother took her on picnics and tried to comfort her as much as possible. Both the mother and a Christian Science practitioner who took an interest in the child tried to help her speak correctly.

When Mary was 10 years old, her father made sexual advances toward her: "He told me I had to do things like this as no man would ever want me anyway." When this occurred a second time, the child became worried and told her mother. The mother promptly made her husband leave the home, and from then on, was forced to support the children herself.

Although Mary was of average intelligence, her school performance was poor. Because the family had moved so often, she had attended eight different grammar schools. Each change involved new and trying situations with other children. "They made fun of me because of the way I talked and the way I looked and said I wasn't normal." When she was 14 and in the eighth grade, it became necessary for her to go to work.

In applying for jobs, Mary found her appearance to be a considerable handicap. A job in a nursery school was refused her on the grounds that children would take exception to her looks. She was denied a minimal office job because "They wanted someone prettier." The only work she was able to obtain was as a domestic. When she was 15, she decided that she had to face her situation and "make the most of it." She worked harder on her speech and spent her free hours reading in the library to educate herself. She was never included in the activities other adolescents cherished but would go to the movies alone or sometimes with a boy she knew. One day when he made sexual advances to her, she submitted to him, though she regarded her behavior as wrong. "Nevertheless," she said, "I did it because he was the first boy who was nice to me, and since I probably would never have anyone, I decided I might as well."

Many years before, she had tried to find a reason for her affliction. When her father had told her she "might as well be bad as no one would want her anyway," she reasoned that she was born to be bad and had been punished for it ahead of time. To this day, she feels this to be true and applies this concept of punishment to other areas in her life. For example, when she and her husband have an occasional argument and some trouble subsequently befalls them, she considers the trouble a form of retribution.

At the age of 18, Mary met a man one year her senior who took her to the movies and for drives in his car, but never in the company of other young people. Since he was kind to her, she accepted his proposal of marriage, but a month after the wedding he told her he had never really loved her and had married her only because he was in trouble with other women. He soon resumed his affairs with them and told Mary, "No man would want to be seen with you." In spite of this, the patient remained with her husband: "I was ashamed to admit I had made a mistake, and besides he would be nice for a day or two, and I tried to believe this would continue." Nevertheless, at the end of two years her husband deserted her; he went to another state and obtained a divorce. Although Mary's mother had disapproved of the marriage, she stood by her daughter and did not condemn her either during the marriage or after the divorce.

Some years later, Mary met the man who is now her second husband. He too was divorced and had had a wife who had been unfaithful to him. For four years he was extremely attentive to the patient and made numerous proposals of marriage. Although Mrs. Benchley confessed she was afraid to marry again after her first experience and was skeptical of the motives of the elder man, he finally convinced her of his sincerity. When she was 28, they were married and moved to New York City. She says that she has not regretted this marriage because her husband has been good to her. She was glad to leave her home town and move to New York "where people seem kinder." The Benchleys led a quiet and rather isolated life until the birth of the baby. Except for occasional movies or ball games, both of them preferred to stay home; Mrs. Benchley, particularly, wished to avoid public places as much as possible. After the birth of the baby, however, it became necessary for her to take the child out for airings, and at these times she could not avoid talking to the neighbors in the apartment house. One neighbor, who was soon to have a child, became friendly with Mrs. Benchley and invited her to a women's coffee club. The patient described this with pleasure as her first real social participation with other women of her own age.

Mrs. Benchley claimed that her whole life had been greatly influenced by her appearance and by her speech defect. While she found it exceedingly embarrassing and difficult to make people fully understand her when she talked (she carried a slip of paper with her name written on it), she felt that her appearance had been the greater handicap in obtaining jobs and making friends. She stated that not only had people ridiculed her and stared at her, but she had been the victim of pity, questions, jokes, and nicknames. All her life she felt rejected by others because of her deformity, and this caused her to feel depressed, inferior, and anxious. Even so, she persisted in her attempts to cope with her situation. While her second marriage and, particularly, the birth of her child gave her a greater sense of security, and while the friendly neighbor and inclusion in the women's coffee club made her feel more accepted, she was still extremely shy and fearful of strangers or of being in public places.

In some ways Mary Benchley was lucky. She was able to make her appearance acceptable by plastic surgery. After that, the barriers to social participation were down. Sometimes the rejected individual can do very little about the characteristics which reduce his acceptability. The physically handicapped come to mind at once: the blind, the deaf, and the crippled. Perhaps the worst situation of all is that in which the individual hopes he can do something to correct his deficiency but finds he cannot. The pathos of stuttering, for example, comes from the stutterer's desperate effort to speak fluently.

Sometimes, of course, the individual does not correctly perceive social standards. In the following excerpts from Lucy Freeman's account of her psychoanalysis, *Fight Against Fears,*[2] it

[2] From *Fight Against Fears* (pocket book edition) by Lucy Freeman, pp. 31–32, 79–80, 102–103. Copyright 1951 by Lucy Freeman. Used by permission of Crown Publishers, Inc., New York.

appears that Lucy, as a child, misinterpreted her parents' standards. What she construed as condemnation of her inadequacies may have been merely impatience or preoccupation with adult problems. Nevertheless, the pain the young girl suffered was real.

Suddenly a scene flashed into memory, forgotten for twenty-one years. I stood alone in the street outside that school. January's ice-wind snapped in from the water. I waited for Mother to pick me up, as she usually did, to drive me home for lunch.

I was still there, long after lunch hour, my face blood-red from the cold. A teacher walked by, asked why I stood in the street.

"My mother's forgotten me," I told her, teeth chattering. She led me indoors. She found out Mother had telephoned, asking that I eat at school as she was unable to call for me. The switchboard girl had neglected to tell me. As apology the school fed me a mammoth meal including double dessert.

But that could not remove the hurt in my heart. I was convinced Mother had finally forsaken me. She liked my brother and sister much better. She never would have left either of them standing alone in the street.

Why is it always me? I wondered, then and now.

. . . .

After the curtain fell and we bowed graciously to "an enthusiastic audience," I raced to find my parents. They must be proud of me, I thought, in this, my first public appearance.

I caught a glimpse of my father in the parental mob. When I reached his side he said crossly, "Let's go. It's late."

"How was I?" I asked excitedly. I expected him to say he now stood ready to put me through the Academy of Dramatic Arts.

"Couldn't hear a word you said," he replied. "Get your mother and let's go home."

"Couldn't hear?" I gasped. "Where were you sitting? In the balcony?"

"Third row, center," he said. "Are you ready to go?"

. . . .

I recalled one time I felt mad enough to kill my Mother. I was eleven. I closeted myself in my room to compose a poem for Mother's Day.

At the appropriate moment I handed it to her, blushing. She read it through, looked up, pleased.

She said, "This is a good poem." Then she laughed nervously. "Where did you copy it?"

I was too stunned to answer. She must be joking, I thought. Feeling like a prisoner, I stuttered, "I-I wrote it myself. Last night."

By that time she was thinking of something else. I was sure she had not heard me. I thought, what's the difference? She would never believe me anyhow.

Now I know Mother was probably embarrassed by my flowery tribute. But all I could feel then was:

She has everything—my father, my brother, my sisters—and she cannot let me have even one lousy little poem as my own without accusing me of stealing.

Perhaps because she felt unloved (insecure), Lucy also felt inadequate. She needed to excel in her schoolwork, in dramatics, in writing. When her parents did not recognize her accomplishments as superlative, she regarded herself as inadequate and worthless. Lucy Freeman was a sick girl. She suffered far more —and for less reason—than most American children. But all children suffer to some extent. Growing up is painful because it is only gradually that the child develops (a) the skills and the characteristics which enable him to fulfill adult standards of adequacy and worthiness, and (b) the understanding that enables him to appreciate adult standards of gratification and security. Perhaps this is not true of all societies, but the stage of life considered ideal in the United States is adulthood. Children may be well cared for and even indulged, but they are not fully accepted and they know it. American voting requirements are simply one manifestation of the assumption that children are immature, irresponsible, unable to meet adult standards. Curiously enough, American adults romanticize youth at the same time that they patronize children. Perhaps this explains why adults usually consider the pain of growing up amusing rather than pathetic. Consider the following excerpt from a novel about a twelve-year-old Southern girl (Frankie).[3] Is her misery funny?

There was in the neighborhood a clubhouse, and Frankie was not a member. The members of the club were girls who were thirteen and fourteen and even fifteen years old. They had parties with boys on Saturday night. Frankie knew all of the club members, and until this summer she had been like a younger member of their crowd, but now they had this club and she was not a member. They had said she was too young and mean. On Saturday night she could hear the terrible music and see from far away their light. Sometimes she went around to the alley behind the clubhouse and stood near a honeysuckle fence. She stood in the alley and watched and listened. They were very long, those parties.

"Maybe they will change their mind and invite you," John Henry said.

"The son-of-a-bitches."

Frankie sniffled and wiped her nose in the crook of her arm. She sat down on the edge of the bed, her shoulders slumped and her elbows resting on her knees. "I think they have been spreading it all over town that I smell bad," she said. "When I had those boils and that black bitter smelling ointment, old Helen Fletcher asked what was that funny smell I had. Oh, I could shoot every one of them with a pistol."

She heard John Henry walking up to the bed, and then she felt his hand patting her neck with tiny little pats. "I don't think you smell so bad," he said. "You smell sweet."

"The son-of-a-bitches," she said again. "And there was something else. They were talking nasty lies about married people. When I think of Aunt Pet and Uncle Ustace. And my own father! The nasty lies! I don't know what kind of fool they take me for."

[3] The selections from Carson McCullers, *The Member of the Wedding,* 1946, pp. 14–15, 39–41, 50–52, 176, are reprinted by permission of and arrangement with Houghton Mifflin Company, Boston, Massachusetts, the authorized publishers.

"I can smell you the minute you walk in the house without even looking to see if it is you. Like a hundred flowers."

"I don't care," she said. "I just don't care."

"Like a thousand flowers," said John Henry, and still he was patting his sticky hand on the back of her bent neck.

Frankie sat up, licked the tears from around her mouth, and wiped off her face with her shirttail. She sat still, her nose widened, smelling herself. Then she went to her suitcase and took out a bottle of Sweet Serenade. She rubbed some on the top of her head and poured some more down inside the neck of her shirt.

"Want some on you?"

John Henry was squatting beside the open suitcase and he gave a little shiver when she poured the perfume over him. He wanted to meddle in her traveling suitcase and look carefully at everything she owned. But Frankie only wanted him to get a general impression, and not count and know just what she had and what she did not have. So she strapped the suitcase and pushed it back against the wall.

"Boy!" she said. "I bet I use more perfume than anybody in this town."

. . . .

. . . "And you know what Janice remarked?" asked Frankie. "When Papa mentioned about how much I've grown, she said she didn't think I looked so terribly big. She said she got the major portion of her growth before she was thirteen. She did, Berenice!"

"O.K.! All right."

"She said she thought I was a lovely size and would probably not grow any taller. She said all fashion models and movie stars —"

"She did not," said Berenice. "I heard her. She only remarked that you probably had already got your growth. But she didn't go on and on like that. To hear you tell it, anybody would think she took her text on the subject."

"She said—"

"This is a serious fault with you, Frankie. Somebody just

makes a loose remark and then you cozen it in your mind until nobody would recognize it. Your Aunt Pet happened to mention to Clorina that you had sweet manners and Clorina passed it on to you. For what it was worth. The next thing I know you are going all around and bragging how Mrs. West thought you had the finest manners in town and ought to go to Hollywood, and I don't know what all you didn't say. You keep building on to any little compliment you hear about yourself. Or, if it is a bad thing, you do the same. You cozen and change things too much in your own mind. And that is a serious fault."

"Quit preaching at me," Frankie said.

"I ain't preaching. It is the solemn truth."

"I admit it a little," said Frankie finally. She closed her eyes and the kitchen was very quiet. She could feel the beating of her heart, and when she spoke her voice was a whisper. "What I need to know is this. Do you think I made a good impression?"

"Impression? Impression?"

"Yes," said Frankie, her eyes still closed.

"Well, how would I know?" said Berenice.

"I mean how did I act? What did I do?"

"Why, you didn't do anything."

"Nothing?" asked Frankie.

"No. You just watched the pair of them like they was ghosts. Then, when they talked about the wedding, them ears of yours stiffened out the size of cabbage leaves—"

Frankie raised her hand to her left ear. "They didn't," she said bitterly. Then after a while she added. "Some day you going to look down and find that big fat tongue of yours pulled out by the roots and laying there before you on the table. Then how do you think you will feel?"

. . . .

. . . For a long time now her brother and the bride had been at Winter Hill. They had left the town a hundred miles behind them, and now were in a city far away. They were them and in Winter Hill, together, while she was her and in the same old town all by herself. The long hundred miles did not make her sadder and make her feel more far away than the knowing

that they were them and both together and she was only her and
parted from them, by herself. And as she sickened with this
feeling a thought and explanation suddenly came to her, so that
she knew and almost said aloud: *They are the we of me.* Yesterday, and all the twelve years of her life, she had only been
Frankie. She was an *I* person who had to walk around and do
things by herself. All other people had a *we* to claim, all others
except her. When Berenice said *we,* she meant Honey and Big
Mama, her lodge, or her church. The *we* of her father was the
store. All members of clubs have a *we* to belong to and talk
about. The soldiers in the army can say *we,* and even the
criminals on chain-gangs. But the old Frankie had had no *we*
to claim, unless it would be the terrible summer *we* of her and
John Henry and Berenice—and that was the last *we* in the
world she wanted. Now all this was suddenly over with and
changed. There was her brother and the bride, and it was as
though when first she saw them something she had known inside of her: *They are the we of me.* And that was why it made
her feel so queer, for them to be away in Winter Hill while she
was left all by herself; the hull of the old Frankie left there in
the town alone.

"Why are you all bent over like that?" John Henry called.

"I think I have a kind of pain," said Frankie. "I must have
ate something."

John Henry was still standing on the banisters, holding to the
post.

"Listen," she said finally. "Suppose you come on over and
eat supper and spend the night with me."

"I can't," he answered.

"Why?"

John Henry walked across the banisters, holding out his arms
for balance, so that he was like a little blackbird against the
yellow window light. He did not answer until he safely reached
the other post.

"Just because."

"Because why?"

He did not say anything, and so she added: "I thought maybe

me and you could put up my Indian tepee and sleep out in the back yard. And have a good time."

Still John Henry did not speak.

"We're blood first cousins. I entertain you all the time. I've given you so many presents."

Quietly, lightly, John Henry walked back across the banisters and then stood looking out at her with his arm around the post again.

"Sure enough," she called. "Why can't you come?"

At last he said. "Because, Frankie, I don't want to."

"Fool jackass!" she screamed. "I only asked you because I thought you looked so ugly and so lonesome."

Lightly John Henry jumped down from the banisters. And his voice as he called back to her was a clear child's voice.

"Why, I'm not a bit lonesome."

Frankie rubbed the wet palms of her hands along the sides of her shorts and said in her mind: Now turn around and take yourself on home. But in spite of this order, she was somehow unable to turn around and go.

. . . .

. . . The wedding was like a dream outside her power, or like a show unmanaged by her in which she was supposed to have no part. The living room was crowded with Winter Hill company, and the bride and her brother stood before the mantelpiece at the end of the room. And seeing them again together was more like singing feeling than a picture that her dizzied eyes could truly see. She watched them with her heart, but all the time she was only thinking: I have not told them and they don't know. And knowing this was heavy as a swallowed stone. And afterward, during the kissing of the bride, refreshments served in the dining room, the stir and party bustle—she hovered close to the two of them, but words would not come. They are not going to take me, she was thinking, and this was the one thought she could not bear.

When Mr. Williams brought their bags, she hastened after with her own suitcase. The rest was like some nightmare show in which a wild girl in the audience breaks onto the stage to take upon herself an unplanned part that was never written or meant to be. You are the we of me, her heart was saying, but could only say aloud: "Take me!" And they pleaded and begged with her, but she was already in the car. At the last she clung to the steering wheel until her father and somebody else had hauled and dragged her from the car, and even then she could only cry in the dust of the empty road: "Take me! Take me!" But there was only the wedding company to hear, for the bride and her brother had driven away.

Clearly, Frankie could not solve her problems by accompanying her brother and her sister-in-law on their honeymoon. But how else could she be a full-fledged human being? She felt big and clumsy; she thought she had an unpleasant body odor; she knew that the older girls did not want her in their club; there were some "nasty lies" about older people that she did not understand. Eventually, the reader smiles, Frankie's troubles will disappear; in two or three years they will be only a painful memory. But new troubles are possible. Consider, for example, the anxieties which some women develop because they think that their sexual skills do not measure up to American standards. The following is a selection from an article by a physician about so-called frigidity.[4]

There are very few really frigid women, yet in my practice as a psychiatrist I am surprised at the number of women who come to me because their marital happiness is threatened by fears of frigidity.

These fears are the result of a grave and widespread misunderstanding of what frigidity is and who suffers from it. It simply is not true, as we hear so often, that 50 or 60 per cent of American women are frigid. It is not true all or even part of the time. Nor is it true that their lack of responsiveness is caused by their husbands' incompetence, selfishness or ignorance, any more than it stems from their own basic indifference or revulsion to or fear of the sexual act.

[4] Anonymous, "The Doctor Talks About Frigidity," copyright *McCall's* © 1957. Used by permission of the Editorial Department of *McCall's*, New York.

True frigidity has deep-seated psychological roots and usually requires prolonged psychiatric treatment. While the term is not ever applied to men, they can and do suffer from it, with much more disastrous consequences than women. A man who is sexually unresponsive is powerless in sexual relations. A woman may not betray her problem at all. This kind of consistent inability to derive any pleasure or relaxation from sexual relations is what we mean by frigidity. It is extremely rare.

A woman who reacts pleasurably to her husband's embraces and caresses is not frigid. She feels warmth and tenderness, and there are physical reactions that she is familiar with as well. Her responsiveness will vary constantly, depending on the whole complex of environmental factors that affect all the emotional aspects of life. But whether or not a woman comes to an easily recognized climax most of the time, if she and her husband enjoy their love-making she is sexually responsive. If she reaches orgasm a little more than half the time, she is very normal and healthy sexually.

However, even the normally responsive woman may go through a period of time in marriage when she fails to reach a climax in intercourse. This may become a source of tension and dissatisfaction. Before it does she should talk to her partner about it. Pretense, lack of frankness and concealment in sex can only make things worse. If a husband can understand his wife's feelings, he may be able to change his approach to love-making so that she can gain satisfaction with him.

These periods of failure to achieve satisfaction in the sexual relationship are usually not important in themselves, but they can and do arouse false fears of frigidity. I have seen marriages deteriorate as a consequence of imagined fears until they are beyond repair.

Anxiety about sexual adequacy seems to be an almost inevitable result of the present-day sex education of many women. They have been told in exaggerated and often unscientific treatises on love and marriage that anything short of 100 per cent perfection in love-making is failure. As a result they are worried about performance even before they have experienced pleasure. A minor upset in marital relations is always the signal for a renewed upsurge of anxiety. Finally the fear becomes chronic.

At best the consequence is temporary maladjustment, dissatisfaction and unhappiness that can be easily straightened out between two partners with candor and courage. But we have put such emphasis on performance that few are able to confess difficulties. Sexual inhibition in our time is frowned on more fiercely than the whole subject of sex was frowned on by our grandfathers. As a result a great many young couples' marriages today go from bad to worse because they won't express their sexual fears. Instead they worry along, pretending that everything is fine—or they are constantly tired or they become slightly ill fairly often or they just find more and more irrelevant reasons for being altogether dissatisfied with their marriage partners.

I think of Roger and Mary. Mary came to me first with the kind of report I hear so often. She just felt "awful." She was tired all the time but she couldn't sleep at night. She stayed up later and later, but when she finally did smoke the last cigarette and read the last magazine and put out the light she still wasn't sleepy. The slightest rustle, the sound of a car in the street might wake her again.

Mary didn't feel like eating and she did look thin. She had lost fifteen pounds in her five years of marriage. She was worried about her temper. She loved her child, yet often she knew that she treated her as if she were nothing but badness and trouble. Then tossed in as if an afterthought, she added the statement: "I don't have any interest in sex *at all*."

Though it came last, I was sure that Mary's worry about no longer getting pleasure, fulfillment, release and greater closeness to her husband through the sexual relationship was enough to trigger all her other complaints.

It was some time before Mary admitted that her husband too seemed uninterested in sex. She was sure he was disappointed in their marriage and would be having an affair with someone else if he could afford the time and money.

Finally, after she had given me approximately fifty more reasons why their marriage didn't work, she came back to the point. She asked, "How often *should* you have sexual relations?"

I told her that I didn't know how often she *or* her husband should have sexual relations. "But suppose you tell me how often you do?" Mary told me that they rarely ever did. In fact, she said, she had just about given up trying because Roger was so obviously uninterested. Mary was convinced that he didn't love her at all.

I was reasonably certain that this wasn't true, but I told Mary it was important to try to find out how their life had deteriorated to the bad state which she described.

The marriage had started well. They were deeply in love and intensely attracted to each other physically. Both were well versed in the lore of marriage manuals and their early sex experiences were utterly satisfactory. After the honeymoon Mary and Roger settled down. Roger was a young hopeful in the insurance business who knew that success depended on hard work. Many of his calls had to be made during the evening hours.

Five months after their marriage Mary became pregnant. They were still paying for their furniture and the little English car (just room for two) that they'd bought that summer. But while they weren't prepared, they wanted their baby. And they wanted the best for it, just as they wanted the best for themselves. Of course this meant even more effort on Roger's part. He spent more nights on his job and this meant more evenings alone for Mary.

It was not until after their daughter Wendy was born that the lonely nights began to tell on Mary and the extra strain of responsibility and the extra hours that went with it began to have their effect on Roger. Probably because she had more time to think, Mary noticed a difference. Roger seemed preoccupied and indifferent. More and more Mary would find Roger asleep when she came to bed. Sometimes Mary would try to wake him.

One night after giving the baby her eleven-o'clock feeding she felt especially affectionate to Roger and succeeded in arousing him. But he could not make love to her. After this experience she felt that Roger was no longer interested in her. She attributed the episode to her own inadequacy as a sexual partner. For Roger it was equally devastating. He began to avoid Mary for fear of a repetition of this humiliating experience.

Mary redoubled her efforts to interest Roger in order to prove to herself that she, at least, was still normally interested in sex. Of course the results were unsatisfying for her, because she was too preoccupied to enjoy herself or consider her partner. She found she was *feeling* less and less. The less she felt, the more anxious she became and the less important the sexual experience became to her as an expression of love. With the real inability to experience sexual pleasure came a new and overpowering fear—frigidity. This was what brought her to my office.

Was she frigid? Absolutely not. The frigid woman is one who consistently fails to develop any interest in the sexual act with the man she loves, even though she and her husband are living under fairly normal conditions without undue emotional strain.

But unreal as their problem seemed a month later, both Roger and Mary had failed to see how it had been building up for several years.

The first thing I did for both of these two young people was to assure them that they were normal in every way. Roger, like Mary, was well educated in the textbooks and believed that a really virile man should be able to make love to his wife on demand, patiently stimulating her interest to match his own. Mary, for her part, believed that she should always be excited at the thought of sexual relations and should always reach a climax.

As a matter of fact, many marriages start off this way. A young woman in love and recently married may be stimulated merely by the thought of her husband when she feels a very deep need for him. The progress of her sexual excitement is not impeded by thoughts of work, children, responsibilities, worry about bills or anything else. Neither is her husband's.

But there comes a point in marriage, as there did in Mary's, where strain or worry or fatigue affects one or the other or both the partners. Something alters the sexual drive. In Roger's case it was too much work and uncertainty about his ability to be an adequate father so soon.

This should have been no problem, except that Mary was living up to unreal standards of sexual behavior. Judging her husband's performance by those standards, she concluded that his lack of interest was induced by her inadequacy. He concluded that his tiredness and lowered sexual vitality were evidence of his failure as a man. Because he couldn't bear that failure he tried to avoid making love to his wife.

If Mary had recognized that her husband had reason to be tired after months of working many evenings a week, she might have been able to relax her expectations temporarily. If she had been aware that her husband might be worried about becoming a father so soon after marriage and so early in his career, she might have tried to build up his confidence with her thoughtful attention. Her insistence, instead, on keeping their marriage up to absolute sexual standards was the worst thing she could have done for him. What he needed more than anything else was the assurance of her trust and love instead of added pressure.

Mary and Roger felt sexually inadequate because they judged themselves in terms of *romantic* standards of erotic performance. The books they had read and the movies they had seen had not provided them with a *realistic* basis for married love. Nothing was wrong with their perceptions; the trouble lay in the definitions of sexual adequacy provided by American culture.

In the following scene from William Inge's play, *Picnic*,[5] desperate effort is expended to avoid still a different type of failure. Rosemary, a school teacher, does not want to be an "old maid," and she regards Howard as her last chance at matrimony.

HOWARD: Honey, you're not yourself tonight.
ROSEMARY: Yes, I am. I'm more myself than I ever was. Take me with you, Howard. If you don't I don't know what I'll do with myself. I mean it.
HOWARD: Now look, Honey, you better go upstairs and get some

[5] From *Picnic*, by William Inge, pp. 76–79. Copyright 1953 by William Inge. Reprinted by permission of Random House, Inc., New York.

sleep. You gotta start school in the morning. We'll talk this
over Saturday.

ROSEMARY: Maybe you won't be back Saturday. Maybe you
won't be back ever again.

HOWARD: Rosemary, you know better than that.

ROSEMARY: Then what's the next thing in store for me? To be
nice to the next man, then the next—till there's no one left
to care whether I'm nice to him or not. Till I'm ready for
the grave and don't have anyone to take me there.

HOWARD (*in an attempt to be consoling*): Now Rosemary!

ROSEMARY: You can't let that happen to me, Howard. I won't
let you.

HOWARD: I don't understand. When we first started going together, you were the best sport I ever saw, always good for
a laugh.

ROSEMARY (*in a hollow voice*): I can't laugh any more.

HOWARD: We'll talk it over Saturday.

ROSEMARY: We'll talk it over *now*.

HOWARD (*squirming*): Well—Honey—I . . .

ROSEMARY: You said you were gonna marry me, Howard. You
said when I got back from my vacation, you'd be waitin'
with the preacher.

HOWARD: Honey, I've had an awful busy summer and . . .

ROSEMARY: Where's the preacher, Howard? Where is he?

HOWARD (*walking away from her*): Honey, I'm forty-two years
old. A person forms certain ways of livin', then one day it's
too late to change.

ROSEMARY (*grabbing his arm and holding him*): Come back
here, Howard. I'm no spring chicken either. Maybe I'm a
little older than you think *I* am. I've formed my ways too.
But they can be changed. They *gotta* be changed. It's no
good livin' like this, in rented rooms, meetin' a bunch of
old maids for supper every night, then comin' back home
alone.

HOWARD: *I* know how it is, Rosemary. My life's no bed of roses
either.

ROSEMARY: Then why don't you do something about it?

HOWARD: I figure—there's some bad things about every life.

ROSEMARY: There's too much bad about mine. Each year, I keep tellin' myself, is the last. Something'll happen. Then nothing ever does—except I get a little crazier all the time.

HOWARD (*hopelessly*): Well . . .

ROSEMARY: A *well's* a hole in the ground, Howard. Be careful you don't fall in.

HOWARD: I wasn't tryin' to be funny.

ROSEMARY: . . . and all this time you just been leadin' me on.

HOWARD (*defensive*): Rosemary, that's not *so!* I've not been leading you *on.*

ROSEMARY: I'd like to know what else you call it.

HOWARD: Well—can't we talk about it Saturday? I'm dead tired and I got a busy week ahead, and . . .

ROSEMARY (*she grips him by the arm and looks straight into his eyes*): You gotta marry me, Howard.

HOWARD (*tortured*): Well—Honey, I can't marry you, *now.*

ROSEMARY: You can be over here in the morning.

HOWARD: Sometimes you're unreasonable.

ROSEMARY: You gotta marry me.

HOWARD: What'll you do about your job?

ROSEMARY: Alvah Jackson can take my place till they get someone new from the agency.

HOWARD: I'll have to pay Fred Jenkins to take care of the store for a few days.

ROSEMARY: Then get him.

HOWARD: Well . . .

ROSEMARY: I'll be waitin' for you in the morning, Howard.

HOWARD (*after a few moments' troubled thought*): No.

ROSEMARY (*a muffled cry*): Howard!

HOWARD: I'm not gonna marry anyone that says, "You gotta marry me, Howard." I'm not gonna. (*He is silent. Rosemary weeps pathetic tears. Slowly Howard reconsiders.*) If a woman wants me to marry her—she can at least say "please."

ROSEMARY (*beaten and humble*): "Please" marry me, Howard.

HOWARD: Well—you got to give me time to think it over.

ROSEMARY (*desperate*): Oh, God! Please marry me, Howard.

Please . . . (*She sinks to her knees.*) Please . . . please
. . .

HOWARD (*embarrassed by her suffering humility*): Rosemary
. . . I . . . I gotta have some time to think it over. You go
to bed now and get some rest. I'll drive over in the morning
and maybe we can talk it over before you go to school.
I . . .

ROSEMARY: You're not just tryin' to get out of it, Howard?

HOWARD: I'll be over in the morning, Honey.

ROSEMARY: Honest?

HOWARD: Yah. I gotta go to the courthouse anyway. We'll talk
it over then.

ROSEMARY: Oh, God, please marry me, Howard. Please.

HOWARD (*trying to get away*): Go to bed, Honey. I'll see you in
the morning.

ROSEMARY: Please, Howard!

HOWARD: I'll see you in the morning. Good night, Rosemary.
(*Starting off.*)

ROSEMARY (*in a meek voice*): Please!

HOWARD: Good night, Rosemary.

When a woman passes the age where her chances of marriage are regarded as good, say, thirty, a subtle change usually
takes place in the attitudes of her family and friends. She is no
longer "single"; she is an unplucked blossom on the family tree.
Similarly, when a man passes thirty-five or forty without marrying, he moves into "bachelor" category. He is suspected of
lecherous motives, of irresponsibility, of an Oedipus complex.
His best friends conspire to ensnare him in the bonds of matrimony—"for his own good." Bachelors and spinsters do not
suffer legal disabilities: There are no laws requiring them to
marry. They do not suffer economic disabilities either. It is true
that the single person pays more income tax than the married
person with the same income, but the cost of raising a family
usually outweighs the exemptions by far. On the other hand,
there *are* social disabilities. Whereas teen-aged friendship groups
are composed almost exclusively of the unmarried, with older
people the unit of social participation tends more and more to
be the married couple. The bachelor notices that casual dating
is less and less possible as he moves into the thirties and forties.

Those girls who are not yet married are less interested in a "good time" than in a serious suitor. They want to begin raising a family. His former chums do not offer him the companionship of bygone days because (a) they are involved in their own families and have little time for recreation and (b) they and their wives have mutual friends—other married couples—with whom he does not always "fit in." There are similar barriers to the social participation of the spinster. The walls of loneliness close in. Thus, social pressures are mobilized to coerce the timid and fearful into marriage. And this promotes social continuity. On the other hand, there are always some individuals who, in a courtship system based on mutual choice, will not be chosen. These, as Rosemary shows, have serious difficulty maintaining their self-respect.

Even when socio-cultural standards have nothing to contribute to societal functioning, even when standards are condemned by scientists and religious leaders as the product of ignorance and malice, failure to meet them is painful. Thus, members of races, nationalities, and religious groups which are discriminated against suffer from feelings of inferiority. This effect of prejudice on the victim was taken account of by the Supreme Court in its May, 1954, decision outlawing racial segregation in the public schools. In the following passage from Richard Wright's autobiography, *Black Boy*,[6] he tells of the humiliation which made him resolve, as a young Negro, to leave the South forever.

The next morning I was outside the office of the optical company long before it opened. I was reminding myself that I must be polite, must think before I spoke, must think before I acted, must say "yes sir, no sir," that I must so conduct myself that white people would not think that I thought I was as good as they. Suddenly a white man came up to me.

"What do you want?" he asked me.

"I'm reporting for a job, sir," I said.

"O.K. Come on."

I followed him up a flight of steps and he unlocked the door of the office. I was a little tense, but the young white man's manner put me at ease and I sat and held my hat in my hand.

[6] From *Black Boy*, by Richard Wright, pp. 163–169. Copyright 1945 by Richard Wright. Reprinted by permission of Harper & Brothers, New York.

A white girl came and began punching the typewriter. Soon another white man, thin and gray, entered and went into the rear room. Finally a tall, red-faced white man arrived, shot me a quick glance and sat at his desk. His brisk manner branded him a Yankee.

"You're the new boy, eh?"

"Yes, sir."

"Let me get my mail out of the way and I'll talk with you," he said pleasantly.

"Yes, sir."

I even pitched my voice to a low plane, trying to rob it of any suggestion or overtone of aggressiveness.

Half an hour later Mr. Crane called me to his desk and questioned me closely about my schooling, about how much mathematics I had had. He seemed pleased when I told him that I had had two years of algebra.

"How would you like to learn this trade?" he asked.

"I'd like it fine, sir. I'd like nothing better," I said.

He told me that he wanted to train a Negro boy in the optical trade; he wanted to help him, guide him. I tried to answer in a way that would let him know that I would try to be worthy of what he was doing. He took me to the stenographer and said:

"This is Richard. He's going to be with us."

He then led me into the rear room of the office, which turned out to be a tiny factory filled with many strange machines smeared with red dust.

"Reynolds," he said to a young white man, "this is Richard."

"What you saying there, boy!" Reynolds grinned and boomed at me.

Mr. Crane took me to the older man.

"Pease, this is Richard, who'll work with us."

Pease looked at me and nodded. Mr. Crane then held forth to the two white men about my duties; he told them to break me in gradually to the workings of the shop, to instruct me in the mechanics of grinding and polishing lenses. They nodded their assent.

"Now, boy, let's see how clean you can get this place," Mr. Crane said.

"Yes, sir."

I swept, mopped, dusted, and soon had the office and the shop clean. In the afternoons, when I had caught up with my work, I ran errands. In an idle moment I would stand and watch the two white men grinding lenses on the machines. They said nothing to me and I said nothing to them. The first day passed, the second, the third, a week passed and I received my five dollars. A month passed. But I was not learning anything and nobody had volunteered to help me. One afternoon I walked up to Reynolds and asked him to tell me about the work.

"What are you trying to do, get smart, nigger?" he asked me.

"No, sir," I said.

I was baffled. Perhaps he just did not want to help me. I went to Pease, reminding him that the boss had said that I was to be given a chance to learn the trade.

"Nigger, you think you're white, don't you?"

"No, sir."

"You're acting mighty like it," he said.

"I was only doing what the boss told me to do," I said.

Pease shook his fist in my face.

"This is a *white* man's work around here," he said.

From then on they changed toward me; they said good morning no more. When I was just a bit slow in performing some duty, I was called a lazy black sonofabitch. I kept silent, striving to offer no excuse for worsening of relations. But one day Reynolds called me to his machine.

"Nigger, you think you'll ever amount to anything?" he asked in a slow, sadistic voice.

"I don't know, sir," I answered, turning my head away.

"What do niggers think about?" he asked.

"I don't know, sir," I said, my head still averted.

"If I was a nigger, I'd kill myself," he said.

I said nothing. I was angry.

"You know why?" he asked.

I still said nothing.

"But I don't reckon niggers mind being niggers," he said suddenly and laughed.

I ignored him. Mr. Pease was watching me closely; then I

saw them exchange glances. My job was not leading to what Mr. Crane had said it would. I had been humble, and now I was reaping the wages of humility.

"Come here, boy," Pease said.

I walked to his bench.

"You didn't like what Reynolds just said, did you?" he asked.

"Oh, it's all right," I said smiling.

"You didn't like it. I could see it on your face," he said.

I stared at him and backed away.

"Did you ever get into any trouble?" he asked.

"No, sir."

"What would you do if you got into trouble?"

"I don't know, sir."

"Well, watch yourself and don't get into trouble," he warned.

I wanted to report these clashes to Mr. Crane, but the thought of what Pease or Reynolds would do to me if they learned that I had "snitched" stopped me. I worked through the days and tried to hide my resentment under a nervous, cryptic smile.

The climax came at noon one summer day. Pease called me to his workbench; to get to him I had to go between two narrow benches and stand with my back against a wall.

"Richard, I want to ask you something," Pease began pleasantly, not looking up from his work.

"Yes, sir."

Reynolds came over and stood blocking the narrow passage between the benches; he folded his arms and stared at me solemnly. I looked from one to the other, sensing trouble. Pease looked up and spoke slowly, so there would be no possibility of my not understanding.

"Richard, Reynolds here tells me that you called me Pease," he said.

I stiffened. A void opened up in me. I knew that this was the showdown.

He meant that I had failed to call him Mr. Pease. I looked at Reynolds; he was gripping a steel bar in his hand. I opened my mouth to speak, to protest, to assure Pease that I had never called him simply *Pease,* and that I had never had any intention of doing so, when Reynolds grabbed me by the collar, ramming my head against a wall.

"Now, be careful, nigger," snarled Reynolds, baring his teeth. "I heard you call 'im *Pease.* And if you say you didn't, you're calling me a liar, see?" He waved the steel bar threateningly.

If I had said: No sir, Mr. Pease, I never called you *Pease,* I would by inference have been calling Reynolds a liar; and if I had said: Yes sir, Mr. Pease, I called you *Pease,* I would have been pleading guilty to the worst insult that a Negro can offer to a southern white man. I stood trying to think of a neutral course that would resolve this quickly risen nightmare, but my tongue would not move.

"Richard, I asked you a question!" Pease said. Anger was creeping into his voice.

"I don't remember calling you *Pease,* Mr. Pease," I said cautiously. "And if I did, I sure didn't mean . . ."

"You black sonofabitch! You called me *Pease,* then!" he spat, rising and slapping me till I bent sideways over a bench.

Reynolds was up on top of me demanding:

"Didn't you call him *Pease*? If you say you didn't, I'll rip your gut string loose with this f—k—g bar, you black granny dodger! You can't call a white man a liar and get away with it!"

I wilted. I begged them not to hit me. I knew what they wanted. They wanted me to leave the job.

"I'll leave," I promised. "I'll leave right now!"

They gave me a minute to get out of the factory, and warned me not to show up again or tell the boss. Reynolds loosened his hand on my collar and I ducked out of the room. I did not see Mr. Crane or the stenographer in the office. Pease and Reynolds had so timed it that Mr. Crane and the stenographer would be out when they turned on the terror. I went to the street and waited for the boss to return. I saw Griggs wiping glass shelves in the jewelry store and I beckoned to him. He came out and I told him what had happened.

"Then what are you standing there like a fool for?" he demanded. "Won't you ever learn? Get home! They might come down!"

I walked down Capitol Street feeling that the sidewalk was unreal, that I was unreal, that the people were unreal, yet expecting somebody to demand to know what right I had to be on the streets. My wound went deep; I felt that I had been slapped out of the human race. When I reached home, I did not tell the family what had happened; I merely told them that I had quit, that I was not making enough money, that I was seeking another job.

That night Griggs came to my house; we went for a walk.

"You got a goddamn tough break," he said.

"Can you say it was my fault?" I asked.

He shook his head.

"Well, what about your goddamn philosophy of meekness?" I asked him bitterly.

"These things just happen," he said, shrugging.

"They owe me money," I said.

"That's what I came about," he said. "Mr. Crane wants you to come in at ten in the morning. Ten sharp, now, mind you, because he'll be there and those guys won't gang up on you again."

The next morning at ten I crept up the stairs and peered into the office of the optical shop to make sure that Mr. Crane was in. He was at his desk. Pease and Reynolds were at their machines in the rear.

"Come in, Richard," Mr. Crane said.

I pulled off my hat and walked into the office; I stood before him.

"Sit down," he said.

I sat. He stared at me and shook his head.

"Tell me, what happened?"

An impulse to speak rose in me and died with the realization that I was facing a wall that I would never breech. I tried to speak several times and could make no sounds. I grew tense and tears burnt my cheeks.

"Now, just keep control of yourself," Mr. Crane said.

I clenched my fists and managed to talk.

"I tried to do my best here," I said.

"I believe you," he said. "But I want to know what happened. Which one bothered you?"

"Both of 'em," I said.

Reynolds came running to the door and I rose. Mr. Crane jumped to his feet.

"Get back in there," he told Reynolds.

"That nigger's lying!" Reynolds said. "I'll kill 'im if he lies on me!"

"Get back in there or get out," Mr. Crane said.

Reynolds backed away, keeping his eyes on me.

"Go ahead," Mr. Crane said. "Tell me what happened."

Then again I could not speak. What could I accomplish by telling him? I was black; I lived in the South. I would never learn to operate those machines as long as those two white men in there stood by them. Anger and fear welled in me as I felt what I had missed; I leaned forward and clapped my hands to my face.

"No, no, now," Mr. Crane said. "Keep control of yourself. No matter what happens, keep control . . ."

"I know," I said in a voice not my own. "There's no use of my saying anything."

"Do you want to work here?" he asked me.

I looked at the white faces of Pease and Reynolds; I imagined their waylaying me, killing me. I was remembering what had happened to Ned's brother.

"No, sir," I breathed.

"Why?"

"I'm scared," I said. "They would kill me."

Mr. Crane turned and called Pease and Reynolds into the office.

"Now, tell me which one bothered you. Don't be afraid. Nobody's going to hurt you," Mr. Crane said.

I stared ahead of me and did not answer. He waved the men inside. The white stenographer looked at me with wide eyes and I felt drenched in shame, naked to my soul. The whole of my being felt violated, and I knew that my own fear had helped to violate it. I was breathing hard and struggling to master my feelings.

"Can I get my money, sir?" I asked at last.

"Just sit a minute and take hold of yourself," he said.

I waited and my roused senses grew slowly calm.

"I'm awfully sorry about this," he said.

"I had hoped for a lot from this job," I said. "I'd wanted to go to school, to college . . ."

"I know," he said. "But what are you going to do now?"

My eyes traveled over the office, but I was not seeing.

"I'm going away," I said.

"What do you mean?"

"I'm going to get out of the South," I breathed.

"Maybe that's best," he said. "I'm from Illinois. Even for me, it's hard here. I can do just so much."

He handed me my money, more than I had earned for the week. I thanked him and rose to leave. He rose. I went into the hallway and he followed me. He reached out his hand.

"It's tough for you down here," he said.

I barely touched his hand. I walked swiftly down the hall, fighting against crying again. I ran down the steps, then paused and looked back up. He was standing at the head of the stairs, shaking his head. I went into the sunshine and walked home like a blind man.

An individual ignored or rejected because socio-cultural standards require a certain age, sex, race, cast of feature, or physique is indeed unfortunate. Perversity does not distinguish him from the majority, only circumstance. Hence social punishment can make him miserable but cannot change him. Usually, people do not mean to be cruel. They fail to realize (a) that the individual cannot help the characteristic which they dislike or (b) that their behavior toward him isolates him and therefore increases his problem of self-acceptance. They can understand readily enough that a man isn't short or a woman homely out of preference. But, as long as they do not vilify or assault an unattractive person, as long as they confine their response to ignoring him, they do not grasp the extent of his frustration. For there is consensus on socio-cultural standards. Individual neglect becomes social rejection because the same response occurs frequently. Thus, reluctance to hire the elderly and the physically handicapped is widespread. The *cumulative* impact of many refusals from employers creates the feelings of worthlessness and inadequacy. In the following passage from Irving Shulman's novel, *The Square Trap*,[7] Vidal, a middle-aged Mexican-American reacts to the loss of his job.

What would he have given for a job? Anything, even his soul to the devil. Anything, to have once again been privileged to get up in the early morning, eaten his breakfast, taken his lunch pail in his right hand, and gone off to work. Then time would not have been a slow, tortuous and stagnant condition, time would not have been a strangling web of inactivity. Time would have meant work, being with people, having purpose and reason, talk and banter and anger and curses at foremen and bosses. And time would have also meant the weariness of arms and legs, and back, luxurious sighs and stretchings, the wonderful feeling of ease after the removal of a pair of shoes, and deep sleep and healthy snoring; sleep without turning and tossing or mutterings of despair. Work meant belonging and feeling well; enforced idleness meant shameful loneliness and illness of the spirit.

Then why didn't he look for a job? What could he do? Attempt the stoop labor of the fields? There were younger men and their families in the Coachella and San Joaquin valleys who fought for jobs as pickers. There were the wetbacks and border jumpers who scattered from Juarez, Tijuana, and Mexicali to gain illegal entrance into the United States and were willing to work for nothing if a rancher would conceal them and help them stay in California and Texas. The railroads didn't want him because he was too old and the building trades couldn't use him because he lacked skill—and he was too old. The all-night restaurants recruited their dishwashing and porter help from Skid Row. The mills in Vernon were retrenching and cutting their payrolls to the minimum. And competing against him were more skilled men, who offered, in addition to their knowledge,

[7] From *The Square Trap* by Irving Shulman, pp. 216, 217–219, 224–228, 230–231, by permission of Little, Brown & Company, Boston, Massachusetts. Copyright 1953 by Irving Shulman.

strength and youth, physical assets he no longer possessed. After decades of work there was no tapering off but a sharp and decisive closing of all doors and because Vidal had never known anything but labor to keep him going, idleness became a cave within which he was entombed by listlessness and apathy. He might as well have been dead. Again: why didn't he look for a job? Because there were no jobs for him. This was what he had discovered after his discharge from the yard . . . There were no jobs for him. This is what he had to believe, and once he could accept this belief, the long silences were best for him.

But nothing, nothing could speed up time. Long ago Vidal had used up talk, going to the movies, long walks, drinking beer and wine in the saloons and at home, attempting to garden and make household repairs, shopping for his wife, disciplining his children, and roaming throughout downtown Los Angeles and far out on South Main Street to seek work.

At the expiration of his first year's unemployment insurance he had hunted in the greatest panic for a job, anything. Of course Helen worked, Tomas contributed to the household, and they insisted that he need not work and should stay home, and Tomas talked of the stand he was going to buy him, but not in recent months. And Vidal wondered if he could accept the stand from his son, especially if the stand were made possible by his son's defiance. But he couldn't stay home forever and permit them to support him. Staying at home meant the end of his authority; he would no longer be master of his household— was he the master now?—he would be expected to remain quiet and have no opinions.

Six months after his last unemployment insurance payment he became eligible for his second year's insurance. For reasons he couldn't define he had refused to apply for it except that he was less and less inclined to leave the Ravine for other areas of the city where people had businesses and jobs and went to work. But Helen with long patience had convinced him this was foolish. If he went to collect his insurance they might have a job for him, and so he permitted himself to be persuaded, had endured the questions and the many signings of his name, and Helen was accompanying him again while he collected his first check. The following week he would go alone, do so for twenty-four weeks more, and be paid for staying home, for feeling miserable and useless and dead. . . .

Helen saw her father through the door, waved to him, and Vidal, self-conscious because she had seen him, waved once before he concentrated upon a display of engagement and wedding rings.

Helen took his arm. "Waiting long, Father?"

"Not too long," Vidal replied. "I looked in the store windows and had a cup of coffee."

"We'll have to hurry," Helen moved rapidly through the crowd toward Seventh Street.

"We're busy today."

"Then business is good?"

"Very good. I'll make several dollars more in commissions this week, I hope."

"I could have gone alone."

Helen nodded. "It's all right, Father. You'll go alone next week."

Vidal smiled maliciously. "Then you're certain I won't be working next week."

.   .   .   .

Vidal began to walk toward Spring and Second Streets, and as he walked he felt some of the old purpose in his step, the rush of excitement which had always made his heart pound before the first morning of a new job, which might be the job that would mean his security and good fortune. Everything was happening as it should and he walked rapidly, humming to himself, feeling alive and vital, full of plans.

. . . On Spring Street he . . . finally chose to enter a store whose windows advertised second-hand machinery, tools, and cut-rate leather findings. The raw smell of hides and leather stirred memories long dormant, and with excited gestures Vidal touched the spools of waxed thread, the supple and stiff leathers, cans of wax and polish, and the hand tools of his trade, much better and finer than those he had used as a boy. But he recognized the tools, knew what they were for, and this knowledge made him feel like striking himself proudly on the chest. A trade was never forgotten. A trade was an everlasting gift. A trade was a heritage.

Deliberately, with great care, he put aside leathers for soles and uppers, choosing them for strength, texture, and finish, and picked over inner linings, thongs, waxed threads, heels, buckles, needles, cutting and shaping knives, augers, tacks, and several patterns.

. . . [When he had selected the items he could afford, Vidal thanked the clerk and said], "Please put them in a strong bag for me."

"You don't want them wrapped?"

Vidal shook his head and laughed. "A strong bag. I want to look at what I've bought."

. . . In the street Vidal hefted the bag, enjoyed its weight, and wondered what Rosa would say when she saw him spread the patterns, leather, and tools on the kitchen table. And as he conjured and saw the tableau, his excitement and optimism began to leave him. His wife might think he was a fool but she would never say so. What Pepe thought didn't matter. Helen and Tomas would not approve of his plan, would think it was stupid and impractical. Furthermore, they would say to him: He, who preached constantly about saving money, had gone off and foolishly squandered almost ten dollars. After this had been thoroughly yelled out, they would begin to insult the old country and the old days and tell him there was no room in the United States for skilled handicrafts, at least not for people of their class.

They couldn't be right. They didn't dare to be right. But maybe they were right and as Vidal considered this unhappy possibility he realized that he needed some fortification for his courage, and in a drugstore he bought a bottle of wine, uncorked the bottle in a doorway, raised the lip to his mouth and took a long drink. Then another drink. Then a third one, but not quite as long. Still the doubts persisted. In ten minutes Vidal had finished the bottle and although he felt lighter on his feet he had not been able to recapture the first enthusiasm which had warmed far more and far better than the wine.

. . . He muttered aloud to himself and noticed his lips and tongue seemed to be thick and expression was difficult. Tonight he wanted to explain very carefully and thoroughly to his family his reasons for buying the articles in the paper bag. Another bottle of wine—just half a pint—was what he needed and he still had enough money in his pocket to buy one.

With considerable gravity Vidal greeted his family, placed the bag on the kitchen table, and sat down heavily.

"We were worried," his wife said to him. "Shall I put away your hat?"

"If you want to," Vidal replied. "I'm not going out any more tonight. . . . It's very warm in here, Rosa. Very warm."

His wife hurried to open the back door and the kitchen window.

"Help your mother, Pepe," Vidal barked at his son.

Pepe stood up as if getting to his feet were a nuisance. "Sure, Pop."

Vidal restrained himself; this wasn't the time for quarrels or shouting. . . . "Do you want to know what I've done?" he asked his wife and daughter. "Would you like to see what I have in the bag? Would you Pepe?"

"We would," Helen replied and calmed her mother's anxiety by a quick look and wave of the hand.

Helen, Pepe, and their mother crowded around the table and watched Vidal remove his shoemaking supplies, tools, and patterns from the bag. And as Vidal arranged them on the table, Rosa started as she saw the leather and shoemaker's twine, but Helen again restrained her mother with a touch on the arm. Pepe pursed his lips and shook his head; this was a new pitch for his father.

"You know what these are?" Vidal pointed to the spread-out articles on the table.

His wife nodded and turned away as she replied, "To make shoes."

"Sandals," Vidal corrected her as he stood up, swayed, and sat down quickly. Although it was difficult to be impressive sitting down, it was safer. "These are the tools and materials of my craft. You remember, Rosa?" he asked her, "how well I made sandals?"

His wife looked anxiously at her daughter as the glimmerings of Vidal's purpose penetrated her bewilderment. "You have gotten a job with a shoemaker?" she asked hopefully.

Vidal smiled drunkenly. "Better than a job," he said to her, "I am going into business for myself. I am going to become a maker of sandals."

"Father!" Helen stared at him with amused anger.

"Geez, Pop, you're kiddin'," Pepe said to him.

. . . As they watched in silence Vidal removed his coat, loosened his tie, and rolled the sleeves of his shirt. Individually and as a group, they feared the tragedy which was about to take place, yet none could stop its performance . . . [They watched him] blink his eyes as he opened one of the patterns, smoothed it on the table, and stagger as he held the pattern in place with both hands. Breathing heavily he stared at the designs, oriented them, and looked for a moment at his family. They were no encouragement to him as he chose a piece of hard leather for the soles, and almost like a magician who is about to pull a rabbit from his hat showed it to Pepe before he placed it underneath the pattern. With great and deliberate care he began to choose a knife, but an uncertain movement of his hand swept all the tools from the table to the floor.

"Vidal—" his wife kneeled to help him recover the tools— "show us tomorrow. It would be a better time."

"This very night!" Vidal shouted and flung the tools on the table. "That was an accident. Every shoemaker needs more than a table to work on. And I'll show you," he said with emphatic challenge, "that I can still make sandals."

He ruined one section of leather.

Then Vidal tore the pattern. Stubbornly, and with anger, he cut into the leather and traced the rough outline of a sole, but nothing seemed to come right to him. The tools were strange, as if he had never used them before, and he was unable to cut the sharp and precise sections required for a pair of sandals. His wife, sons, and daughter watched silently, knowing they could not stop him and alarmed by the thought of what might happen if they attempted an interruption of this labor by which their father attempted to prove to them that he was still master of his household. And they watched him as they might have a sorry and grotesque comedy single, in which the performer is incompetent, unskilled, and ill versed in his part, but determined, despite the catcalls and jeers of the audience, to play his role through to the last gesture and point of punctuation.

Slowly Vidal raised his hands and turned them. There were his fingers: thickened, scarred, and stiff with age and the punishment of unyielding manual labor; these were the fingers and hands of a sandalmaker. And he had forgotten much. But his hands: the blunt nails; the crooked middle and index fingers of his left hand, broken by a falling crate and set by a friend so they had not healed properly; the crisscross ridges of scars caused by brambles and thorns and gravel; the thickened calloused rings of flesh on his palms. His hands; ugly and crippled, unable to measure up to the demands he made of them.

"I can't do it," he admitted to his family.

Something had to be said, but no one knew what to say.

"I can't do it," Vidal repeated, "I've wasted the money," he looked at the laden table. "Everything," he swept the leather, pattern, and tools to the floor. "Everything."

"It's all right," his wife whispered. "It's all right, Vidal."

"I can't go on," Vidal turned his hands slowly. "I can't—I can't make sandals. My hands are dead."

In the American occupational system, having a job means respectability; unemployment is something that must be explained. Except for children and housewives, part-time employment is not considered acceptable. Thus, when a worker grows too old to follow his trade full time, as Vidal did, retirement may be equivalent to social death. In business and professional occupations, it is usually possible to continue one's career until an advanced age. In professional sports, one is old at thirty-five. For an unskilled laborer, like Vidal, fifty years of age is usually the end of the road. This is especially true of workers who flit from job to job, from community to community. Unless the loyalty of continuing association mitigates the rigor of performance standards, the older worker cannot help but appear inadequate. Thus, the mobility of the American population, the lack of deep roots, is related to the failure to meet standards.

Americans move from one community to another so frequently that, even in rural areas, it is difficult to find someone who has spent a lifetime within a few miles of the spot where he was born. Contrast this with the situation in a Sicilian village where a man might be regarded with suspicion because his family has been in the locality for a mere two hundred years. In world perspective, Americans are vagrants. We can't understand the love of the French peasant for his farm because to Americans a farm is real estate, not an heirloom. You consider a man "irrational" to turn down an attractive business or professional opportunity because it requires him to pull up his roots and cross the country. Most Americans are willing to follow the example of the early settlers: Migrate as soon as you see a chance for better opportunities. The automobile plays a part in American mobility—as anyone who has seen a traffic jam can testify. It made it possible to cover more ground, faster. Even those of us who are not truck drivers, railroad engineers, sailors, and traveling salesmen like to dash about. Americans travel for the sheer pleasure of getting away from the place where they have been. Going on grueling trips by ship, plane, car, bus, or train is called "vacationing."

In spite of all this, American standards show no special consideration for persons seeking new roots. A nation of recent immigrants, they dislike foreigners. A nation of wanderers, they are suspicious of strangers. A nation of recent arrivals in the city, they ridicule "hicks." To put the matter bluntly, it is another case of the pot calling the kettle black. Americans do not seem one whit more sympathetic to the hobo or the migrant laborer because they lack deep roots themselves. Even the Serviceman, who is usually a wanderer by virtue of age, health, and the Selective Service System, finds acceptance difficult. In the vicinity of every Army camp, lonely soldiers wander the streets aimlessly. Aside from bars, movies, and U.S.O. clubs, they may not have any place to go. They miss their home towns where people are "friendlier." But they forget that "back home," people were friendlier to *them*, members of the community, not to strangers. Even there, no one makes it easy for uprooted people to establish a satisfactory self-image. The following case history from Harvey W. Zorbaugh's *The Gold Coast and the Slum*[8] illustrates the difficulties a young girl had in the anonymity of Chicago.

[8] From Harvey W. Zorbaugh, *The Gold Coast and the Slum* (Chicago: The University of Chicago Press, 1929), pp. 71–73.

Emporia, Kansas, was my home until I was twenty-two. My father had a small business there. He was an upright, God-fearing man. . . . He taught us to obey the Ten Commandments, to go to church on Sunday, to do all the things the "respectable" do in a small, gossiping place.

We were a large family but father managed to save enough to send me, the oldest, to a small college in the state. And from the time I was a little girl I had music lessons. It is about these music lessons that the story of my life revolves. . . .

The first few weeks [in the city] went by like magic. It was all so strange and maddeningly stimulating to my smalltown soul. . . .

I soon found a rooming-house was the only place I could live. But it was hard to find a rooming-house where I wanted to live. The rooms I could afford were in gloomy old houses on La Salle Street, bleak and bare, and so large that usually I had to share them with one or two other girls. The beds were hard, and often vermin-infested. The landladies were queer-looking and dowdy, tight-lipped and suspicious of eye, ignorant and coarse. They rarely took any other interest in you than to see that you paid your week in advance. The men and women living in the house were mostly a tough lot. There were goings on that shocked me then—though I would pay scant attention to them now. . . .

I had come to the city in June. By Christmas my loneliness amounted almost to desperation. I had made no friends—a girl brought up on the Commandments doesn't make friends in rooming-houses or as a waitress very readily. I didn't talk the same language as the girls I worked with. At the theater or the restaurant men often came up to me and said things in a way that made me blush, though often I had no idea what they meant, unsophisticated little fool that I was. Mother was ill, and letters from home came less and less frequently. Shortly after Christmas she died, and the last tie that bound me to Emporia was gone. I was "on my own," and very nearly "on my uppers" as well. But I still had my ambition—I would some day be a great *artiste,* and all this loneliness and hardship would be for-gotten. . . .

There were occasional little dramas—as when a baby was found in the alley, and when the woman in "the third floor back" took poison after a quarrel with her husband, or when police came to arrest a man who had eloped from Pittsburgh with his wife's sister, and a new trio of roomers robbed most of the "guests" on the second floor; there were these occasional little dramas when the halls and bathrooms were the scenes of a few minutes' hurried and curious gossip. But the next day these same people would hurry past each other on the stairs without speaking. . . .

[A year of this had gone by, when one day her music teacher told her there was no hope of her ever realizing her ambitions.] I turned dazedly from the piano . . . I scarcely heard him. I picked up my music and tossed it into a waste-basket in the corner; and then I walked out of the room. . . .

Then I began to look at my life in Chicago. What was there in it, after all? My music was gone. I had neither family nor friends. In Emporia there would at least have been neighborhood clubs or the church. But here there was neither. Oh, for someone or something to belong to!

My roommate had been going to Sunday night services at the Fourth Presbyterian Church, over on the Lake Shore Drive. She told them about me, and one day some pastor's assistant's assistant came to call on me. I went one night after that. I was greeted with ostentatious and half-hearted civility. It was all so impersonal . . . I never went back; and no other church ever took an interest in me. The only other group I had had anything to do with, outside of my work, had been a social agency from which I had tried to get a little help in the spring. They treated me as impersonally as though I had been a rag doll. There was ringing of buzzers, long documents with endless questionings to be filled out—and not a human touch in it all. . . .

SUMMARY

When you fail to measure up to the standards by which you have learned to judge yourself, you feel pain that only human beings can experience. It may be a standard of physical attractiveness, a standard of excellence in acting or poetising; a standard that makes marriage a necessary condition of self-respect;

a standard compelling a man to be the money-earning head of his family; or a standard which insists that life is empty without love and friendship. Whatever the standard, failure to meet it produces frustration.

Given the fact of such frustration, and given the fact that people will struggle desperately to avoid it, it is essential to look closely at the nature of the values prevailing in American society in order to see how *they* might be responsible for the suffering you have glimpsed in the foregoing pages. Part Three turns to such an analysis.

ANNOTATED BIBLIOGRAPHY

Bakke, E. Wight, *The Unemployed Man* (New York: E. P. Dutton & Company, Inc., 1934). ([An intensive study of the reactions of unemployed men in England to their position and their attitudes toward unemployment insurance.

Davis, Kingsley, Bredemeier, Harry C., and Levy, Jr., Marion J., *Modern American Society* (New York: Rinehart & Company, 1949). ([Chapter 22 of this book of readings contains several analyses of the ways in which Americans go about finding mates, their frustrations, and the factors affecting their chances of success.

Drake, St. Clair, and Cayton, Horace R., *Black Metropolis* (New York: Harcourt, Brace and Company, Inc., 1945). ([An excellent description and analysis of life in the Negro section of Chicago. Both the frustrations of northern Negroes and their modes of adjustment are vividly detailed.

Erickson, Erik H, *Childhood and Society* (New York: W. W. Norton & Company, 1950). ([A valuable analysis of the psychological and cultural mechanisms of the growth of a sense of identity and of ego-ideals. The author is a leading psychoanalytic psychologist.

Frazier, E. Franklin, *The Negro in the United States* (New York: The Macmillan Company, 1949). ([The definitive history of the Negro in America. The frustrations of pre-Civil War slavery and of contemporary discrimination are reported with a wealth of illustrative material.

Griffith, Beatrice W., *American Me* (Boston: Houghton Mifflin Company, 1948). ([A fictionalized account of the humiliations and the frustrations of Mexican-Americans in Los Angeles.

Kardiner, Abram, *The Mark of Oppression* (New York: W. W. Norton & Company, 1951). ([A well-known psychoanalyst's report of the scars left on Negro personalities by the frustrations they experience.

Kinsey, Alfred C., et al., *Sexual Behavior in the Human Male* (Philadelphia: W. B. Saunders, 1948). ([On the surface this book is a scientific survey of actual male sexual activities in the United States. By implication it is a plea for greater tolerance toward those whose sexual needs bring them into collision with social and legal rules.

PART THREE

The pursuit of success:
Governing principles

In every society people strive to live up to adequacy, worthiness, gratification, and security standards. To do otherwise is to expose themselves to the suffering illustrated in Chapter Two. In some societies, it is relatively easy to live up to these standards; in other societies, it is difficult. Part Three of this book is concerned with *American* society and, more specifically, with principles having implications for the search for a favorable self-image in the United States. We, the authors, maintain that American social problems, which will be considered in Part Four, cannot be understood without prior discussion of American values.

Let us begin this discussion by raising the question of American goals. What do Americans want out of life? To achieve individual salvation? To conquer the world? To earn as much money as possible? The United States is a large and heterogeneous country. A simple answer to the question about American goals is not possible. Some Americans seek a state of grace; some are imperialists; some pursue financial success. However, in general terms the sociologist might characterize the philosophy of living implicitly held by *most* Americans. Americans are not ascetics or mystics. Church membership to the contrary notwithstanding, most Americans appear to be more concerned with the material benefits they are getting in this world than with their prospects for salvation in the next. Frequently, material rewards are desired as a symbol of success rather than for hedonistic gratification, but whatever the ultimate motivation the overt goal is the same. In Chapter 3, we summarize this tendency to place the concerns of this world first by calling one of the four governing principles of American society, "materialism." "Secularism" would be an equally apt descriptive tag. This fact about American society—the emphasis on acquiring goods and services of a tangible sort as the primary fulfillment of life —has important implications for social problems. It means that the search for a favorable self-image is more likely to end in failure in the United States than in a society where the emphasis is on a different type of goal. Consider why this is so. Material things are intrinsically distributive. That is, they cannot be given to everybody *to the same extent*. Thus, in the United States, as in every other society, the population is divided into rich and poor (those who have a larger claim on available production and those who have a smaller claim). You may say, "Oh, but in the United States, even the poorest person has more food and better clothing and shelter than the wealthiest members of certain other societies." This may be of great interest to biologists, but to the sociologist it is an irrelevancy. Remember that human beings never react to *situations,* only to their *symbolic definitions of situations.* The Hollywood writer who said, ". . . I'm snubbed socially because I only get a thousand dollars a week. That hurts," genuinely felt poor. As a matter of fact, the *feeling* of poverty is greater in the United States than in societies where less emphasis is placed on material goods. To put it another way, in a society oriented to the hereafter, material deprivations will probably exist to an even greater extent but they will not be so threatening to the individual's self-respect. In a more secular society, material goals are so prominent that it may be unbearable to have less income than one's neighbor. That is the explanation of a seeming paradox: If poverty causes crime, how can the United States be the richest country in the world and have the highest crime rate? Poverty causes crime in the United States because the American emphasis on material goals threatens the self-conceptions of persons who are *relatively* unsuccessful in terms of wealth and income.

Having observed (a) that most Americans tend to define the meaning of life in terms of their acquisition of material rewards and (b) that such a goal is inherently distributive, you must next consider the principles governing the distribution of facilities and rewards in American society. First of all, how do Americans *come into contact* with persons who can give them what they want? How do you locate an employer who has a job to fill? How do you discover the automobile that will satisfy your need for transportation or your desire to "show off"? One principle institutionalized in American society is to set up specialist organizations which bring together people who mutually need one another. Employment bureaus refer job-seekers to employers; guidance counselors describe to students the merits of various colleges. This is not the dominant principle, however. The principle followed by most Americans in attempting to obtain material rewards is self-reliance. You are expected to fend for yourself, to eschew the assistance of others, in the pursuit of the symbols of success—in short, to "shop around." Chapter 4 attempts to specify how the self-reliance principle works in American life.

There is a *second* distributive problem which all societies must solve: Which members of the society have control over what scarce facilities and rewards? Who in America become business executives, government officials, physicians? One principle institutionalized in American society is to have specialized authorities who assign people to various roles. Thus, the Selective Service System conscripts young men into the Army; government officials are selected by a Civil Service Commission. American society also assigns people to roles without formal appointment. Thus, some government officials are *elected,* presumably on the basis of ability, but it is not easy to specify the kind of ability that is being evaluated when the evaluation results from the consensus of a large number of anonymous individuals. A similar consensual process of selection is at work in the economy. Consumers decide—in an anonymous vote conducted in supermarkets and other retail stores—who is going to produce canned peas for the American housewife. Note that appointment by an authority and nomination by consensus are equally compatible with free choice on the part of the role seeker. The canned pea manufacturer *wants* to produce peas; the candidate *wants* to get elected. Note also that appointment by an authority and nomination by consensus are equally compatible with the definition of eligibility for the role in terms of capacity to perform it. These two criteria, voluntary choice of the role on the part of the role seeker and eligibility for the role in terms of the abilities which it is presumed to call for, define competition, the major principle of role allocation in the United States. This is not to say that competition is the only role allocation principle in American life. Remember that age and sex roles are assigned on the basis of biological qualities; persons possessing the relevant characteristics are not judged in terms of their ability to perform the role. Similarly, the housewife role is assigned to the wife of the breadwinner regardless of her interests or abilities; she does not have to compete with other candidates. Further illustrations of *noncompetitive* role assignment are jobs given to relatives or to members of the same political club and voting rights given to literate citizens who happen to be over twenty-one years of age. Chapter 5 attempts to specify how the *competitive* principle works in American society. For the present, let us simply point out that the competitive principle throws an enormous number of statuses open to multiple candidates. As a result of this principle, you almost invariably anticipate that many other persons have an equal right to the statuses you seek to occupy.

Besides assigning the members of the society to roles which control scarce facilities and rewards and establishing some principle which brings together persons who mutually need one another, each society faces a third distributive problem: Settlement of the *terms* on the basis of which the occupant of role A exchanges material benefits with the occupant of role B. Why should an employer pay a worker X dollars rather than Y dollars per week? Why should a husband give his wife money for her dental bills? One principle institutionalized in American society defines the provision of such service as an end in itself. The physician is supposed to *want* to cure patients entirely apart from their ability to pay. College professors are supposed to respond to the student's craving for knowledge outside as well as inside the classroom. But this is not the dominant principle for satisfying wants in the United States. The principle followed by most Americans is *negotiated exchange*. Chapter 6 attempts to specify how the negotiated exchange principle works in American life. For the present, let us point out merely that negotiated exchange implies a mutual expectation on the part of each negotiator that the other is going to give him as little as he can for as much as possible.

To sum up: The search for a favorable self-image goes on in every society. In the United States this search is more likely to end in failure than in some other societies because Americans pursue material rewards, and material rewards cannot be allocated to everybody to the same extent. Furthermore, this inherent difficulty is exacerbated by the institutionalization in the United States of self-reliance, competition, and negotiated exchange.

CHAPTER THREE

Materialism—by default

Americans live in a scientific age. To say that a man's thinking is unscientific or irrational is almost as insulting as to call him a Communist. But, as scientists are the first to admit, science is a method of acquiring knowledge, not a source of the values by which men live. Thus, a criminologist tries to learn why some people commit crimes and others do not. He does not necessarily *care* which they do. The detachment of the scientist, his willingness to be objective about the subject of his study, is regarded by contemporary America as an intellectual triumph. At the same time, his skepticism about established beliefs, a prerequisite for objectivity, is incompatible with unquestioning faith in God, in country, in family. Joseph Wood Krutch, in a passage from his book, *The Modern Temper,*[1] shows how the critical examination of life has taken some of the meaning out of it.

It is not by thought that men live. Life begins in organisms so simple that one may reasonably doubt even their ability to feel, much less think, and animals cling to or fight for it with a determination which we might be inclined to call superhuman if we did not know that a will to live so thoughtless and so unconditional is the attribute of beings rather below than above the human level. All efforts to find a rational justification of life, to declare it worth the living for this reason or that, are, in themselves, a confession of weakness, since life at its strongest never feels the need of any such justification and since the most optimistic philosopher is less optimistic than that man or animal who, his belief that life is good being too immediate to require the interposition of thought, is no philosopher at all.

In view of this fact it is not surprising that the subtlest intellectual contortions of modern metaphysics should fail to establish the existence of satisfactory aims for life when, as a matter of fact, any effort to do so fails as soon as it begins and can only arise as the result of a weakening of that self-justifying vitality which is the source of all life and of all optimism. As soon as thought begins to seek the "ends" or "aims" to which life is subservient it has already confessed its inability to achieve that animal acceptance of life for life's sake which is responsible for the most determined efforts to live and, in one sense, we may say that even the firmest medieval belief in a perfectly concrete salvation after death marks already the beginning of the completest despair, since that belief could not arise before thought had rendered primitive vitality no longer all-sufficient.

[1] From *The Modern Temper,* by Joseph Wood Krutch, pp. 233–236; copyright 1929, by Harcourt, Brace and Company, Inc., New York; renewed 1956, by Joseph Wood Krutch. Reprinted by permission of the publishers.

The decadent civilizations of the past were not saved by their philosophers but by the influx of simpler peoples who had centuries yet to live before their minds should be ripe for despair. Neither Socrates nor Plato could teach his compatriots any wisdom from which they could draw the strength to compete with the crude energy of their Roman neighbors, and even their thought inevitably declined soon after it had exhausted their vital energy. Nor could these Romans, who flourished longer for the very reason, perhaps, that they had slower and less subtle intellects, live forever; they too were compelled to give way in their time to barbarians innocent alike both of philosophy and of any possible need to call upon it.

The subhuman will to live which is all-sufficient for the animal may be replaced by faith, faith may be replaced by philosophy, and philosophy may attenuate itself until it becomes, like modern metaphysics, a mere game; but each of these developments marks a stage in a progressive enfeeblement of that will to live for the gradual weakening of which it is the function of each to compensate. Vitality calls upon faith for aid, faith turns gradually to philosophy for support, and then philosophy, losing all confidence in its own conclusions, begins to babble of "beneficent fictions" instead of talking about Truth; but each is less confident than what went before and each is, by consequence, less easy to live by. Taken together, they represent the successive and increasingly desperate expedients by means of which man, the ambitious animal, endeavors to postpone the inevitable realization that living is merely a physiological process with only a physiological meaning and that it is most satisfactorily conducted by creatures who never feel the need to attempt to give it any other. But they are at best no more than expedients, and when the last has been exhausted there remains nothing except the possibility that the human species will be revitalized by some race or some class which is capable of beginning all over again.

Krutch argues that contemporary literature reflects the progressive disenchanment with the world which science has helped to bring about. Specifically, he points out that we no longer can

enjoy tragedies—or even understand them. The plays of Sophocles and Shakespeare are "documents" instead of dramas because the assumptions upon which they were based are no longer
believed.[2]

It is, indeed, only at a certain stage in the development of
the realistic intelligence of a people that the tragic faith can
exist. A naiver people may have, as the ancient men of the north
had, a body of legends which are essentially tragic, or it may
have only (and need only) its happy and childlike mythology
which arrives inevitably at its happy end, where the only ones
who suffer "deserve" to do so and in which, therefore, life is
represented as directly and easily acceptable. A too sophisticated
society on the other hand—one which, like ours, has outgrown
not merely the simple optimism of the child but also that vigor-
ous, one might almost say adolescent, faith in the nobility of
man which marks a Sophocles or a Shakespeare, has neither
fairy tales to assure it that all is always right in the end nor
tragedies to make it believe that it rises superior in soul to the
outward calamities which befall it.

Distrusting its thought, despising its passions, realizing its
impotent unimportance in the universe, it can tell itself no
stories except those which make it still more acutely aware of
its trivial miseries. When its heroes (sad misnomer for the pitiful
creatures who people contemporary fiction) are struck down it
is not, like Oedipus, by the gods that they are struck but only,
like Oswald Alving, by syphilis, for they know that the gods,
even if they existed, would not trouble with them, and they cannot attribute to themselves in art an importance in which they
do not believe. Their so-called tragedies do not and cannot end
with one of those splendid calamities which in Shakespeare seem
to reverberate through the universe, because they cannot believe
that the universe trembles when their love is, like Romeo's, cut
off or when the place where they (small as they are) have gathered up their trivial treasure is, like Othello's sanctuary, defiled.
Instead, mean misery piles on mean misery, petty misfortune fol-

[2] *Ibid.*, pp. 128–134 and 24–26.

lows petty misfortune, and despair becomes intolerable because it is no longer even significant or important.

Ibsen once made one of his characters say that he did not read much because he found reading "irrelevant," and the adjective was brilliantly chosen because it held implications even beyond those of which Ibsen was consciously aware. What is it that made the classics irrelevant to him and to us? Is it not just exactly those to him impossible premises which make tragedy what it is, those assumptions that the soul of man is great, that the universe (together with whatever gods may be) concerns itself with him and that he is, in a word, noble? Ibsen turned to village politics for exactly the same reason that his contemporaries and his successors have, each in his own way, sought out some aspect of the common man and his common life—because, that is to say, here was at least something small enough for him to be able to believe.

Bearing this fact in mind, let us compare a modern "tragedy" with one of the great works of a happy age, not in order to judge of their relative technical merits but in order to determine to what extent the former deserves its name by achieving a tragic solution capable of purging the soul or of reconciling the emotions to the life which it pictures. And in order to make the comparison as fruitful as possible let us choose *Hamlet* on the one hand and on the other a play like *Ghosts* which was not only written by perhaps the most powerful as well as the most typical of modern writers but which is, in addition, the one of his works which seems most nearly to escape that triviality which cannot be entirely escaped by any one who feels, as all contemporary minds do, that man is relatively trivial.

In *Hamlet* a prince ("in understanding, how like a god!") has thrust upon him from the unseen world a duty to redress a wrong which concerns not merely him, his mother, and his uncle, but the moral order of the universe. Erasing all trivial fond records from his mind, abandoning at once both his studies and his romance because it has been his good fortune to be called upon to take part in an action of cosmic importance, he plunges (at first) not into action but into thought, weighing the

claims which are made upon him and contemplating the gran-
diose complexities of the universe. And when the time comes at
last for him to die he dies, not as a failure, but as a success. Not
only has the universe regained the balance which had been upset
by what *seemed* the monstrous crime of the guilty pair ('there
is nothing either good nor ill but thinking makes it so'), but in
the process by which that readjustment is made a mighty mind
has been given the opportunity, first to contemplate the magnificent scheme of which it is a part, and then to demonstrate the
greatness of its spirit by playing a role in the grand style which
it called for. We do not need to despair in *such* a world if it has
such creatures in it.

Turn now to *Ghosts*—look upon this picture and upon that.
A young man has inherited syphilis from his father. Struck by
a, to him, mysterious malady he returns to his northern village,
learns the hopeless truth about himself, and persuades his
mother to poison him. The incidents prove, perhaps, that pastors
should not endeavor to keep a husband and wife together unless
they know what they are doing. But what a world is this in which
a great writer can deduce nothing more than that from his greatest work and how are we to be purged or reconciled when we
see it acted? Not only is the failure utter, but it is trivial and
meaningless as well.

Yet the journey from Elsinore to Skien is precisely the journey which the human spirit has made, exchanging in the process
princes for invalids and gods for disease. We say, as Ibsen would
say, that the problems of Oswald Alving are more "relevant" to
our life than the problems of Hamlet, that the play in which he
appears is more "real" than the other more glamorous one, but
it is exactly because we find it so that we are condemned. We
can believe in Oswald but we cannot believe in Hamlet, and a
light has gone out in the universe. Shakespeare justifies the ways
of God to man, but in Ibsen there is no such happy end and
with him tragedy, so called, has become merely an expression of
our despair at finding that such justification is no longer possible.

Modern critics have sometimes been puzzled to account for
the fact that the concern of ancient tragedy is almost exclusively
with kings and courts. They have been tempted to accuse even

Aristotle of a certain naiveté in assuming (as he seems to assume) that the "nobility" of which he speaks as necessary to a tragedy implies a nobility of rank as well as of soul, and they have sometimes regretted that Shakespeare did not devote himself more than he did to the serious consideration of those common woes of the common man which subsequent writers have exploited with increasing pertinacity. Yet the tendency to lay the scene of a tragedy at the court of a king is not the result of any arbitrary convention but of the fact that the tragic writers believed easily in greatness just as we believe easily in meanness. To Shakespeare, robes and crowns and jewels are the garments most appropriate to man because they are the fitting outward manifestation of his inward majesty, but to us they seem absurd because the man who bears them has, in our estimation, so pitifully shrunk. We do not write about kings because we do not believe that any man is worthy to be one and we do not write about courts because hovels seem to us to be dwellings more appropriate to the creatures who inhabit them. Any modern attempt to dress characters in robes ends only by making us aware of a comic incongruity and any modern attempt to furnish them with a language resplendent like Shakespeare's ends only in bombast. . . .

. . . .

To this fact many are not yet awake, but our novels, our poems, and our pictures are enough to reveal that a generation aware of its predicament is at hand. It has awakened to the fact that both the ends which its fathers proposed to themselves and the emotions from which they drew their strength seem irrelevant and remote. With a smile, sad or mocking, according to individual temperament, it regards those works of the past in which were summed up the values of life. The romantic ideal of a world well lost for love and the classic ideal of austere dignity seem equally ridiculous, equally meaningless when referred, not to the temper of the past, but to the temper of the present. The passions which swept through the once major poets no longer awaken any profound response, and only in the bleak, torturous complexities of a T. S. Eliot does it find its moods given ade-

quate expression. Here disgust speaks with a robust voice and
denunciation is confident, but ecstasy, flickering and uncertain,
leaps fitfully up only to sink back among the cinders. And if the
poet, with his gift of keen perceptions and his power of organization, can achieve only the most momentary and unstable adjustments, what hope can there be for those whose spirit is a less
powerful instrument?

And yet it is with such as he, baffled, but content with nothing which plays only upon the surface, that the hope for a still
humanized future must rest. No one can tell how many of the
old values must go or how new the new will be. Thus, while
under the influence of the old mythology the sexual instinct was
transformed into romantic love and tribal solidarity into the
religion of patriotism, there is nothing in the modern consciousness capable of effecting these transmutations. Neither the one
nor the other is capable of being, as it once was, the *raison d'etre*
of a life or the motif of a poem, which is not, strictly speaking,
derivative and anachronistic. Each is fading, each becoming as
much a shadow as devotion to the cult of purification through
self-torture. Either the instincts upon which they are founded
will achieve new transformations or they will remain merely instincts, regarded as having no particular emotional significance
in a spiritual world which, if it exists at all, will be as different
from the spiritual world of, let us say, Robert Browning as that
world is different from the world of Cato the Censor.

As for this present unhappy time, haunted by ghosts from a
dead world and not yet at home in its own, its predicament is
not, to return to the comparison with which we began, unlike
the predicament of the adolescent who has not yet learned to
orient himself without reference to the mythology amid which
his childhood was passed. He still seeks in the world of his experience for the values which he had found there, and he is
aware only of a vast disharmony. But boys—most of them, at
least—grow up, and the world of adult consciousness has always
held a relation to myth intimate enough to make readjustment
possible. The finest spirits have bridged the gulf, have carried
over with them something of a child's faith, and only the coarsest
have grown into something which was no more than finished

animality. Today the gulf is broader, the adjustment more difficult, than ever it was before, and even the possibility of an actual human maturity is problematic. There impends for the human spirit either extinction or a readjustment more stupendous than any made before.

Can it be that Krutch is right, that science has pulled the rug from under us by destroying the beliefs men live by? Or is his pessimism unjustified? After all, the current revival of interest in religion would seem to belie the notion that faith is dead. Let us see how Will Herberg analyzes America's return to religion.[3]

What do Americans believe? Most emphatically, they "believe in God"; 97 per cent according to one survey, 96 per cent according to another, 95 per cent according to a third. About 75 per cent of them, as we have seen, regard themselves as members of churches, and a sizable proportion attend divine services with some frequency and regularity. They believe in prayer: about 90 per cent say they pray on various occasions. They believe in life after death, even in heaven and hell. They think well of the church and of ministers. They hold the Bible to be an inspired book, the "word of God." By a large majority, they think children should be given religious instruction and raised as church members. By a large majority, too, they hold religion to be of very great importance. In all of these respects their attitudes are as religious as those of any people today, or, for that matter, as those of any Western people in recent history.

Yet these indications are after all relatively superficial; they tell us what Americans say (and no doubt believe) about themselves and their religious views; they do not tell us what in actuality these religious views are. Nowhere are surface appearances more deceptive, nowhere is it more necessary to try to penetrate beyond mere assertions of belief than in such ultimate matters as religion.

We do penetrate a little deeper, it would seem, when we

[3] From *Protestant, Catholic, Jew* by Will Herberg, pp. 85–104. Copyright © 1955 by Will Herberg. Reprinted by permission of Doubleday & Company, Inc., Garden City, New York.

take note of certain curious discrepancies the surveys reveal in the responses people make to questions about their religion. Thus, according to one trustworthy source, 73 per cent said they believed in an afterlife, with God as judge, but "only 5 per cent [had] any fear, not to say expectation, of going [to hell]." Indeed, about 80 per cent, according to another source, admitted that what they were "most serious about" was not the life after death in which they said they believed, but in trying to live as comfortably in this life as possible. And in their opinion they were not doing so badly even from the point of view of the divine judgment: 91 per cent felt that they could honestly say that they were trying to lead a good life, and 78 per cent felt no hesitation in saying that they more than half measured up to their own standards of goodness, over 50 per cent asserting that they were in fact following the rule of loving one's neighbor as oneself "all the way"! This amazingly high valuation that most Americans appear to place on their own virtue would seem to offer a better insight into the basic religion of the American people than any figures as to their formal beliefs can provide, however important in themselves these figures may be.

But perhaps the most significant discrepancy in the assertions Americans make about their religious views is to be found in another area. When asked, "Would you say your religious beliefs have any effect on your ideas of politics and business?", a majority of the same Americans who had testified that they regarded religion as something "very important" answered that their religious beliefs had no real effect on their ideas or conduct in these decisive areas of everyday life; specifically, 54 per cent said no, 39 per cent said yes, and 7 per cent refused to reply or didn't know. This disconcerting confession of the irrelevance of religion to business and politics was attributed by those who appraised the results of the survey as pointing to a calamitous divorce between the "private" and the "public" realms in the religious thinking of Americans. There is certainly a great deal of truth in this opinion, and we shall have occasion to explore it in a different context, but in the present connection it would seem that another aspect of the matter is more immediately pertinent. *Some* ideas and standards undeniably govern the conduct of Americans in their affairs of business and politics; if they are not ideas and standards associated with the teachings of religion, what are they? It will not do to say that people just act "selfishly" without reference to moral standards of any kind. All people act "selfishly," of course; but it is no less true of all people, Americans included, that their "selfishness" is controlled, mitigated, or, at worst, justified by some sort of moral commitment, by some sort of belief in a system of values beyond immediate self-interest. The fact that more than half the people openly admit that their religious beliefs have no effect on their ideas of politics and business would seem to indicate very strongly that, over and above conventional religion, there is to be found among Americans some sort of faith or belief or set of convictions, not generally designated as religion but definitely operative as such in their lives in the sense of providing them with some fundamental context of normativity and meaning. What this unacknowledged "religion" of the American people is, and how it manages to coexist with their formal religious affirmations and affiliations, it is now our task to investigate.

"Every functioning society," Robin M. Williams, Jr. points out, "has to an important degree a *common* religion. The possession of a common set of ideas, rituals, and symbols can supply an overarching sense of unity even in a society riddled with conflicts." What is this "common religion" of American society, the "common set of ideas, rituals, and symbols" that give it its "overarching sense of unity"? Williams provides us with a further clue when he suggests that "men are always likely to be intolerant of opposition to their central ultimate values." What are these "central ultimate values" about which Americans are "intolerant"? No one who knows anything about the religious situation in this country would be likely to suggest that the things Americans are "intolerant" about are the beliefs, standards, or teachings of the religions they "officially" acknowledge as theirs. Americans are proud of their tolerance in matters of religion: one is expected to "believe in God," but otherwise religion is not supposed to be a ground of "discrimination." This is, no doubt, admirable, but is it not "at least in part, a sign that the crucial values of the system are no longer couched in a religious framework"?

What, then, is the "framework" in which they *are* couched? What, to return to our original question, is the "common religion" of the American people, as it may be inferred not only from their words but also from their behavior?

It seems to me that a realistic appraisal of the values, ideas, and behavior of the American people leads to the conclusion that Americans, by and large, do have their "common religion" and that that "religion" is the system familiarly known as the American Way of Life. It is the American Way of Life that supplies American society with an "overarching sense of unity" amid conflict. It is the American Way of Life about which Americans are admittedly and unashamedly "intolerant." It is the American Way of Life that provides the framework in terms of which the crucial values of American existence are couched. By every realistic criterion the American Way of Life is the operative faith of the American people. . . .

The American Way of Life is, of course, conceived as the corporate "way" of the American people, but it has its implications for the American as an individual as well. It is something really operative in his actual life. When in the *Ladies' Home Journal* poll, Americans were asked "to look within [themselves] and state honestly whether [they] thought [they] really obeyed the law of love under certain special conditions," 90 per cent said yes and 5 per cent no when the one to be "loved" was a person belonging to a different religion; 80 per cent said yes and 12 per cent no when it was the case of a member of a different race; 78 per cent said yes and 10 per cent no when it concerned a business competitor—but only 27 per cent said yes and 57 per cent no in the case of "a member of a political party that you think is dangerous," while 25 per cent said yes and 63 per cent said no when it concerned an enemy of the nation. These figures are most illuminating, first because of the incredible self-assurance they reveal with which the average American believes he fulfills the "impossible" law of love, but also because of the light they cast on the differential impact of the violation of this law on the American conscience. For it is obvious that the figures reflect not so much the actual behavior of the American people—no people on earth ever loved their neighbors as themselves as much as the American people say they do—as how seriously Americans take transgressions against the law of love in various cases. Americans feel they *ought* to love their fellow men despite differences of race or creed or business interest; that is what the American Way of Life emphatically prescribes. But the American Way of Life almost explicitly sanctions hating a member of a "dangerous" political party (the Communist party is obviously meant here) or an enemy of one's country, and therefore an overwhelming majority avow their hate. In both situations, while the Jewish-Christian law of love is formally acknowledged, the truly operative factor is the value system embodied in the American Way of Life. Where the American Way of Life approves of love of one's fellow man, most Americans confidently assert that they practice such love; where the American Way of Life disapproves, the great mass of Americans do not hesitate to confess that they do not practice it, and apparently feel very little guilt for their failure. No better pragmatic test as to what the operative religion of the American people actually is could be desired.

It is not suggested here that the ideals Americans feel to be indicated in the American Way of Life are scrupulously observed in the practice of Americans; they are in fact constantly violated, often grossly. But violated or not, they are felt to be normative and relevant to "business and politics" in a way that the formal tenets of "official" religion are not. That is what makes the American Way of Life the "common religion" of American society in the sense here intended.

. . . The "common faith" of American society is not merely a civic religion to celebrate the values and convictions of the American people as a corporate entity. It has its inner, personal aspects as well; or rather, side by side and in intimate relation with the civic religion of the American Way of Life, there has developed, primarily through a devitalization of the historic faiths, an inner, personal religion that promises salvation to the disoriented, tormented souls of a society in crisis.

The inner, personal religion is based on the American's *faith in faith*. We have seen that a primary religious affirmation of the American is his belief in religion. The American believes that religion is something very important for the community; he also believes that "faith," or what we may call religiosity, is a kind of "miracle drug" that can cure all the ailments of the spirit. It is not faith in *anything* that is so powerful, just faith, the "magic of believing." "It was back in those days," a prominent American churchman writes, recalling his early years, "that I formed a habit that I have never broken. I began saying in the morning two words, 'I believe.' Those two words *with nothing added* . . . give me a running start for my day, and for every day" (emphasis not in original).

The cult of faith takes two forms, which we might designate as introvert and extrovert. In its introvert form faith is trusted to bring mental health and "peace of mind," to dissipate anxiety and guilt, and to translate the soul to the blessed land of "normality" and "self-acceptance." In earlier times this cult of faith was quite literally a cult of "faith healing," best expressed in what H. Richard Niebuhr has described as the "man-centered, this-worldly, lift-yourselves-by-your-own-bootstraps doctrine of New Thought and Christian Science." Latterly it has come to vest itself in the fashionable vocabulary of psychoanalysis and is offering a synthesis of religion and psychiatry. But at bottom it is the same cult of faith in faith, the same promise that through "those two words, 'I believe,' with nothing added," all our troubles will be dissipated and inner peace and harmony restored.

The cult of faith has also its extrovert form, and that is known as "positive thinking." "Positive thinking," thinking that is "affirmative" and avoids the corrosions of "negativity" and "skepticism," thinking that "has faith," is recommended as a powerful force in the world of struggle and achievement. Here again it is not so much faith in anything, certainly not the theocentric faith of the historic religions, that is supposed to confer this power—but just faith, the psychological attitude of having faith, so to speak. And here too the cult is largely the product of the inner disintegration and enfeeblement of the historic religions; the familiar words are retained, but the old meaning is voided. "Have faith," "don't lose faith," and the like, were once injunctions to preserve one's unwavering trust in the God from Whom comes both the power to live and the "peace that passeth understanding." Gradually these phrases have come to be an appeal to maintain a "positive" attitude to life and not to lose confidence in oneself and one's activities. "To believe in yourself and in everything you do"; such, at bottom, is the meaning of the contemporary cult of faith, whether it is proclaimed by devout men from distinguished pulpits or offered as the "secret of success" by self-styled psychologists who claim to have discovered the "hidden powers" of man. What is important is faith, faith in faith. Even where the classical symbols and formulas are still retained, that is very often what is meant and what is understood.

Herberg seems to be saying that American society retains the outward forms of religiosity but has emptied it of biblical content. Or, to put it another way, our faith in faith reflects a widespread recognition that we need something to believe in. If we lack faith in Divine purpose, we will worship at lesser shrines. We may make a religion out of self-gratification (hedonism). We may make a religion out of our nationality or our social class (groupism). We may also make a religion of *things,* of the tangible entities which seem more real to a population impressed with the triumphs of atomic physics and antibiotics. The worship of things (materialism) is not, however, undertaken with a clear conscience. Americans are far more interested in the symbolic rather than the physical aspect of cars and houses and clothes. Americans are materialistic by default—because they try to use "things" to express their search for the meaning of existence. Aldous Huxley, in the following excerpt from his book, *Jesting Pilate,*[4] captures this paradoxical quality of American materialism.

Turning over the pages of the Chicago telephone directory, I came upon a full-page advertisement of a firm of undertakers, or "morticians," as they are now more elegantly styled in Amer-

[4] From *Jesting Pilate,* by Aldous Huxley, pp. 305–314. Copyright 1926, 1954 by Aldous Huxley. Reprinted by permission of Harper & Brothers, New York.

ica. The type was large and bold; my eye was fatally caught. I
interrupted my search to read, in twenty lines of lyrical prose, an
appreciation of the incomparable Service which Kalbsfleisch and
Company were rendering to Society. Their shop, I learned, was
a mortuary chapel in the Gothic style; their caskets (the grosser
English would call them coffins) were elegant, silk-lined and
cheap; their motor-hearses were funereally sumptuous; their
manners towards the bereaved were grave, yet cheering, yet pur-
posefully uplifting; and they were fortunate in being able to
"lay the Loved Ones to rest in — graveyard, the Cemetery Unusual." Service was their motto and always would be. Service
wholehearted and unflagging. And to prove that they meant it,
personally and individually, they had reproduced two photo-
graphs, one of Mr. Kalbsfleisch, the Governing Director of the
Firm, and the other of charming Mrs. Kalbsfleisch, Licensed
Embalmer.

I remained for some time in meditative contemplation of
Mrs. Kalbsfleisch's smile; I re-read more than once her husband's poetical and uplifting prose. The page on which I now
gazed was something more, I reflected, than a mere page of
advertising in a telephone book. It was a page out of contemporary American history. Something is hapening on the Western
shore of the Atlantic, something that has already made America
unlike any other country in the world, something that threatens
to separate it still further from the older civilisations, unless
(which God forbid) the older civilisations should themselves
fall victims to the same distorting process. To any one who reads
and inwardly digests Mr. Kalbsfleisch's advertisement in the
Chicago telephone book, the nature of this strange historical
process becomes clear. The page is a symptom and a revealing
symbol [of changes in established values]. . . .

There are two ways in which the existing standards of value
may be altered. In the first case, the very existence of values may
be denied. In the second, values are admitted, but the mode in
which they are assigned is changed: things which in the past had
been regarded as possessing great value are disparaged or, more
often, things which were previously considered of small value
come to be regarded as precious.

In Europe such attempts as have been made to alter the existing standard of values have generally taken the form of denials of the existence of values. Our belief that things possess value is due to an immediate sense or intuition; we feel, and feeling we know, that things have value. If men have doubted the real existence of values, that is because they have not trusted their own immediate and intuitive conviction. They have required an intellectual, a logical and "scientific" proof of their existence. Now such a proof is not easily found at the best of times. But when you start your argumentation from the premises laid down by scientific materialism, it simply cannot be discovered. Indeed any argument starting from these premises must infallibly end in a denial of the real existence of values. Fortunately human beings are capable of enormous inconsistencies, and the eighteenth- and nineteenth-century men of science, whose conception of the universe was such that values could not be regarded by them as possessing any sort of real existence, were in practice the most ardent upholders of the established standards of values.

Still the materialist conception of the universe could not fail to exert an influence. The generation of Arnold and of Tennyson sat uncomfortably on the horns of what seemed an unescapable dilemma. Either the materialist hypothesis was true; in which case there was no such thing as value. Or else it was false; in which case values really existed, but science could not. But science manifestly *did* exist. The electric telegraph and the steam engine were there to prove it. The fact that you could go into any post office and communicate almost instantaneously with the antipodes was felt to be a confirmation of the materialistic hypothesis then current among men of science. It worked, therefore it was true, and therefore our intimate sense of the existence of values was a mere illusion. Tennyson and Arnold did not want it to be an illusion; they were distressed, they were inwardly divided. Their intellects denied what their feelings asserted; and the Truth (or rather what was at that time apparently the Truth) was at war with their hopes, their intuitive convictions, their desires. The European intellectuals of a later generation accepted the conclusions logically derivable from the scientific-materialist hypothesis and resigned themselves—almost with glee—to living in a devaluated world. Some of them are still with us, and the theories which they propounded, as corollaries to the main value-denying theory from which they started, are still influential. Claiming to speak as the apostles of scientific truth, they stripped art of its significance, they reinterpreted human life in terms, not of its highest spiritual aspects, but of its lowest. (I am using the terms "highest" and "lowest," which they, of course, would repudiate as nonsensical.) A less sophisticated generation had regarded the Sistine frescoes as being somehow superior to a prettily patterned rug, *Macbeth* as more important than *The Rape of the Lock*. Illusion! According to the apostles of scientific truth, one was really just as good as the other. Indeed, the *Rape* and the patterned rug were actually superior to *Macbeth* and the Michelangelo frescoes, as being more finished and perfect works of art: they aroused, it was explained, intenser "esthetic emotions." Art thus satisfactorily disposed of, religion was next "explained" in terms of sex. The moral conscience was abolished (another illusion) and "amuse yourself" proclaimed as the sole categorical imperative. The theories of Freud were received in intellectual circles with acclaim; to explain every higher activity of the human mind in terms of incest and coprophily came to be regarded not only as truly scientific, but also as somehow virile and courageous. Freudism became the *realpolitik* of psychology and philosophy. Those who denied values felt themselves to be rather heroic; instinctively they were appealing to the standards which they were trying, intellectually, to destroy. . . .

But the influence of these *ci-devant* "scientific" deniers of value has not been wide. In most human beings the intuitive sense of values is too strong to be seriously affected by intellectual arguments, however specious. They are revolted by the denial of values; they insist on interpreting the world in terms of high and low. Unfortunately, however, they are apt to make mistakes and to call things by the wrong names, labelling "high" what should rightly be low, and "low" what ought to be high. . . .

The morticians, and with them all the Business Men of America, are as whole-heartedly enthusiastic about Service as was ever St. Francis or his divine Master. But the activities which they designate by the word "Service" happen to be slightly different from those which the Founder of Christianity called by the same name. . . .

. . . It is on the same ground that they perform necessary jobs well that American Business Men claim to be doing Service, and Service of the highest value. They overlook the significant historical fact that all the valuable things in life, all the things that make for civilisation and progress, are precisely the unnecessary ones. All scientific research, all art, all religion are (by comparison with making coffins or breakfast foods) unnecessary. But if we had stuck to the merely necessary, we should still be apes. . . . By exalting the merely necessary to an equality with the unnecessary, the American Business Man has falsified the standard of values. The service rendered by a mortician or a realtor has come to be regarded as the equivalent of the service rendered by an artist of a man of science. Babbitt can now honestly believe that he and his kind are doing as much for humanity as the Pasteurs and the Isaac Newtons. Kalbsfleisch among his silk-lined caskets knows himself to be as good as Beethoven. Successful stockbrokers, certain that Business is Religion, can come home after a day of speculation on the Exchange, feeling as virtuously happy as Buddha must have felt when he had renounced the world and received his great illumination.

Note that Aldous Huxley's argument involves two points: (a) a misinterpretation of science tends to undermine faith generally, and (b) the everyday business of life tends to be regarded as the main point of life. Although he does not explicitly denounce the American preoccupation with "things," Huxley implies that materialistic standards of evaluation have crept into sectors of American life where they should not be. As an example of this phenomenon, consider that the "leading" minister of a community is the minister with the largest and wealthiest congregation, not the minister whose life comes closest to Christian ideals. In the following excerpt from Walter Clark's article, "Education by Facade," [5] observe a similar tendency in the field of education.

A certain third-rate college in the Middle West recently raised several million dollars in a succesful campaign for funds. Despite the fact that the professors were wretchedly paid, all of the money went into a complete renovation of the campus. It is still a third-rate college, but the public now is not so aware of it. A Southern university accepted an enormous gift which, by the terms of the donation, could be spent only on building. The campus is now one of the showplaces of the region, but since none of the funds received could be put aside for upkeep or faculty, the university scrimps along, able to maintain only the most meager teaching force with the thinnest possible salaries. . . . Much can be made of the point that an opportunity to live amid scenes of beauty and good taste is one of those experiences that should be offered by every college and university. Certainly there is no virtue in the ugliness of a campus. Yet, as one looks back over the last three decades or so, one has the feeling that the reaction against ugliness has been overdone. Such lavish appointments as characterize the residential units of Yale and Harvard or the clubs of Princeton represent something that few undergraduates will ever experience again, and then only if they enter the most lucrative vocations. A man is rich in proportion to the number of things he can afford to let alone, as Thoreau reminds us, and nearly every commencement orator makes much of the devotion of the liberal arts to non-material values; yet through these very expensive expressions of beauty the undergraduates are taking a very subtle but very effective course in the rewards of materialism. Good taste is not synonymous with great expense.

Again, we hear the continual cries of the heads of private colleges asserting their independence of the government and their determination to have no part of public funds. Independence

[5] Walter Houston Clark, "Education by Facade," *American Association of University Professors Bulletin,* Vol. 38 (Winter, 1952–53), pp. 528–31. Reprinted by permission of Walter Houston Clark and the editors of the *American Association of University Professors Bulletin.*

is indeed a commodity precious to the educational enterprise, but it is relative rather than absolute, and one may question whether dependence on business—which is the chief source of financial supply for the independent colleges—is always more ennobling or fruitful than the dependence on government, which characterizes public institutions. Doubtless it is more "respectable." But at any rate there is the possibility of a holier-than-thou hypocrisy that is more dangerous because it so often goes unrecognized. One would not want to carp at all the representatives of business who receive honorary degrees on commencement day, for many are the statesmen of the market place whose vision and public-spiritedness well deserve recognition. Yet the academic honors heaped on mediocre men, whose chief claim on fame is the hall of business administration this one has donated or the swimming pool that another has endowed, must give one pause. They can have but two effects on the wide-eyed seniors who watch these individuals join a procession of celebrities who step forward in rotation to receive the academic hood. The keener-eyed and better informed will react with a measure of cynicism that will cheapen in their eyes their own degrees; the average senior, however, despite the brave words of the commencement speaker, will adulate and feel the urge to imitate the careers of those who can afford such largess.

A certain businessman, through dubious financial transactions, acquired a large fortune, and when the government began to inquire into his affairs, he deftly changed to foreign citizenship and so thwarted the curiosity of the law. He nevertheless has been generous toward his *alma mater* and the church in the village in which his college is situated. Here he returns at frequent intervals, where he is feted and dined by those unwilling to believe that so rich a man could not be respectable. His chief gift to the college, to date, is the principal classroom building, where the powers, not content with merely giving the building his name on its construction, have recently seen fit to install his photograph in the lobby. . . .

Of course, it would be too much to ask of college administrators, already harassed by the specters of inflation and the difficulty of competing with the government in the feverish chase after funds, that they track down every gift dollar to its source to see that it has been honestly come by. . . . In the cruel necessity of choosing between subsistence and ideals, facade and worth, it is too often that subsistence and facade come first and the others worry along behind if they can be afforded.

SUMMARY

Krutch, Herberg, Huxley, and Clark criticize what seems to them the absence of meaningful goals in American life, and all of them recognize American "materialism." Krutch echoes Hamlet's lament about being "sicklied o'er with the pale cast of thought." Civilized man has lost the élan that comes from a commitment to some important purpose. Since it is impossible for human beings to live without *some* conception of a point to life, Westerners seem often to be engaged in a desperate effort to fill the void left by the disappearance of earlier and "naive" faiths. Turning specifically to America, Will Herberg believes that the resurgence of traditional religion, although it may be motivated by a search for identity and meaning, results in an empty formalism. Whether or not Americans are Godless, they do not dare to be churchless.

What is left for many Americans, says Huxley, is an escape from the dread fear of "pointlessness" into a mad round of materialistic preoccupations and distractions. They try to persuade themselves and others that they *are* doing something important: They are, they are, they are! Perhaps Huxley goes too far. To anticipate Chapter 17, we might ask whether the "service orientation" which Huxley considers mere hypocrisy is a genuine, not a fake, discovery of the meaning of life. Maybe Huxley is so blinded by the gaucherie of the words of Kalbsfleisch that he misses the embryo of a valid new faith.

Certainly, there is a real problem here—the problem of what is America *for?* And doubtless, "materialism" is a strong contender for the answer. As the reader will see in forthcoming chapters, this answer gives rise to not a few "social problems."

ANNOTATED BIBLIOGRAPHY

Durkheim, Emile, *Suicide* (Glencoe, Illinois: The Free Press, 1951).
⟨ A classic study by the great French sociologist. Durkheim's discussion of *"anomie"* here and in his *Division of Labor* adds considerably to understanding the nature and consequences of self-oriented materialism.

Merton, Robert K., "Social Structure and Anomie," and "Continuities in the Theory of Social Structure and Anomie," in Robert K. Merton, *Social Theory and Social Structure* (Glencoe, Illinois: The Free Press, 1957), Chapters 4 and 5. ❨ We are greatly indebted for this present book to the original essay and a later development of its theme. We refer the reader to it in the present context for Merton's excellent brief descriptions of the cult of success in America.

Parrington, Vernon Louis, *Main Currents in American Thought* (New York: Harcourt, Brace and Company, Inc., 1927). ❨ A classic among historians' efforts to capture the spirit of an age or society through its literature. Parrington's description of the "Great Barbecue" in Volume II is an impressive account of the heyday of one form of American materialism.

Rosten, Leo C., *Hollywood* (New York: Harcourt, Brace and Company, Inc., 1941). ❨ A searching yet sympathetic study of the people who make motion pictures. Rosten shows how the values of the market place, money, and prestige dominate this branch of the entertainment industry.

Weber, Max, *The Protestant Ethic and the Spirit of Capitalism* (London: George Allen & Unwin, 1930), Chapter 3. ❨ An analysis of the interrelations between capitalism and Protestantism. According to Weber, the spirit of capitalism required, in order to flourish, a religious orientation different from that of medieval Europe.

Whitehead, Alfred North, *Science and the Modern World* (New York: The Macmillan Company, 1925). ❨ A brilliant history of the impact of science on the intellectual climate of society.

CHAPTER FOUR

Self-reliance

Alfred P. Doolittle sings in "My Fair Lady,"

> The Lord above made man to help his neighbor,
> No matter where—on land or sea or foam.
> But, with a little bit of luck,
> When he comes around you won't be home.

The song is supposedly English, but the sentiment is characteristically American. Its folklore expressions are legion: "Trust in God—but keep your powder dry"; "God helps him who helps himself"; "Do unto others as they would do unto you, only do it first." These are the pungently irreverent summaries of a basic American principle: You sink or swim on your own. That principle is the other side of the coin of freedom of choice: If I am free to choose what to do with my own life, then so are you— but your freedom means (in the American version) that I cannot expect help from you.

Americans admire "self-made" men and tend to feel superior to those who cannot survive without the guidance or charity of others. Receiving charity is regarded as a sign of moral decay because charity is a clear violation of the self-reliance principle. Help from one's family is one of the few exceptions to the principle which Americans permit—and even that is regarded suspiciously.

In short, success and failure in America are considered a problem of individual achievement. The individual has the responsibility not only to select his roles in life but also to train himself to play them; and in a complex society, this is not always easy. Ruth Benedict's article, "Continuities and Discontinuities in Cultural Conditioning," [1] contrasts the difficult transitions of American society with the easier transitions in many nonliterate communities. We, the authors, assume that a major factor underlying the discontinuity from child to adult in contemporary America is just this implicit norm of self-reliance: Not only are expectations for an adult radically different from expectations for a child; more important, there is very little social guidance in achieving the transition. As Dr. Benedict put it toward the end of the article, ". . . far from redoubling efforts to help children bridge this gap, adults in our culture put all the blame on the child when he fails to manifest spontaneously the new behavior . . ."

All cultures must deal in one way or another with the cycle of growth from infancy to adulthood. Nature has posed the situation dramatically: on the one hand, the newborn baby, physiologically vulnerable, unable to fend for itself, or to par-

[1] From an article by Ruth Benedict entitled "Continuities and Discontinuities in Cultural Conditioning." Reprinted by special permission of The William Alanson White Psychiatric Foundation, Inc., Washington, D. C., and Patrick Mullahy from *A Study of Interpersonal Relations,* edited by Patrick Mullahy and published by Thomas Nelson and Sons, New York. Copyright 1949 by Hermitage Press. (Originally published in *Psychiatry,* 1938, **1**:161–167.)

ticipate on its own initiative in the life of the group, and, on the
other, the adult man or woman. Every man who rounds out his
human potentialities must have been a son first and a father later
and the two roles are physiologically in great contrast; he must
first have been dependent upon others for his very existence and
later he must provide such security for others. This discontinuity
in the life cycle is a fact of nature and is inescapable. Facts of
nature, however, in any discussion of human problems, are ordinarily read off not at their bare minimal but surrounded by all
the local accretions of behavior to which the student of human
affairs has become accustomed in his own culture. For that reason it is illuminating to examine comparative material from other
societies in order to get a wider perspective on our own special
accretions. . . .

From a comparative point of view our culture goes to great
extremes in emphasizing contrasts between the child and the
adult. The child is sexless, the adult estimates his virility by his
sexual activities; the child must be protected from the ugly facts
of life, the adult must meet them without psychic catastrophe;
the child must obey, the adult must command this obedience.
These are all dogmas of our culture, dogmas which in spite of
the facts of nature other cultures commonly do not share. In
spite of the physiological contrast between child and adult these
are cultural accretions.

It will make the point clearer if we consider one habit in our
own culture in regard to which there is not this discontinuity of
conditioning. With the greatest clarity of purpose and economy
of training, we achieve our goal of conditioning everyone to eat
three meals a day. The baby's training in regular food periods
begins at birth and no crying of the child and no inconvenience
to the mother is allowed to interfere. We gauge the child's
physiological make-up and at first allow it food oftener than
adults, but, because our goal is firmly set and our training consistent, before the child is two years old it has achieved the adult
schedule. From the point of view of other cultures this is as
startling as the fact of three-year-old babies perfectly at home
in deep water is to us. Modesty is another sphere in which our
child training is consistent and economical; we waste no time in

clothing the baby and in contrast to many societies where the child runs naked till it is ceremonially given its skirt or its public sheath at adolescence, the child's training fits it precisely for adult conventions.

In neither of these aspects of behavior is there need for an individual in our culture to embark before puberty, at puberty or at some later date upon a course of action which all his previous training has tabued. He is spared the unsureness inevitable in such a transition. . . .

I shall select for discussion three . . . contrasts that occur in our culture between the individual's role as child and as father: 1. responsible—non-responsible status role; 2. dominance—submission; 3. contrasted sexual role. It is largely upon our cultural commitments to these three contrasts that the discontinuity in the life cycle of an individual in our culture depends.

1. RESPONSIBLE—NON-RESPONSIBLE STATUS ROLE

The techniques adopted by societies which achieve continuity during the life cycle in this sphere in no way differ from those we employ in our uniform conditioning to three meals a day. They are merely applied to other areas of life. We think of the child as wanting to play and the adult as having to work, but in many societies the mother takes the baby daily in her shawl or carrying net to the garden or to gather roots, and adult labor is seen even in infancy from the pleasant security of its position in close contact with its mother. When the child can run about it accompanies its parents still, doing tasks which are essential and yet suited to its powers, and its dichotomy between work and play is not different from that its parents recognize, namely the distinction between the busy day and the free evening. The tasks it is asked to perform are graded to its powers and its elders wait quietly by, not offering to do the task in the child's place. Everyone who is familiar with such societies has been struck by the contrast with our child training. Dr. Ruth Underhill tells me of sitting with a group of Papago elders in Arizona when the man of the house turned to his little three-year-old granddaughter and asked her to close the door. The door was heavy and hard to shut. The child tried, but it did not move. Several times the grandfather repeated, "Yes, close the door." No one jumped to the child's assistance. No one took the responsibility away from her. On the other hand there was no impatience, for after all the child was small. They sat gravely waiting till the child succeeded and her grandfather gravely thanked her. It was assumed that the task would not be asked of her unless she could perform it, and having been asked the responsibility was hers alone just as if she were a grown woman.

The essential point of such child training is that the child is from infancy continuously conditioned to responsible social participation while at the same time the tasks that are expected of it are adapted to its capacity. The contrast with our society is very great. A child does not make any labor contribution to our industrial society except as it competes with an adult; its work is not measured against its own strength and skill but against high-geared industrial requirements. Even when we praise a child's achievement in the home we are outraged if such praise is interpreted as being of the same order as praise of adults. The child is praised because the parent feels well disposed, regardless of whether the task is well done by adult standards, and the child acquires no sensible standard by which to measure its achievement. The gravity of a Cheyenne Indian family ceremoniously making a feast out of the little boy's first snowbird is at the furthest remove from our behavior. At birth the little boy was presented with a toy bow, and from the time he could run about serviceable bows suited to his stature were specially made for him by the man of the family. Animals and birds were taught him in a graded series beginning with those most easily taken, and as he brought in his first of each species his family duly made a feast of it, accepting his contribution as gravely as the buffalo his father brought. When he finally killed a buffalo, it was only the final step of his childhood conditioning, not a new adult role with which his childhood experience had been at variance. . . .

2. DOMINANCE—SUBMISSION

Dominance—submission is the most striking of those categories of behavior where like does not respond to like but where
one type of behavior stimulates the opposite response. It is one
of the most prominent ways in which behavior is patterned in
our culture. When it obtains between classes, it may be nour-
ished by continuous experience; the difficulty in its use between
children and adults lies in the fact that an individual conditioned
to one set of behavior in childhood must adopt the opposite as
an adult. Its opposite is a pattern of approximately identical
reciprocal behavior, and societies which rely upon continuous
conditioning characteristically invoke this pattern. In some
primitive cultures the very terminology of address between father
and son, and more commonly, between grandfather and grandson or uncle and nephew, reflects this attitude. In such kinship
terminologies one reciprocal expresses each of these relationships
so that son and father, for instance, exchange the same term
with one another, just as we exchange the same term with a
cousin. The child later will exchange it with his son. "Father—
son," therefore, is a continuous relationship he enjoys throughout life. The same continuity, backed up by verbal reciprocity,
occurs far oftener in the grandfather-grandson relationship or
that of mother's brother-sister's son. When these are "joking"
relationships, as they often are, travellers report wonderingly
upon the liberties and pretensions of tiny toddlers in their dealings with these family elders. In place of our dogma of respect
to elders such societies employ in these cases a reciprocity as
nearly identical as may be. The teasing and practical joking the
grandfather visits upon his grandchild, the grandchild returns
in like coin; he would be led to believe that he failed in propriety if he did not give like for like. If the sister's son has right
of access without leave to his mother's brother's possessions, the
mother's brother has such rights also to the child's possessions.
They share reciprocal privileges and obligations which in our
society can develop only between agemates.

From the point of view of our present discussion, such kinship conventions allow the child to put in practice from infancy
the same forms of behavior which it will rely upon as an adult;

behavior is not polarized into a general requirement of submission for the child and dominance for the adult.

It is clear from the techniques described above by which the child is conditioned to a responsible status role that these depend chiefly upon arousing in the child the desire to share responsibility in adult life. To achieve this little stress is laid upon obedience but much stress upon approval and praise. Punishment is very commonly regarded as quite outside the realm of possibility, and natives in many parts of the world have drawn the conclusion from our usual disciplinary methods that white parents do not love their children. If the child is not required to be submissive, however, many occasions for punishment melt away; a variety of situations which call for it do not occur. Many American Indian tribes are especially explicit in rejecting the ideal of a child's submissive or obedient behavior. Prince Maximilian von Wied who visited the Crow Indians over a hundred years ago describes a father's boasting about his young son's intractability even when it was the father himself who was flouted; "He will be a man," his father said. He would have been baffled at the idea that his child should show behavior which would obviously make him appear a poor creature in the eyes of his fellows if he used it as an adult. Dr. George Devereaux tells me of a special case of such an attitude among the Mohave at the present time. The child's mother was white and protested to its father that he must take action when the child disobeyed and struck him. "But why?" the father said, "he is little. He cannot possibly injure me." He did not know of any dichotomy according to which an adult expects obedience and a child must accord it. If his child had been docile he would simply have judged that it would become a docile adult—an eventuality of which he would not have approved. . . .

3. CONTRASTED SEXUAL ROLE

Continuity of conditioning in training the child to assume responsibility and to behave no more submissively than adults is quite possible in terms of the child's physiological endowment if his participation is suited to his strength. Because of the late development of the child's reproductive organs continuity of conditioning in sex experience presents a difficult problem. So far as their belief that the child is anything but a sexless being is concerned, they are probably more nearly right than we are with an opposite dogma. But the great break is presented by the universally sterile unions before puberty and the presumably fertile ones after maturation. This physiological fact no amount of cultural manipulation can minimize or alter, and societies therefore which stress continuous conditioning most strongly sometimes do not expect children to be interested in sex experience until they have matured physically. This is striking among American Indian tribes like the Dakota; adults observe great privacy in sex acts and in no way stimulate children's sexual activity. There need be no discontinuity, in the sense in which I have used the term, in such a program if the child is taught nothing it does not have to unlearn later. In such cultures adults view children's experimentation as in no way wicked or dangerous but merely as innocuous play which can have no serious consequences. In some societies such play is minimal and the children manifest little interest in it. But the same attitude may be taken by adults in societies where such play is encouraged and forms a major activity among small children. This is true among most of the Melanesian cultures of Southeast New Guinea; adults go as far as to laugh off sexual affairs within the prohibited class if the children are not mature, saying that since they cannot marry there can be no harm done.

It is this physiological fact of the difference between children's sterile unions and adults' presumably fertile sex relations which must be kept in mind in order to understand the different mores which almost always govern sex expression in children and in adults in the same culture. A great many cultures with preadolescent sexual license require marital fidelity and a great many which value premarital virginity in either male or female arrange their marital life with great license. Continuity in sex experience is complicated by factors which it was unnecessary to consider in the problems previously discussed. The essential problem is not whether or not the child's sexuality is consistently exploited—for even where such exploitation is favored in the majority of cases the child must seriously modify his behavior at puberty or at marriage. Continuity in sex expression means rather that the child is taught nothing it must unlearn later. If the cultural emphasis is upon sexual pleasure the child who is continuously conditioned will be encouraged to experiment freely and pleasurably, as among the Marquesans; if emphasis is upon reproduction, as among the Zuni of New Mexico, childish sex proclivities will not be exploited for the only important use which sex is thought to serve in his culture is not yet possible to him. The important contrast with our child training is that although a Zuni child is impressed with the wickedness of premature sex experimentation he does not run the risk as in our culture of associating this wickedness with sex itself rather than with sex at his age. The adult in our culture has often failed to unlearn the wickedness or the dangerousness of sex, a lesson which was impressed upon him strongly in his most formative years.

Benedict's comparative analysis enables the American reader to gain perspective on the problem of growing up in other societies. Thereby it helps him to understand the extent to which Americans are left to their own resources.

Professor Kingsley Davis—in the following excerpt from his article, "Adolescence and the Social Structure" [2]—also points up the implications of the self-reliance principle for the socialization process. For one thing, as Davis indicates, adolescence in American society is not clearly marked off from adulthood. In some respects the individual boy or girl is treated as an adult, in other respects as a child. This ambiguity of social definition, extending as it does over several years, throws considerable responsibility on the adolescent for defining his own role.

Whereas American youth think that getting a job and getting married entitle them to independence, the case is quite different in many other societies. In old India, Ireland, China, and Japan, for example, the authority of the parent tended to continue until death. The end of adolescence did not mean a sig-

[2] Kingsley Davis, "Adolescence and the Social Structure," *The Annals of the American Academy of Political and Social Science,* Vol. 236 (November, 1944), pp. 8–15. Reprinted by permission of the editor of *The Annals of the American Academy of Political and Social Science.*

nificant change in authority, and hence the adolescent phase, for that reason at least, did not stand apart as a separate period. In addition, there was little conflict over authority, not only because complete emancipation did not occur, but also because such emancipation as did occur developed by well-grooved, mutually accepted, publicly ritualized steps.

In modern society, by contrast, the child is supposed to become completely emancipated from the parental power, but the exact time, manner, and cause of such emancipation remain uncertain, a subject of dispute, recrimination, and remorse. The individual may become a full-fledged wage earner as early as childhood or as late as adulthood. Marriage is often postponed so long that there tends to arise a distinction between the adolescent and the unmarried adult. Neither employment nor matrimony, therefore, may be accepted as a standard criterion of emancipation. There is no such standard criterion. Each family must virtually settle the matter for itself as a result of private interaction. This in spite of the fact that the emancipation, once it does come, is relatively more complete than in most societies.

In Peter Blos's book, *The Adolescent Personality,* one of the three major goals of adolescence is claimed to be "emancipation from the family." Achieving this goal is viewed as a long and hard psychic struggle. Yet in most societies it either comes in the normal course of affairs or never comes at all. Among us, it comes as a struggle because the adolescent needs the protection of his family at the same time that he rebels against its authority, because he dreads to leave the glamorous irresponsibility of youth for the humdrum cares of adulthood, and because he has no standardized steps by which emancipation can be automatically and publicly achieved.

In relation to older persons outside his family, the adolescent, if he has a separate status at all, usually has a subordinate one. . . . The adolescent boy is most likely to be accorded full adult status in simple, mobile, warlike societies, where physical prowess is emphasized as a societal necessity. Even so, it is only during the latter part of the adolescent period, say between the ages of 18 and 22, that he achieves virtual parity. The Comanche culture, for example, prior to the coming of the whites placed considerable emphasis on youth but the older men nevertheless retained a superiority in magic which partially compensated them for their loss of prestige due to physical decline.

In our society, even apart from the family, the adolescent finds an absence of definitely recognized, consistent patterns of authority. Because of the compartmentalization of the culture he is defined at times as an adult, at other times as a child. Furthermore, he is subjected to a confusing array of competing authorities, of which the school is the principal but not the happiest one.

The principle of self-reliance is also imbedded in the American courtship system. Americans have gone further than any other society in making marriage a matter of the personal preference of the bride and groom. It is built into the household arrangements of families. The "normal" household consists of a man, his wife, and their dependent children; and the necessity of having parents or other relatives in the household on anything but a temporary basis is regarded as little short of a misfortune. Note that this means that the American family is structurally isolated. When death or illness strikes, there is no father or mother substitute to take over the relinquished role—as there would be in a society where the conjugal unit is less on its own. Finally, the principle of self-reliance receives its fullest expression in the occupational system. The individual decides on the line of work he wishes to pursue; he obtains whatever training he feels is necessary; and he is free to look for a job in whatever way he decides to do it. In the article which follows, the authors show some of the floundering which results from the responsibility to find one's own job.[3]

Throughout the last 150 years "equality of opportunity" has been an effective slogan of liberal and radical social reformers. It has also been a slogan dear to Americans who proudly compared their own society with that of the Old Country. It is in the nature of such slogans that they gain in appeal what they lack in clarity. In this case, to distribute anything "equally," one

[3] S. M. Lipset, Reinhard Bendix, and Theodore Malm, "Job Plans and Entry into the Labor Market," *Social Forces,* Vol. 33 (March, 1955), pp. 224–232. Reprinted by permission of the publishers, The Williams & Wilkins Company, Baltimore, Maryland.

would have to know how much there is of "it," and one would also have to decide that the manifest differences between people did not or should not affect their role as "equal recipients." Actually, people have rallied to the cause of "equality of opportunity" in a protest against specific inequalities, and the slogans have turned their specific grievances into a vague principle of universal appeal. A factual study of inequality must begin with the recognition that equality or inequality are relative terms. Just as an individual is not "highly mobile" but rather more mobile than another, so two individuals are not equal as such but rather equal or unequal in some specific respect.

In another article the authors were concerned with the effect of family background on educational attainment and the relation between the education attained and the subsequent careers of respondents. It was found that existing educational opportunities are unequally distributed in the sense that individuals do not have an equal chance to stay in school during their formative years. This finding points to important aspects of the chances for occupational advancement other than those having to do with education. For the sample as a whole, about 30 percent never went beyond grammar school and another 22 percent did not complete their high school education. Educational attainment did not constitute, therefore, a major step in the occupational careers of over one-half of the sample. As has been seen earlier, a relative lack of education has an adverse effect on the occupational level at which the individual enters the labor market as well as on his subsequent career. Since so much depends on these initial steps it may be useful to analyze somewhat more closely the factors which facilitate or obstruct the individual's career at this point.

It has been suggested that young people entering the labor market are in effect floundering around in a new world for which they are ill prepared and for which they have made few plans. The majority of the respondents are no exception to this generalization, for 55 percent of the total sample reported that they had no specific job plans while in school. As one would expect, the proportion of those without specific job plans declines as they continue their education, both because of growing personal maturity and because of the greater urgency of making a deci-sion. When respondents are classified by level of education, 78 percent of those with an eighth-grade education or less stated that they had no job plans, while the proportion for high school graduates was only 47 percent, and for college graduates 13 percent.

Because respondents were asked at the time of the survey to remember what, if any, plans they had while in school, it may well be that the above results are not entirely accurate. Some are likely to have forgotten that they did have definite plans when they were in school, while others are perhaps prompted by the question to attribute to their school days particular plans which are in fact only a reflection of their later experience. But however inaccurate in detail, the data suggest that the pro-longed availability of educational opportunities in this country enables some American youngsters to postpone a decision on occupational choice which most of their European agemates, for example, must make at the age of 14 or before.

This postponement of decisions on careers has other reasons which are related to the educational system. Job plans crystallize only in the later years of high school and college, partly because at an earlier time respondents received advice concerning their future careers rather infrequently. Among those in the sample with an eighth-grade education or less, 67 percent had not re-ceived vocational advice from their parents, teachers, or any other persons; among high-school graduates the proportion fell to 45 percent, and for college students to 31 percent.

The disadvantages which beset the careers of individuals with little education tend to be cumulative. Such persons receive little vocational guidance in school. Specifically, 87 percent of those who did not go beyond grammar school reported that they received no vocational advice from their teachers. It is true that 63 percent of the college students and even 53 percent of the graduate students did not receive vocational advice from their teachers either. But it is apparent that this lack of advice falls most heavily on those whose very lack of education presumably accentuates their need for advice. And aside from this lack of guidance there is the further fact that those who *do* receive advice in school are mostly ill-advised. Of those who were advised by their teachers, between 60 and 75 percent say that they were advised to choose a professional career. And this advice is apparently given regardless of whether the individual student attends grammar school, high school, or college. The comments of our respondents indicate that few teachers took the trouble to advise their students concerning their future plans, and those few who did give such advice made no attempt to brief their students for the real labor market.

Whether or not the individual student receives advice concerning his future plans does not depend solely on how far he goes in school. He is likely to receive advice from his parents. Moreover, if the parents are well-to-do, they will be in a relatively better position to offer helpful advice concerning his future plans than if they are poor. Advice is given somewhat more frequently when the father is a professional worker or a business executive than it is when he is a manual laborer; however, the percentage difference (namely 57 percent as against 42 percent) is not as large as one might expect. It is possible that this may be due in part to the fact that most fathers advise their sons in some fashion or other. The question was not focused clearly enough to ascertain whether or not the father had given specific advice concerning job plans for the future. . . .

. . . [T]he occupational status of an individual's family and his own educational attainment have considerable effect on the first job he obtains in the labor market. But the manner in which he obtained this first job is interesting in itself. Persons differ significantly in terms of whether their first job is obtained in response to some immediate pressure or whether it is obtained "at the proper time." Two other differences, related to those already noted, are the means by which the individual obtains information concerning available jobs and the extent to which he can choose among a number of jobs *available to him* once he has begun to look for his first job. Given the importance of the first job for a person's career one might expect that the individual would spend some time in examining the opportunities which are available. Actually the majority of respondents report that they took the only job they knew about.

This is in part related to the way in which different persons hear about job opportunities. To secure such data, respondents were asked how they heard about their first job. The data suggest that the means of obtaining job information in the labor market vary with one's position in the occupational structure. . . . The labor market appears to operate for the young manual and white-collar worker through haphazard contacts with friends and relatives. Only the trained individuals with higher education and initial skills (the professionals and semi-professionals) can fruitfully use the formal channels of communication to learn of job opportunities. The white-collar workers were next in order in using the formal channels. It is interesting that the best jobs in the manual group, the skilled and apprentice positions, as well as entry into farm occupations, tended to be secured through members of one's own family. Persons obtaining semi-skilled and unskilled jobs made somewhat greater use of the formal channels than did skilled workers. However, more than half of the young workers who began in manual employment learned about their first job through a friend or a relative. Clearly they were not likely to learn much about available job opportunities unless these friends and relatives themselves knew of many. Since the latter are likely to be manual workers as well, it is improbable that they would have such knowledge. Thus, inadequate knowledge concerning job opportunities as well as avenues of advancement is handed down from generation to generation.

The cumulation of advantages or disadvantages is also reflected in the manner in which knowledge of other job opportunities was distributed among respondents. Of the children of families in the professions and in business (owners and executives) 48 percent indicated that they knew of other jobs available to them at the time they entered the labor market. For the other occupational groups an average of 30 percent knew of such alternatives. These and similar data show that a person's knowledge of job opportunities increases with education and that such knowledge is consequently more available to those whose first jobs placed them on the upper levels of the occupational hierarchy. However, data from other studies suggest that this knowledge of available opportunities is not solely a matter of information or of the immediate urgency which prevents the individual from "shopping around." It is also a question of the psychological disposition, of the apathy or the drive with which the individual enters into the labor market. It is difficult to make this point without indulging either in a "Horatio Alger" argument or without suggesting that middle class families are distinguished from working class families by the degree of striving which they instill in their children. Both of these explanations, the one naively and the other in sophisticated psychological terms, attribute such "drive" exclusively to psychological causes. They fail to recognize that "drive" or "apathy" may be greatly strengthened or weakened by the cumulative pressure of external factors; some of which we have reviewed.

Some conclusions derived from this analysis of the effect of family background and educational attainment on entry into the labor market can be summarized here.

The importance of family background for the education and the careers of respondents is seen in the characteristic cumulation of advantages and disadvantages. Vocational advice from many sources is more often given to those individuals whose families can afford to keep them in school. It also seems to be more realistic and helpful than such advice as is given to the children of working-class parents. The effect of these and other background factors may be discerned in an individual's choice of his first job.

If an individual comes from a working-class family, he will typically receive little education or vocational advice; his job plans for the future will be vague while he attends school; and when he leaves school he is likely to take the first available job he can find. Unfavorable economic circumstances, lack of education, absence of personal "contacts," lack of planning, and failure to explore fully the available job opportunities which characterize the working-class family are handed down from generation to generation. The same cumulation of factors which in the working-class case adds up to mounting disadvantages works to the advantage of the child coming from a well-to-do family. The social status of parents and the education of their children are therefore closely related both to the nature of the children's first jobs and to the pattern of their later careers.

Almost identical conclusions were reached by Paul Lazarsfeld in summing up the results of the rather extensive pre-Hitler Austrian and German studies of the factors which affect the job choice of adolescents.

> The more socially oppressed a group is, the more restricted in advance is the range of occupational choice of its children.
>   . . . The effect of the material limitations acts in part so as to narrow the perspectives of those faced with the occupational choice. The socially underprivileged adolescent has seen less, read less, heard about less, has experienced less variety in his environment in general, and is simply aware of fewer opportunities than the socially privileged young person.

SUMMARY

American culture insists that each individual "find his own way." Few devices exist for guiding the young child along a well-defined road to maturity, and there is a good deal of inconsistency in what he is expected to learn. In adolescence, especially, relatively few social arrangements tell him what to do and when and how to do it.

The pioneer spirit of independence and self-reliance has been so deeply ingrained in the American character that even the important process of occupational choice and job placement tends to be left to the individual's own resources, resources which are often inadequate to the task.

ANNOTATED BIBLIOGRAPHY

Davis, Kingsley, "Final Note on a Case of Extreme Isolation," *American Journal of Sociology,* Vol. 45 (January, 1940), pp. 554–65. (A description of one of the rare but illuminating cases of almost total "self-reliance." Davis' report very effectively shows the vital dependence of human beings on others and the impossibility of thoroughgoing self-reliance.

Hofstadter, Richard, *Social Darwinism in American Thought,* rev. ed. (Boston: Beacon Press, 1955). (A historian's description and analysis of the tendency for "Darwinism" to be interpreted by Americans as both meaning and justifying a self-reliant and self-oriented struggle for survival. Hofstadter makes clear both the arbitrariness and the functional significance of such an interpretation.

Landieu, Gloria; Hanfman, Eugenia; and Dembo, Tamara, "Studies in Adjustment to Visible Injuries: Evaluation of Help by the Injured," *Journal of Abnormal and Social Psychology*, Vol. 42 (1947), pp. 169–192. ¶ An unintended commentary on the institutionalization of self-reliance in America. What was most frustrating to the injured persons studied was the necessity of accepting the help of others, in many cases when it was not actually needed.

Sumner, William Graham, *What Social Classes Owe to Each Other* (New York: Harper & Brothers, 1883). ⟨ ". . . above all, an exhortation to independent thought and action, self-reliance, and individual initiative." Barnes, Harry Elmer, *An Introduction to the History of Sociology* (Chicago: University of Chicago Press, 1948), p. 156.

Thoreau, Henry David, *Walden* (New York: Random House, Inc., Modern Library, 1937). ⟨ The great individualist's account of the glories of self-reliance. Thoreau writes of life at Walden Pond, where he lived alone for two years. See also his famous essay, *On the Duty of Civil Disobedience*.

CHAPTER FIVE

Competition

When an American schoolboy refers to the United States as "the land of opportunity," he does not mean that everyone has the same opportunities. Obviously, some children are born more intelligent than others, some better looking, some healthier. Some homes have greater financial resources than others. What is usually meant by "opportunity" is that *nobody in this society is chained to the social status he receives as an infant.* Within the limits of age and sex roles, which have a biological basis, you are free to make of your life what you can. You have a wide choice of jobs, of places to live, of persons to marry. You can decide whether or not to go to college, and you can restrict your friends to people who are personally congenial. Americans can hardly believe that there are peoples whose lives follow a different pattern: who are born in the same house in which their great-great-grandfather was born, who use household utensils which have been in the family for generations, who have little to say about whom they marry or how their children are to be raised. For Americans such existence would be misery. You would be restless with traditional patterns of behavior. You would wonder whether improvements could not make life more convenient, more interesting, more varied. You would resent the lack of opportunity to "better yourself." In short, Americans prefer a competitive system, where serious mistakes are possible, to an unalterable blueprint specifying exactly what they can and cannot do from birth until death.

From an objective point of view, however, competition is only one of several possible methods of allocating persons to roles. It expands enormously the range of alternative roles available to the individual but, by the same token, he cannot claim a role merely by virtue of being born. He must *earn* the right to a role. He must demonstrate qualities or perform actions which are then evaluated by society and compared with the qualities and performances of all the other people who wish to occupy that role. In short, a competitive system is a little like a jungle. Only the fittest obtain the highest rewards of the system.[1] You live in a world filled with rivals and potential rivals, with persons who want your job, your reputation in the community, your girl friend. Lewis Carroll might have been describing a competitive system when he had the Red Queen say in *Through the Looking Glass,* "Now, *here,* you see, it takes all the running *you* can do, to keep in the same place. If you want to get somewhere else, you must run at least twice as fast as that!" In a competitive society, every aspect of life tends to be defined as a contest, and one's sense of adequacy, of worthiness, of security, and even of pleasure hinges on whether one is a winner or a loser. This has at least two consequences. For one, contests are usually set up so that there are many losers and few winners; this means that the majority, in addition to not getting the rewards which con-

[1] In the history of social thought, the analogy between a competitive system and a jungle has often been made. See, for example, Richard Hofstadter, *Social Darwinism in America* (Boston: Beacon Press, 1955).

tests allocate, are publicly humiliated. Second, the winners are never sure how long they can continue to be winners. They know that their margin of superiority is small; rivals are close behind. Thus fear of failure haunts the successful.

Although the layman thinks of competition as primarily an economic phenomenon, the sociologist regards competition as a general principle of role assignment. Thus, in the excerpt which follows—from Willard Waller's article, "The Rating and Dating Complex" [2]—observe that the competitive struggle for dates on a college campus can be just as rugged as the competitive struggle for customers in the garment district.

X College, a large state-supported school, is located in a small city at a considerable distance from larger urban areas. The school is the only industry of the community. There are few students who live at home, and therefore the interaction of the young is but little influenced by the presence of parents. The students of this college are predominantly taken from the lower half of the middle classes, and constitute a remarkably homogeneous group; numerous censuses of the occupations of fathers and of living expenses seem to establish this fact definitely. Nevertheless, about half of the male students live in fraternities, where the monthly bill is usually forty-five or fifty dollars a month, rarely as high as fifty-five. There is intense competition among the fraternities. The desire for mobility of class, as shown by dozens of inquiries, is almost universal in the group and is the principal verbalized motive for college attendance.

Dating at X College consists of going to college or fraternity dances, the movies, college entertainments, and to fraternity houses for victrola dances and "necking"; coeds are permitted in the fraternity parlors, if more than one is present. The high points of the social season are two house parties and certain formal dances. An atypical feature of this campus is the unbalanced sex ratio, for there are about six boys to every girl; this makes necessary the large use of so-called "imports" for the more important occasions, and brings it about that many boys do not date at all or confine their activities to prowling about in small industrial communities nearby; it also gives every coed a

[2] Willard Waller, "The Rating and Dating Complex," *American Sociological Review,* Vol. 2 (October, 1937), pp. 727–737. Reprinted by permission of The American Sociological Society.

relatively high position in the scale of desirability; it would be difficult to say whether it discourages or encourages the formation of permanent attachments. Dating is almost exclusively the privilege of fraternity men, the use of the fraternity parlor and the prestige of fraternity membership being very important. Freshman men are forbidden by student tradition to have dates with coeds.

Within the universe which we have described, competition for dates among both men and women is extremely keen. Like every other process of competition, this one determines a distributive order. There are certain men who are at the top of the social scramble; they may be placed in a hypothetical Class A. There are also certain coeds who are near the top of the scale of dating desirability, and they also are in Class A. The tendency is for Class A men to date principally Class A women. Beneath this class of men and women are as many other classes as one wishes to create for the purpose of analysis. It should be remembered that students on this campus are extremely conscious of these social distinctions and of their own position in the social hierarchy. In speaking of another student, they say, "He rates," or "He does not rate," and they extend themselves enormously in order that they may rate or seem to rate.

Young men are desirable dates according to their rating on the scale of campus values. In order to have Class A rating they must belong to one of the better fraternities, be prominent in activities, have a copious supply of spending money, be well-dressed, "smooth" in manners and appearance, have a "good line," dance well, and have access to an automobile. Members of leading fraternities are especially desirable dates; those who belong to fraternities with less prestige are correspondingly less desirable. I have been able to validate the qualities mentioned as determinants of campus prestige by reference to large numbers of student judges.

The factors which appear to be important for girls are good clothes, a smooth line, ability to dance well, and popularity as a date. The most important of these factors is the last, for the girl's prestige depends upon dating more than anything else; here as nowhere else nothing succeeds like success. Therefore the clever coed contrives to give the impression of being much sought after even if she is not. It has been reported by many observers that a girl who is called to the telephone in the dormitories will often allow herself to be called several times, in order to give all the other girls ample opportunity to hear her paged. Coeds who wish campus prestige must never be available for last minute dates; they must avoid being seen too often with the same boy, in order that others may not be frightened away or discouraged; they must be seen when they go out, and therefore must go to the popular (and expensive) meeting places; they must have many partners at the dances. If they violate the conventions at all, they must do so with great secrecy and discretion; they do not drink in groups or frequent the beer-parlors. Above all, the coed who wishes to retain Class A standing must consistently date Class A men.

Cressey has pointed out that the taxi-dancer has a descending cycle of desirability. As a new girl in the dance hall, she is at first much sought after by the most eligible young men. Soon they tire of her and desert her for some newer recruit. Similarly the coed has a descending cycle of popularity on the campus which we are describing, although her struggle is not invariably a losing one. The new girl, the freshman coed, starts out with a great wave of popularity; during her freshman year she has many dates. Slowly her prestige declines, but in this case only to the point at which she reaches the level which her qualities permanently assure her. Her descent is expedited by such 'mistakes,' from the viewpoint of campus prestige, as 'going steady' with one boy (especially if he is a senior who will not return the following year), by indiscretions, and by too ready availability for dates. Many of the girls insist that after two years of competitive dating they have tired of it and are interested in more permanent associations. . . .

This competitive dating process often inflicts traumas upon individuals who stand low in the scale of courtship desirability. "While I was at X College," said a thirty year old alumnus, "I had just one date. That was a blind date, arranged for me by a friend. We went to the dorm, and after a while my girl came down and we were introduced. She said, 'Oh, I'm so sorry. I forgot my coat. I'll have to go get it.' She never came down again. Naturally I thought, 'Well what a hit I made!' " We have already seen that nonfraternity men are practically excluded from dating; it remains to note that many girls elect not to date rather than take the dates available to them. One girl writes as follows: "A girl's choice of whom to fall in love with is limited by the censorship of the one-sex group. Every boy that she dates is discussed and criticized by the other members of the group. This rigid control often keeps a girl from dating at all. If a girl is a member of a group in which the other girls are rated higher on the dating scale than she, she is often unable to get dates with boys who are considered desirable by her friends. In that event she has to decide whether to date the boys that she can and choose girl friends who would approve, or she must resign herself to not dating."

Since the class system, or gradient of dating desirability on the campus, is clearly recognized and adjusted to by the students themselves, there are interesting accommodations and rationalizations which appear as a result of inferior status. Although members of Class A may be clearly in the ascendant as regards prestige, certain groups of Class B may contest the position with them and may insist upon a measuring stick which will give them a favorable position. Rationalizations which enable Class D men and women to accept one another are probably never completely effective.

The accommodations and rationalizations worked out by one group of girls who were toward the bottom of the scale of campus desirability are typical. Four of these girls were organized in one tightly compact "bunch." All four lived off campus, and worked for their room and board. They had little money to spend for clothes, so there was extensive borrowing of dresses. Members of the group cooperated in getting dates for one another. All of them accepted eleventh hour invitations, and probably realized that some stigma of inferiority was attached to such ready availability but they managed to save their faces by seeming very reluctant to accept such engagements, and at length doing so as a result of the persuasion of another member of the bunch. The men apparently saw through these devices, and put these girls down as last minute dates, so that they rarely received any other invitations. The bunch went through "dating cycles" with several fraternities in the course of a year, starting when one of the girls got a date with one member of the fraternity, and ending, apparently, when all the girls had lost their desirability in that fraternity.

The "rating and dating" analysis points up an inherent difficulty of a competitive system: There is every likelihood that victory in the struggle has nothing to do with the needs of the competitors. As a classroom demonstration of this generalization, Jackson Toby sometimes asks his students about their criteria for selecting dates. They say they seek girls who are pretty, well-poised, good conversationalists, good sense of humor, and so forth. And what about girls who do not meet these standards? "Oh, they are pigs, and we steer clear of them." But what happens to "pigs"? Don't they want dates too? "Perhaps," a student will suggest, "the unpopular boys date the unpopular girls, thus taking care of everybody." Unfortunately, if Waller's data are correct, this does not happen. *Common* standards of attractiveness exist; the same girls are liked (or disliked) by most of the boys. Even an unpopular boy does not want to date an unpopular girl.

Competition for dates and, ultimately, for spouses is a symmetrical process; that is to say, girls and boys *mutually* choose one another. Mutuality of choice is characteristic of much role allocation in the United States, although sometimes one of the choosers is a collectivity rather than an individual. For example, on American campuses freshmen compete among one another for fraternity bids and fraternities compete among themselves for pledges. The following analysis is an attempt to explain the operation of the fraternity system in terms of prestige competition very similar to that involved in dating behavior.[3]

The key that unlocks most of the mysteries of the fraternity system is that on every campus some fraternities are good, others are better, and one, perhaps, is the best. These terms refer, of course, not to their moral character but to their prestige. Whereas membership in a high ranking fraternity is a notable

[3] Jackson Toby, "Competition for Prestige: the Engine That Drives the Fraternity System," unpublished lecture.

achievement, it is hardly worth joining a low ranking one at all. Freshmen realize quite soon that one fraternity is not just as good as another, although amnesia sets in by the sophomore year—after the pledging and the initiations are over. Those who have settled for a less desirable fraternity seem convinced that theirs is the best little old fraternity in the world. They are boosters. They will tell you about the "swell bunch of guys" at their House and the wonderful times they have.

It's not all talk. If their fraternity does not have the recognition on the campus that is clearly its due, the members try to build it up, to put it across. That means winning intra-mural contests, electing the brothers to Student Council, participating in extra-curricular activities—especially Varsity sports, and, last, and probably least, keeping up the scholastic average of the House. No fraternity is reconciled to a humble position in the campus firmament. Since those occupying a place in the sun show no inclination to move out of it, a fraternity man works as hard as he can to keep his fraternity in the same relative position it was a year ago. Occasionally changes take place in the prestige hierarchy. One fraternity is ruined by scandal; another manages to attract personalities who improve its relative position. But, more often, the years come and go; the best fraternity is still the best; and the fraternity of last resort is still, to speak frankly, the last resort.

There are at least two factors in this stability. One is real estate. Some fraternity houses are more attractive than others: they are more expensive, better furnished, or more conveniently located. Second, and more important, the pledging system handicaps the fraternities of *lesser* prestige. Promising freshmen are snapped up by the best fraternity because it can generally exercise first choice. The less the prestige of the fraternity, the lower the standards it can afford to maintain in recruiting pledges. After all, there is a limit to the choosiness of a rushing committee. Men must be found to carry the financial burden of the House. But the less glamorous the pledge of today, the less glamorous the brother of tomorrow. Thus, the pledging system operates as a kind of flywheel, perpetuating the competitive advantages and disadvantages of each fraternity.

Of course, freshmen are shopping around for the right fraternity just as diligently as rushing committees are searching for pledges who will add luster to their House. So it is not enough for the brothers to be favorably impressed by a freshman. *He* has to be convinced that he can do no better. He weighs the relative desirability of pledging himself to some other fraternity. It is not uncommon for a half a dozen fraternities to solicit the membership of a particularly attractive freshman. This fortunate fellow usually accepts the bid of the highest ranking fraternity among them, if he knows which is which—but not always. He may have a close friend who has not been invited to pledge to that fraternity. As a result, he may pledge himself to a fraternity of lesser prestige or to none at all. Were it not for such instances, where the logic of pledging is modified by the human beings who apply it, the fraternities constituting the college Inter-Fraternity Council might be as rigidly ordered as Indian castes.

The human element is involved in pledging in yet another way. Someone must decide who will and who will not be an asset to the fraternity. This entails not only correct assessment of the freshman while he is a freshman but a prediction of what he will be like as a senior. Each fraternity has a rushing committee saddled with this task. Smokers are specially arranged during rushing season to help the committee get personal impressions. However, it is no secret to the freshman that he is being looked over. The tension which this knowledge contributes to the situation does not make the committee's work any easier. Nevertheless, rushing committees have definite ideas about candidates. They do not abandon the attempt to evaluate freshmen because of the obvious difficulty of the problem. Nor should it be thought that their criteria are so vague that any freshman desirous of joining a fraternity will be invited to pledge to one fraternity if not to another. Many a freshman attends the smokers of half a dozen fraternities and does not receive a bid from any of them. This is because the notion of the type of fellow who is an asset varies little from fraternity to fraternity. A boy who is sufficiently poised, outgoing, and well-rounded to look promising to one rushing committee will very likely attract attention elsewhere. On the other hand, the freshman who is obviously ill-at-ease despite the forced cordiality of the brothers, who drinks the beer he is offered as though it were his first glass, who is frightened because he has no idea what is expected of him, and who reacts to a conversational gambit like a stag brought to bay, such a freshman is not likely to strike *any* fraternity as a good prospect.

Occasionally, a boy whom no rushing committee considered worth bothering with as a freshman becomes a Big Man On Campus by his junior or senior year. This is, however, unusual. It is not that the appraisals of the rushing committees are necessarily good—although the committees certainly *try* to recruit potential B.M.O.C.'s. It is simply that fraternities wield great power; hence they are usually able to prevent a barbarian, however remarkable, from becoming, say, president of the Student Council. To put it another way, the chances for becoming a B.M.O.C. are so much greater if one is a member of a prominent fraternity that its rushing committee could probably choose freshmen for membership at random and make a disproportionately large number of them into campus leaders by the time they are seniors. Hence, it is not often apparent that the rushing committees overlooked good fraternity material. The boys missed by the rushing committees do not have equality of opportunity for campus social and political success. Furthermore, it is always possible to recruit the Varsity athlete, who slipped through unnoticed as a freshman or sophomore, after he makes the team and establishes his reputation. This is the common explanation when a prominent barbarian joins a fraternity in his junior year.

Mistakes in the other direction are more visible. Boys who struck the rushing committee as nuggets at the smoker may, on closer examination, turn out to be clinkers. Every fraternity has a few members that the majority would like to see drafted or graduated in a hurry. Of course, pledging is only apprenticeship, not membership. It is *possible* to rectify the error of inviting an albatross to pledge before fastening it around the neck of the fraternity by an initiation. But rectification at this stage is not easy. Although the vote of a single brother is technically enough to blackball a pledge, fraternity members are reluctant to dash the expectations of someone they have gotten to know. Sentiment against him must be quite strong, and even then a few friends may be able to persuade the majority to let him in. A supporter of an unpopular pledge in one fraternity threatened to blackball all the other pledges that year if his friend were not admitted to membership. His friend got in. In other words, a fraternity is usually stuck with the pledges it has started with. Hence, every rushing committee has nightmares about the current batch of pledges.

The rushing committee has a twofold problem. One is to select freshmen who are personally congenial to the brothers. The other is to maintain—and, if possible, augment—the relative standing of the fraternity by pledging freshmen who will be a credit to it. There are occasions when these two objectives are incompatible. For instance, a wealthy freshman may be personally unappealing, but he may be invited to pledge because the fraternity cannot afford to let another fraternity get him. Or, a boy with many social graces may be relegated to the shadow-world of the barbarians because the fraternity dares not pledge a Catholic, a Jew, or a Negro. Thus, actions which appear snobbish on the surface often turn out to be motivated by an excess of competitive zeal. They are hastily disposed of and conveniently forgotten.

What worries rushing chairmen most is that a hectic scramble to choose and be chosen is not conducive to accurate evaluation. Fraternities which select pledges on the run may repent their selections at leisure. Consequently, many fraternities start lining up pledges long before the rushing period officially opens. Far from waiting for candidates to make a beaten path to the fraternity door, some fraternities do not even wait for the freshmen to arrive on the campus. They launch an aggressive campaign as soon as the Admissions Committee of the college makes known the names of the high school students entering college in the fall. Besides providing more time for study of the freshman class, an early start may enable the rushing committee of one's own fraternity to indoctrinate promising freshmen *first*.

An early start depends on the resources of the fraternity for contacting and assessing incoming freshmen when they are still in high school. Will the brothers take time out of their summer vacations to visit remote corners of the state? Can the alumni be counted on to snoop in the fraternity's behalf? Sometimes the brothers and the alumni show diligence on its behalf above and beyond the call of loyalty. For example, confidential information from the office of the Dean of Students or the Admissions Office may find its way mysteriously to a rushing committee. Many fraternities make a preliminary investigation of a prospective pledge before he occupies his dormitory room. What was his high school record? Athletics? Politics? Cheer leading? Scholarship? Debating? Does he come from a respectable family? Would his parents fit in if asked to be chaperons at a fraternity function? Did they go to college? Is his father an alumnus of the fraternity—or of some other good fraternity? Is his family able to give him a substantial allowance? Will he have a car at college? The simplest way to get answers to these questions is personal recommendations. Perhaps one of the brothers comes from the same town as the freshman and knew him in high school. Such testimony can be decisive because it is presumed that the brother is fully aware of fraternity standards and would call attention to any deficiency in the candidate's qualifications. But a recommendation from an alumnus, especially an active one, also carries weight. Sometimes a freshman will arrive on the campus shortly after letters introducing him have been received by the fraternity.

It would be wrong to conclude that, except for relative prestige, one fraternity is exactly like another. Each has its distinctive rituals; each is unique in the particular personalities it has combined within it. Moreover, there are variations in interests from one House to another. One has a reputation for mountaineering; another harbors the campus poker sharks. But every fraternity, regardless of size, religious affiliation, or financial resources, is competing with other fraternities for campus glory. Success in this competition is not promoted by too scrupulous a regard for youngsters unable to get into the fraternity of their choice—or to any fraternity at all. Of course, some students do not join fraternities even though the fraternities would be glad to have them. All barbarians are not disappointed Greeks. Some

boys believe fraternities to be undemocratic or immoral. Some
are forbidden to join by their parents. Some avoid membership
because of the time, the expense, or the possible obstacles to
study which membership entails. But there are others who feel
themselves rejected by the fraternities. They suffer in silence,
yearning for the convivial life which appears to go on behind
the pillared facades.

The irony of the fraternity system is that fraternities do not
practice brotherhood toward the loneliest students on the campus. Freshmen sever their social roots in coming to live at
college. They are homesick until the gap created in their lives
by reduced contact with family and with hometown chums is
filled by college friends. Those who become members of fraternities fill the gap quickly, almost automatically. Those who
do not join fraternities have to make new friends slowly, one by
one. And, paradoxically, it is precisely those who find the readjustment from home to college most difficult that the fraternities
are least likely to want. They are boys who are sometimes rebuffed but, more often, just ignored, for they are too shy to
make advances. On the other hand, freshmen sufficiently endowed with social skills to make their way without the help of
ready-made friendships are much more likely to be recruited by
the fraternities. Whereupon they get the benefit of additional
opportunities to ease the transition from home to college.

Of course, competitive role allocation can occur without
mutuality. Voters choose senators and representatives; Congressmen do not choose voters—unless election laws can be considered "choice." In the economic system, where competitive
role allocation is very prominent, choices are usually mutual,
although the mutuality may be disguised by the impersonal
mechanism of the market. Thus, employers of unskilled labor
compete among themselves for workers by offering to pay varying wage rates; laborers compete among themselves for jobs by
a differential willingness to work for a given wage. However,
even in the occupational realm competition is not always reciprocal. Corporation executives frequently feel committed to
one firm for life. Thus, General Electric executives compete
among themselves for promotions, but those who are not promoted do not necessarily seek other jobs with other companies.

Commitment to a career within a corporation may be as permanent as marriage. Needless to say, this irrevocability of the commitment adds to the pressures of competition. As the assistant managing editor of *Fortune* shows, despite the ideological climate which extols cooperation, each junior executive looks anxiously over his shoulder at potential rivals.[4]

The figures of speech younger executives use to describe the situation they now find themselves in are illuminating. The kind of words they use are "treadmill," "merry-go-round," "rat race" —words that convey an absence of tangible goals but plenty of activity to get there. The absence of fixed goals, . . . may make them seem less ambitious, less competitive than their forebears, but in the more seemingly co-operative climate of today lies a prod just as effective. They are competing; all but the fools know this—but for what, and against whom? They don't know, and there is the trap. To keep even, they must push ahead, and though they might like to do it only slightly, who is to say what slightly is. Their contemporaries are in precisely the same doubt, and thus they all end up competing against one another as rapaciously as if their hearts were set on the presidency itself.

This co-operative competition can be observed rather clearly in the postgraduate business schools. At one school an up-and-coming plant manager told me that he was puzzled at the apparent lack of ambition in the others. Since they represented a good chunk of the cream of their age group in U. S. corporation life, he couldn't understand why so few of them had no specific goal in mind. (He wanted to be president of his corporation's major subsidiary.) "But the funny thing is," he told me, "that they work just as hard as I do. Frankly, I'm knocking myself out to get top grades because that will mean a lot to the people back in New York. The only thing the others here are working for is just to get an okay grade. But the grades here depend on how everybody else does, so how can you tell what a good grade is? They can't take any chances so they do just as much night work, give up just as many week ends as I do."

[4] From *The Organization Man* by William H. Whyte, Jr., pp. 177–178. Reprinted by permission of Simon and Schuster, Inc., New York.

Back at the office the job of steering the right middle course requires more and more skill. The increasingly "democratic" atmosphere of management has opened up opportunities for the executive, but it has also made more difficult the task of sizing up the relative rankings around the place and judging the timing of one's pushes. The overt differences in status and office amenities are much less than before, but the smaller the differences the more crucial they can become to the individual. It is easy to joke about whether or not one has a thermoflask on his desk or whether the floor is rubber tiled or carpeted, but the joking is a bit nervous and a number of breakdowns have been triggered by what would seem a piddling matter to the observer. Where does one stand in this shifting society in which standing depends so largely on what other people think? Even a thermo-flask is important if it can serve as a guidepost—another visible fix of where one is and where others are.

"You get into a certain position," one forty-year-old execu-tive explains, "and you start getting scared that somebody else might want the job you have. You can't tell who he might be, so you take on the protective coloring so you won't look as if you are ambitious and have the others move in on you." The best defense against being surpassed, executives well know, is to sur-pass somebody else, but since every other executive knows this also and knows that the others know it too, no one can ever feel really secure. Check vacation records, and you will find that the higher up the man is, the more likely is the vacation to be broken up into a week here and a week there and, furthermore, to be rescheduled and postponed to suit the company rather than the family. "I like to take my vacation in two or three stretches instead of three or four weeks," one executive confesses. "I don't do it for my health. If you go away for three weeks, when you come back you find that they have rearranged your entire job. Someone has to carry on while you are gone and they are in your files, and when you get back the people will ask you questions about your job on account of what others did while you were away. I don't blame them, mind you; I would do ex-actly the same thing." (In *Blandings' Way,* Eric Hodgins has sketched a commuter's reverie that has occurred to many a management man. Today, the executive thinks miserably to himself, is the day they *find me out*.)

The business executive with such unpleasant daydreams has put all his eggs in one basket—he is a "company man"—and he is afraid he cannot outperform his rivals. In short, he is trapped. C. Wright Mills, a sociologist who has studied lower-level white-collar workers, suggests that occupational competition can produce less conclusive and therefore less traumatic results—in the American metropolis at any rate. The struggle for status goes on in the neighborhood and on vacation as well as in the world of work. The white-collar worker may not himself know whether he has won or lost, and those who came into contact with him in some specific segment of his existence may be even less sure.[5]

The sharp split of residence from work place, characteristic of urban life since the Industrial Revolution, is most clearly manifested in the big city suburb, where work associates are formally segregated from neighbors. This means that the subordinate may compete in two status worlds, that of work place in the big city and that of residence in the suburb.

At the work place, it is difficult, even in large enterprises, to inflate real occupational status, although great status tensions are likely to be lodged there. But actual job position is not so well known to those whom one meets away from work. It may be that to the extent that status aspirations and claims are frustrated at work, there is a more intense striving to realize them off the job. If the status struggle within the job hierarchy is lost, the status struggle outside the job area shifts its ground: one hides his exact job, claims prestige from his title or firm, or makes up job, title, or firm. Among anonymous metropolitan throngs, one can make claims about one's job, as well as about other bases of prestige, which minimize or override actual occupational status.

The place of residence, which is a signal of income and style of life, limits this inflation of status; for neighbors, like job

[5] From *White Collar* by C. Wright Mills, pp. 254–258. Copyright 1951 by Oxford University Press, Inc., New York. Reprinted by permission of the publishers.

associates, will not readily cash in higher claims. Among them, the first, often the only, impression one makes may permit a brief success in status claiming, sometimes as a sort of mutual deal.

"Under modern conditions," Thorstein Veblen wrote, "the struggle for existence has, in a very appreciable degree, been transformed into a struggle to keep up appearance." Personal worth and integrity may count for something but "one's reputation for excellence in this direction does not penetrate far enough into the very wide environment to which a person is exposed in modern society to satisfy even a very modest craving for respectability. To sustain one's dignity—and to sustain one's self-respect—under the eyes of people who are not socially one's immediate neighbors, it is necessary to display the token of economic worth, which practically coincides . . . with economic success." . . .

"One does not 'make much of a showing' in the eyes of the large majority of the people whom one meets with," Veblen continued, "except by unremitting demonstration of ability to pay. That is practically the only means which the average of us have of impressing our respectability on the many to whom we are personally unknown, but whose transient good opinion we would so gladly enjoy. So it comes about that the appearance of success is very much to be desired, and is even in many cases preferred to the substance . . . the modern industrial organization of society has practically narrowed the scope of emulation to this one line; and at the same time it has made the means of sustenance and comfort so much easier to obtain as very materially to widen the margin of human exertion that can be devoted to purposes of emulation."

Of an eighteenth-century nobility, Dickens could say that "dress was the one unfailing talisman and charm used for keeping all things in their places," but in a mass society without a stable system of status, with quick, cheap imitations, dress is often no talisman. The clerk who sees beautifully gowned women in the movies and on the streets may wear imitations if she works hard and, skipping the spiced ham sandwich, has only cokes for lunch. Her imitations are easily found out, but that is not to say they do not please her. . . .

The prestige enjoyed by individual white-collar workers is not continuously fixed by large forces, for their prestige is not continuously the same. Many are involved in status cycles, which, as Tom Harrison has observed, often occur in a sort of rhythmic pattern. These cycles allow people in a lower class and status level to act like persons on higher levels and temporarily to get away with it.

During weekdays the white-collar employee receives a given volume of deference from a given set of people, work associates, friends, family members, and from the transient glimpses of strangers on transport lines and street. But over the week end, or perhaps a week end once a month, one can by plan raise oneself to higher status: clothing changes, the restaurant or type of food eaten changes, the best theater seats are had. One cannot well change one's residence over the week end, but in the big city one can get away from it, and in the small town one can travel to the near-by city. Expressed claims of status may be raised, and more importantly those among whom one claims status may vary—even if these others are other strangers in different locales. And every white-collar girl knows the value of a strict segregation of regular boy friends, who might drop around the apartment any night of the week, from the special date for whom she always dresses and with whom she always goes out.

There may also be a more dramatic yearly status cycle, involving the vacation as its high point. Urban masses look forward to vacations not "just for the change," and not only for a "rest from work"—the meaning behind such phrases is often a lift in successful status claims. For on vacation, one can *buy* the feeling, even if only for a short time, of higher status. The expensive resort, where one is not known, the swank hotel, even if for three days and nights, the cruise first class—for a week. Much vacation apparatus is geared to these status cycles; the staffs as well as clientele play-act the whole set-up as if mutually consenting to be part of the successful illusion. For such experiences once a year, sacrifices are often made in long stretches of gray weekdays. The bright two weeks feed the dream life of the dull pull.

SUMMARY

That American society relies upon competition to allocate roles in the economic area of life needs no particular documentation. This chapter has illustrated the *pervasiveness* of competition as a governing principle in noneconomic activities. Toby and Waller show how the principle operates in dating and fraternity life, and both emphasize an important implication of the principle—that "others" are threats to one's success because one's chances of being chosen depend on how one is invidiously compared with others. Toby, moreover, calls attention to one rather little-noticed consequence of competition: The tendency for competition to perpetuate a ranking system when competitors are mutually choosing and being chosen.

Whyte describes the operation of competition among junior executives in the modern corporation and calls attention to the diffuse anxiety generated by the awareness that productivity is measured in competitive terms, that adequacy depends on how much others are doing and getting. On lower white-collar levels, Mills shows how the struggle for symbols of competitive success extends into the leisure time activities of white-collar workers.

ANNOTATED BIBLIOGRAPHY

Barker, Roger G., "Success and Failure in the Classroom," *Progressive Education,* Vol. 19 (1942), pp. 221–224. ⟨ An analysis of the impact of the competitive system in the classroom. The author shows how children compete for the approval of the teacher and what success or failure in this competition means to the individual child.

Dashiell, John F., "An Experimental Analysis of Some Group Effects," *Journal of Abnormal and Social Psychology,* Vol. 25 (1930), pp. 190–199. Reprinted in Newcomb, Theodore M. and Hartley, Eugene L. (eds.), *Readings in Social Psychology* (New York: Henry Holt and Company, Inc., 1947), pp. 297–303. ⟨ One of many attempts by psychologists to discover the effect of competition (and other group relationships) on performance. Dashiell summarizes some of the early literature and reports the results of his own experimental evidence showing how rivalry affects speed and accuracy in problem-solving.

Goodman, Walter, "Bicker at Princeton," *Commentary,* Vol. 25 (May, 1958), pp. 406–415. ⟨ A report of a problem which arose on the

campus of Princeton University: How could the more exclusive
Eating Clubs take in sophomores who were not sufficiently elite to
maintain such Clubs' competitive standing? The problem arose because of pressure from the students as well as from the University
administration to admit all sophomores wishing to join Eating
Clubs.

Mead, Margaret, *And Keep Your Powder Dry* (New York: William
Morrow and Company, 1942). ⁅ A description of the American
character by a leading anthropologist. The varied ways in which the
American is taught to compare himself competitively with others are
described at length and in (impressionistic) detail.

Montague, Ashley, *On Being Human* (New York: Henry Schuman,
1951). ⁅ A polemic against the position that "the survival of the
fittest" is a law of nature. Montague claims that cooperativeness is
at least as conspicuous in the animal world and, by extension,
should characterize human communities.

Polanyi, Karl, "Our Obsolete Market Mentality," *Commentary* (February,
1947), pp. 109–117. Reprinted in Wilson, Logan, and Kolb, William
L., *Sociological Analysis* (New York: Harcourt, Brace and Company, Inc., 1949), pp. 557–67. ⁅ A spirited protest against the "com-
moditization" of labor. Polanyi argues that the competitive market
system (when combined with "bargaining") is based on a dysfunc-
tional but powerful ideology and on erroneous psychological assumptions about the nature of man.

Veblen, Thorstein, *Theory of the Leisure Class* (New York: The Macmillan Company, 1915). ⁅ Another classic by a master of irony and
iconoclasm. Veblen here describes the competition among consumers
for symbols of superiority, a competition in "conspicuous consumption," which some current writers now maintain has turned into a
competition in "inconspicuous consumption."

CHAPTER SIX

Negotiated exchange

American society has gone very far in institutionalizing a market mentality. That is to say, an American usually asks himself, when contemplating an arrangement with other persons, "What's in it for me?" And, on the other hand, he expects others to agree to the arrangement only if he can make it "worth their while." It would be a mistake to infer from this that Americans are more selfish than members of other societies. The point is

124

rather that one of the governing principles of American society is that of *negotiated exchange*. The individual is expected to secure what he needs and wants from others by contracting a mutually advantageous arrangement. Thus, your claim to an income rests on the wages you can induce an employer to give you; the quality of housing you obtain depends on the bargain you make with landlords or mortgage companies; your chance for favorable legislation depends on the pressure you can exert on your representatives.

No principle, of course, is institutionalized with thoroughgoing consistency; thus there are exceptions to the principle of negotiated exchange. Americans do not expect small children to make it worth their parents' while to feed them.[1] Certain categories of persons—children, the mentally ill, the very old—are not expected to negotiate on their own behalf. Actually, the boundary separating those capable of negotiating on their own behalf and those needing the protection of society has been redrawn again and again in American history. Thus, legislation regulating the working conditions of women and children was once held to be unconstitutional. Note the reasoning in the Supreme Court decision of Adkins vs. Children's Hospital (1923); the legislation was struck down because it infringed the right of women to bargain freely on their own behalf.[2]

Mr. Justice Sutherland delivered the opinion of the Court.

The question presented for determination by these appeals is the constitutionality of the Act of September 19, 1918, providing for the fixing of minimum wages for women and children in the District of Columbia. . . .

The act provides for a board of three members, to be constituted, as far as practicable, so as to be equally representative of employers, employees and the public. The board is authorized to have public hearings, at which persons interested in the matter being investigated may appear and testify, to administer oaths, issue subpoenas requiring the attendance of witnesses and production of books, etc., and to make rules and regulations for carrying the act into effect.

By § 8 the board is authorized—

[1] On the other hand, the claim of an American child for food, clothing, and shelter does depend on the bargain his parents are able to drive with other persons in the economy.

[2] *Adkins* vs. *Children's Hospital,* 261 U. S. 525 (1923).

"(1), To investigate and ascertain the wages of women and minors in the different occupations in which they are employed in the District of Columbia; (2), to examine, through any member or authorized representative, any book, pay roll or other record of any employer of women or minors that in any way appertains to or has a bearing upon the question of wages of any such women or minors; and (3), to require from such employer full and true statements of the wages paid to all women and minors in his employment."

And by § 9, "to ascertain and declare, in the manner hereinafter provided, the following things: (a) Standards of minimum wages for women in any occupation within the District of Columbia, and what wages are inadequate to supply the necessary cost of living to any such women workers to maintain them in good health and to protect their morals; and (b) standards of minimum wages for minors in any occupation within the District of Columbia, and what wages are unreasonably low for any such minor workers." . . .

. . . .

. . . a woman twenty-one years of age was employed by the Congress Hall Hotel Company as an elevator operator, at a salary of $35 per month and two meals a day. She alleges that the work was light and healthful, the hours short, with surroundings clean and moral, and that she was anxious to continue it for the compensation she was receiving and that she did not earn more. Her services were satisfactory to the Hotel Company and it would have been glad to retain her but was obliged to dispense with her services by reason of the order of the board and on account of the penalties prescribed by the act. The wages received by this appellee were the best she was able to obtain for any work she was capable of performing and the enforcement of the order, she alleges, deprived her of such employment and wages. She further averred that she could not secure any other position at which she could make a living, with as good physical and moral surroundings, and earn as good wages, and that she was desirous of continuing and would continue the employment but for the order of the board. . . .

The feature of this statute which, perhaps more than any other, puts upon it the stamp of invalidity is that it exacts from the employer an arbitrary payment for a purpose and upon a basis having no causal connection with his business, or the contract or the work the employee engages to do. The declared basis, as already pointed out, is not the value of the service rendered, but the extraneous circumstance that the employee needs to get a prescribed sum of money to insure her subsistence, health and morals. The ethical right of every worker, man or woman, to a living wage may be conceded. One of the declared and important purposes of trade organizations is to secure it. And with that principle and with every legitimate effort to realize it in fact, no one can quarrel; but the fallacy of the proposed method of attaining it is that it assumes that every employer is bound at all events to furnish it. The moral requirement implicit in every contract of employment, *viz.*, that the amount to be paid and the service to be rendered shall bear to each other some relation of just equivalence, is completely ignored. The necessities of the employee are alone considered and these arise outside of the employment, are the same when there is no employment, and as great in one occupation as in another. Certainly the employer by paying a fair equivalent for the service rendered, though not sufficient to support the employee, has neither caused nor contributed to her poverty. On the contrary, to the extent of what he pays he has relieved it. In principle, there can be no difference between the case of selling labor and the case of selling goods. If one goes to the butcher, the baker or grocer to buy food, he is morally entitled to obtain the worth of his money but he is not entitled to more. If what he gets is worth what he pays he is not justified in demanding more simply because he needs more; and the shopkeeper, having dealt fairly and honestly in that transaction, is not concerned in any peculiar sense with the question of his customer's necessities. Should a statute undertake to vest in a commission power to determine the quantity of food necessary for individual support and require the shopkeeper, if he sell to the individual at all, to furnish that quantity at not more than a fixed maximum, it would undoubtedly fall before the constitutional test. The fallacy of any argument in support of the validity of such a statute would be quickly exposed. The argument in support of that now being considered is equally fallacious, though the weakness of it may not be so plain. A statute requiring an employer to pay in money, to pay at prescribed and regular intervals, to pay the value of the services rendered, even to pay with fair relation to the extent of the benefit obtained from the service, would be understandable. But a statute which prescribes payment without regard to any of these things and solely with relation to circumstances apart from the contract of employment, the business affected by it and the work done under it, is so clearly the product of a naked, arbitrary exercise of power that it cannot be allowed to stand under the Constitution of the United States. . . .

It has been said that legislation of the kind now under review is required in the interest of social justice, for whose ends freedom of contract may lawfully be subjected to restraint. The liberty of the individual to do as he pleases, even in innocent matters, is not absolute. It must frequently yield to the common good, and the line beyond which the power of interference may not be pressed is neither definite nor unalterable but may be made to move, within limits not well defined, with changing need and circumstance. Any attempt to fix a rigid boundary would be unwise as well as futile. But, nevertheless, there are limits to the power, and when these have been passed, it becomes the plain duty of the courts in the proper exercise of their authority to so declare. To sustain the individual freedom of action contemplated by the Constitution is not to strike down the common good but to exalt it; for surely the good of society as a whole cannot be better served than by the preservation against arbitrary restraint of the liberties of its constituent members.

The liberty which the Supreme Court was protecting in this decision was, in short, the liberty to receive whatever one could succeed in bargaining for. Since this decision, the principle of negotiated exchange has been tempered considerably; and the Supreme Court, since 1937, has validated legislation regulating wages, hours, and working conditions, not only for women and children, but for men as well.

Another departure from the negotiated exchange principle is this: American society provides some services to its members without regard to what they contribute in exchange. Thus, all children are entitled to elementary education; and all members of the community are entitled to police and fire protection. Finally, in application, the exchange principle is softened; Americans insist on certain ethics in negotiations. They frown on lying and other kinds of deliberate deception. They are shocked when a surgeon performs unnecessary operations even though his patients agree to them. Nevertheless, despite the exceptions, the principle is clear: Ideally, Americans feel entitled only to what they are able to get through free negotiation in the market place.

Economists have stated the principle with relentless logic. They call it the exchange theory of value. According to this theory, the remuneration received by a factor of production (including human beings) should be equal to the value added by the last unit of that factor. Here is the way Harvard professor Thomas Nixon Carver put it in a book entitled *Essays in Social Justice.*[3]

We are concerned, in the problem of distribution, with the question how much income a man ought to have, assuming that whatever income he has he may consume or not according to his choice. . . .

If we may begin with the rather obvious assumption that the value of a transferable thing depends upon how much it is wanted in comparison with other transferable things, we have next to inquire what determines how much such a thing is wanted. Some of the more difficult phases of this question, so far as goods sold to consumers are concerned, have been satisfactorily answered by the marginal utility theory of value. To answer the same question concerning productive agents requires further analysis. It may be assumed, to begin with, that productive agents are wanted primarily because of their products. Doubtless there is also a certain element of consumers' satisfaction, coming directly to the owner or user of producers' goods,

[3] Reprinted by permission of the publishers, Harvard University Press, Cambridge, Massachusetts, from Thomas Nixon Carver, *Essays in Social Justice,* 1915, pp. 177, 184, 200–201, by the President and Fellows of Harvard College.

in addition to that which comes from their products. The farmer takes a certain amount of pride and satisfaction in the style and appearance of his horses and cattle, and the workman in the quality and finish of his tools. These qualities, therefore, increase somewhat the desirability of such goods and enhance their value. Nevertheless, it is safe to say that productive agents are wanted chiefly for the sake of their products rather than for their own sakes. . . .

. . . a factor of production is worth as much as it specifically produces, that is to say,—if you can find out in any given situation how much more you can produce with it than without it you will have a physical measurement of its productivity, and this determines its value. But it must be remembered that this applies to specific units of the factor. The law is the same whether it be a material factor or a human factor. On a piece of swamp land the question is one of more or less, not how much could he produce without any water, but how much difference in his product would be made by more or less water. So with the valuation of nitrogen as the element of soil fertility; not how much he could produce without nitrogen, for he could produce none, but how much more or less would he produce with one hundred pounds more or one hundred pounds less of nitrogen on his farm. That would determine for him the value of one hundred pounds of nitrogen. So in a given situation not how much could be produced without labor, for nothing could be produced, but how much more could be produced with one more laborer, or how much less could be produced with one less laborer; that would determine the value of one laborer of the kind in question at the spot where the valuation is made. If there should be too many of one kind of laborers at one particular spot, so that no more could be produced with one more of that kind, and no less with one less of that kind, the physical product of a man of that kind at that spot is exactly nothing, and therefore his value is exactly nothing. But if the number of a particular kind of laborers is so small and the other factors are so abundant that one more laborer of this particular kind would add greatly to the product of the combination, then it is not in-

accurate to say that his physical product is very high. That being
the case, his value is very high. This, therefore, is the principle
which determines how much a man is worth, and consequently,
according to our criterion of justice, how much he ought to have
as a reward for his work. To pay him more than that would take
something from other producers. If the total addition which a
certain individual can make to the total product of the community is one dollar a day, or, which means the same thing, if
the total reduction in the production of the community when he
ceases to work is one dollar a day, and if he is actually consuming two dollars a day, then there would be one dollar a day
more for some one else if he should emigrate or die. The extra
dollar which he receives, at the expense of some one else, is
either given him for love or benevolence, according as the others
look upon him. It is not given him for the sake of justice.

The principle of negotiated exchange answers the question,
"How much is a man worth?" by finding out what other people
are willing to pay for his services. Obviously, this principle is
relevant to economic activities, but it also settles the terms of
trade in other areas of American life. Recall the discussion of
"rating and dating" in the previous chapter. Boys who "rated"
—that is, who enjoyed high prestige on the campus—insisted on
dating girls of equivalent status. To date a girl with a lower comparative ranking on the prestige scale would have been giving away something for nothing. Similarly, the analysis of the fraternity system in the previous chapter could be translated into
the language of the market place. Each fraternity bought as
valuable pledges as it could afford; each freshman sold himself
to the fraternity willing to pay the highest price. Note that these
campus exchanges are of the take-it-or-leave-it variety; haggling
is not considered proper. The forces which set a valuation on
dates and pledges are impersonal—just like the forces on the
New York Stock Exchange. However, the absence of attempts at
mutual persuasion should not obscure the principle underlying
the process. Negotiated exchange is just as much involved in
dating and pledging and in a large department store where a
one-price system is meticulously observed as in a Malayan fishing village where customer and fisherman haggle for an hour.
The exchange principle becomes more obvious when shifts

in bargaining power occur. Here is a relevant excerpt from "The Rating and Dating Complex":[4]

During the winter term the preponderance of men assures to every coed a relatively high bargaining power. Every summer witnesses a surprising reversal of this situation. Hundreds of women school teachers flock to this school for the summer term, and men are very scarce; smooth, unmarried boys of college age are particularly scarce. The school teachers are older than the boys; they have usually lost some of their earlier attractiveness; they have been living for some months or years within the school-teacher role. They are man-hungry, and they have a little money. As a result, there is a great proliferation of highly commercialized relations. The women lend their cars to their men friends, but continue to pay for repairs and gasoline; they take the boys out to dinner, treat them to drinks, and buy expensive presents for them. And many who do not go so far are available for sex relations on terms which demand no more than a transitory sort of commitment from the man.

The school teachers accepted unfavorable terms of exchange not because the boys persuaded them to do so but because girls were worth less on the dating market during summer months. Note what is meant by inequality of bargaining power: One party to the negotiations, A, has *many* potential suppliers of his needs while the other party, B, is dependent on A because he has *few* alternative suppliers. B bargains under a severe handicap. One measure of American commitment to the principle of negotiated exchange can be obtained from the American formula for dealing with such situations. Thus, during the nineteenth century it became apparent that individual workers were in a poor position to negotiate with large industrial corporations. One solution to the problem might have been the abandonment of negotiated exchange as the principle governing wage determination; the government could have assumed this responsibility. Such a possibility was not seriously considered. Instead, unionization was permitted—and then encouraged—so that *collective* bargaining could replace *individual* bargaining as the means for

[4] Willard Waller, "The Rating and Dating Complex," *American Sociological Review*, Vol. 2 (October, 1937), p. 736. Reprinted by permission of the American Sociological Society.

arriving at fair contracts. Here is how an industrial sociologist describes the background of collective bargaining in America:[5]

Legal emphasis upon a contractual social order stems from a period in Anglo-American law when economic activities were being freed from feudalistic rituals, customs, and personal fealty. The legal theory of individual contractual freedom fitted rather admirably an economic order comprising chiefly independent producers in agriculture and handicrafts, and petty traders supplying the market. The factory system, to say nothing of the corporation and modern industrialism as we know it, developed after the main lines of legal prescription had been laid down. Thus the power to give or withhold employment, and the attendant power to determine all of the conditions of employment, was only economic coercion: It did not exist in the eyes of the law. The relations of employer and employee were officially assumed to be determined by a process of bargaining between equals.

Now it is well known that even if the employer is an independent enterpriser—a single individual—the power he exercises by virtue of his control over employment is much greater than the power of the individual employee who controls only his own labor. If the "employer" is actually a combination of investors, directors, and managers—that is, a corporation—the bargaining equality of employer and employee becomes a fiction straining the imagination of pedestrian minds. But this is precisely the fiction upon which the courts insisted until very recent times, and it is against such a background that the contemporary law and practices of collective bargaining must be understood.

Collective bargaining between employers and unions makes it possible to apply the negotiated exchange principle without outraging American standards of "fairness." However, an incidental and probably unintended consequence of unionization was the increased mutual dependence of employers and workers. Nowadays giant corporations and giant unions face one another

[5] This selection is from Wilbert E. Moore, *Industrial Relations and the Social Order*, pp. 373–374, copyright 1946, by The Macmillan Company, New York, and is used with the permission of The Macmillan Company.

in what the economist calls bilateral monopoly. That is, neither employer nor worker has alternative "suppliers" to negotiate with. This means that each is more desperate. Each feels he must persuade or coerce the other; the alternative to a contract with his usual supplier is no contract at all. In this context, the warlike features of the American labor market become more understandable.[6]

A "lockout" by an employer is the reverse of a strike initiated by employees. By suspending work and precipitating a dispute the employer hopes to gain an advantage over the representatives of labor. In practice, however, it is very difficult to distinguish the strike and the lockout in a full-fledged industrial dispute, and it is not infrequently true that spokesmen for management will declare that the workers are on strike, whereas the union leaders will maintain that they are locked out. . . .

Just as employers have taken precautionary measures to protect that power already granted by law and custom, and definitely coercive measures to meet challenges to that power, so organized groups of employees have developed over a considerable period of time the fundamental strategy and varying tactics of battle. It is understandable that some of the methods used by management and labor are similar, and that each may learn "tricks" from the other. Management may follow a "divide and conquer" policy by securing individual contracts or by creating dissension between rival organizations; the striking labor union may find it expedient to settle with one employer in a competitive field while the remainder are forced to come to terms or lose part of their sales. Similarly, the occasional counterpart of the industrial spy may be found in the striker who secures employment as a strikebreaker to add even further damage to that normally perpetrated by professional or amateur "scabs."

But there are also marked differences in the range of effective weapons available to management and labor arising from their different resources and normal power. Thus, the labor organization is usually in the position of the challenger (or "aggressor") in an industrial dispute, and must perfect the strategy

[6] *Ibid.,* pp. 405, 425–428.

of offense rather than defense. Furthermore, the management of a business enterprise is already a cooperative organization; this is not equally true of the employees. Thus, a good deal of the effort of the union leaders and members must be expended on maintaining unity of purpose, preventing "scabbing," and persuading workmen that concerted demands have more chance of success than individual petitions for redress of grievances or rewards for merit. These differences, and others that follow from them, account for the disparity in weapons and in the importance of those weapons available to both parties to industrial disputes. The significance of these observations may be pointed up by a survey of the battle resources of organized labor.

The significance of the position of organized labor as the customary challenger in industrial disputes is given immediate point by the importance of direct action in the union strategy of combat. Purely defensive measures are a luxury of assured strength and status. American labor unions have rarely enjoyed such luxury. Nowhere is the predominantly direct action better illustrated than in the elaboration and perfection of the strike.

. . . It is frequently asserted that for American organized labor the strike is the center and substance of organizational policy: that other tactics of conflict are either subsidiary to or designed to protect the weapon of collective refusal to work. Although objection might be made to this generalization in specific instances, it is certainly true in a statistical sense. That is, of the various weapons used by various labor organizations, the strike is certainly the most frequent and the one customarily regarded by the unions as most effective.

Essentially the strike is an organized work stoppage, directed against the economic interests of the employer, but also against any sympathizers or supporters of the employer (including "loyal" employees). It is true that strikes, like wars, may also be undertaken to solidify the ranks of the combatants and thus gain a united front for future and more successful action. On the other hand, such unification is not likely to follow from resounding defeat by the selected "enemy," and a union will not willingly call a strike which is patently foredoomed to complete failure at the hands of the employer. Thus, even an "organizational" strike has as its immediate or ultimate goal a successful challenge to the power of management.

The strike is sometimes referred to as a "primary boycott," since its aim is to bring direct economic pressure on the employer by the members of the union and their immediate sympathizers. Although occasionally this pressure consists partly in withholding patronage for the products or services of the company, the strike is primarily designed to withhold the labor necessary for the employer to continue normal operation of the business. For this reason the strike is also commonly called an "economic weapon." However, such a designation should not be thought to mean too much. For example, it does not mean that strikes are called only to wrest economic concessions from employers, or even that during an actual strike the workers' sole hope of victory rests upon the cost of the strike to the company. The designation of a strike as an economic weapon certainly does not mean that it is also an "economical" one, since both parties to the dispute lose income while the plant is shut down. Whether or not the results of the strike are worth the expense even to the victors is a question to which there may be no answer capable of evaluation on a balance sheet. Both sides are likely to feel that there is more at stake in a strike than simply a question of monetary advantages and disadvantages.

. . . Viewed as a fairly standardized form of collective action, the strike involves preliminary planning and organization, the strategy and tactics of concerted stoppage of work, and a "settlement" which may range all the way from complete victory for the workers to various forms of defeat, the most disastrous of which may be not only the collapse of the organization but general loss of employment. Obviously, the exact outcome of such a complex and highly variable situation cannot be predicted exactly, although both managers and union leaders who have had long experience in industrial conflict are able to predict and control the outcome to a marked extent. On the other hand, strikes are not necessarily undertaken on purely rational grounds, and there is a notable and understandable tendency to overestimate the chances for victory. But even shrewd and cautious contestants may be forced to resort to trial by ordeal in order to determine relative power.

Whatever may be the grievances of the workers, or their more positive aims which can only be achieved through some form of exertion of power and control, a union leader must recognize that simple conviction in the justice of the cause is not sufficient to win battles. The order of decision is likely to be: whether, and if so, when? Naturally the decision to strike, and certainly the decision concerning the time of a strike, will depend upon a judgment of relative strength. Thus, the most propitious time for a strike is when the union is well organized and equipped with sufficient reserve funds, when the demand for labor is high and increasing, and when the employer is in the poorest bargaining position—especially, at a peak season in production, so that a shutdown will really constitute an effective weapon.

Still another area in which the trading principle of American relationships may be viewed is that of politics. True, students of democratic government have long debated whether legislators should primarily represent their constituents or should, through "study of the issues," arrive at their own independent judgment of what is "best for the country." The fact is, however, that the American device for protecting the country against "despotism" —the device of making lawmakers responsive to the electorate— means in practice that legislators receive and hold their positions only so long as they make it "worth their constituents' while" to vote for them. It also means that legislators who wish to be retained in office must please those persons to whom they owe their positions—not others, and not posterity, because posterity cannot vote yet.

In other words, the principle that you are entitled to what you can make it worth someone's while to give you applies here also. Alistair Cooke expresses this fact in the following comparison of the American Congress and the British Parliament.[7]

. . . Englishmen usually leave Washington with the complaint that Congress is not, and seems to have no intention of

[7] From an address delivered by Alistair Cooke, "Ethics in Congress and Parliament," at the Twentieth Annual Herald Tribune Forum. Reprinted by permission of Alistair Cooke and the *New York Herald Tribune*.

becoming, the House of Commons. I spend some part of every year begging British and French journalists to start their study of American government not in Washington but in the places the men in Washington come from; so they may understand why a man from the goat country of Texas, west central Texas, keeps up such a lively interest in mohair and army uniforms, and why a man from California sometimes seems to have nothing on his mind but water, unless it is the oil that flows under it.

By such little expeditions it is possible for a foreigner to learn at the start one of the great differences between a Congressman and a member of Parliament. . . .

When a man goes to Westminster, he does not go as a one-man delegation from an industry or a crop. . . . Very often he may have only a rough idea of what his constituents do for a living. For there is no locality rule in the British system, which is not an oversight but a provision meant to leave the member of Parliament comparatively free to give his best to the affairs that concern the nation as a whole. This is quite different from watching the Congress bring up a bill and expecting your man to amend it in your interest.

A small glimpse of the pressures imposed on a Congressman by this principle of "responsiveness to his constituents" is provided by Stephen K. Bailey and Howard D. Samuel in their book, *Congress at Work*. We quote below a brief section of that study.[8]

"Let's be realistic," a member [of Congress] might say. "I owe my election in part to an organization. Sad as it may seem, the support of those who make the electoral machinery spin is not always conditional upon my voting record. In fact, most of what in political parlance is called 'the mob' don't care how I vote. They want to know what I have done for *them*—and done for them lately: aid in getting a government contract, assistance in straightening out an immigration case, help in getting a judgeship for a loyal party member. If I want to be returned next

---

[8] From *Congress at Work* by Stephen K. Bailey and Howard D. Samuel, pp. 4–5. Reprinted by permission of the publishers, Henry Holt and Company, Inc., New York.

election, this is a part of the hidden cost of campaigning, and the necessary price for having a Congress at all. Do I have to compromise my ethics occasionally? Of course I do."

The principle of negotiated exchange—like the principles of self-reliance and of competition—is an institutionalized procedure for the allocation of goods and services in American society. These procedures solve the basic distributive problem. However, they also have implications for the personality of the individual—quite apart from what they allocate to him in the way of material benefits. They become principles of self-assessment. Thus, the individual's feelings of adequacy, worthiness, security, and gratification stem in part from his success in applying the principles of self-reliance, competition, and negotiated exchange. Erich Fromm, the famous psychoanalyst, comments on the process whereby the distributive principle of negotiated exchange can emerge in the personality as a basis for self-assessment.[9]

The marketing orientation developed as a dominant one only in the modern era. . . .

Barter is one of the oldest economic mechanisms. The traditional local market, however, is essentially different from the market as it has developed in modern capitalism. Bartering on a local market offered an opportunity to meet for the purpose of exchanging commodities. Producers and customers became acquainted; they were relatively small groups; the demand was more or less known, so that the producer could produce for this specific demand.

The modern market is no longer a meeting place but a mechanism characterized by abstract and impersonal demand. One produces for this market, not for a known circle of customers; its verdict is based on laws of supply and demand; and it determines whether the commodity can be sold and at what price. No matter what the use value of a pair of shoes may be, for instance, if the supply is greater than the demand, some shoes will be sentenced to economic death; they might as well

[9] From *Man for Himself*, by Erich Fromm, pp. 67–69, 72–74. Copyright 1947 by Erich Fromm. Reprinted by permission of Rinehart & Company, New York, publishers.

not have been produced at all. The market day is the "day of judgment" as far as the exchange value of commodities is concerned. . . .

The market concept of value . . . has led to a similar concept of value with regard to people and particularly to oneself. The character orientation which is rooted in the experience of oneself as a commodity and of one's value as exchange value I call the marketing orientation.

In our time the marketing orientation has been growing rapidly, together with the development of a new market that is a phenomenon of the last decades—the "personality market." Clerks and salesmen, business executives and doctors, lawyers and artists all appear on this market. It is true that their legal status and economic positions are different: some are independent, charging for their services; others are employed, receiving salaries. But all are dependent for their material success on a personal acceptance by those who need their services or who employ them.

The principle of evaluation is the same on both the personality and the commodity market: on the one, personalities are offered for sale; on the other, commodities. . . .

Since modern man experiences himself both as the seller and as the commodity to be sold on the market, his self-esteem depends on conditions beyond his control. If he is "successful," he is valuable; if he is not, he is worthless. The degree of insecurity which results from this orientation can hardly be overestimated. If one feels that one's own value is not constituted primarily by the human qualities one possesses, but by one's success on a competitive market with ever-changing conditions, one's self-esteem is bound to be shaky and in constant need of confirmation by others. Hence one is driven to strive relentlessly for success, and any setback is a severe threat to one's self-esteem; helplessness, insecurity, and inferiority feelings are the result. If the vicissitudes of the market are the judges of one's value, the sense of dignity and pride is destroyed.

But the problem is not only that of self-evaluation and self-esteem but of one's experience of oneself as an independent entity, of one's identity with oneself. . . . the mature and productive individual derives his feeling of identity from the experience of himself as the agent who is one with his powers; this feeling of self can be briefly expressed as meaning "I am what I do." In the marketing orientation man encounters his own powers as commodities alienated from him. He is not one with them but they are masked from him because what matters is not his self-realization in the process of using them but his success in the process of selling them. Both his powers and what they create become estranged, something different from himself, something for others to judge and to use; thus his feeling of identity becomes as shaky as his self-esteem; it is constituted by the sum total of roles one can play: "I am as you desire me." . . .

The way one experiences others is not different from the way one experiences oneself. Others are experienced as commodities like oneself; they too do not present themselves but their salable part. The difference between people is reduced to a merely quantitative difference of being more or less successful, attractive, hence valuable. This process is not different from what happens to commodities on the market. A painting and a pair of shoes can both be expressed in, and reduced to, their exchange value, their price; so many pairs of shoes are "equal" to one painting. In the same way the difference between people is reduced to a common element, their price on the market. Their individuality, that which is peculiar and unique in them, is valueless and in fact, a ballast. The meaning which the word, "peculiar," has assumed is quite expressive of this attitude. Instead of denoting the greatest achievement of man—that of having developed his individuality—it has become almost synonymous with "queer." The word, "equality," has also changed its meaning. The idea that all men are created equal implied that all men have the same fundamental right to be considered as ends in themselves and not as means. Today, "equality" has become equivalent to "interchangeability," and is the very negation of individuality. Equality, instead of being the condition for the development of each man's peculiarity, means the extinction of individuality, the "selflessness" characteristic of the marketing orientation. Equality was conjunctive with difference, but it has become synonymous with "in-difference" and, indeed, indifference is what characterizes modern man's relationship to himself and to others.

SUMMARY

The way in which the measurement of "worth" by exchange-value has traditionally been linked in America with the values of freedom and efficiency is revealed in the decision of the United States Supreme Court in the *Adkins* case and in the writings of Thomas Nixon Carver. Freedom means, according to this reasoning, the right to pay as little as you must for what you need; the right to get as much as you can for what you offer; and the correlative duty to accept what you can get. Moreover, adds Carver, this is both efficient and just.

Nor, as Willard Waller observes, is that principle confined to the money-market; it is to be observed also in sexual relations. Furthermore, so strongly is the principle embedded in the American culture that even the other principle, competition, is subordinated to it: Unionized workers do not compete among themselves because this would interfere with collective *bargaining* vis-a-vis employers, who also act collectively.

The same exchange principle underlies American politics, where votes and political support are exchanged for legislation and political favors.

Given the widespread institutionalization of this principle, Erich Fromm suggests that people inevitably come to judge themselves in terms of their marketability. We have then the paradoxical result that a principle justified by Justice Sutherland and Thomas Nixon Carver in terms of individualism ends up in the eyes of a modern psychoanalyst as a major threat to individualism.

ANNOTATED BIBLIOGRAPHY

Goffman, Erving, *The Presentation of Self in Everyday Life* (University of Edinburgh, Social Science Research Centre, 1956). ([A sensitive and skillful dissection of the devices used in everyday life to create in one's audience the image of oneself that will best serve one's purpose. With examples drawn from a wide variety of familiar situations, Goffman analyzes the function of otherwise taken-for-granted activities for "selling" an image; the pitfalls that confront the individual seeking a favorable response from others; and the precautions and reactions to those pitfalls commonly employed.

Green, Arnold, "The 'Cult of Personality' and Sexual Relations," *Psychia-*

try: Journal of the Biology and Pathology of Interpersonal Relations, Vol. 4 (August, 1941), No. 3, pp. 344–348. Reprinted in Davis, Kingsley, Bredemeier, Harry C., and Levy, Jr., Marion J. (eds.), *Modern American Society* (New York: Rinehart & Company, 1949), pp. 604–609. ⟦ A vivid description and explanation of the unequal bargaining power prevailing among young women and men in a community of Polish immigrants. Green shows the consequences for personality adaptation and for marriage of the bargaining principle when it operates in the field of mate selection.

Heilbroner, Robert, "Who Are the American Poor?", *Harper's Magazine,* Vol. 200 (June, 1950), pp. 27–33. ⟦ A description of the low income group in the United States. According to Heilbroner, poverty is not a social heritage in America—as it is in some societies. Poverty results from the inability of certain individuals or groups to bargain successfully in the economic system, for example, the physically handicapped are not readily employable.

Kornhauser, Arthur, Dubin, Robert, and Ross, Arthur M. (eds.), *Industrial Conflict* (New York: McGraw-Hill Book Company, 1954). ⟦ A collection of essays by leading social scientists on problems of industrial conflict. An invaluable starting point for the understanding of issues, techniques, and implications of collective bargaining.

Wootton, Barbara, *Lament for Economics* (New York: Farrar and Rinehart, 1938). ⟦ A critique by a well-known British economist (author also of *Plan or No Plan*) of classical economic theory. The author criticizes in lucid style some basic assumptions of the bargaining model of distribution.

PART FOUR

The costs of an acquisitive society

During World War II signs like the following hung in war plants and in military installations: "The difficult we do immediately. For the impossible, give us 24 hours." These signs, sometimes facetious, sometimes braggadocio, reflected American optimism, the tendency to regard any problem as capable of solution—and fast. This optimism in American culture helps to account for the range of phenomena discussed in social problems courses: disease and premature death, race prejudice, industrial conflict, mental illness, waste of natural resources, economic cycles, crime, illiteracy, divorce, political corruption, and atomic war. Situations which might be regarded fatalistically in another society are labeled "social problems" in America and studied from the viewpoint of ultimate amelioration. "Let's not just stand there. Let's *do* something about it!"

Unfortunately, the desire to alleviate suffering and to fulfill wasted potentialities is not enough. Without an analytical framework, activism may conspire with humanitarianism to produce waste motion. Something more than the binding should hold a social problems textbook together. In an effort to develop a theoretical framework for understanding and, ultimately, doing something about social problems, the authors of this book are using a more limited definition of "social problems" than the catalogue of "pathology" found in the usual textbook. A situation must fulfill *all three* of the following conditions in order for it to be considered a social problem in this book.

1. It involves people who are frustrated because they fail to meet the adequacy, security, worthiness, or gratification standards of their society—or who anticipate failing to meet these standards.

2. It involves their attempts to cope with this frustration and,

145

in particular, the channeling of these attempts by the governing principles of American society.[1]

3. The form that this attempt to cope with frustration takes arouses widespread concern within the society.

These conditions do not succeed in demarcating the social problems field with complete rigor. Condition 3 requires "widespread concern," a vague requirement if there ever was one. One reason for the vagueness is that public concern is *fickle*. Today juvenile delinquency is on every tongue, and tomorrow an international crisis has superseded it. Another reason is that public concern *lacks a uniform direction*. To some people divorces are too easy to get; to others they are too difficult to get. Lack of consensus on the issues forces the authors to be somewhat arbitrary in their choice of material for inclusion in this book. On the other hand, the interpretive framework imposed by these three conditions is not so flexible that anything can be called a social problem. Furthermore, this framework fits the analysis of deviance provided by leading sociological theorists.[2] To illustrate, consider an individual who faces a situation threatening to his self-respect. He needs a certain response from other people or some turn of events, because otherwise he feels himself sexually inadequate ("The Doctor Talks about Frigidity") or an occupational failure (*The Square Trap*) or worthless (*Black Boy*) or rejected by his family (*Fight against Fears; The Member of the Wedding*) or ungratified (*Picnic*).

He can, as one mode of adjustment, give up the struggle. He commits suicide, the ultimate act of withdrawal. Or he can retreat to a dream world less painful to his self-respect than the world of reality. He develops delusions and hallucinations; or he uses liquor or heroin to deaden the feelings of frustration he would otherwise experience. Not every form of withdrawal, of course, arouses "public concern." And "public concern" is one of the criteria of a social problem for the purposes of this book. Although psychiatrists, social workers, poets, and bartenders may be aware of the "lives of quiet desperation" led by inconspicuous persons, withdrawal from suffering does not constitute a social problem in itself. It must be recognized as a problem by the general public. As long as the desperation is quiet and the withdrawal inconspicuous, the public tends to ignore it. In Chap-

[1] This textbook is concerned with the social problems of *American* society. In principle, the same theoretical framework could be used to analyze the problems of other societies.

[2] See Talcott Parsons, *The Social System* (Glencoe, Illinois: The Free Press, 1951), Chapter VII, and Robert K. Merton, *Social Theory and Social Structure* (Glencoe, Illinois: The Free Press, 1949), Chapter III.

ter 7, a few forms of the withdrawal adjustment which arouse public concern are described.

Another alternative open to the individual who faces a situation threatening to his self-respect is to build his self-respect on some other basis. He acknowledges his defeat—he perceives himself as inadequate or insecure or worthless or deprived—but he derives satisfaction from his conformity to the governing principles of his society. (Professor Robert K. Merton calls this mode of adjustment "ritualism." We shall call it "submission.") Again note that this mode of adjustment does not necessarily produce a social problem. From the point of view of Christianity, submission to the vicissitudes of life may be a virtue. In Chapter 8, a few forms of the submissive adjustment which *do* arouse public concern are described.

Withdrawal and submission constitute the *passive* reactions to anticipated defeat. The individual may also *refuse* to give up; he may devote himself relentlessly to living up to the standards in terms of which he has learned to judge himself. Whether he achieves inner satisfaction is questionable. But, at least on the surface, he seems to get what he wants. (George Santayana, the Harvard philosopher, defined a fanatic as a person who, after losing sight of his original goal, redoubles his efforts.) The *active* responses to anticipated defeat can be distinguished by ascertaining *which* governing principle is mangled by the individual in his effort to make life bearable for himself.

In Chapter 9, we show how *self-reliance* can be carried to lengths where it becomes a social problem; in Chapter 10, on the other hand, we describe problems generated by the *repudiation of self-reliance*. In Chapter 11, the problems produced by fanatical adherence to the *bargaining* principle and, in Chapter 12, those produced by *rejection of bargaining* are considered. In Chapter 13, we describe the consequences of relentless adherence to the *competitive principle* and, in Chapter 14, the results of the *rejection of competition*. Finally, in Chapter 15, we take up the consequences of fanatical *materialism* and, in Chapter 16, those of the *rejection of materialism*.

CHAPTER SEVEN

The acceptance of defeat:

Withdrawal

Some people give up the struggle for self-respect when their situation appears to hold nothing but defeat. In effect, they say, "The hell with everything!" Suicide is perhaps the clearest expression of this mode of adjustment. Whatever his particular reasons, the suicide decides that life is not worth living. More than 16,000 persons commit suicide every year in the United States, and several times that number attempt suicide unsuccessfully.[1] The daily newspaper reports suicides, especially the more dramatic ones, but newspaper readers cannot usually reconstruct the life history that culminated in self-destruction. Consider the following case history.[2]

Miriam Patterson seems to have been rather an ordinary girl who grew up in a rapidly growing midwestern metropolis. Her father and mother were divorced when Miriam was eight years old, but she continued to live in the "small-townish" residential community in which she was born until her marriage to Alfred Donaven.

Alfred and Miriam met at a high school dance when Miriam was nineteen and Alfred twenty. Alfred's background seems to have been very much like that of Miriam except for a somewhat more puritanical up-bringing, the rigors of which, being a male, he was able to escape through the conveniently culturally approved double standard of his time. After a five-months' acquaintance, Alfred and Miriam were married and moved to a rapidly deteriorating residential area. Here the first disillusionments of marriage were experienced. Alfred did not conform to the romantic ideal of a husband fostered by the popular literature of the time. Neither does it appear that Miriam lived up to the role of a wife as defined in the expectations of Alfred and reinforced in the conventional attitudes of his mother. Miriam disliked housework, and yet she was little prepared for remunerative activities which might have provided an outlet for her nervous energy and bolstered Alfred's not too adequate income.

After a few months of marriage, Miriam became pregnant. Alfred did not want a child yet and so she had an abortion. Later she regretted this step whenever Alfred was inattentive and forgot it when her husband was solicitous. Periods of estrangement followed others of contentment. Quarrels became more violent and occurred more frequently. Miriam went to work in a department store and there stole things for Alfred in

[1] U. S. Bureau of the Census, *Statistical Abstract of the United States: 1956* (Washington: Government Printing Office, 1956), p. 69.

[2] From *Disorganization, Personal and Social*, by Ernest R. Mowrer (Chicago: J. B. Lippincott Company, 1942), pp. 363–364. Reprinted by permission of Ernest R. Mowrer.

an ever-increasing effort to win more attention. About this time they took in a roomer, and Miriam developed a casual interest in him which irritated Alfred. Quarrels came to involve some physical conflict. At times they became so estranged that they scarcely spoke to each other for days, and upon one occasion Miriam left for a day. Miriam had an escapade with a "pickup" acquaintance, and soon after this she and Alfred talked about divorce. After this, one flirtation followed another. They moved to another part of the city. Shortly in the new surroundings, Alfred left Miriam but later returned, following an orgy of dissipation and adventure upon Miriam's part. Alfred had his adventures with other women. They quarreled and made up, yet never seemed to be able to make a final decision. Miriam's flirtations seem to have represented attempts to taunt Alfred for his inattention. Finally, however, there was little left of the marriage, and after some mutual bargaining in which Alfred threatened to leave and Miriam left, to return later, Alfred agreed to give Miriam cause for divorce. But before this had been accomplished, Miriam thought of killing first Alfred and then herself, even expressed the second in a letter to her mother. Divorce ended the relationship five years after marriage, but not without an interlude in which Alfred returned for a short time after months of separation.

After Alfred and Miriam separated, Miriam turned to prostitution to supplement the support given her by her husband. This she continued after the divorce until she finally entered into a free alliance with Robert Timmins, a married man who lived a double life. With this alliance began again a struggle to rebuild a romantic relationship. In this second attempt the same essential sequence of contentment and dissatisfaction was reproduced which had characterized her life with Alfred. At times, she achieved the romantic ideal in her relationship with Robert Timmins; at other times she felt neglected and despaired of being able to "hold" her lover. She tried to persuade Robert to divorce his wife and marry her, but he refused to do so. On occasions they quarreled about his inattention, his refusal to give up his wife, and his selfish refusal to see her side of the relationship. Slowly she saw him drift from her, yet was unable to do anything about it. Finally, he told her that this relationship could go on no longer, and she carefully planned both his and her death. Consequently, three years after her divorce from Alfred Donaven, Miriam shot first her lover as he lay in bed and then herself beside him. Both bodies were later discovered lying much as if in sleep as Miriam had planned it.

More prevalent than suicide as a form of escape is mental breakdown. About 160,000 first admissions to public and private mental hospitals are reported every year, and the inmates of mental hospitals in the United States number more than 600,-000.[3] Many of these are so-called functional disorders; that is, no organic basis for the symptoms can be found. Thus, psychologists consider a great deal of mental illness a flight into the world of fantasy, a grossly exaggerated—and sometimes irreversible—form of daydreaming. The following selection from the tremendous literature on mental disorders describes a case of paranoia, which is characterized by highly organized suspicions about other people.[4]

The following case is presented because it represents a type of case which was frequently observed in military installations —that of the homosexual panic. . . .

S. F., a 19-year-old, white, married male private, with nine months' service, was admitted ambulatory to the closed ward of the N. P. Section of a Station Hospital in an Infantry Advance Replacement Training Center. At the time of his admission the patient was disheveled and unkempt in appearance. He was quite vague about his personal history and responded to the initial questions of his interview with "I don't remember." He did recall, however, that he was described as being 'nervous' by his family physician, following an attack of diphtheria at the age of eight. He was also forced to discontinue employment as an auto repairman when a young man because of "nervousness and stomach trouble." Following this, he became a wholesale

[3] U. S. Bureau of the Census, *op. cit.*, pp. 81, 252.

[4] Howard H. Kendler, "S. F., A Case of Homosexual Panic," *Journal of Abnormal and Social Psychology,* Vol. 42 (1947), pp. 112–119. Reprinted by permission of Howard H. Kendler and the Publications Office of the American Psychological Association, Washington, D. C.

drug salesman in a medium-size city of a southeastern state. The only spontaneous conversation elicited during the initial interview was the vehement statement, "I'm mad at the whole works." The patient was described by the interviewing psychiatrist as being "lachrymose and constantly tugging at his clothing."

The nurse's report of his behavior that night read as follows:

2230—Patient leaped from bed and began running wildly about. Seemed very tense and frightened—was questioned, stated "dull" and held his head. Placed in a private room, given 3 grains of seconal, wept profusely for about 20 minutes and finally fell asleep.

The nurse's report on his activities on the following day was as follows:

Patient refused to get up and eat breakfast. Is confused and disoriented. States someone bothered him all night by ringing a bell. 1100—Patient disturbed, yelling. States there is a man in the room after him. Appears very frightened, is crying, peers under the bed and in the corner in a furtive manner.

During this day he was interviewed by the enlisted psychiatric social worker, and it was observed that, as well as being markedly fearful, he was now disoriented as to time and place. He was under the impression that he was born in 1926, but was ignorant of the specific date. He denied having siblings and was unable to provide any information about his parents. To the question of where he was, the patient cried, "I'm in jail. I've been in jail before only they don't ring bells and talk to me all night. They ask me to go help ring the bell, and then they get mad. Sometimes they laugh at me. They won't get me—but if I stay here, they might—so I'm not staying!" Patient was incapable of identifying his pursuers.

A physical examination produced only negative findings. An Army-Wechsler Intelligence Test revealed that the patient was functioning at a mental age level of eight years and six months. There was marked scatter between the various weighted subtest scores, and within any one subtest the patient's performance was uneven. This finding was consistent with the belief that we were dealing with an individual in a disturbed emotional state, who was not functioning efficiently, rather than a mentally deficient individual. The test pattern was not similar to those reported for known syndromes. The Rorschach cards elicited only four responses, and this paucity of responses precluded interpretation. During this time a request for marihuana was made by the patient in order to "clear my head." For several days his behavior remained unchanged. He spent all his time in his room and would crouch in a corner when someone approached. He continued to complain of bells ringing and being pursued by someone with homicidal intent.

The nurse's notes for the third day read as follows:

Patient continues to be confused, disoriented and hallucinatory. Ate fairly well at breakfast this morning.

The next day's note read:

Lachrymose, apprehensive and continues hallucinatory state. Patient cries, "He's been in here again. He talks all the time. I'll kill myself. He'll never get me!" Patient must be coaxed to eat.

Several days later the patient was given 7½ grains of sodium amytal, preceded by an injection of 7½ grains of caffeine sodium benzoate. . . .

The information obtained in approximately the same order of its expression was that the bells that he was constantly hearing were church bells, and were being rung by a person possessing horns and a tail. The identity of this representation of the devil varied throughout the abreaction. Initially, it was his father, then his Platoon Sergeant, then it was his Junior Officer. It always represented some captious father surrogate. For his mother, he expressed only great fondness. He revealed that he had a sister, a few years his senior, but refused to comment on their relationship. He then spontaneously expressed violent resentment toward all aspects of Army life, particularly toward his relationships with his commissioned and noncommissioned officers. When expressing this hostility toward his superiors he suddenly broke into "soap box oratory," denouncing the president's role in the beginning of World War II. His appearance changed; his voice took on a deep and resonant quality, his southern accent became thick, and a sardonic expression appeared.

Because of the paranoid component of his clinical picture, probing of the sexual area of his personality was begun. He revealed that he was married and had a child. He began boasting about his numerous heterosexual affairs. Suddenly he sarcastically commented, "You can have the women the way you want, I'll take the boys the way I want them." The patient then returned to previous topics and no new material was elicited. It was suggested to the patient that he go to sleep and he did so.

About an hour later, patient awoke and became very buoyant. He walked about the ward and acted the part of a lawyer, referring to the various persons around the ward as his assistants. He requested additional sodium amytal, referring to it as "Schenleys." He confidentially told the therapist that he had at times sold drugs and was himself a drug addict.

Approximately five hours after the administration of the drug the patient returned to his old behavior patterns except that he now revealed more psychomotor activity.

Time was found to interview the patient for a short period the following day. He was given reassurance that he would recover. He spontaneously asked, in case he returned home, if he would be forced to indulge in sexual relations with his wife. He was told nobody would force him, and asked what instigated the question. He stubbornly answered, "I don't want to sleep with anybody." When asked whether he ever used drugs, he admitted the use of marihuana and cocaine in cigarettes, using the latter when the former was unavailable. He stated that he felt slightly improved from the sodium amytal interview, but it was evident he was still hallucinatory. . . .

Patient attributed his present difficulty to "psychoneurosis," a diagnosis which had been given to him at a previous installation. "I did not want to admit it to myself, but it is true." He acknowledged the great conflict instigated by living in barracks. This conflict of desiring to make homosexual advances toward his barrack mates and the ensuing fear of being caught and punished was usually solved by patient physically fleeing from the barracks. It was suggested to him that this conflict was one of the causes of his present difficulty. This he denied, insisting his present trouble stemmed from Army life. "Army doesn't know that a man has a sense of feeling. Man is just another S.O.B. They can shoot me tomorrow, and I would like it." It was then suggested that he was not facing his problem squarely, thereby precluding any opportunity to solve it. To this, the patient responded that because of marihuana it was unnecessary to face "problems squarely."

Patient was then asked about his attitude toward women, and he stated, "A woman has a pretty face, but that is as far as it goes." He explained his aversion to heterosexual relationships by saying, "A woman wants too much of you." He said that he enjoyed effeminate men and had on several occasions gone "drag." [5] . . .

Freud was the first to emphasize the close association between homosexuality and paranoia. In the Armed Services this relationship is frequently seen. S. F. attempted to frustrate his desires by concealment and self-denial, but was unable to restrain himself. His feelings of guilt led to strong ideas of persecution necessitating hospitalization.

Still another form of withdrawal generally considered a social problem is compulsive drinking. Alcoholism is not merely *excessive* drinking; it is a condition wherein the individual becomes slavishly *dependent* on liquor. Although there are more than sixty million adult drinkers in the United States, only four million of these are problem drinkers or alcoholics.[6] Like the mentally ill person, the alcoholic finds that his mode of adjustment to his problems—problems that may originally have been no worse than average—multiplies his difficulties. Whereas he may have increased his drinking in order to feel more adequate in a difficult job, he reaches the point where he cannot hold any job at all. Perhaps his family did not give him the emotional response he craved before he became an alcoholic. Afterwards, his wife divorces him and his children refuse to see him. In

---

[5] "Drag" is a homosexual slang expression meaning to be dressed in female garments.

[6] Robert Straus, "Alcoholism," in Arnold Rose (ed.), *Mental Health and Mental Disorder* (New York: W. W. Norton & Company, 1955), pp. 434–435.

short, the alcoholic becomes a person all of whose bridges have been burned. He needs liquor because he has nothing else left. In the following selection, bear in mind that Harry and Bud have become blood-producing machines in order to get enough liquor to make life "bearable." [7]

Harry Ross, an amiable bum of about fifty who lives in the cellar of a Chinese laundry near Abingdon Square in lower Manhattan, has an unusual vocation. He is a professional blood donor. Paradoxically, Mr. Ross prefers to keep his only visible means of support invisible, since no blood bank will accept his merchandise while the puncture from the last sale can still be seen on the inside of his elbow above the cubital vein. The Health Code naively stipulates a forty-two-day interval between bleedings, but only an unhealed puncture or a low blood count is considered a trade barrier by Harry or by Bud Williams, his roommate and business associate. They simply hide the scars with cosmetics, keep their hemoglobins above the required eighty-five percent by eating iron pills like salted peanuts, and play the blood market every two weeks.

"We manufacture blood like Du Pont does paint," says Bud. "And we peddle a very high-class product. We never had jaundice, goiter, malaria, TB, heart trouble, or diabetes. We can't afford no social diseases, and how the hell could you get hay fever in this hole?"

The hole, reached by a precipitous flight of steps from the street, is a small grotto for which they pay the Chinese laundryman fifteen dollars a month. The cozy little flat, choked with fairly good furniture, is marred only by a total absence of daylight and a large pile of egg coal in the bedroom. The coal, provided by the landlord, feeds a stove in the kitchen which supplies heat and hot water for both establishments. Looking after the stove is the responsibility of the tenants and is part of their rent. The furnishings, mainly overstuffed chairs and box springs, are artifacts of a former tenant. "A drunken upholsterer used to

[7] From "Blood Is Cheaper than Brandy," by Poyntz Tyler, as it appeared in *The Reporter,* July 6, 1954, pp. 31–33. Copyright 1954 by The Reporter Magazine Company. Reprinted by permission of Poyntz Tyler and the Editorial Department of The Reporter Magazine Company.

have the place," says Harry in explanation of the munificence, "and when his customers couldn't pick up the tab he kept their furniture. When he couldn't pay the rent the Chinaman kept the furniture. When we can't pay the rent he'll probably keep our right arms. They're our only liquid assets."

By a combination of sporadic work, scavenging, panhandling, and treasure trove, they get enough food to sustain life and enough fortified wine to make it bearable. But a sum large enough to impress the landlord is hard to come by. So every fortnight, to propitiate their household gods and in flagrant violation of the health regulations, each sells a pint of blood for five or six dollars, less than the cost of most good liqueurs. Immaculate and cold sober for the occasion, they make the business trip together and deliver the proceeds to the landlord together, lest one, alone and affluent, succumb to temptation on the way home. Keeping their sanguinary account straight requires considerable dexterity on the laundryman's abacus, but the Chinaman always rewards their financial integrity with some sound advice and a pint of the grain alcohol he uses to heat his irons. They file the advice and use the alcohol to spike a jug of claret —held in donor circles to have a therapeutic effect on the blood stream.

Bud and Harry are not typical professional blood donors. Many are working men and women who consider it a painless way to pick up extra cash. They know their health won't be impaired—the most learned medicos advocated phlebotomy as a cure-all until fairly recently, and the best medical brains out of jail in Russia used leeches on Stalin—and they pride themselves that they are helping to meet an urgent need.

There are only four basic blood types: O, A, B, and AB. But the ten RH combinations multiply this to forty, and if certain other important blood factors are taken into account, there are 360 types in all. The rarest type, which courses through the veins of only one out of ten million people, is A_2, B_1, N_1, P negative Rh prime, Rh double prime, and its owners are invariably snobs.

The Red Cross blood program gets few alcoholics, but the commercial banks are plagued with them. The craving for five dollars' worth of oblivion brings donors whose blood would probably give the recipient delirium tremens. Drunks, people with tropical diseases who vehemently deny ever having been south of Perth Amboy, cardiac cases who claim their symptoms are simply the temporary signs of overwork, Negroes who interpret a low hemoglobin report as racial bias, and indiscreet repeaters make life so hectic for the bank personnel that Harry and Bud are welcome visitors. They are momentarily clean and reasonably healthy, and although the examining doctor generally harbors a suspicion that they are being tapped too often, their blood is known to be free of transmittable diseases.

While selling blood barely outranks bird watching in financial returns, Bud and Harry have too much at stake to risk their earning power with any dietary foolishness—other, that is, than claret and grain alcohol. Neither ever saw the inside of a high school, but they have combined native intelligence with a sporadic accumulation of knowledge gained in public libraries on rainy days to formulate a cheap diet that allows them to ply their trade in reasonable security. The entree is usually some kind of viscera, with beef kidneys and lamb liver leading in popularity and value. Other staples are cabbage, kale, root vegetables, potatoes, macaroni, rice, toasted day-old bread, and a generous helping of the iron pills that are dispensed freely by all blood banks. Coffee is often scarce or indifferent, but tobacco, in the form of butts, is plentiful. These are gleaned around subway entrances and bus stops, both fertile fields, and smoked whole or in pipes.

Most of their supplies are bought in chain supermarkets, and while shopping they will sometimes violate their own rule against larceny by having lunch on the house. Their method, while not undetectable, is practically unprovable. It consists of dining directly from the shelves, so that the checker would need a stomach pump to produce the corpus delicti. Cold cuts, cheese, rolls, candy, and fruit are the usual luncheon snacks on these occasions, and beer is the favorite beverage because the empty bottles can be turned in for what the management believes to be a refund.

Bleeding, or rent, days are set in advance to allow time for tapering off the *vino,* and the market is carefully cased. Including hospitals, which buy for their own needs only, there are over twenty-five blood banks in New York City, but Harry and Bud confine their patronage to a favored ten where they are well known and even slightly pampered. Weather conditions affect the choice, and care must be taken they aren't "overdrawn" (under the forty-two-day limit) at the selected "branch." They try to allow three months between visits, but this rule is often abrogated for a few choice spots. One hospital is especially esteemed because it not only pays an extra four bits to compensate for its inconvenient location but paints the lily with a generous slug of whiskey. The big commercial outfits, with their more cursory physical examinations, are held in reserve against the days when hemoglobins are suspected of being low. One large bank, known to the profession as "The Abattoir," is visited with reluctance and only when the Chinaman appears restive.

"It's strictly from hunger," Harry says, "but it's easy to make a sale once you get past an old hag who crawls out from under the linoleum every now and then to pull her rank."

"I figure her a frustrated nympho," explains Bud, whose brief tour of matrimony made him an authority on the behavior of the human female. "She could be saved by the love of a good man, but she's strictly in restraint of trade at the moment. Me and Harry and some bums will be standing there beating our gums and she comes storming out for inspection like a top sergeant. She picks a couple of the best-looking stiffs in the line—present company excepted, naturally—and gives them the old heave because they need a shave or their hair ain't combed."

Once past this obstacle, Harry claims they could peddle tomato catchup if not deterred by professional ethics. "You pass along this counter," he says, "and give your life history and your identification to a babe and she hands you a card. This card tells the doctor exactly what you just told the babe—and it also has a liability release. So you sign it and hand it to another babe who checks to see if you're jumping the gun. Then you hand it to the babe who takes your blood count. She sticks a needle in your pinky and collects a few drops of blood—sort of a free sample— and drops it into a whiskey glass full of copper sulphate solution.

If it floats you're anemic and she ties the can on you right there."

"All these babes," Bud breaks in, "act like they are strictly from Vassar—and there ain't one couldn't use a transfusion herself."

"If it sinks," Harry continues, "it means your blood is heavier than the solution in the glass, so you're O.K. and she marks your card with a black pencil. But if it only sinks a little, and then bobbles around like it can't make up its mind, it shows you're a borderline case. So she marks your card with a red pencil. That means the doc is supposed to test it again to make sure, so you stay in line—but the doc always comes up with the same score."

"The same score with everyone but us, that is," Bud interrupts again, "because old Harry here spots the hole in the gimmick right off. So if one of us gets the red hook, we just change cards until we pass the doc. Then we switch back."

"Nothing to it," Harry says modestly, "but it gets us both by, and the way we work it, they don't get all balled up in their typing records. Soon as the doc tests the guy with the red mark, his blood plunks to the bottom like buckshot. So the doc figures the babe outside with the needle is nuts. He may be right.

"The doc is O.K. He takes your blood pressure and tests your heart and asks if you're pure in mind and body. If your ticker's O.K. he congratulates you as if you'd made it yourself. If it's jumpy he says you'd better take it easy at the office or get off to Bermuda for a week or so.

"Once you pass the doc you're all set for your dough, but jeeze, boy, you earn it. The doc sends you out into sort of a hallway that's so jammed with lugs it looks like the Jerome Avenue Express. Everybody telling the next guy what a big shot he is. Or what a big shot he used to be. Or what a big shot his brother is. Me and Bud don't say nothing and we could probably buy the whole bunch. At retail.

"It takes over an hour to work your way down that hall. Standing up and no smokes. Then when you finally get to the butcher shop you're lying there with a big needle in your arm and your arm sticking out in the aisle. And the joint's so crowded everybody goes by bumps your arm. Jeeze, by the time you're finally through, you need your blood back."

To some donors the five or six dollars for a pint of blood is the payment on the family's health insurance. To others it's a night's lodging, some new soles, the first meal in days, a quart of rye. To Harry and Bud it's dignity.

Without it they would be homeless bums. With it they are bums in residence. To eat they collect bottles, shovel snow, deliver packages, wash cars, or peddle the early tabloids. To drink they beg. Neither will ever do any better, and when their blood streams balk or someone perfects artificial plasma, they will do worse. But right now they are grateful—and a little proud.

"How else," Harry inquires, "could bums like us help anybody? They can't brew blood like it was beer. But me and Bud are blood factories. A guy's all busted up he don't give a damn where the stuff comes from. It could be his brother or his wife or his priest or me."

Drug addiction is another form of escape from life, one which is regarded with peculiar horror by the general public— as the phrase, "dope fiend," indicates. Actually, heroin does not make addicts fiendish. An addict who has just taken "horse" is less likely to behave aggressively or boisterously than a student who has just visited the neighborhood tavern. It is true, however, that an addict who cannot get the drug his body demands becomes desperate; he will do almost anything for a "shot." (Some students of addiction have suggested that making heroin available to addicts under medical supervision would not only reduce the considerable crime associated with the traffic in illegal drugs but also the physical suffering of addicts.[8]) The following case history of a sixteen-year-old Negro addict, Charlie Reed, shows the underprivileged background from which most addicts come.[9] It is no accident that drug addiction is found disproportionately among Negroes and Puerto Ricans.

[8] Alden Stevens, "Make Dope Legal," *Harper's Magazine,* November, 1952, pp. 40–47.
[9] From an article by Eugene Kinkead, entitled "Sixteen," in the November 10, 1952, issue of *The New Yorker,* pp. 44–63; copyright 1951 by The New Yorker Magazine, Inc. Reprinted by permission of the Editorial Department of *The New Yorker.*

Mr. Hargraves turned at East 100th Street and headed toward the slum block lying between First and Second Avenues, where Charlie has his home. It is part of a wretched area in which the police records show an alarming incidence of narcotic addiction. Six-story cold-water tenements, their fronts fretted with moldering fire escapes, line both sides of the street, except at a point in the middle of the block where the city has torn down one of the most decrepit buildings, leaving a makeshift play lot that is strewn with debris. Seven grocery stores and five churches, including a synagogue and Mr. Hargraves' branch of the East Harlem Protestant Parish, occupy ground floors in the tenements, as do a barbershop, a social club, and a primitive steam laundry, whose tiny doors were open as we went by, giving us a glimpse of some incredibly antique wooden tubs teetering above a suds-sloshed floor that was overrun by a swarm of scrawny cats. The windows of the groceries were piled with grimy tins of Treet and Spam, and the façades of the churches bore crudely hand-lettered legends along the lines of "Jesus Calls" and "Sinners, Repent!" Even on that shining spring morning, the street looked drab and lifeless, as though it had not yet awakened from the activities of the night before. Mr. Hargraves had told me that in this section of the city three-year-olds can be seen playing happily on the street two or three hours after midnight. . . .

After locking the station wagon, Mr. Hargraves led me to what he called the parish house, a ground-floor flat at the rear of 311 East 100th Street, across the street from his church. Its clean, freshly painted three rooms contrasted sharply with the dark, strong-smelling hall outside. I had told Mr. Hargraves that before talking with Charlie about his experiences as a junkie—as a person who uses dope is generally called in the world of narcotics—I wanted to learn a little about the boy's background and the community in which he lived, and when we had settled ourselves in chairs, he started out by giving me a brief picture of the parish he works in. He said that most of his colleagues in the parish are, like himself, recent graduates of Union Theological Seminary. The parish, which was organized in 1948, extends from Ninety-ninth to 104th Street and from Lexington to First Avenue.

"When we first came here, we went around and knocked on doors to get acquainted," Mr. Hargraves said. "It was an eye-opening adventure. Across the hall from Charlie's apartment, for example, I found two Puerto Rican families who had been living together in three rooms for six months without knowing each other's last names. In another house, an old Negro lady of seventy-five was living all alone with six cats and six dogs, each with its own little filthy bowl in the center of the room. Poverty, love, and ignorance are all mixed up here. Last Christmas-time, one woman took in a family of five—utter strangers to her—to give them a bed and a warm place to stay over the holy season. Usually, in this neighborhood, apartments have a kitchen and just two or three other rooms. The gas range is the principle source of heat. In cold weather, it's kept burning most of the day."

Mr. Hargraves turned to the matter of family economics in the block. Family incomes, he said, vary widely, but individual earnings are for the most part low. Relief money is, of course, a big factor in the life of the community. "The Department of Welfare has a schedule of payments designed to take care of almost every conceivable domestic situation of the needy," Mr. Hargraves said. "Its checks—they're usually cashed around here in Jenny's Market, on Second Avenue—arrive on the fifth and twentieth of the month. Those are red-letter days for the block. I'd say that five distinct economic groups live here, and—as far as the adults are concerned, at least—they keep quite separate. First, there are the aristocrats, amounting to about five per cent of the total—Jews, Italians, and West Indian Negroes who came here around 1910 as immigrants. They're familiar with the scene, regard it as their home, and keep on living here because they like it, despite the fact that there are apt to be high-salaried individuals in their families, such as pressers in the strictly unionized garment industry. Next—about ten per cent, I imagine—are Puerto Ricans who came to New York in the first wave of emigration from the island, around 1920. They've brought up their children as Americans and are better off financially than the third group—some thirty per cent—who are Southern Negroes who came here during the twenties. This third class is the one Charlie Reed's family is in. These people form a hard-working lower stratum of society, with obscure jobs that often require several hours' travel to get to and from each day. It's odd how far people around here seem to have to go to find work. Well, next there's the largest unit—about forty per cent—made up of newly arrived Southern Negroes and Puerto Ricans. Right now, they're in a state of ferment. Some of their customs tend to make them the laughing stock of the block, but, of course, they're only going through the same period of adjustment that the other groups went through before them. They seem to have a corner on menial kitchen and hospital work. The last, and in many ways the most difficult, group is the shady class. It runs to around fifteen per cent, and is composed of people who have broken off from the other groups. Its children rarely go to school. Their parents never look out for them. Both young and old are always either on the border line of crime or right in the midst of it—mixed up in the numbers racket, muggings, prostitution, and selling dope, to adults as well as to minors like Charlie Reed.

"From youngsters like Charlie who have come to us for help, we know that there are still more than twenty juvenile addicts in this block alone. We also know that in this district more than half the young people who have reached eighteen have taken dope in some form or other. Of these, a substantial percentage, ranging somewhere from a quarter to a third, have got hooked—become addicted, that is. The stronger boys seem to use drugs a few times and then stop. That's the end of it for them. But with the weaker ones the whole pattern of life is likely to be changed."

Mr. Hargraves said that the hub of a slum boy's social life in East Harlem is his gang. The neighborhood gangs are much more democratic than the adult groups; they tap all levels for membership. Organized to provide excitement in an otherwise dull society, the gangs have junior, intermediate, and senior divisions, and take in boys of anywhere from around twelve to twenty. The main juvenile gangs in Charlie Reed's area are the Latin Lords, the Viceroys, the Turbens [sic], and the Redwings, none of which are to be confused with the 107th Street gang of adults that testimony at the Kefauver Committee hearings here linked with Charles Luciano in the dope-smuggling racket.

"Boys join their neighborhood gangs to improve their social status," Mr. Hargraves said. "It's a perfectly natural, boylike thing to do, I suppose. The bad part about it is that when trouble—or what's called a rumble—with another gang starts, they find that even if they're afraid to fight, they'd better not show it. It's a funny thing, though. Some boys don't like to go in for that sort of thing, and refuse to join gangs, and the other boys look up to them for it. And here's another funny thing. Although boys usually get their first experience with drugs through their older friends in the gang, the ones who get hooked drop out of the gang and drift off in little knots by themselves. That's what happened to Charlie and his two friends. They were prominent members of their gang until six months ago, when they started using heroin. For the last two months before they went to Bellevue, they'd been main-lining—you know, injecting the drug directly into a vein. Gradually, they drew away from the people and activities they'd formerly liked, and began wandering around the neighborhood like wraiths. Then their families got in touch with me, and two weeks ago I took them down to Bellevue to see if something could be done to cure them. They were in pretty bad condition by that time—thin and dirty, with their clothes unkempt and their eyes glazed. They had taken a shot somewhere just before getting in the car, and were on the nod—sitting there with their eyes open, but hardly able to talk and practically asleep, and their heads bobbing like mechanical dolls. Of course, they're all cleaned up now. Inside and outside, they're different boys. But in view of the case histories we've had on the block, all I can say is that we *hope* they'll stay this way."

I asked Mr. Hargraves about Charlie's family. "That's an important part of it, of course," he said. "Like so many other young users on the block, Charlie comes from a broken home. Up here, society tends to be matriarchal in the less prosperous families. That is, couples live together and have children, and sometimes they're married and sometimes they're not, but almost always the man is a transient or a weakling and the lease of the apartment is in the woman's name. She gets the relief check, too, and tries to hold the family together. Charlie's home is a good example of that. Some twenty-five years ago, as a teen-age girl, his mother came up here with *her* mother from South Carolina and settled in the block. She married and had Charlie and Sammy, his brother, who is a year older, before she and her husband separated. Then, by a second man, she had two girls, who are now ten and twelve, and a boy, who's nine. Finally, she married her present husband, and they have a son of two. Charlie's older brother Sammy is a settled boy and a good student, but the mother doesn't seem to care much for him. The eight members of the family live in a three-room-and-kitchen flat on the third floor rear that she gets rent free by acting as superintendent of the building—cleaning the halls, collecting the rents, and such. She also does part-time work in a laundry, and her husband is a dishwasher, and what they earn, together with relief, comes to about sixty dollars a week, and they manage fairly well financially. The mother is popular as the building superintendent because she does a good job and looks after her neighbors when they're sick. Charlie is crazy about her. He doesn't get along with his stepfather so well, but he just loves his mother. She's a big, handsome mulatto. Very much the queen of her household, I'd say."

I thanked Mr. Hargraves and set out down the street for Charlie's flat. He opened the door at my knock, and I stepped into the kitchen, as one usually does in tenements of ancient architectural vintage. Sammy was down on his knees mopping the floor. A little dog was tied to a leg of the sink. Beside the sink were some paper bags of refuse topped by soggy coffee grounds. The door of a closet hung open, revealing a toilet inside, and nearby was a tiny bathtub of the old-fashioned claw-foot kind. A string of wash hung drying in the hall leading from the kitchen to the other rooms. In the first room, although it was mid-morning, three of Charlie's brothers and sisters were still sleeping. This did not surprise me, for Mr. Hargraves had told me that children in that region often don't get up until afternoon, at least on weekends.

I had been in the kitchen only a few minutes when Charlie's

mother came in from the landing with a mop and a pail with
which she had been cleaning the stairs. She stood erect, with animated eyes and a face that was still attractive for all her many
years of backbreaking existence. "This is a friend of Archie's,
Mom," said Charlie.

She greeted me warmly. "Won't you sit down?" she said,
indicating a sagging sofa against the kitchen wall.

"No, let's go up on the roof," said Charlie quickly. "We can
talk better up there."

Charlie and I climbed the stairway to the roof, where we sat
down on a wall in the bright sunshine, and Charlie began telling
me about his difficulties and frustrations. He said he wanted to
become a city fireman, but most of the time he doubted whether
he would ever be able to pass the tests. When I said I couldn't
see why he didn't have as good a chance as the next fellow, he
looked grateful. "Firemen ain't like cops," he said. "They *save*
people." I asked him if he had a girl, and he replied that he was
fond of a Puerto Rican girl in the block but that he felt hopeless
about his chances of marrying her. "For all the color the Puerto
Ricans got in their race, they sure act strictly like white people
about their women," he said bitterly. "They're Jim Crow just like
down South that way. A Puerto Rican girl's family will whip her
if she's going out with a colored boy, even if he's three shades
lighter than her. If she don't stop going out with him, they'll
throw her off the roof. And yet this girl I'm talking about, her
brother and me is good friends in the gang." . . .

Charlie told me he had been led to taking dope by smoking
marijuana early in the winter that he became fifteen. The first
time he tried it was when he and some of the other members of
his gang were coming back from Ward's Island after watching
a soccer game. One of the boys handed him a butt and told him
to inhale on it if he wanted to feel good. He took a few drags
but felt nothing. In fact, he smoked marijuana off and on that
whole winter without experiencing any kick. Then the warm
weather came, and the drug hit him. "You feel peppy," he said.
"You want to dance. When you walk, you really got that nine-
foot glide. And it's good to listen to music when you been smoking reefers. It feels so nice just to hear it." Charlie did some of

his smoking at stag parties in neighboring flats, but most of the time he smoked outside—in yards and parks and on rooftops— where the telltale sweetish herbal odor of the drug wouldn't be so likely to draw attention. Charlie said he learned that for the best results, marijuana smoke should be inhaled deeply and the smoke then blown out into cupped hands and inhaled again through the nose.

Tolerance to marijuana can be acquired fairly quickly, and shortly after Charlie became sixteen, he found he was no longer walking with that nine-foot glide. Then he started on heroin, or "horse." He and Bugsy first tried the white powder together, taking turns snuffing in the phone booth of a candy store. Buff had given it to them, saying that he'd tried it and that it was better than marijuana. Both Charlie and Bugsy knew what heroin was. They had even heard that some Harlem boys had died from taking it. I asked Charlie why, under the circumstances, he and Bugsy so much as accepted the stuff from Buff. He looked at me with surprise. "Buff was our pal, wasn't he?" he said stoutly. "Hell, I wasn't going to miss nothing." The snuffing stage lasted about a month. Then the trio turned to skin injections, using hypodermic syringes that they bought at a drugstore, and from that it was only a step to main-lining. Charlie said that when he realized he was hooked, he grew frightened. He tried to switch back to marijuana, but found he couldn't. "It made me sick at my stomach and left a terrible taste in my mouth," he told me. "It never works, the fellows say. You have to stay on the horse kick until you kick it."

Charlie said that heroin made him feel separated from the rest of the world. "It's a different feeling than when you're on marijuana," he went on. "You're relaxed. You ain't got a care from here to Brooklyn. A cop can come up to you and talk to you, and you won't get nervous or anything. When you're on marijuana and a cop comes up and talks to you, you're leery and you want to run. But not on horse. You talk right back to him." One of Charlie's favorite pastimes when he was taking heroin was to give himself a shot and then go to a movie, often at the Triboro Theatre, on 125th Street, which daily offers three features of the more lurid sort. He would buy a ticket, take a seat

in the balcony, and stay there for hours, smoking regular cigarettes, one after another, and aimlessly watching the fantasies
on the screen, which helped heighten and prolong his own fantasies. Often, during these reveries, his cigarette would burn his
fingers. "I'd just sit there and goof," he said. Always in his
fantasies he was big, important, powerful. "If somebody was to
come up to me then and say, 'Let's have a swimming race or a
home-run-hitting contest or something like that,' I wouldn't pay
no attention to him," he told me. " 'What the hell,' I'd say to
myself, 'I know I can lick him.' "

During the last two months before Charlie went to Bellevue,
when he was main-lining, he injected himself with heroin three
times a day—in the morning, at noon, and at night. When he
couldn't manage it on time, he told me, he felt weak in the
knees, headachy, and feverish, and cigarettes tasted like hay.
He took the morning and evening shots in the toilet in his
family's flat and the other in a washroom wherever he happened
to find himself around noon. In those days, he would frequently start out for his high school—Samuel Gompers, in the
Bronx—and never get there. He carried his hypodermic outfit
around with him in a pocket of his jacket. It consisted of a
syringe, some capsules of heroin, a soot-blackened spoon in
which he diluted the drug with water and warmed it over a
match, a thick rubber band to raise a vein in his arm, and a
dab of cotton. Charlie said he never injected himself outdoors,
because he had been told that if a person should be touched by
a breeze while using a hypodermic needle, a bubble of air would
enter the vein and later "freeze the heart."

As a main-liner, Charlie used three capsules of heavily cut
heroin a day. He bought the drug, at a dollar a capsule, mostly
from a twenty-three-year-old dope peddler—or pusher—named
Pete, who lived on East Ninety-ninth Street and whom Charlie
would meet in a lunchroom on Second Avenue. Once or twice,
he bought his supply from a Puerto Rican who walked brazenly
down the street calling *"Caballo! Caballito!"* ("Horse! Horsie!")
Pete told Charlie he didn't really know where the stuff was coming from; he said he thought it might be from New Jersey. The
biggest dealer in the neighborhood, whom Charlie said he was

acquainted with but didn't patronize, ran his business right in his second-floor tenement apartment, and some of his customers, after making a purchase, would "take off"—as young addicts call injecting themselves—in the hallway just outside the door of the flat. During Charlie's two months of main-lining, he got hold of the three dollars a day he needed for the drug by working as a runner in the numbers racket and by some lucky breaks in a floating dice game. Buff had a job in a grocery store, and Bugsy became a petty thief. "We helped each other out with money," Charlie said. All three of the boys lost their interest in the gang, and were unconcerned when, toward the end, the other members wouldn't let them hang out on the gang's favorite street corner. "They told us, 'We don't want you junkies lousing us up,'" Charlie said. "I don't blame them. Hell, the gang has enough trouble with the cops as it is, without no junkies underfoot." . . .

. . . I went up to Charlie's flat. I arrived as the family was finishing supper, which had apparently consisted only of thick cold-meat sandwiches. Charlie and his stepfather, a slight, pimply Negro of about forty, were arguing over which one of them should take the day's garbage downstairs to the cans in front of the building. "Take it down, Charlie, you hear me?" said the stepfather.

"Like hell I will," said Charlie.

"It's your turn, God damn you!" the stepfather yelled.

"Don't you cuss at me, you skin-dirty louse!" Charlie yelled in return, whereupon the man rushed at him with upraised fist.

Charlie's mother stepped decisively between them, and sent each sprawling backward with a push. "Mind your manners!" she said. "Both of you! You hear me?"

"I'll take it down," said Sammy.

"Come on," Charlie said to me, picking himself up off the floor. "Let's get out of this stinking hole." On the way down the stairs, he denounced his stepfather profanely. "I don't see how Mom puts up with him, nohow," he said. "I'd as soon touch a rat. She's going to get rid of him one of these days, too. You mark my words." . . .

. . . Charlie and I went into a lunchroom down the block

for a Coke and a piece of pie. We were joined by Bugsy, who proved to be congenial and talkative. Bugsy told me about a swell job he had had the year before. He had been a mortician's assistant, he said, at ninety-five dollars a week, and had had a luxurious apartment over the mortician's shop, with dim lights, flowered curtains at the windows, a tile floor, and a tile fountain with bubbling water. Bugsy also gave me a full description of his job—of going to people's homes to pick up bodies, of comforting grief-stricken families, and of preparing the remains. "But I gave up the work because it was too unfriendly," Bugsy said. "Nobody ever came to see me."

Charlie gave him a look. "You sure feeling comfortable," he observed.

Later that night, I dropped in to see Mr. Hargraves. He told me Bugsy was back on heroin again. I asked him about the boy's ninety-five-dollar-a-week job and the fancy apartment. "Rubbish," he said. "Just a junkie's fantasy."

Two weeks afterward, Mr. Hargraves called me to say that Charlie himself had gone back on heroin—less than two months after being discharged from Bellevue. He was slinking in and out of doorways again, and often stayed out all night. A few days later, Mr. Hargraves called me a second time. Charlie, he told me, had been arrested by a plainclothesman, who, as they say in Harlem, had lucked out on him; that is, the officer had picked him up merely on suspicion, searched him in a hallway, and found his dope outfit. So Charlie was held for possession and remanded to the Tombs to await trial.

A couple of days later, I went to see Charlie's mother. From time to time, as we sat and talked on the sofa in the kitchen, she plucked despairingly at a bright-colored scarf she wore around her head. Charlie, she said, had been in the hands of the police once before. "And that wasn't his fault," she added. "That was when a crazy Spanish man stabbed him." She explained that Charlie on that occasion had been down on the street, leaning through the window of a car talking to a friend, when a Puerto Rican he had never seen before came by and knifed him in the back. "Man *must* have been crazy," she said. "Drunk or crazy. But the cops took Charlie along, too. This here's different. Now he's in trouble with the law on his own. I don't know what to do," she went on. "It just worries me and worries me all the time." For a couple of weeks before Charlie's arrest, she told me, he had been sleeping either at Buff's or Bugsy's. "He had trouble with my husband," she said. "My husband miss his overcoat, a real beautiful California wrap. Them boys must of pawned it. And some of my rent money was gone, too. I don't know which one of them done it. They all stick together."

Charlie had grown crankier and crankier in the days just before his arrest, his mother told me. "I used to think I understood that boy," she said, in a low voice. "I had real trouble raising him up. He had asthma bad, you know. But now I don't know if I knows him at all. I could tell when he started taking that stuff again, though. I says to him, 'You promised me, Charlie, when you came out of the hospital, you ain't never going to do that no more.' I never knew how he take it, or nothing. I was awful stupid. Then, one day about three weeks ago, I pull out of his pocket this thing all wrop round with a rubber band, with a needle and a black spoon in it. I says, 'Glory God, this is it!' I shows it to him. 'Son,' I says, 'you deep in wrong.' He beg me so hard to give it back to him, and say he going to throw it away, that I give in and do. But he trick me. He hide it someplace, and I never did find it no more. Later, when I says to him, 'I see you taking that stuff again,' he lies. He says, 'You ain't see me take nothing.' I says, 'I may not *see* you take nothing, but I can tell when you done did it. I can tell the difference in you.' Then he yells at me, 'You see how you is? You talking like that *makes* somebody take something.' Oh, he was terrible cranky." The mother told me she suspected that her son, Buff, and Bugsy had been injecting themselves off and on in the bedroom that Charlie shared with Sammy in the flat. The door to it could be fastened on the inside with a hook. "The three of them would go in there and set the hook," she said. "After a while, I says to Charlie, 'Why you fasten that door?' 'I just want to talk secrets with my friends,' he says. 'You don't have to hear everything we talking about.' "

I asked Charlie's mother how she could tell when her son had been taking heroin. "Right off, he seems happy," she replied. "Wants to dance. Comes around and kisses me. Says, 'Mom, I love you!' Then he gets a book. He tries to read and falls asleep. I'd sure like to know where he was getting it. I talked to Archie about this, and he say the police made a lot of arrests of pushers, but every time they do, new ones pop up in the same place. It seem just like some big business company." She asked me what I thought they would do with Charlie. I said I had no idea. "I sure hope they cures him this time," she said.

Drug addiction is a good example of clinging to a ruinous habit. For whatever reason the individual began taking opiate drugs, to relieve pain or fatigue, for thrills, because his friends were using them, he soon discovers disadvantageous aspects of the practice: (a) Heroin is extremely expensive because he must purchase it from illegal "peddlers." (b) Once he is physiologically habituated, he cannot stop using the drug without experiencing violent nausea and other unpleasant physical symptoms. (c) Being known as a "dope fiend" isolates him psychologically; his family and friends condemn him in words or action; employers have no desire to hire him; he is liable to arrest and imprisonment. Nevertheless, it is difficult to effect permanent cures. At the United States Public Health Service Hospital in Lexington, Kentucky, addicts from all over the country come for treatment. Not only is physiological dependence on the drug eliminated, but the patient also gets considerable psychological help. When he leaves the hospital, he is "cured" in a medical sense. Notwithstanding, he is likely to go back to the drug, sooner or later. Why? Because he knows that opiates provide relief from physical and psychic pain. When he encounters defeats and discouragement in his effort to readjust himself, there is a temptation to fall back upon them. True, drugs brought him trouble as well as relief, but at a low moment he is more likely to remember the relief than the trouble. He takes a small "shot." Having failed to resist temptation once, he will probably put up less objections to the drug the next time that troubles beset him. Soon he is "hooked" again.

Usually, vicious circles are involved whenever individuals resort to the withdrawal mode of adaptation. The alcoholic *knows* that drinking broke up his marriage. Withdrawers expose themselves to social rejection, not because of ignorance but because of a vested interest. That is to say, they are loath to give up their mode of adjustment because, in the short run, there are only meager compensations for such a sacrifice. True, both foresight and hindsight point in the same direction: Give it up; it is ruining you. But at any one moment the choice is between a familiar escape and vague, uncertain hopes for the improvement of a bad situation. Furthermore, as the situation worsens—a consequence of the withdrawal—it looks to the individual less and less probable that giving up his solace will do any good.

SUMMARY

When people are damned if they do and damned if they don't—when what they have learned to need they have also learned they should not want, or cannot have—then they are under pressure to withdraw. Withdrawal represents an admission of defeat in the struggle to maintain a favorable self-image; it is also a repudiation of the governing principles of American society. Whether the individual commits suicide, suffers a mental breakdown, or becomes an alcoholic or a drug addict, he is fleeing from the stresses of the real world. He can be termed a social problem because, in one sense or another, Americans evaluate such flight as undesirable.

ANNOTATED BIBLIOGRAPHY

Anderson, Nels, *The Hobo* (Chicago: University of Chicago Press, 1923). ⟨ The famous study of Chicago's West Madison Street: ". . . the Pennsylvania Avenue of the anarchy of Hobohemia." Anderson describes the lives and motivation of the men who have withdrawn from responsible roles and become "homeless men."

Bacon, Seldon D., "Alcohol and Complex Society," in *Alcohol, Science and Society* (New Haven: *Quarterly Journal of Studies on Alcohol,* 1945), pp. 179–194. ⟨ An analysis of the functions of alcohol in overcoming the tensions of modern competitive and impersonal society.

Deutsch, Albert, *The Mentally Ill in America* (New York: W. W. Norton & Company, 1944). ⟨ The history and current status of care for the mentally ill in the United States.

Erikson, Erik H., *Childhood and Society* (New York: W. W. Norton & Company, 1950). ⟨ A justly famous psychoanalyst's account of the problems of maturity and immaturity. Erikson presents some vivid descriptions and illuminating explanations of psychic withdrawal from threatening social environments.

Faris, Robert, and Dunham, Warren L., *Mental Disorder in an Urban Area* (Chicago: University of Chicago Press, 1939). ⟨ The pioneer ecological study of the relation between mental illness and social structure. The authors report on the concentration of certain types of mental illness in various areas of the city.

Freud, Sigmund, Lectures on Psychoanalysis, *American Journal of Psychology*, Vol. 21 (April, 1910), No. 2. Excerpts are reprinted in Naftalin, Arthur, et al. (eds.), *An Introduction to Social Science* (Chicago: J. B. Lippincott Company, 1953), Book I, pp. 145–162. ⟨The famous lectures given at Clark University in 1909. These lectures, showing Freud's brilliant ability to explain his ideas to lay audiences, remain among the most lucid expositions of psychoanalytic theory yet published.

Harris, Sara, *Skid Row, U.S.A.* (Garden City, New York: Doubleday & Company, Inc., 1956). ⟨ A perceptive and sympathetic account of the inadequate personalities who gravitate, in surprisingly large numbers, to the flophouse districts of large American cities. Contrary to popular belief, Miss Harris suggests that alcoholism is the result rather than the cause of Skid Row residence.

Hirsh, Joseph, *The Problem Drinker* (New York: Duell, Sloan and Pierce, 1949). ⟨ A popular book about alcoholic withdrawal by the Executive Director of the Research Council on the Problems of Alcohol. The alcoholic, according to Hirsh, is a person who is compulsively dependent upon liquor as a means of dealing with his problems.

Lindesmith, Alfred R., *Opiate Addiction* (Bloomington, Indiana: Principia Press, 1947). ⟨ An explanation of drug addiction by the leading sociological investigator of this problem. Lindesmith shows how the term "escapist" may be appropriate in describing the addict but not the term "dope fiend."

Menninger, Karl A., *The Human Mind* (New York: Alfred A. Knopf, Inc., 3rd edition, 1945). ⟨ An outstanding psychiatrist's readable and reliable discussion of human psychic mechanisms and their control.

Strecker, Edward A., *Fundamentals of Psychiatry* (Philadelphia: J. B. Lippincott Company, 1944). ⟨ A good account of the differences among different kinds of psychoses.

CHAPTER EIGHT

The acceptance of defeat:
Submission

The mode of adjustment which we call "submission" is not as thoroughgoing an admission of defeat as is "withdrawal." True, submission implies renouncing the struggle to live up to standards of adequacy, security, gratification, or worthiness. But it does not necessarily mean loss of self-respect. Those who submit try to sustain a favorable self-image by conforming to one or more of the governing principles of American society. They say, in effect, "I may not be successful, but I do my best. Besides,

I can take it; I'm a good sport." The substitution of conformity
to the institutional rules for realization of culturally approved
goals is no easy road to self-respect. Frequently, the individual is
haunted by feelings of inferiority, unconsciously if not consciously. Psychologists describe some neuroses along these lines.
The individual conforms outwardly; he is able to play the social
roles that he is assigned. But he suffers; he is torn by inner conflicts. Submission is not necessarily accompanied by inner turmoil. Sometimes submission is a problem precisely because the
public feels there is not *enough* resistance. Consider the unskilled
worker in modern industry. Most Americans are disturbed by his
lack of ambition, his absenteeism, his frequent changes of job.
Of course, when his home conditions are taken into account, and
this is especially true if he is a Negro or a Puerto Rican, his behavior becomes more understandable.[1]

The miserable housing, and recurrent homelessness of the
underprivileged workers are the most costly of all drains upon
his efficiency. A study of working-class Negroes in Chicago in
1944–1945 revealed that most of them had less than five hours'
sleep per night. Children and adults must sleep three to five in a
bed. Beds are usually filled day and night in Chicago's slums,
as workers await their turn to sleep. The density of the population on the Negro South Side is the second highest in the United
States.

Ruth sleeps in a kitchenette apartment rented by a mother
with eight children. Ruth shares a bed with five other adolescents
and children, sleeping crosswise the bed. She counts it a windfall
when there are only three in the bed, and she may sleep length-
wise. A record of her hours of sleep was kept last winter, for
two periods of two weeks each, one in November and one in
January. She was in bed an average of 4½ hours out of each 24.
During these 10 working days, she was absent 4. Her work was
extremely heavy, so heavy that she was given a half hour's rest
by the plant for each hour on the job. Without more sleep, she
said, she could not stand the work even five days a week. She has
been trying since Christmas to find a room to rent. Last fall she

---

[1] Reprinted by permission from "The Motivation of the Underprivileged
Worker" by Allison Davis in *Industry and Society,* edited by William F. Whyte,
pp. 84–106, copyright 1946, McGraw-Hill Book Company, Inc., New York.

tried to find a kitchenette apartment, so that she could marry, but, as anyone who knows the South Side's residential "lock-in" understands, she had no chance.

Similar conditions prevail among white workers in many parts of the city, of course. In one large area restricted to whites on the South Side, the great majority of *families with children* live in single rooms, or in kitchenette apartments. No matter whether the people in these modern, urban ratholes in which human children and their parents must live are white or Negro, the social and economic results are the same. The children are forced out into the streets, day and night; they are 'movie children' or completely vagrant children. Life cannot be lived as a family group in these packed rooms; it has to be lived on the streets, in the motion-picture theaters, the taverns, the bars, and the night clubs. Under such unimaginable living conditions, all the effort, training, and money, which in the case of the middle-class worker goes into his home, is blocked and diverted to sex, recreation, and gambling. How can a worker be motivated to work to furnish or to improve his home, when he cannot get an apartment, or even a bed to sleep in? . . .

The physical disabilities of underprivileged workers in Chicago are far more extensive than the favorite publicity concerning their lack of orange juice and milk, and the occasional rat-bites, would suggest. Unemployment and inadequate income resulting in chronic malnutrition decrease both their physical resistance and their working efficiency. A series of recent scientific studies of the children of underprivileged workers, as contrasted with children of middle-class parents, have revealed that the vitamin and chemical levels in the blood of working-class children are greatly below those of middle-class children and are seriously deficient. A study of the bone structure of children in two such groups, by means of X ray, revealed that these nutritional and other environmental deprivations of working-class people leave their marks upon the very bones, themselves. In Chicago, the rates of infection and death from tuberculosis are far higher among underprivileged working-class groups, both white and Negro, than among middle-class groups, as revealed by a survey made at the University of Illinois. At the same time, hospital and medical care is far more limited and is critically limited for Negroes.

For the employer, the most important consideration here is that *the underprivileged worker becomes accustomed to these conditions; he learns to accept poor habits of nutrition and medical care and to accept physical impairment as a natural part of his life.*[2] Ruth, for instance, eats only one meal a day, even when doing heavy labor. She has never been to a physician, or an optician, or an opthalmologist. Yet she is so nearsighted that she has to be within six inches of a newspaper or clock to read them; she is partly deaf from an early childhood accident, and she lived with a tubercular father for several years. But like Pearl, the white underprivileged worker, whose stamina is sufficient only for periods of a few weeks on a job, Ruth regards her physical impairment as "natural." She has not had the money nor the training requisite to secure good medical attention and to learn good health habits. Thus, both cultural attitudes toward nutrition and medical care, as well as severe limitations in housing and hospital facilities work together to reduce the efficiency of such workers. These social and economic drains accustom them to accept high absenteeism and chronic physical impairment as normal aspects of their work adjustment. . . .

In short, one reason that submission is frequently regarded as a social problem is the belief that the individual ought to strive more actively to solve his difficulties. Sometimes, of course, objective circumstances are so crushing that the individual does not feel capable of resisting. Take, for example, the situation of Negroes in the South. Shorty—the Negro elevator operator in the following selection—gives up the struggle for a favorable self-image because, as long as he lives in Memphis, Tennessee, he cannot perceive any better alternatives.[3]

The most colorful of the Negro boys on the job was Shorty, the round, yellow, fat elevator operator. He had tiny, beady eyes that looked out between rolls of flesh with a hard but humorous

[2] Italics added by Bredemeier and Toby.

[3] From *Black Boy* by Richard Wright, pp. 198–200. Copyright 1945 by Richard Wright. Reprinted by permission of the publishers, Harper & Brothers, New York.

stare. He had the complexion of a Chinese, a short forehead, and three chins. Psychologically he was the most amazing specimen of the southern Negro I had ever met. Hardheaded, sensible, a reader of magazines and books, he was proud of his race and indignant about its wrongs. But in the presence of whites he would play the role of a clown of the most debased and degraded type.

One day he needed twenty-five cents to buy his lunch.

"Just watch me get a quarter from the first white man I see," he told me as I stood in the elevator that morning.

A white man who worked in the building stepped into the elevator and waited to be lifted to his floor. Shorty sang in a low mumble, smiling, rolling his eyes, looking at the white man roguishly.

"I'm hungry, Mister White Man. I need a quarter for lunch."

The white man ignored him. Shorty, his hands on the controls of the elevator, sang again:

"I ain't gonna move this damned old elevator till I get a quarter, Mister White Man."

"The hell with you, Shorty," the white man said, ignoring him and chewing on his black cigar.

"I'm hungry, Mister White Man. I'm dying for a quarter," Shorty sang, drooling, drawling, humming his words.

"If you don't take me to my floor, you will die," the white man said, smiling a little for the first time.

"But this black sonofabitch sure needs a quarter," Shorty sang, grimacing, clowning, ignoring the white man's threat.

"Come on, you black bastard, I got to work," the white man said, intrigued by the element of sadism involved, enjoying it.

"It'll cost you twenty-five cents, Mister White Man; just a quarter, just two bits," Shorty moaned.

There was silence. Shorty threw the lever and the elevator went up and stopped about five feet shy of the floor upon which the white man worked.

"Can't go no more, Mister White Man, unless I get my quarter," he said in a tone that sounded like crying.

"What would you do for a quarter?" the white man asked, still gazing off.

"I'll do anything for a quarter," Shorty sang.

"What, for example?" the white man asked.

Shorty giggled, swung around, bent over, and poked out his broad, fleshy ass.

"You can kick me for a quarter," he said, looking impishly at the white man out of the corners of his eyes.

The white man laughed softly, jingled some coins in his pocket, took out one and thumped it to the floor. Shorty stooped to pick it up and the white man bared his teeth and swung his foot into Shorty's rump with all the strength of his body. Shorty let out a howling laugh that echoed up and down the elevator shaft.

"Now, open this door, you goddamn black sonofabitch," the white man said, smiling with tight lips.

"Yeeeess, siiiiir," Shorty sang; but first he picked up the quarter and put it into his mouth. "This monkey's got the peanuts," he chortled.

He opened the door and the white man stepped out and looked back at Shorty as he went toward his office.

"You're all right, Shorty, you sonofabitch," he said.

"I know it!" Shorty screamed, then let his voice trail off in a gale of wild laughter.

I witnessed this scene or its variant at least a score of times and I felt no anger or hatred, only disgust and loathing.

Shorty's mode of adjustment to his situation is not clearly a source of social concern. Submissive persons sometimes are ignored; they are the expendable underdogs of American society. The selection that follows deals with two such underdogs, Katherine and Bernard Lavery. They would never have come to public attention had they not committed a crime, but otherwise they are indistinguishable from tens of thousands of young people who were caught up in the hardships of the Great Depression. Their story is included here *despite* their crime, which, after all, represented a departure from a generally submissive style of life.[4]

[4] From an article by St. Clair McKelway entitled "A Case of Abandonment," in the July 14, 1934, issue of *The New Yorker*. Reprinted by permission of the author; copyright © 1934, The New Yorker Magazine, Inc.

When Mrs. Bernard Lavery abandoned her twin girl babies one October morning, leaving one in a subway lavatory and the other in the vestibule of a church, she violated a law, or, as the legal phrase has it, she committed an act "against the peace of the People of the State of New York, and their dignity." She was arrested the same afternoon—detectives had merely to canvass the hospitals on Manhattan Island to find out what mother of newly born girl twins had been discharged that morning—and for about a year after that the People of the State of New York, represented by sundry individuals and agencies, tried very hard to decide what to do about Mrs. Lavery.

Five or six newspaper reporters, including myself, were in the police station on West Sixty-eighth Street when Mrs. Lavery was brought in. The detectives told us they had also tracked down the woman's husband and that, at the moment, he was on his way to the station house. Then we learned that the husband hadn't had anything to do with the crime of which Mrs. Lavery was accused. She had written him from the hospital (she had been in a charity ward at the City Hospital on Welfare Island) and told him the babies were dead. His job as bellhop at a cheap hotel in the West Forties had prevented him from going to see her, because the visiting hours at the hospital came during his working hours at the hotel, and he couldn't afford to take any time off. So the telephone call from a detective had brought to the bellhop the first word that his wife was under arrest and the first word that his twins were alive. There were no secrets in this case, from the detectives' point of view, because the woman had confessed and the case was already cleared up. They left the door open, and we could see her sitting there. She was not unattractive. A slim woman, tired and pale, she was dressed rather smartly and looked very much like any one of the thousands of young working women you may see on the subway any day at the rush hour. On the police blotter her age was given as thirty. The reason she had abandoned her babies, she had told the detectives, was that her husband made only fifteen or twenty a week and that she knew he wouldn't be able to support twins. She had thought, when she was pregnant, that he might be able to support the one child they had expected.

The husband came into the station house after a while and was shown to the detectives' room. He sat down without touching his wife, and they talked earnestly, facing one another on two chairs the detectives had placed in a corner of the room. After two or three minutes, he turned half away from her and, looking at the ceiling, doubled up his fist and struck his own temple twice, sharply. Then his wife leaned forward awkwardly and put her head on his shoulder. He did not embrace her then; he let his arms hang down and kept his eyes on the ceiling. They sat like that, silently, until the detectives left them there together, coming out and closing the door. About a half hour later they took Mrs. Lavery to jail to await her arraignment before a magistrate the next morning. Lavery himself watched her get into the patrol wagon; then he walked off down the street. I walked after him and asked him whether he wanted to talk about it. "I could have supported them," he said immediately. "But *she* . . ." Somehow he put a large quantity of his own bewilderment and anger and hopelessness into the single pronoun. "She," he began again, and then, *"Listen,"* he said in a different voice, "you can't do anything for me. Leave me alone, now, will you? Will you leave me alone?" He was a short, slight man with one of those ageless faces that bellhops seem to have more often than not. It was easy to picture him in his uniform, waiting for a call, bringing ginger ale or soda water, accepting a tip with a nod of thanks. At the hotel where he worked, they told me he was a faithful employee and that, while he was paid no salary, he averaged fifteen or twenty dollars a week in tips. Next day I learned that Lavery, having no money for a railroad or bus fare, had hitchhiked to Hartford and back the night before. There he had borrowed from a relative some money with which to bail out his wife. It had taken him all night long to make the trip, he was in the Magistrates' Court the next morning, and that afternoon, when I telephoned the hotel, they said he was back at work again—taking things to people in the rooms, standing around in his bellhop's uniform, holding out his hand for tips. A number of times in the weeks that followed, I found myself wondering what had happened to the Laverys and their twins, and so one day a few months later I spent an hour going over the records at the Criminal Courts Building. A good deal had happened, I found, and a great many facts about the Laverys had been gathered, but the case had not been disposed of. It wasn't until almost eleven months had passed that the courts decided what to do about Mrs. Lavery.

The history of the Lavery twins is brief. Both were discovered that October morning soon after their mother abandoned them, and they were taken to the New York Foundling Hospital, where they died, one after the other, within the month. Doctors said their death could not be blamed on anybody, that much more had been done for them at the hospital than the mother could have done for them in her home, and that they had been destined to die soon after birth because of a condition called marasmus—a wasting away, a withering, caused by prenatal malnutrition. The twins simply had no chance from the start, the doctors said.

Mrs. Lavery herself remained in jail only that one night. She appeared before a magistrate the next day, pleaded guilty to the charge of abandoning her babies, and was released on cash bail of fifty dollars, which was put up by her husband. The Laverys had lived in a furnished room on West Sixty-fifth Street before this, but now they moved to a furnished room in Long Island City. The bellhop kept his job and continued to earn fifteen or twenty dollars a week in tips. Mrs. Lavery's case proceeded automatically from the Magistrates' Court to the Court of General Sessions. There a Judge accepted her plea of guilty and paroled her in custody of the Probation Department of the Court. He would pronounce sentence three months later, he said, after the case had been thoroughly investigated.

One of the first things the probation officers found out was that Mrs. Lavery was not legally Mrs. Lavery. She had lived with Lavery for more than six years, but they had never been married. Her real name, it turned out, was Katherine Ryan. Dating from this revelation, the papers in the case refer to her as "Katherine Ryan, alias Mrs. Katherine Lavery." She was subjected to a mental and physical examination, when the investigation commenced, and it showed that she was "of average intelligence, but with a neurotic personality, emotionally unstable," and that she was "undernourished." The examining physician added that "from a purely and strictly psychiatric standpoint, without considering the social, environmental, and other factors in the case, it is respectfully suggested that the social rehabilitation possibilities are good, in view of the fact that the personality findings also indicate a number of favorable characteristics." Probation officers then investigated the social, environmental, and other aspects of the case. They found that Mrs. Lavery, as she preferred to be called, was one of four children. Her father, a bartender, had been unemployed for the past two years; her mother, who was described as "a quiet, well-spoken individual," had been taking in roomers. They owned a small house in Queens. Mrs. Lavery's elder brother, they found, was married and "maintaining his own home," as the report put it. One of her sisters had been totally blind since infancy; the other had been crippled since she was two years old, as a result of spinal meningitis. Until Katherine was eighteen, the probation officer found, she had been "an intelligent, normal child and most helpful to her mother, who was naturally preoccupied with the other two daughters." At that age, however, Katherine had become independent, had moved away from her home, had supported herself by working as a telephone operator in hotels in Manhattan, and had rarely visited her family.

Katherine had her first child about a year after she met Lavery. She quit her job at a small hotel on Columbus Avenue three months before it was born. When the baby—a girl—was about two months old, she brought it to her parents' home in Queens. The child's name, she told them, was Caroline Lavery. She left the baby there, saying she would be back, but she did not come back, and after some months the grandparents turned the child over to a foundling home. This baby lived. The probation officers found that the mother had visited her several times at the foundling home. During the six years Katherine was living with Lavery, she paid for her own clothes and contributed her share of the room rent and grocery bills, according to the probation officers' report. She worked as a telephone operator in various hotels in Manhattan, and in each case is remembered as a faithful employee. Her salary, at times, was as high as thirty-five dollars a week. It was in one of these hotels that she first met Lavery and, as the report says, "formed a strong attachment for him." The report is laconic about the Laverys. "They have always made their home in a furnished room," it says. Of the woman, "Her leisure is spent at home with her paramour, and save for an occasional visit to the motion pictures, she leads a rather colorless life."

Because Mrs. Lavery had pleaded guilty to the crime of which she was accused, it was entirely up to the General Sessions Judge to decide what to do about her. No trial was necessary, of course; no jury of twelve good men and true would sit in judgment and say, "We find the defendant guilty" or "We find the defendant not guilty." It was not necessary for one of the public prosecutors to build up a case against her, to denounce her as an enemy of society, to demand a heavy penalty. Mrs. Lavery was guilty, she admitted she was guilty, and when she appeared for sentence, the Judge had before him only the information gathered by the probation officers. He was evidently puzzled. "I do not know," he told her, "whether to put you in the House of the Good Shepherd or the Bedford Reformatory. It would probably be a good thing to put you in one or the other, because the way you are living I do not know but what you will abandon a couple more children. . . . But it goes against my grain to send a woman of your age to the House of the Good Shepherd or the Bedford Reformatory—one who is not a criminal, whose only offense is that she sins like a fool and then throws her progeny onto society." The Judge decided to defer the pronouncement of sentence for three months longer. "I want to be satisfied," he told her, "that you are going to make some kind of a genuine effort to live straight."

The fact that Lavery and Katherine had neglected to get married became from this time on the major issue of the case. A fairly nice legal technicality was involved. Under the old law pertaining to domestic relations in the state of New York, the Laverys' relationship might have been called a common-law marriage. They had lived "before the world," as the old law phrased it, as man and wife. But the status of such couples was made more explicit by the Legislature in a law which became effective in May, 1933. This law provided that no marriage should be valid unless solemnized by a clergyman, by an authorized official of a city or county, or by a written contract signed by both parties. People who lived together 'before the world' as man and wife no longer were to be regarded as legally married in this state, the new law provided. So the various individuals and agencies concerned with the case of the Laverys concentrated on this question of legal status and made a good deal of it. The Catholic Big Sisters were called in at the suggestion of the Judge, and a Miss Kelly was delegated to arrange a marriage between the telephone operator and the bellhop. Mrs. Lavery was given to understand that the Judge would have much more sympathy for her if the marriage were duly solemnized. But there were obstacles in the way of this denouement. Mrs. Lavery was a Catholic; Lavery was a Protestant. He refused to be married in her church, and she would not have the ceremony performed in his. The reports made by the probation officers on this phase of the case are voluminous. When it was evident that an impasse had been reached, Miss Kelly of the Catholic Big Sisters ceased her efforts to arrange the ceremony. No solution had been found when, on June 7th, ten months after the now dead babies had been abandoned, Mrs. Lavery appeared before the Judge to be sentenced. She looked extremely well; she had gained weight since her discharge from the maternity ward that October morning, and the fatigue had gone out of her face. She was, as before, smartly dressed—a white straw hat, long white gloves, a flowered dress clasped at her throat with a neat little stock. She was more than ever representative of the young women you see on the subway at the rush hour. Lavery did not come to court with her; he was working.

An attorney who had been acting for Mrs. Lavery without charge since her first arraignment spoke briefly in her behalf. He said that the religious difficulties had now been straightened out, and that he himself was to be a witness at the wedding, which was to be performed the next week at the Municipal Building.

"Well, I want to see the certificate," said the Judge. "I will defer sentence until two weeks this day."

"Couldn't Your Honor make it next week this day?" the

attorney asked. "I'm not making anything out of this case, as you know, and I want to be rid of it as soon as possible."

"This day next week, then," said the Judge, and Mrs. Lavery departed, having spoken not a word.

Mrs. Lavery appeared before the Judge the next week, dressed in an attractive brown ensemble. The attorney began his speech a little hesitantly. He explained that Lavery worked until five P.M. every day. On the preceding Wednesday, he said, Lavery had got off a little early and had gone to the Municipal Building, with Mrs. Lavery and himself, but had arrived a few minutes too late; the Marriage License Bureau was closed, and nothing could be done. Lavery, the attorney said, had been afraid that he would be discharged by his employers if he asked for more time off that week, so now the marriage would have to take place the following week. The Judge was incensed. He talked for ten minutes or so, in angry tones. "I look more like a fool every day," he said. "I know you for what you are," he went on, turning to Mrs. Lavery. "You are a cruel, wicked woman who abandoned her children—you will come before this court one week hence, married, or this travesty on consideration will cease and you will go to the Bedford Reformatory. Just you think that over!" he told her, and Mrs. Lavery departed. Again, she had not spoken. Then the next week Mrs. Lavery's attorney handed the Judge a certificate of marriage, proving beyond all doubt that the telephone operator and the bellhop had been married the day before. The Judge chuckled with pleasure, looked at the attorney, at the court attendants, at Mrs. Lavery, still chuckling. The attorney grinned, the court attendants grinned, and Mrs. Lavery, standing at the bar awaiting sentence, smiled in a restrained way and looked around the courtroom self-consciously.

"All right," said the Judge, turning again to Mrs. Lavery, and letting out a final chuckle, "I suspend sentence. You are free. You need have no more worries about this case as long as you live straight. I have nothing further to say, as I do not wish to embarrass you further." Mrs. Lavery nodded and smiled and left the courtroom. The indictment that had charged her with committing an act "against the peace of the People of the State

of New York, and their dignity" was handed to a clerk, who put
it in an outgoing basket, to be taken to the file-room. I learned
afterward from the attorney that Mrs. Lavery is working again
now. She is a telephone operator in a hotel on the upper West
Side and is making thirty dollars a week. She and the bellhop
have moved away from Queens and are back in Manhattan
again. They are living not far from their former address, in a
furnished room.

SUMMARY

Ruth, the underprivileged Negro girl in Chicago; Shorty, the
boot-licking Negro man in Memphis; and the Laverys, the white
couple in New York City, all have in common a passive submission to their defeat. They have not retreated along the road of
suicide, alcohol, or dope; they accept the "rules of the game"
and they live with their defeat under those rules.

In what sense, then, are they "social problems"? In two
senses.

In the first place, many people are disturbed by the enormous
discrepancy between such "lives of quiet desperation" on the one
hand, and the Greco-Judeo-Christian vision of man's potentialities on the other. Hold the image of Ruth, Shorty, and Bernard
and Katherine Lavery in your mind while you read Sophocles'
ode on man:

> Numberless are the world's wonders, but none
> More wonderful than man; the stormgrey sea
> Yields to his prows, the huge crests bear him high;
> Earth, holy and inexhaustible, is graven
> With shining furrows where his plows have gone
> Year after year, the timeless labour of stallions.
>
> The lightboned birds and beasts that cling to cover,
> The lithe fish lighting their reaches of dim water,
> All are taken, tamed in the net of his mind;
> The lion on the hill, the wild horse windy-maned,
> Resign to him; and his blunt yoke has broken
> The sultry shoulders of the mountain bull.
>
> Words also, and thought as rapid as air,
> He fashions to his good use; statecraft is his,

And his the skill that deflects the arrows of snow,
The spears of winter rain. . . .

In the second place, how long does desperation remain quiet? As Edwin Markham put it in his poem, "The Man with the Hoe,"

Oh, masters, lords, and rulers in all lands,
How will the future reckon with this man?
How answer his brute question in that hour
When whirlwinds of rebellion shake all shores?
How will it be with kingdoms and with kings—
With those who shaped him to the thing he is—
When this dumb terror shall rise to judge the world,
After the silence of the centuries?

ANNOTATED BIBLIOGRAPHY

Bibliographical Note: Conspicuously few references are included in the bibliography for this chapter, and the reason for this deserves note. "Submission" as a mode of adjustment to frustration is different from the other modes of adjustment (withdrawal, relentless conformity, and rejection) in that there are no overt *behavioral* signs to distinguish it. The submissive individual *behaves* in conformity to the governing principles, but he has given up any hope that his conformity will "pay off." His distinguishing characteristic, then, is a certain *state of mind,* which influences his behavior in subtle ways that are difficult to detect. We suggest that for this reason little successful work has yet been done on this mode of adjustment to which we can refer in this bibliography.

Bakke, E. Wright, *Citizens Without Work* (New Haven: Yale University Press, 1940). (["A study of the effects of unemployment upon the workers' social relations and practices." In this book and its companion by the same author, *The Unemployed Worker,* Bakke describes in sympathetic detail what acceptance of unemployment means to workers in their familial, religious, and recreational lives, and in terms of their self-respect.

Davis, Allison and Dollard, Charles, *Children of Bondage* (Washington, D. C.: American Council on Education, 1940). ([Case studies of the adjustment of Negro children and adults to their deprived status. The individuals described provide a clear contrast among several modes of adjustment, including the submissive one.

Fromm, Erich, "Individual and Social Origins of Neurosis," *American Sociological Review,* Vol. 9 (1944), pp. 380–384. ([A revision of the Freudian theory of the origins of the neurosis. Insofar as a neurosis consists of behavioral conformity despite inner turmoil, it is an example of submission. Fromm tends to emphasize this approach to the neurosis and, in particular, submission of the child to the authority of his parents.

CHAPTER NINE

The refusal to accept defeat:
Relentless self-reliance

This chapter—as well as the ones to follow—is concerned with the modes of adjustment of those who *refuse* to withdraw or submit. Faced with the prospect of suffering, some people fight and fight hard. But how? A few geniuses invent new techniques of struggling for their place in the sun. But the ordinary fighter gets his inspiration from the governing principles of American society. He may apply them so relentlessly as to reduce them to an absurdity; or he may reject them so violently that only precisely contrary behavior appeals to him. In either case, the point of departure of his behavior is the culture of his society.

How can social problems arise from overzealous application of the self-reliance principle? Easily. According to the principle, the individual is supposed to "make his own way," "stand on his own feet," "take care of Number 1." Of course, it is understood that he should respect the rights of others. If he finds, however, that concern for the welfare of other people makes it more difficult for him to look after himself, he is tempted to shade the doubts in his own favor. "This is a hard world. If I don't look out for myself, nobody else will." In the selection that follows, William Manchester has drawn a portrait of a slum landlord whose self-reliance adds to the problems of his unfortunate community.[1]

A man I shall call Dan Marner, a typical metropolitan slum landlord, once had a friend. He was a real friend, not just another useful contact in the local Bureau of Buildings or land-record office, and before he and Dan broke up over a roofing contract he gave him a Christmas present. It was a game of Monopoly.

Dan never used it. He studied the rules carefully and then shelved it. For several years it has lain in a ledger case beside his scarred desk, gathering office dust. "It was those 'Community Chest' cards you got to pick," said the estranged friend later. "Dan Marner couldn't bring himself to give anything to charity even in a game."

Dan himself explains that the game sounds foolish. To him it probably does: In Monopoly, the winning player usually must acquire the most expensive properties on the board—"Park Avenue" and "the Boardwalk." Dan knows that real estate doesn't work that way. In the twenty years he has been working the shabby side of his city's map, he hasn't had to pay the "Community Chest" or "Go to Jail" once, and he has been a consistent winner. On paper, indeed, he is a millionaire, the title

[1] From "The Life and Times of a Slum Landlord" by William Manchester, as it appeared in *The Reporter,* November 15, 1956, pp. 24–26. Copyright 1956 by The Reporter Magazine Company. Reprinted by permission of Harold Matson Company, New York.

owner of 327 deeds. Each month he grosses $6,000 from rents
and auxiliary sources. His expenses are comparatively small—
his three sons act as office and field assistants, slum tax assessments are low, and Dan never repairs houses voluntarily.

At sixty-two, Dan is a dour, bespectacled man, wise in the
ways of the drab districts that dot every metropolis on the eastern seaboard—districts built before the Civil War, paved with
Victorian cobblestones, and peppered today with pawnshops,
cut-rate drugstores, and warped doors bearing the crudely
chalked names of tenants. The increase of traffic in the interiors
of cities long ago sent the original householders to suburbs on
the perimeter. Into the vacuum they left, men like Dan moved—
first as managers, later as landlords.

Dan's headquarters is in a dingy office building on the edge
of the slum. There his tenants—some colored, some white—
bring their weekly money and humbly wait in line while his sons
stamp their rent books, which are small and black and resemble
bankbooks. Some tenants send money orders, but none mail
cash. Long ago they learned that since there is no record of a
cash mailing, they have no recourse if Dan tells them their
envelopes have been lost in the mails. Like many professional
slum landlords, he has a reputation for sharp practice. The office
building, which he shares with several competitors, is known in
the trade as "the Den of the Forty Thieves."

Dan's reputation doesn't affect his business, and so it doesn't
bother him. Within obvious limits, he is candid, and he will open
his records to the outsider who guarantees him anonymity. They
reveal that his typical house was built about forty-five years ago,
is on the outskirts of the downtown area in his city, is overcrowded, lacks plumbing, has no central heating, and frequently
lacks heating equipment altogether. Dan rents it for $28 a
month. It costs the occupant $9 more for utilities, which means
that the typical tenant, who makes less than $2,000 a year,
spends a quarter of it on housing characterized by defective
wiring, blind rooms, an outside toilet, a leaking roof, and massive rat infestation.

Unless he is goaded by the law, Dan pockets the two per
cent depreciation allowed him under the Federal tax laws and

mends nothing. Suggestions that he should do otherwise baffle him. To Dan, his career is not merely defensible; it is admirable.

"What I did," he says, peering over his steel-rimmed glasses at the files of paying tenants, "any of them could do."

That is a difficult argument to answer, because it is literally true. Like most of the other Forty Thieves, Dan is a product of the slum. His rise is a kind of twisted Horatio Alger story. Tubercular as a youth, he left school in the seventh grade, married early, and was earning $18 a week in a canning factory when the depression threw him on relief. In 1934, after two years on the dole, he rented a vacant house, agreeing to clean it for the first two weeks' rent. He swiped a rusty bedspring from a junk yard, set it up on four soapboxes, and advertised a room for rent. Saving his coins and assembling other makeshift beds, he converted the vacant building into a profitable flophouse.

The owner of the house, an elderly woman who had inherited money and moved to a suburb, admired Dan's ingenuity. She owned five occupied buildings in the same block. Times were hard, the occupants were in arrears, and she appointed Dan her rent collector. He was so persistent at extorting money from his neighbors that one, in exasperation, slugged him. The story made the papers. The public may have disapproved of Dan's methods but other absentee property owners decided he was just the man they needed. He became the busy manager of several estates, charging, under standard practice, a five per cent commission on the rents he collected.

Actually he charged much more, if those who knew him then are to be believed. According to them, Dan, knowing that absentee landlords rarely visit their properties, extracted money from them for repairs he never made. At the same time, it is contended, he jacked up rents on his own authority and kept the difference. Dan admits none of this. But it is a matter of record that in two years he had saved enough to buy his first house, a two-story shack offered by the city in a tax sale.

The following year he bought his second house in a low-income white neighborhood. Dan moved a Negro family in and took advantage of the neighbors' panic to buy four more homes in the same block at bargain prices. He had to mortgage everything he had to do it, but today the street is a respectable colored district, a faithful producer of weekly money orders. He has acted as a "blockbuster" on several occasions since, serving as an incidental agent of desegregation.

Dan goes into debt frequently. Every cent he makes goes into new property. In courthouse circles he has a reputation for not being able to answer a judgment without selling a house. If a house becomes burdensome, he usually finds it profitable to have the mortgage foreclosed. He will keep it until he has cleared his investment and then cut off payments to the building-and-loan association. Occasionally the auctioneer will fail to meet his expectations, and he will be obliged to pay the association a small deficiency decree, but as a rule he finds foreclosure cheaper than a broker's commission.

All other things being equal, Dan prefers colored tenants to white. Negroes, confined to the slum by social pressures, are of all types. White families can live elsewhere, however, and those he gets are inclined to be irresponsible. There is one exception to this: The handicapped of all races are sound risks. Late in the 1930's, for example, Dan took in a veteran of the Argonne, a chronic victim of combat shock. The man, unmarried, received $125 a month from the Veterans Administration. He regularly turned his check over to Dan, who saw to it he was supplied with coffee and beans from the corner grocery until his death, which Dan deeply regretted.

Exploiting the handicapped may seem beneath a millionaire, but Dan doesn't look at it that way. "Life is dog eat dog," he says, shrugging and spreading his hands. "It's survival of the fittest." His fortune has been built from stacks of small change, and no device is too petty for him. If a Department of Highways inspector insists he repair one of his sidewalks—a twenty-five-dollar job—Dan dutifully takes out a Bureau of Buildings permit, indicating that he intends to do the work. The permit costs one dollar and gives him thirty days' grace. By then the inspector is looking over another neighborhood. When he returns next year and finds the walk worse, Dan will explain that he has been unable to find a contractor. He will take out another permit as evidence of his good faith. He is prepared to go on from permit to permit, always promising and never performing, to avoid paying that $25.

On the other hand, he knows all his rights. Since Dan's days as a rent collector, the city has established a small-claims court, and he is one of its steadiest customers. In theory, the court is for taxpayers who cannot afford to press extensive suits. Actually, two-thirds of its docket entries are rent cases, with the city acting as agent for complaining landlords. If a tenant falls into arrears, Dan drops into the court, fills out a slip, and pays a one-dollar fee. A policeman then serves a summons on the tenant. Most occupants of slum homes are terrified of authority. Frequently the lax tenant will borrow the cash that day and rush to Dan, who will also recover the one-dollar summons charge from him.

Dan's big property gains were made during the war. On the eve of Pearl Harbor, he was worth about $100,000. He held title to thirty-four houses, acquired at public tax sales, from out-of-town heirs unfamiliar with local values, or from hard-pressed owners needing quick cash. Each month, his records show, he was grossing between $850 and $900 in rentals, and he was branching out. He had become a professional bondsman, pledging his property as collateral. His eldest son hung around police stations soliciting business. Dan always made certain his bonds were secured by chattel mortgages, and he always demanded the maximum legal interest—ten per cent in Federal court, five in local courts. Each year he met a score of bonds and took in upward of two thousand dollars in bail fees. He had plenty of free capital—too much, indeed, to suit him. "I was uneasy," he says. "I figured someone would find out and make an excuse to sue me for something."

Unfortunately, investment opportunities were limited. The specter of competition was rearing its head: Other landlords were bidding against Dan at auctions, and the market was tight. He wanted to pioneer a new field by buying a block of Victorian mansions on the slum fringe and converting them into apartments, but the zoning statute prohibited it. Then, at the appropriate time, the Japs attacked. War industry boomed, and the city was invaded by Southerners who wanted to work but had no place to live. Dan took a plunge. He bought the block, went to the zoning-appeals board, and explained he would house the war workers if the board would overlook the law. It worked: His peculiar contribution to the war effort was accepted.

"I didn't get the Army-Navy 'E'," he recalls, "but I got a precedent, and in 1946 I got rid of all those hillbillies by moving one Negro family in."

Dan's one serious challenge has come from the local Health Department. Late in the war the department set up a housing bureau, and under its leadership a team of inspectors invaded the slum, looking for infractions of the law. In one fourteen-block area, with 791 properties, they found 13,589 health, building, fire and electrical violations. Notices were issued ordering repairs, and the team moved on, checking off kerosene space heaters, outdoor hoppers, exposed wiring, and sagging walls. A week later they struck the first of Dan's blocks.

The campaign was a real threat to him. Structural repairs are expensive—mending his houses properly would have taken more money than he had, or so he now says. He began by protesting that his property rights were being invaded, but the inspectors had strong public support. Protest failing, Dan quietly told each of his tenants he could buy the house he was renting with no down payment. The terms were farcical; Dan retained the deeds, and he was permitted to cancel the contract if one weekly payment was one day late. Most occupants fell for the "buy-instead-of-rent" gimmick, however, until Dan started forwarding Health Department notices to them. Ownership, he piously explained, implies responsibility.

The department argued that Dan was still the landlord, and a legal battle opened to determine where ownership really lay. Meanwhile, Dan had opened a contracting sideline. He outfitted a man in neat white coveralls, with the word INSPECTOR embroidered over the left breast pocket, and sent him out to trail bona fide Health Department inspectors. After the Health Department men had gone, Dan's "inspector" would call and ask the bewildered tenant if he might look at the house. Usually he was admitted without question.

Inside, he would explain that this or that had to be done.

When the frightened occupant, thinking of himself as the house's owner, asked where repairmen might be found the "inspector" said he had friends who did work at cut-rate prices. The prices were, of course, inflated, for Dan extracted a referral fee from the plumbers and roofers he sent out. Under this ingenious arrangement, the repairs were not only made; Dan made a profit on them. According to one report, Dan's "inspector" dismantled a furnace on the coldest day of 1949, left, and returned the following day with an installment-sale furnace contract. The shivering householder signed.

The courts decided that Dan, as deed holder, was legally responsible. Since then he has been erecting cardboard partitions and installing inferior wiring—doing the work, in short, but in the worst possible fashion. The Health Department keeps after him, and he has paid a few ten-dollar fines for failure to comply with its notices. But he is still the winner. Ten years after its ambitious opening, the department's campaign is hopelessly bogged down in detail. By fighting it every step of the way, Dan is defeating it.

Outside the Health Department and a few civic organizations interested in slum clearance, there is little local interest in Dan. The business community is almost wholly indifferent. Some of its members, one suspects, secretly admire him. They think of him as a shrewd trader, a self-made man, an individualist who is defying bureaucracy and managing to get away with it.

Dan is all those, and more. He is a symbol of the spreading rot in metropolitan areas, and his story has as many implications for economists as for moralists. Since 1935, when Dan bought his first house, the assessed value of his properties has dropped twenty-seven per cent, meaning his municipality gets nearly $8,000 less in taxes from them each year. The city is spending forty-five per cent of its income in the slums and getting six per cent of its taxes there.

The forty-five per cent is spent in many ways. The neighborhood Dan converted to apartments during the war now leads the city in juvenile delinquency, with twenty cases per thousand population annually. Patrolmen are necessary in every block: after midnight they meet under street lamps and pivot, back to back, like sentries. About one-third of the city's inhabitants live in the slums, but they account for eighty-three per cent of its syphilis and seventy-one per cent of its tuberculosis—one of Dan's blocks has five active TB cases today. The cost of slums in petty thefts, bastardy cases, and social parasites is incalculable, but census figures show that eighty-one per cent of the welfare cases are concentrated there.

Dan's admirers may not know it, but they all contribute to his loot through the relief rolls. A home-owner with an assessment of $9,500 pays three weeks' rent each year in taxes. Through their unfortunate tenants, Dan and his colleagues get a big slice of this.

Such implications have no interest whatever for Dan. His outlook is expressed in a few catch phrases: dog eat dog, tooth and claw, survival of the fittest. He came up the hard way, and he argues anyone else can do it, though if pressed he will modestly admit that stamina, brains, and what he calls "realism" are necessary for success.

Dan Marner was self-reliant at the expense of his neighbors. Edwin H. Sutherland, in the following excerpt from his book, *White Collar Crime,* tells about business executives who were self-reliant at the expense of their companies.[2]

Executives and directors of a corporation are trustees, in the eyes of the law, and have the duty of managing the affairs of the corporation in the interest of the corporation as a unit. At the same time, these executives have personal interest and other interests, which may conflict with their duties as executives of the corporation. While every person in a position of responsibility confronts this situation, many corporate executives make strenuous efforts to secure positions in which they may have an opportunity to violate the trust for which they are legally responsible.

A total of 64 accusations of violation of trust and misap-

[2] From Edwin H. Sutherland, *White Collar Crime* (New York: Dryden Press, 1949), pp. 153–158. Reprinted by permission of Mrs. Myrtle C. Sutherland.

plication of corporate funds has been made against executives of 41 of the seventy large corporations. These include violations of trust in the interest of a particular executive, of a small group of executives, of a particular group of security holders, of investment banks, and of other corporations with which these executives are connected. In some of these cases, the crime is committed against the corporation rather than by the corporation, but it is difficult to differentiate the two types of offenders in most of the cases.

These violations of trust are of several types. One of the most clear-cut, as well as least frequent, violations of trust is ordinary embezzlement of corporate funds by executives of a corporation. The chief executive of one corporation, after he had been displaced, was found to be short in his account with the corporation by more than three million dollars. He was permitted to make a settlement without an official court action.

A second way in which executives of corporations have violated trust is by organizing personal companies to render services to their corporations. In doing this they act both as buyers and sellers of the services and make bargains which are advantageous to their personal companies. Some of these personal companies may be limited to specific services, such as foreign sales or lighterage service, and these probably cause no serious loss to the corporation; other personal companies may be placed in the corporate structure so that they can drain off a large share of the corporate profits. The stockholders of one corporation sued the executives in connection with such a personal company for $50,000,000 which was claimed to have been misapplied.

The third way in which executives violate trust is by using their knowledge to make private purchases of stocks or of commodities and selling these to the corporation at a large profit. The executive of a corporation has inside knowledge that his corporation must purchase more land for the plant; he makes a private purchase of the best available land and sells it at a considerable profit to the corporation.

A fourth way in which executives violate trust is by using their official positions for personal advantage rather than for corporate advantage. A stockholder of a corporation offered to sell a large block of stock to the corporation; several of the directors of the corporation influenced the Board to vote against the purchase of this stock; then they organized a syndicate and purchased this stock privately.

The fifth type of behavior which may involve violations of trust is the appropriation of enormous salaries and bonuses by the executives of a corporation. Accusations have been made on this count against the executives of 25 of the seventy corporations. These huge awards are described in the charges as illegal appropriations by officers who are in a position to manage the corporation in their own interest and as cognate with embezzlement. On the other hand, the defense is made by the executives that the number of persons qualified for executive positions in large corporations is small, that large awards are necessary in order to secure good executives, that these huge payments are incentives to greater efficiency, and that they are therefore economical in the long run. John C. Baker, however, in a statistical analysis found a slight tendency for corporations which paid high salaries to have smaller earnings, and greater fluctuations in earnings than in those which paid low salaries.

Stockholders are seldom able to determine from the corporate reports the salaries paid to their executives. In some of the earlier cases not even the directors knew the salaries of the executives. One of the large corporations recently was fined for making false reports to the Securities and Exchange Commission in the effort to conceal a special fund for executive bonuses. Also, in some cases an executive received a large salary from a parent corporation and additional large salaries from each of several subsidiaries. Many executives of corporations have protested vigorously against publicity regarding salaries and bonuses.

These huge salaries and bonuses are frequently paid in years when the corporations have a net loss as well as in years when they have a net gain. The chief executive of one of the seventy corporations received a salary and bonus of approximately $1,000,000 a year, plus additional payments to cover his income tax, although this corporation had paid no dividends on common stocks for many years. The principal executives of another corporation received bonuses over a twenty-year period, which exceeded the dividends on common stocks for that period.

Many stockholders have sued the executives of corporations for misapplication of corporate funds in the payment of these bonuses to themselves, generally with little success. In one of these cases a judge was convicted of taking a bribe. In other cases it has been revealed that the executives have paid the complainants large sums from corporate funds to drop the suits. In one suit, however, the executives were ordered to reimburse the corporation by approximately $6,500,000 for funds illegally appropriated to themselves as bonuses, with a part of the period of illegal appropriation exempted by the statute of limitations.

The sixth type of violation of trust is the profit of one group of security holders, including the executives of a corporation, at the expense of other security holders. Several decisions have been made on this point against the seventy corporations. In two cases the courts enjoined corporations from paying dividends on common stocks until the accrued dividends on preferred stocks had been paid. In another case the court enjoined a corporation from issuing new bonds which took precedence over previous mortgages. The stockholders of another corporation voted in favor of a plan of reorganization, on information supplied to them by the executives of the corporation. They discovered later that the reorganization was very favorable to certain securities which were held principally by the executives of the corporation. Charges have been made that unsecured bank creditors are frequently given precedence in reorganization proceedings; A. J. Sabath, chairman of the Congressional Committee on Reorganizations, stated regarding one reorganization that it was marked by "collusion, fraud, and conspiracy." In some cases corporations in financial difficulties were managed for a period of years by agents of investment banks, who controlled the corporation through special management shares. In at least one case of this kind, the agents of the investment bank looted the corporation.

The final method of violation of trust is through the looting of a subsidiary by a parent corporation, when the subsidiary is controlled but not wholly owned by the parent corporation. A simple example of this is the purchase of the assets of the subsidiary by the parent company at a price far below the amount that could have been secured from other purchasers. In this case, the parent company was, in substance, both buyer and seller, but the minority stockholders of the subsidiary secured a decision which forced a higher payment. In another case in which a subsidiary was about to be separated by court action from the parent company, the subsidiary paid to the parent company approximately $50,000,000 for rights which were of no value. A settlement was made in this case, with the approval of the court.

Some of these businessmen were unscrupulous; they would steal whether they were executives or taxi-drivers. Most of them, however, simply believed in self-reliance. They did not feel they were stealing from the stockholders—any more than customers who cheat the Bell Telephone Company worry about the widows and orphans who own shares of American Telegraph and Telephone.[3] In short, many Americans do not consider it *wrong* to put personal interests ahead of loyalty to a corporate employer or of honesty with the tax collector. For the same reason, many Americans vote for candidates who will protect their interests as veterans, farmers, businessmen, or old people rather than for candidates who, they think, will promote the general welfare of the nation. Clearly, this creates difficulties. The American economy, characterized as it is by giant corporations, cannot function efficiently unless employees make the best judgment they can on behalf of their companies. Similarly, the American political system, characterized as it is by swarms of regulatory agencies, cannot function efficiently unless officials and voters place societal goals ahead of personal advantage.

Under special circumstances, the self-reliance principle tends to generate social problems in quite a different way. Consider an individual who has failed to earn enough money to realize his goals in terms of esteem, adequacy, security, or gratification. He interprets the self-reliance principle to mean that he must not let other people know about his failure. For one thing, he cannot

[3] In a fascinating study of attitudes toward corporate and personal property among the rubber workers in Akron, Ohio, Alfred W. Jones showed that many persons regarded stealing from a corporation as less reprehensible than stealing fom a human being. See *Life, Liberty, and Property* (Philadlephia: Lippincott, 1941).

let them know how lacking in self-reliance he is. For another, he does not feel he has any right to expect anybody to help him. This is the sort of situation in which the idea occurs to him of "borrowing" other people's money, if it happens to be temporarily accessible to him. By violating his trust—temporarily, he believes—he can still regard himself as self-reliant. As an example of this process, take the following case cited by Donald R. Cressey in his book about embezzlers:[4]

. . . At the time of his commitment this man was forty-two and had been the president of his bank. He was sentenced for violating the law in connection with operations calculated to keep his bank open during the depression. . . . He became the cashier of a country bank in another state and advanced rapidly [but] he was called back to Wisconsin to manage a bank which needed to be extricated from financial difficulties. He says, however, that he did not know how serious the difficulties were. . . . He succeeded in putting the bank on a better-paying basis temporarily, but the depression again placed it in jeopardy. To keep the bank open he falsified the statements, hoping that time would dispel its difficulties. Matters went from bad to worse, however, until it was necessary to close the bank. . . .

Why did this man who had been brought up in a good home, who had made money and was highly respected, and who had been trained in banking methods, finally engage in legal embezzlement, while his brother, also a bank manager, brought his institution through the same severe crisis successfully? . . . Two or three aspects of this man's history may furnish a clue. 1. As the oldest child in the family he had been thrown upon his own resources early and had gradually learned to trust his own judgment. His youngest brother frequently pleaded with him during the difficulties to cut down on his scale of living, resign from an impossible situation, and allow the bank to be closed. *His pride doubtless prevented his accepting this advice, for to do so would have been to admit poor judgment in accepting the*

[4] From *Other People's Money*, 1953, by Donald R. Cressey, pp. 45–47. Reprinted by permission of Donald R. Cressey and the publishers, The Free Press, Glencoe, Illinois. Cressey quotes in this excerpt from John L. Gillin, *The Wisconsin Prisoner* (Madison: The University of Wisconsin Press, 1946), pp. 186–188, by permission of the publisher.

presidency of the bank without a more thorough investigation, but also the failure of his efforts to solve its difficulties, and loss of prestige in the community. . . . His previous success had engendered a pride in his ability to handle difficult situations which his resignation would have hurt. Like many a banker, he took chances during the depression and finally lost. He seems to have made no personal profit from any of the illegalities. He had no intention of cheating anyone, but only a strong desire to save the bank and with it not only his own investment but that of his stockholders and depositors.

One essential difference between this man and his brother, who is cited as a "control" case, lies in the fact that the latter had no occasion to define his banking problems as non-shareable [with other people who might have helped him].

The history of the brother differs at some points. He was an extrovert, whereas the prisoner was an introvert. His reputation in the community was based on sound business practices and modest social activities which intrenched him in the esteem of the inhabitants; the prisoner moved about and had to rebuild his reputation anew in each town he lived in. *The brother sought help in his banking deals both from his board of directors and from other bankers; the prisoner had learned to play a lone hand and did so in the management of the Wisconsin bank.* The brother had been careful never to be involved in the disputes of the community, with whose social and business life he was intimately familiar. The prisoner had been thrust into a bitter feud between social and business groups of the community and had become the punching bag of both factions. The brother's bank was examined regularly by the State Banking Commission; the prisoner was encouraged to adopt shady methods by a "hands off" policy of the examiners, who hoped he might succeed in pulling the bank through. The brother was governed to some extent in his personal life by the standards of his depositors, and his wife always lived simply, particularly during the depression. The prisoner, on the other hand, though he kept within his income, always lived on a higher scale than his country depositors. He invited criticism by keeping polo ponies, building a pretentious home, and sending his wife to Europe many times.

Even when the refusal to appeal for help does not result in clearly deviant behavior like embezzlement, the attempt to "go it alone" may create social problems. Sometimes, as in the following passage from the book, *Families in Trouble,* a reaching out for available community resources is the only way to prevent the situation from proceeding from bad to worse.[5]

Troubles don't cast their shadows before them, in most instances. The research worker studying the life of the family or the social worker treating its problems may see premonitory symptoms of troubles in some instances, but for the most part, to the family at least, they drop like lightning from the sky. Caught in its own worries, bogged down by the exigencies of urban existence, and confused by the changing scene about it, the family knows only that yesterday it got along without too much difficulty and today it faces what appears to be a solid wall of trouble. What does the family do under such circumstances?

The ways in which these families solved or did not solve their one hundred and nine troubles may best be considered from two angles—in relation to institutional aids, and in terms of their own efforts, independent of help from organized sources.

SOLVING PROBLEMS WITH INSTITUTIONAL AIDS

There are four general types of situations to be considered under this heading: (1) where no help was available from a social agency; (2) where help was available for a particular kind of trouble but the existence of such sources was unknown to the family; (3) where help was available and known to the family but rejected for one reason or another; and (4) where help was available and accepted.

Theoretically, at least, there were no situations which could be assigned the first of these. The social agencies of a city as well-organized as New York provided, apparently, for every possible contingency. Readily accessible to the people of this block were social agencies meeting every need which urban man conceivably could have, regardless of race or creed.

[5] From Earl L. Koos, *Families in Trouble* (New York: Kings Crown Press, 1946), pp. 79–85. Reprinted by permission of the author. The 62 families who participated in this survey were residents of one relatively homogeneous city block in a tenement area in Manhattan.

It was impossible, of course, to determine whether or not any given trouble would have been solved by one or another agency; this could have been done only if the family's problem had been submitted to the agencies themselves. One can only judge by the statements of purpose of some of the leading agencies whether or not the family might have expected help, and whether or not social agencies are prepared to serve all families. The following statements of purpose are those of agencies active in the city area in which the study was made:

"The primary purpose . . . is service to individuals and families having problems which interfere with satisfactory and wholesome living. The service aims to help families overcome such obstacles to effective management of their own affairs as may be presented by financial strains, occupational handicaps, mental and physical illness, disturbed relationships."

"To relieve at once acute distress and suffering: . . ."

"By helping people in the early stages of their troubles, by sustaining them through periods of stress, by the provision of resources. . . ."

From these generous statements of purpose it seems reasonable to assume that assistance was certainly available for such troubles as were experienced.

To determine whether or not families knew of agencies which might help in solving troubles, a check list was prepared containing the names of all agencies within a radius of one mile which offered service in the fields of health, family service, relief, day care of children, legal aid, loans, nursing services, and recreation. The families were asked, at the end of the study, to identify the agencies, to tell their approximate location, and to indicate whether or not they had ever had any contacts with them. The results of this survey are summarized in Table [1].

The widespread knowledge of the existence of health agencies, and the use of their services at least once by fifty-seven of the sixty-two families was not surprising, since illness presented problems which could not be solved without recourse to medical facilities. The five families which had not used any of the health facilities had all employed private physicians.

Thirty-four of the fifty-seven families which had used the

TABLE [1]. *Number of Families Identifying and Contacting Specified Types of Social Agencies*

Type of Service Rendered by Agencies	NUMBER OF FAMILIES	
	Identifying at Least One Agency	Having Had Contact with at Least One
Health	62	57
Family Service	27	5
Relief	57	19
Day Care of Children	3	1
Legal Aid*	—	—
Loan agency (private)*	1	1
Nursing service	43	12
Recreation	62	53

* Not within one mile radius.

health agencies did not use them, however, *except in case of extreme need*. A summary of the opinions of these thirty-four families indicates that they considered medical clinics and hospitals impersonal, and rejected them on this basis:

> They don't really care about you there [in the out-patient clinics]. If you're something special the young docs can learn from, you're o.k. and get a break. If you're ordinary sick, they just push you through.

> I saw the doctor eight times—he had to look at my card every time to call me by name. I didn't mean nothing to him. It was my liver he was interested in, not me.

> Hurry, hurry, hurry—the nurse is always pushing you along, because there's somebody else behind you. You can't be last in line and if you are, then the doctor is in a hurry. The nurse acts like you are in the way.

> What I don't like is the way they do it. Pay your money, do this, do that. It isn't like seeing a doctor, it's like being in a machine shop. You go in one end and click right along, only with a lot of waiting in between. . . .

The nursing services in the area were well-known, having been identified by forty-three families. This was to be expected, since the distinctive uniform of the Henry Street Visiting Nurses Association was seen daily on the block. Only twelve families had ever used this service—a smaller number than might be expected—but discussion with the families revealed that there was no objection to the service or its personnel. There was entire satisfaction on the part of those who had used the service—only inertia on the part of those who had not.

In the Botaccio family, where the work of a visiting nurse would not have prevented the trouble but would probably have eased it, the point of view is representative of this latter group:

> I don't know why we didn't get her in [the Henry Street Nurse]. We get all mixed up, we don't think about her—she's a stranger, we don't have strangers in our house, and our house, it ain't too good, anyway. Besides, you hate to have to depend on somebody else.

Here again the "you hate to have to depend upon somebody else" idea prevails, and the stigma attached to needing "help" prevents the use of what institutionalized aids the culture has already set up. . . .

Agencies in the one remaining category, family services, were known to twenty-seven but used by only five families. The statements of purpose given earlier are those of the family service agencies, and recognition of them by less than half the families, and use by only one-twelfth, brings sharply into focus certain questions regarding the relation of these agencies to the families in the study. Two primary questions are: why do more families not know of the existence of agencies intended for their use?, and, why do more families which do know of their exist-ence not turn to them in time of trouble? Some information was gained from the twenty-two families knowing of but not using the services which helps to answer the second question.

A major reason in fourteen of the families was the rejection of such assistance as "charity." Material relief was objectionable to these families, although some of them had been forced to accept relief in depression days, and there was degradation in such acceptance. "Aren't we supposed to stand on our own two feet in America?" While the stigma appears to have lessened in time of depression, it returned with the official closing of that period. To these families there was no appreciable difference between the social worker giving a grocery order in 1936 and a social case worker giving case work service in 1942. It had been "charity" in the past; ergo, it was still "charity," and anyone who used the services of such an agency was "a charity case."

The remaining eight families rejected the idea of assistance from a social agency on the ground that "social workers are Mr. Buttinskis," as Mr. Derber expressed it. As the family agencies have turned from relief-giving to the adjustment of human relations they have leaned heavily upon the findings of dynamic psychology, and have found it necessary to search for the causes of surface maladjustments in the inner recesses of the personality. This requires, legitimately, an investigation of the less-obvious relationships in the family, and it was this probing which created resentment of the social worker. Not, of course, that these families had been subjected to such probings, but rather that they feared such would be the case if they were to apply to an agency for assistance. In all fairness it must be said that not one of these eight families could define its objections to the family agencies; all, however, were specific regarding their not allowing social workers to interfere with their personal lives.

Their interpretation of the self-reliance principle led these slum families to ignore or avoid community resources which could have helped them. There is, however, another side to the coin. More successful members of society may interpret the self-reliance principle so as to justify not helping those more unfortunate than they. The physicians whose behavior is reported in the following newspaper item believed that residents of a low-cost housing project had a right *not* to be helped.[6]

The proposal for a free clinic at the state-aided Carver Houses project was firmly opposed last night by the Medical Society of the County of New York.

The action, approved in a spirited voice vote by the large majority of the 300 doctors present at the society's 148th annual meeting, followed a bitter attack on the plan's sponsor, State Housing Commissioner Herman T. Stichman, and a strong

[6] From *The New York Times,* May 26, 1953, p. 31. Reprinted by permission of *The New York Times.*

defense of a poor man's right to pay his own doctor bills. The session was held at the society's headquarters, Fifth Avenue and 103rd Street.

A small contingent of physicians, shouted down by the vehement majority, tried hard to forestall a vote, contending that it would be "silly" to take action on "something that is still a hole in the ground." By that, the minority meant that construction on the subsidized housing development at Madison Avenue between Ninety-ninth and 106th Streets had scarcely begun, and that it would be wiser to make a decision when the project had been completed.

Another argument advanced against taking a vote was that Mount Sinai Hospital, which would operate the clinic under the plan, "will probably do what it wants to regardless of what the society says."

Adoption of the measure will have no practical effect on the establishment of the clinic by the state or city. Doctors will not be penalized by the society if they participate in the clinic's operation. . . .

Last night, Dr. Murray was one of the chief spokesmen against the Stichman plan. In an impassioned plea in favor of the resolution condemning the proposal, Dr. Murray declared that "too often politicians have ridden to power on the backs of the poor." His remarks were often greeted by applause.

"I have for twenty years," he said, "made a living by treating people in the income groups of $2,100 to $2,800 a year. The indigent are entitled to self-respect. They will not accept charity. Mr. Stichman is trying to give away something that doesn't belong to him. That is, the time and energy which we physicians are giving without pay in the clinics now. The social engineers are staying awake nights now figuring out how to give away your services and mine."

Another leading opponent of the plan was Dr. Samuel Z. Freedman, chairman of the society's committee on legislation, who suggested that Mr. Stichman was not serious in making his proposal. He charged that the Commissioner was "just a politician" and was "making a play for the votes of the poor people."

Permission was refused Mr. Stichman to address the meeting last night. His letter supporting his plan was read, however, by Dr. Herbert S. Ogden, the society's secretary.

To put the same point another way, people who recognize that something is wrong and say, "It's not my business," contribute to the problem. This principle is widely recognized in police work. One reason British police do not carry guns is that they can count on the help of the average citizen in making an arrest. In the following story, entitled, "Bystanders Are Not Innocent," we see what happens when self-reliance turns into callousness.[7]

In the U. S. occupied zone of Germany recently, American authorities were pleasantly surprised to receive valuable de-Nazification assistance from a prominent German educator. His name was not mentioned in the reports—possibly because it was thought wise to shield him from suspicion of currying favor with occupation officials. Suppose we call him Professor Mueller.

It seems that Professor Mueller was chairman of a conference of leading educators called to make recommendations for meeting the No. 1 problem of the German school system: how to get rid of the lingering remnants of Nazi habits of thinking and teaching. Now the traditional German educational conference is as ponderous as it is inconclusive. Each individual reads his own paper aloud, the interminable droning going on for days, after which there is little or no cross-ventilation of ideas through discussion. The participants return to their respective universities to ponder the weighty contributions of their academic brethren. Finally, they convene again months later, each of them prepared to read another paper commenting on a paper read at a previous conference. Decisions are seldom if ever reached; that would be much too arbitrary and unscholarly.

Imagine, then, the stunned reaction of the German educators at this recent conference to the calm, direct opening announcement by Professor Mueller that the chair would rule out

[7] From an article by Norman Cousins entitled "Bystanders Are Not Innocent," in the August 2, 1947, issue of *The Saturday Review of Literature,* pp. 7–9. Reprinted by permission of the Saturday Review.

of order any paper that took more than ten minutes to read. Even before the effects of this academic torpedo were fully felt, Professor Mueller quickly released another: there would be a round-table discussion of all papers the following morning, with afternoon deadline for the final report of recommendations.

A murmur of astonishment instantly followed this announcement; the word "unprecedented!" was easily heard among the protests.

"You seem to forget, gentlemen," the chairman said, "that the very business of this conference is to break with the past. There is a direct relationship between indecision and lack of courage. Little wonder that our schools were so quickly and easily made part of the Nazi propaganda and breeding machine."

That was all that was needed by way of admonition. The conference went off on the chairman's schedule and the recommendations were turned over to the occupation authorities.

An American observer present at the conference afterward sought out Professor Mueller. "I liked the way you took hold of this thing and saw it through," he said. "It reminded me, in the one-two-three way the conference went off, of a quick-trigger American sales meeting."

"What I have done calls for no special credit," the Professor replied. "Anyone exposed to the experiences I had under Nazism would have been just as impatient to help bring about a more open and democratic way of looking at things and doing things."

After some prodding by the American, Professor Mueller explained that early in 1938 he was summoned with Mrs. Mueller to the local police station. There were forms to be filled out; someone had reported to the Nazi Party that Mrs. Mueller's grandmother was a half-Jew, which would make her one-eighth Jewish. If the Nazis could prove that there were other "guilty" fractions in the family background, however far removed, they might be able to add up enough of them to bring Mrs. Mueller and, because of the marriage relationship, the professor himself, within the anti-Semitic decrees.

"It was insane, this grotesque and incredible manhunt in arithmetic among the ancestral records. My wife was confronted with names four and five generations back—names she had never heard of before—and accused of concealing required information concerning their supposedly Jewish or part-Jewish origin.

"This went on for months; it became a ghoulish form of torture—answering questions about people who lived in the eighteenth or even seventeenth century—people about whom we had no knowledge whatever. It was wrecking my wife's health; I need not tell you how it affected my work at the university.

"Finally, however, the summonses stopped. We were notified that the official investigation had been suspended in our favor. I was told that my wife's status was satisfactory and that my own position at the university would not be affected by the inquiry.

"But that was far from the end of this hideous business. In many ways, what was to happen was far more horrible than the official investigation. Less than a week after we thought the nightmare was over, an unofficial investigation was resumed by the local Gestapo. They came, as was their custom, in the middle of the night, rapping on the door with the butt ends of their pistols. They were empowered, they said, to ask some questions which had been previously overlooked. For more than two hours we were prodded and abused before they left.

"Until the war began they would come back two or three nights a month. After Germany conquered France, there was little left at home for the Gestapo to do; virtually all the Jews had been sent away or killed. The Gestapo had to take it out on someone, and all the 'small-fraction cases' had to serve as the outlet for their perverted thirst for authority. For three or four nights each week we would be subjected to this monstrous torture. What fraction of a Jew are you if your great-great-great grandmother was a quarter-Jew? Do you or did you ever have any distant cousins in other countries? Can you guarantee their pure ancestry?

"Sometimes they would break in the doors and windows; frequently they would search the entire house pretending to look for hidden records but actually smiling to themselves as they emptied the contents of drawers upon the floor, or cleaned out our closets, or made us roll up the rugs, or cut open the mattresses and upholstery, or 'accidentally' spilled ink all over our papers.

"Yes, I know what you are thinking. You are thinking that this was mild compared to the concentration camps and the gas chambers; and you are right. Our suffering was Utopian luxury alongside what happened to those who were taken away. But do not think that what we endured was not insidious torture: night after night without sleep, the suction of uncertainty, the daily strain. . . .

"When I arrived home from the university late one afternoon, I found my wife dead in the bathroom. I saw the razor and knew she had taken her own life. Nearby was a note telling me that the police had phoned, that they had finally determined 'officially' that she was quarter-Jewish and had instructed her to be ready to leave within fifteen minutes for a concentration camp. She always knew, she wrote, that she would want to do exactly this if ever the moment came. Besides, she could stand it no longer; she begged my forgiveness but was sure I would understand.

"After a while, I recovered my senses sufficiently to go to the phone. The police denied any knowledge of the notification; there was nothing to be done about the false call, they said, because there was no proof.

"I needed advice. I needed help. I needed someone who could help do the things that have to be done when someone close to you dies. I phoned the universities and spoke to my oldest and closest friends; they were all weirdly taciturn. They were too busy; this thing or that. No one came. . . .

"After several hours, I phoned several undertakers, then gave it up when I realized that none wanted to have it known that he buried a woman one of whose ancestors might have been part Jewish. It might be too incriminating.

"The same was true of the cemetery people and everyone else I phoned.

"That night, shortly after midnight, I carried my wife to a quiet place outside the city, and buried her."

The professor had finished his story, and the American observer understood. It would have been difficult not to understand. The professor was anxious not only to fumigate Nazism but to strike hard at the state of mind that made Nazism possible, for the "innocent bystander's" lack of courage and decisiveness was the lever that enabled the Nazis to move a nation and almost the world. The bystander pretended to see no evil and hear no evil when confronted with evil; and so he became evil's own champion.

It is now more than two years since Nazi Germany lost the war; and episodes such as these, it might be said, have historical value at best. Why, then, do I recount them here?

I suppose that the story of Professor Mueller, which was told to me two weeks ago by a prominent educator at an Ohio university, would never have been retold here were it not for something that I learned only last week at another great American university in the Midwest.

It was the morning after I gave a public lecture under the auspices of the university. I was having my breakfast in the coffee shop of a well-known hotel. A gentleman came over, introduced himself as a fellow Nutmegger from Connecticut who had been at the lecture the previous night. He was teaching and doing graduate work in a field that he knew had been my own special interest as well; namely, the direct relationship between the decay of Greek civilization and the failure of the Greek states to come together under principles of federation.

With so many points of mutuality, I was anxious to have him join me for breakfast. He spoke of the university and the faculty, for both of which he had the highest regard. I liked the basic humaneness of his general approach and attitude; I was impressed with his modesty and bearing and quiet scholarship.

After breakfast, one of the deans met me in the hotel lobby and escorted me over to the campus for the morning roundtable. I told him of my conversation with my breakfast companion, and learned that the dean shared my high opinion of him.

The dean then told me that my companion had just returned from the hospital. He had been painfully injured some ten days earlier in the same coffee shop in which we had just had breakfast. It seems that about 9 P.M. on a week-day evening he had stopped in for a bite after working in the library. At a nearby table were several undergraduates. They began to pass remarks about Jews. Soon they were telling and laughing loudly at coarse jokes.

Then one of them pointed to the Greek scholar. "Look at him, he looks like a Jew!" he yelled.

"Of course he's a Jew," someone else said roughly. "I know all about him. He makes big dough teaching at that damned Hebrew school in town."

"Hey, Jew!" the third one taunted. "Whattaya doin' in a restaurant for white men? Git the hell out before we throw you out!"

The gentleman sat quietly, sipping his coffee, his attention fastened upon a book.

The jibes became increasingly abusive and vulgar. The gentleman got up to leave. An outstretched leg and a quick push sent him spinning to the floor. He was set upon by the undergraduates who punched and kicked him about the head and other parts of the body. There was blood on the hands and shoes of the undergraduates when they finally left, having decided, apparently, that it wasn't much fun beating up a body after it became inert.

But the purpose of these two episodes—about Professor Mueller and my breakfast companion—is not to draw a least common denominator of brutality, nor even to show that the body of Nazism is far from dead—even in America. The purpose is to identify an evil that is even worse—impossible though that may seem—than the evil of raw, unleashed cruelty. This is the evil dramatized so effectively in Laura Hobson's "Gentleman's Agreement"—the evil of conscienceless gentility, the impassive bystander, the "respectable" citizen who looks the other way, the nonparticipant who plays it safe, the circumspect fool. Professor Mueller's "life-long friends" were moral paralytics at whose trembling feet the real crime of Nazism can be laid; their colonic regions broke into a jaundiced and fluttering retreat when the Nazi brute first showed himself and when he could easily have been ground underfoot. Later, of course, the pattern of vicious prudence and servility were so well established that people dared not even help bury the innocent dead.

And if we are appalled at the ominous impotence and guilt of the bystander in Nazi Germany, what are we to say about those in America who are looking the other way today? In the case of my university friend, it wasn't that the bystanders were sympathetic with the tactics of the assailants; probably they deplored the beating and wished that it could somehow be halted —a wish almost as deep, no doubt, as the wish that they might not have been there to have been witnesses to it all. After all, they were the good folk; they contributed as generously as the next fellow when the plate was passed in Church; they were honest, upright souls; people had no right confronting them with violent situations which made it necessary for them to play it safe.

At least in Germany, there was no such tradition as free men enjoy in America. But while a man lay on a floor in a large hotel near the campus of one of the great liberal universities in America, the bystanders—and there were enough of them— found it expedient not to see what they saw. Today, the degenerate young hooligans remain unpunished—by police and college authorities both—though their identities can be easily ascertained. One hesitates to conclude that the university is itself a pusillanimous bystander, more concerned about avoiding unwelcome publicity than about justifying the liberal tradition with which it is so often associated. . . .

If the two episodes described here seem completely lost in the prodigious groundswells that move the world today, at least they are not isolated; they are not unrelated to the most important single question in history: can we save the human race from itself? Whether the answer is world government, the regeneration of the heart of man, a biological mutation, or something that no one has yet thought of, one thing is certain. The answer—if there is an answer—can only rise out of the will of the people themselves. The world is suffering today from a bankruptcy of leadership. It would be folly to suppose that the high fulfillment of responsibility proceeds automatically from high positions of responsibility. Thus, for the individual American citizen, the question "What can I do?" must no longer be a helpless gesture and a rhetorical defense. What he can do must be limited only by his imagination and energy and conscience; and not by what he imagines to be inexorable tides as far beyond his reach as planetary motion.

In any event, this is no time for bystanders. Those who persist in looking the other way in the presence of evil or necessity exempt themselves from nothing except membership in the human family.

This week marks the second anniversary of Hiroshima and the Atomic Age. Happy anniversary, everybody.

SUMMARY

Self-reliance as a governing principle of American society tends to create social problems for three distinct reasons:

1. In a conflict of interest between the individual as an individual and the individual as a member of some larger collectivity, one interpretation of the self-reliance principle justifies the sacrifice of the interests of the collectivity. "What's in it for me?" is an expression of this interpretation.

2. In situations where the individual needs the assistance of others in order to surmount his difficulties, one interpretation of the self-reliance principle requires him to "go it alone," to conceal his mistakes and get by somehow without the help of others —even though he may be fully entitled to that help.

3. In situations where the individual sees other people in need of *his* help, one interpretation of the self-reliance principle counsels him to withhold it on the grounds that they should help themselves.

To take a concrete example, all three of these reasons are relevant to the problem of slum clearance. First, men like Dan Marner are more interested in making a "buck" for themselves than in helping to create a healthy neighborhood. Second, slum residents with disabling difficulties are often ashamed of their poverty and hesitate to appeal for "charity." Third, those members of slum communities with the ability to organize neighborhood improvement do not perceive this as their responsibility. (They are more likely to move out of a blighted area than to try to arrest the blight.)

ANNOTATED BIBLIOGRAPHY

Binger, Carl, *The Doctor's Job* (New York: W. W. Norton & Company, 1945). ⟦ A reliable and interestingly written report on medical and health problems in the United States and on the conditions of medical service.

Cleckley, Harvey M., *The Mask of Sanity* (St. Louis: C. V. Moseby, 1941). ⟦ A classic account of the psychopathic personality, a personality disorder in which the individual is not responsive to the moral claims made on him by other people. The difficulty in diagnosing the psychopathic personality in American society is the thin line separating him from the rugged individualist.

Cressey, Donald R., *Other People's Money* (Glencoe, Illinois: The Free Press, 1953). ⟦ A full-length portrait of trusted employees who turn to embezzlement late in life and without previous criminal associations. According to the author, a necessary and predisposing condition is a financial problem which the employee feels he must solve by himself, that is, without telling anyone else about it.

Josephson, Matthew, *The Robber Barons* (New York: Harcourt, Brace and Company, Inc., 1934). ⟦ A classic account of the fortune-building of Cooke, Morgan, Rockefeller, Vanderbilt, and others of the last half of the nineteenth century. Both the productivity and the dysfunctions of these extremely self-reliant men are detailed.

Hollingshead, August and Fredrick C. Redlich, *Social Class and Mental Illness* (New York: John Wiley & Sons, Inc., 1958). ⟦ Part 4, "Class Status and Treatment," is a careful account of the difference class position makes for the kind of therapy received by patients. "Self-reliance" means that many lower-class patients do not receive adequate treatment.

Schulberg, Budd, *What Makes Sammy Run?* (New York: Random House, Inc., 1941). ⟦ A novel about a ruthlessly self-reliant young man who became a "success" in Hollywood. The author does not answer explicitly the question he asks in the title, but it is clear that he regards "relentless self-reliance" as a form of psychopathology.

Sutherland, Edwin H., *White Collar Crime* (New York: Dryden Press, 1949). ⟦ A compendium of the illegal behavior of business and professional people. Sutherland tried to show that predatory self-reliance is not confined to the lower class.

CHAPTER TEN

The refusal to accept defeat:
Rejection of self-reliance

Sometimes the individual finds the responsibility for his own welfare a crushing burden. He does not want to be free; he wants to be taken care of. When this happens, he rejects the principle of self-reliance in favor of a secure status in some group. In rudimentary form, this rejection of self-reliance can be observed in mob behavior. Individuality is submerged in mass frenzy. The mob is, however, only a temporary phenomenon. It is in the family, the neighborhood gang, the political movement, where the "escape from freedom" can be permanently achieved.[1] The following selection—from Allison Davis' article, "The Motivation of the Underprivileged Worker"—throws light on absenteeism and labor turnover in industry by revealing the group supports of the low-status worker.[2]

Pearl Elno, the white female worker, was born of old native stock in southern Indiana, the daughter of a coal miner. At the beginning of the great depression, her father came to Chicago to seek work, bringing his family. Here Pearl met Jim Elno, a young machinist, the son of a Polish laborer and a charwoman, and, like both his parents, extremely devoted to liquor in general and to schnapps in particular. At eighteen, Pearl married Jim Elno. Both youngsters were ambitious and smart. They were both good workers, anxious to buy a home of their own, and to get ahead in the world. Jim studied hard at his trade; and he bought a derby hat and a pair of spats—just to show his friends that he was a man who took himself seriously and intended to get somewhere in the world.

His young wife was always more practical and conscientious than Jim, and forced him to leave his mother's, set up a home of his own, and to work for goals more enduring than a derby and spats. All her efforts for a house of their own and for a decent standard of living were defeated, however, during the next 10 years, by the rapidly increasing number of their children. Jim was a Catholic, and Pearl was a very fertile woman. In 9 years, she bore seven children.

Unable to secure work during most of the thirties, and presented annually with a new baby by Pearl, Jim began to drink heavily. Any father who has had to come home to five, or six, or seven small children, and has had to try to live and sleep with them, crowded into a three-room flat, will sympathize with Jim, I imagine. During the depression, four children were born to

[1] See Erich Fromm, *Escape from Freedom* (New York: Farrar and Rinehart, 1941).

[2] By permission from "The Motivation of the Underprivileged Worker" by Allison Davis in *Industry and Society,* edited by William F. Whyte, pp. 84–106, copyright 1946, McGraw-Hill Book Company, Inc., New York. Note that another excerpt from this same article appears in Chapter 8.

the Elnos. They had to flee to steadily smaller and poorer apartments, and the children were reduced to half-starvation rations, which kept them sorely undernourished and chronically ill. Unemployment and their hopelessly large family wore away the determination and the morale of the parents, especially of Jim. They separated twice, and Jim deserted once but returned. He was arrested two or three times for panhandling while drunk. He beat his wife several times, when he was drunk. The Elnos and their seven little children were on the rocks and seemed headed for the bottom.

But Pearl still had her own parental family. Her father and mother, and her sisters, together with their husbands, formed a closely organized and loyal clan, which repeatedly rescued her and her seven children. The sisters took them in, when Jim was violently drunk, or when they were evicted for inability to pay the rent. They bought the children clothes, and helped feed them. Pearl's mother, still able to hold a job at sixty, borrowed money on her home to lend to Jim, when he was employed by the Works Progress Administration. She came up from southern Indiana repeatedly to care for the children, so that Pearl could work as a waitress, and as a machine operator, to help feed the children while Jim was unemployed. One of Pearl's sisters opened a tavern recently and employed the mother, who in turn helped Pearl's family. Both the sisters and mother thus have continued to help Pearl. . . .

To improve the underprivileged worker's performance, one must help him to learn *to want* and to be anxious to attain higher social goals for himself and his children. All one can get out of methods of starvation conditions in wages, or of threat and intimidations, is more of the same inferior work and more concealed resistance, as in the case of a man whipping a poorly trained mule. The problem of changing the work habits and motivation of people who come out of families like the Elnos' is far more complex than mere supervision and pressure. It is a problem of changing the goals, the ambitions, and the level of cultural and occupational aspiration of the underprivileged worker.

This change in his cultural motivation cannot be attained by

getting him into the starvation box. For, as the Elno family illustrates, the average working-class family is a large economic
unit, a clan of kin. They can depend upon *each other* for shelter
and food in time of unemployment, or of reduced income, or of
prolonged absenteeism, or when they simply quit the job. In
this working-class culture, one may usually fall back upon his
brothers, or sisters, or aunts, or nieces, or cousins for a bed and
meals, in a way that middle-class people cannot. The middle-
class adult person is ashamed to go to his relations or friends for
food and shelter. "Respectability" prohibits such dependence.
To avoid this embarrassing loss of "face," he will work harder,
take more punishment of a mental and emotional kind on the
job, and cling to the job more desperately than will the average
lower class, underprivileged worker.

That is to say, the masses of working-class people, like the
Elnos, cannot be frightened and forced into better work habits,
simply through having the economic squeeze put on them, or
through being threatened constantly with firing. Such threats
do not intimidate them, as they do the middle-class clerk or
schoolteacher, because the underprivileged worker is thoroughly
accustomed to those conditions of life that middle-class people
call "insecurity." Most important of all, he knows he can always
"bunk in" with a relative, usually on his mother's side of the
family, and he is certain that an extra plate will be filled for him
and his, so long as his relatives have food. The harder the economic *noose* is drawn, the tighter the *protective* circle of the
average working-class family is drawn. Thus economic intimidation is much less effective than with white-collar employees.
Since most working-class people do not get the rewards of social and economic prestige in our society, they do not fear the
loss of the job or the attendant loss of respectability in their communities nearly so deeply as do the white-collar workers.

One other example of this pattern of *group* economic help
and solidarity should be included, before leaving the matter. In
Negro families in the rural South, and generally in those which
have migrated from the farms to Chicago, the circle of relations
who help each other economically is even larger than in the aver-

age white working-class family. There are more children in these families; the average number of children in 300 Negro working-class families in the Chicago area is 4.9. The bonds of kinship, the closeness of feeling, and the number of mutual duties are also greater in the Negro working-class family, owing to its recent experiences as an integrated economic and social unit on the plantations.

There are also many broken white and Negro working-class families, of course. But these individuals, whose families have been scattered by death, disease, desertion, and immigration, are also provided with a communal group, which helps them in times of economic difficulty and illness. The life of Ruth, a Negro factory worker in Chicago, who was born in Mississippi, illustrates this point. Ruth's parents were unskilled workers, far below the Elnos in both education and opportunity for occupational training—at the very bottom of the economic hierarchy. The family came to Chicago in 1935. For a long time, they were unable to secure either work or relief. Both then, and later when the father was given a job as an unskilled laborer on WPA, Ruth, her four sisters and brother, and her parents lived in the large cellar of an old tenement on the South Side. The cellar had been divided into nine rooms, one for each family. There was no kitchen, only an open corner at the back of the cellar, with a small gas stove and a faucet. The nine families shared this corner as their "kitchen." But they had an organized, cooperative system of sharing, which went far beyond the joint use of the so-called "kitchen." They shared their small stocks of furniture, their bedclothes, and their wearing apparel. Most important of all, they shared their food and even their money. When a family was both out of work and off relief, the other families put their money and food into a communal "pot," in which the destitute family shared. This is a hard system to beat, for those who believe in the effectiveness of economic intimidation in making good workers. When workers can survive at this level, and still have the social support and approval of their friends, they can scarcely be threatened or starved into better work habits. They will have to be led, by the offering of concrete rewards of better

job opportunities and wages and better treatment and status on
the job.

In 1942, when Ruth was fifteen, her parents separated, and
her mother remarried. This marriage forced Ruth out of her
home at once. The next year she had to leave school and go to
work. After she had to leave her home, but before she could obtain her working papers, Ruth lived, slept, and ate with the
families of her working-class school friends. Often she had little
sleep because there was no bed available, but she had a roof
over her and at least a meal a day. She also shared the clothes
of her school friends.

This communal, group living has persisted, even though
Ruth has now been working for more than two years. She is
a hard and powerful worker, who carries a man's load. Foremen
pick her for heavy, driving jobs that not 1 woman out of 10
can stand. She likes to do this heavy work thoroughly, but she
also finds it exhausting. Moreover, she is still very young, and
she has no responsibilities except herself. Therefore, she stays
off the job rather frequently and sometimes misses several days
in succession. She can continue this habit, because she still has
her group of friends, her large social clique, who are really her
"adopted" family and who will give her shelter and food and
lend her clothes whenever they have them. Therefore, Ruth dis-
appears from the job even when she has *no* money. Keeping her
broke, by paying her only every two weeks or every three weeks,
will not keep her on the job. She can always "bunk in" with her
group of friends. This is a typical experience of underprivileged
workers, both male and female, and both in the South and in
the North. Groups of people, who have *no families,* live together, share food, money, clothes, and beds, and also share
their work; for example, trading their ironing for another person's washing or cleaning.

"The Motivation of the Underprivileged Worker" emphasizes
the beneficence of friends and family in the slum. The other side
of the picture is the danger of enemies. Especially for the adolescent, the slum is a jungle. To be on one's own is to invite
humiliations and even physical violence. Time and again in the
case histories of delinquent gang members, the theme recurs: "I

had to join for my own protection." The following case is typical.[3]

I used to be a president of the Dukes, but now I tell the younger boys what we used to do. They got respect for me like they want to be like me.

I started going with gangs when I was 10. I used to live then on 159th St. and 111th Av. before they built the South Jamaica housing project.

Now, I live in the project, but I did a lot of gangbusting in my day.

When I was only a little kid, the older boys would make me jump up and down to see if I had any money in my pockets. If I did, they would take it away. Sometimes, they even took my clothes.

So I wanted to get even. I joined a gang.

Everybody in my class in public school belonged to the Dukes, so they asked me if I wanted to get in. I joined. At the time, we had 75 or 80 members. We were all Negroes except Tony. He was Italian and the war counsellor for the club. The Wings, Jokesters and the Ramblers were our rivals. It was mostly fighting over territory. . . .

The Dukes are still operating and are now one of the biggest in Queens. They've wiped out most opposition and most of the other gangs have joined forces. They've got about 900 members now.

The Dukes are tougher and bigger than when I was a junior. Everybody's got a gun now. Most we ever had was 10 guns in a club.

The Dukes have been known in Queens since 1935 and now they're a power. There's not much fighting in the area any more, so they've got to go outside, mostly to Brooklyn, to do their rumbling. . . .

Most of the social workers think the best way to stop the gangs is to set up youth centers. But that's where they often

[3] From an article by Arthur Massolo in the *New York Post*, July 12, 1955. Reprinted by permission of the *New York Post*. Copyright 1955, New York Post Corporation.

start. That's where all the fellers and girls meet and make their plans.

What happens most of the time is that one gang gets control of the center and all the girls. Other gangs try to move in and then there's trouble.

If you're a good kid and don't join up you're always going to have trouble. You have no friends, and they get you. They take your money. You've got to join.

The gang member is gradually more and more submerged in gang activities. He hardly comes home because he "hangs" with fellow gang members at "the store" or on the corner. He loses interest in school. When he leaves school, he isn't eager to go to work. He "kills time" aimlessly with his friends. Much of the trouble gangs get into arises because members seek to inject excitement into what is actually a rather drab existence. The following is a report on a typical day in the life of a gang member.[4]

7 A.M.

It's a swell day. Wonder if any of the gang are around yet. Hey, there's Sam and Georgie coming out of the subway; they sure look like they're still asleep. "Where you guys been?" "Aw, we slept on the train last night. We started to sleep in a car but a cop chased us, so we ended up on the train."

We're heading for the candy store now (that's our hangout). We pass a car, and Sam says, "A couple guys started to sleep in that car last night. Let's see if they're still there." We look, and there they are, one on the front seat and one in the back. I give them a couple of pokes, but they just grunt and curse and turn over, so we leave them there.

Here comes three more of the boys down the street. They're working on the docks this week, unloading ships.

Between a quarter and a half of our gang work. Most of us quit high school in our second or third year and were supposed

[4] From *Intercultural Attitudes in the Making,* by Charles E. Hendry, Russell Hogrefe, and Edward Haydon, edited by William Heard Kilpatrick and William Van Til, pp. 155–165. Copyright 1947 by Harper & Brothers, New York. Reprinted by permission of Harper & Brothers.

to go to work. Our parents think this is a good idea, because when they were our age they had already been working for several years. You can't quit school unless you have a regular job, so we get someone we know to give us a temporary job and sign our working papers.

10 A.M.

We've had some coffee and walked around the neighborhood, and now we've been sitting on the newspaper box by the candy store for a while. Some of the younger kids are starting to show up now. Pretty soon we get into a real bull session. We're talking about a fight we had three or four nights ago. We do a lot of fighting, you know. We fight mostly with strangers—Jigs, Jews, service men, or anybody—usually because of insults. We're not fussy about what the odds are for or against us when we fight. We don't worry about the rules, either. We throw punches, kick, use clubs, bats, and bottles, anything that's handy. We spend a lot more time talking about our fights than we actually do fighting; sometimes we go back several months to hash over a specially good fight.

Right now two of the younger kids are really going to town. They're telling us how tough they are, and what they did in this fight and that fight, and that they're not afraid of anyone; they keep saying that over and over. Several months ago we wouldn't have anything to do with these young guys because they were just kids. Then we finally let them hang around with us a little bit, and now they're with us almost all the time. They're all right, but sometimes we have to put them in their place. If one of these kids gets out of line a couple of us older fellows will gang up on him, just to show that we're still boss.

12:30 P.M.

I'm getting hungry, so some of the boys have come with me to this little restaurant to have coffee. It's time for lunch, but if I go home my mother is going to kick like hell because I haven't got a job.

A bum just walked in. Frank knew him from before and shook hands with him, squeezing his hand real hard, and, of

course, the old guy couldn't take it. We've been kidding the old
guy and teasing him. We sometimes throw him a little money
when he "touches" us for something to eat.

We've been here in the restaurant now for about an hour and
the guy who owns the place is starting to give us some hints so
I think we'll go back over by the candy store and see who's
there.

2:00 P.M.

We just got back to the candy store. One of the boys found
an old table top, so we got some boxes and we are all set to play
cards. One of the boys just got a deck of cards; some of us are
playing, the rest are looking on.

3:30 P.M.

"Hewer cewum thwa bewalls." Oh, that's right, you don't
understand the way we talk. Joey just said, "Here come the
bulls." We're going to keep on playing, we don't see nothing
wrong with it. They play poker over in the station house all the
time, but they never let us do anything like that around here.
Yep, the car's stopping all right, and that son of a b— Sullivan,
who knocked Frank around with a billy club a while back for
no reason at all, tells us we gotta break it up. We explain we
aren't doing anything but playing cards. We're not bothering
anybody. He tells us toughlike that it doesn't matter, we gotta
break it up anyway. As we start walking away, he tells us he
doesn't want to see us around here when he comes back. We stop
at the corner and stand there talking and by God they pull up
and say, "I thought we told you guys to get moving." So we turn
around and start walking again.

The law is out of sight now, so we start drifting back toward
the candy store. Hell, we havta have some place to hang out.
Where else have we got to go? We are all back now, but the guys
are afraid to play cards, so we start fooling around. Some of us
figure that kid Ralphie put on a big deal act in the bull session
this morning, so Frank and I are gonna back him into the hallway and punch the hell out of him. We aren't gonna hurt him
but we'll give him a good hint that he's not a big shot.

Boy, that was some workout. Now Jumbo, who's a little bit older and a heck of a lot bigger than Ralphie, tells us he'll take any four or five guys on. He's got a club about four feet long and he's swinging it around his head so we can't get close to him. We'll wait for a while and then we'll catch up with him, though, you wait and see.

If we keep on fooling around this way (we just threw a garbage can at Kid Ralphie and made a lot of noise), the neighbors will be calling the law and we'll be getting chased again.

5:00 P.M

Willie just came along. He's been painting with his brother. He tells us how his brother gets these painting jobs and then how little work it is to make a lot of money. Then to make it real good he says there's a couple of nice girls in the house they're working on now.

It's funny how the guys who work always feel that they gotta come back and tell us how easy their job is and the big money that they make. Actually, I know Willie makes about $25 or $30 a week, and a lot of times he has to break his hump to keep the job because his brother's wise to him.

The guys that work on the docks just came along, and to hear them talk, they slept all day. I worked on the docks too. I know once in a while you can cut out and sleep for a couple of hours but sooner or later you gotta make up for it. On my last job we had a nice guy for a snapper, but his boss started raising hell because we weren't getting much done. I was sleeping in a lifeboat. The snapper looked in and the boss was right behind him so he had to fire me.

7:30 P.M.

Most of the boys are back here at the candy store. Buddy and Big Ralphie and JoJo are going to a dance with their girls. Kid Ralphie and Riff are going to the movies. The rest of us are just going to hang around.

I'd like to go dancing or go to the movies too, but when you're beat there's not much you can do about it. Kid Ralphie and Riff offered to pay my way to the movies, but of course I wouldn't go with them. I'd feel obligated to them and they're just kids. The rest of the guys in the gang'd think I was brown-nosing just so I could go to the movies. JoJo offered to pay my way to the dance, but I haven't got a girl right now, and anyway JoJo's given me a lot of money since I been out of work. Course, I do the same for him when he's out of a job or is broke, but you can't go on taking money off of your friends forever.

A couple of the boys who work on the docks got paid, so they are playing open-faced poker with an older guy here in the neighborhood for two bits a hand. By Sunday night they'll be broke. But that's the way it is when you work, it comes and goes pretty fast, and anyway money isn't important unless you can do what you want with it and treat your friends right.

Jinx, the king of the bums, just came by and one of the boys gave him a dime and he sang a song and did a dance for us. Larry just gave the old man a rap because he thought he got a snotty answer to some teasing we were giving the old man. Larry is too handy with his hands. The old guy's just a bum, but he's an old man and you gotta have a little respect for him. Larry always wants to be sure the boys know he's a tough guy. Personally, I think he's afraid of some of the boys or he wouldn't put on such a big deal act to impress them.

Milly's coming up the street, she's a good kid but we like to tease her. We just gave Jinx another dime and told him to tip his hat to her and give her a fast line about her going out with him. She just walked by him like he wasn't there. She made some wise crack to us about our instigating.

A couple of boys got money so we had a soda. Kid Ralphie's brother sneaked some cookies off the counter and tossed them to one of the boys sitting at the booth. It's kinda fun to fool around because it's just like a game to see if you can keep from getting caught. We don't like Harry, the candy store guy, too well; he's a Jew and you know how they are. He bitches about our hanging around all the time. But when it's chilly outside, it's nice to stay indoors where it's warm. We don't steal too much on him.

Harry just caught one of us tossing something back to the guys in the booth and he put up a big holler about it. We gave him all the stuff back except a couple of packages and then he chased us out of the store, so we're back out on the sidewalk again.

8:30 P.M.

One of the boys just robbed a ball from the dime store and started a little baseball game in front of the tailor shop where the light is good on the sidewalk. You take a couple of sidewalk squares and bounce the ball back and forth and score just like in baseball. Sometimes people crab about us taking up the whole sidewalk, but we gotta have something to do and that doesn't hurt anybody.

Three or four of the boys are over on the newspaper box talking about girls. Sammy just told the boys that if a girl's been laid, there's no reason why anybody that knows about it shouldn't try to do the same thing, and if she puts up a kick, you give her a smack in the mouth, and she'll probably lay for you too. Sometimes that doesn't seem right to me, but that's what all the boys say. You know sometimes a bunch of us run across a broad who's out to have a good time and we all take a crack at her. Getting in a line-up like that isn't much fun, but it's better than nothing. If you haven't got the dough to take girls out, why you don't have much chance otherwise. The younger guys don't have the guts to make a deal with a broad so they let the guys with a fast line do the talking and then they just get in line. You can get in a hell of a jam with the law if they ever catch you, but the girls almost never holler. Some of 'em like it and others figure it won't do any good to holler, and if they did they'd embarrass themselves and their family anyway.

The squad car just pulled around the corner and I'll bet they stop here and give us the chase. I wonder if Harry called them because he figured we robbed some cookies or maybe that girl that went bouncing by called them because one of the boys made a fast remark. Yep, yep, they're gonna stop all right. Oh, it's all right though. Chippie is a hell of a nice cop. He probably was a knock-around guy just like us when he was a kid. He just told us to move, and kinda grinned and said something about they got a complaint at the station house about us. We're all taking a walk. But there's no place to walk to. In about 15 minutes we'll be back by the candy store again.

9:30 P.M.

Say, that sounds like music. Oh, yeah, this is Friday night. Jerry's gin mill has dancing every week end. He's got a speaker hung outdoors to attract the customers. I think I'll take a walk down there. There's Milly, Rosena, and Fay standing over there. There are three Jigs in this band who really know how to play jump music. The trumpet player is especially good. We know the guys in the orchestra personally because they always come out here on the sidewalk during intermissions and a lot of times we stand and talk to them. They're nice guys. They're really hep. I sure like to listen to that fine jive talk. A couple of times when we've had a bottle, we gave a couple of them a drink. They like us a lot. Fay just started dancing with Milly, so Joey and I split 'em up. The rest of the boys out here on the sidewalk can't dance so good but they formed a circle and they're giving us a little encouragement by clapping their hands. You get tired when you really jump so fast, but then we change off. One of the other guys takes over and by the time we get through the girls are really worn out. The people that come along on the sidewalk always like to watch us dance and before we get through we get quite a crowd. Jerry doesn't care about the crowd just so the neighbors don't complain too much about the sidewalks being blocked up. If the cop makes everybody move on once in a while nobody complains to Jerry.

10:30 P.M.

The law broke up our jump session and we're back by the candy store again. The boys are kinda wound up so we've been horsing around a lot. Kid Ralphie's brother got up on the newspaper box and started being the king of the hill. He didn't stay up there but about two seconds. About half of us have been up there and down again. Harry's been crying about us making so much noise, but he's crying most of the time anyway, so we don't pay too much attention to him. I'm going to take a walk with some of the boys.

11:30 P.M.

We've been back by the candy store for about 15 minutes. We just started a bull session about driving cars. When some of these kids start to drive cars, they don't know nothing about it and they drive all over the streets, and get in all kinds of jams. Sometimes we rob cars just to take a ride. One of the boys robbed a car and kept it for about two months.

I'm going over for coffee now. The guys ought to be back from the movies pretty soon. Yep, they're already in, having coffee. At night we come into this place. It's a big cafeteria with a bar on one side. I don't think the guys who own the place like to have us come here too much, because once in a while we get in a little fight, but they try to be nice to us. They know damn well if they weren't we could make it plenty tough for them.

We've been in here now for about three-quarters of an hour. The paper came out a little while ago and we've been talking about baseball and who's going to win the pennant, and then we got to talking about Rocky Graziano and a couple of other fighters. Georgie, who's kind of a quiet sort of guy, was reading the front part of the paper, and he said that he figures we're gonna have to fight Russia. We had a hot argument about that, because a couple of boys who've been in the service said if we have to fight Russia it's gonna be a hell of a mess, and if we do they're gonna find a nice little place in the mountains till the whole thing blows over.

12 MIDNIGHT

The boys that have been out dancing just came back with their girls. While two of them were over getting the coffee, a guy sitting at the bar figured he'd try to make a deal with one of the girls, so he whistled at her and motioned to her to come over. Larry just walked over to see what he wanted, and the guy said he figured that there was a couple extra girls there and he wanted one of them to have a drink with him. The guy sounded like a rebel (he's a guy from down south) and he made a couple of snotty remarks, so Larry sized him up and dropped him. His buddy started to take a swing at Larry and by then Rudy and a half a dozen of the boys were over there and they gave both of them a good going over. They kicked hell outa one guy and they hit the other guy with a bar stool. The bartender hollered like hell, but we told him to shut up and mind his own business, and if he gets smart with us we'll drop him too. The boys that were in the fight just took a walk because the law will probably be around in a few minutes. Nobody would call up the law from here; they're afraid we might give them the business, too.

Sure enough, the law just walked in. They came right over to the table where we're sitting. I don't know why it is these bulls always have to put on such a big deal act. The guy comes over with the billy club in his hand and says, "I see you guys are getting in trouble again." We tell him we don't know nothing about it, we haven't been in no trouble, we just been sitting here drinking coffee. He tells us to finish up and get the hell out and not to be hanging around in here. The manager just came over and told them that we weren't in the fight—it was somebody else.

1 A.M.

Well, that's how it goes. Every day it's the same old business. I think I'll cut out and go to bed now because the boys who work on the docks think if I go along with them tomorrow they can get me in on their job. I sure hope so because I could use a little extra dough.

You know, I've been thinking since we been telling you about what us guys do. You probably wonder how we like this kind of life. Well, it's like this. It's not so bad. We kinda like it because we can do whatever we want to. We don't have to take any crap off of anyone. At least it's not like in the army or the navy. Around here you take a chance getting your beatings from the law, but except for that you don't get pushed around without having anything to say about what happens to you, like in the army or the navy. You know, a lot of the guys from here get discharged from the service by putting on some kind of an act. One guy acted like he was a homo, another guy acted real nervous, and so on. Pretty soon the army gets disgusted and lets them go. If we had a place where we could play cards and hang out without the cops always figuring we were wrong, it would be good.

A lot of the boys would like to have jobs, but some of them figure they ought to get the money they got when the war was on, and there ain't no such thing any more as a 60-buck-a-week job for just labor. Most of the guys haven't got enough schooling and don't know enough about a trade to get a good job, and they kinda hate to take a cheap one where they have to work so hard. Besides, finding a job is kinda hard. You have to know someone who can get you in. Sometimes I get to thinking about working and I really wish I could find a job that I would like. It's no fun to work like hell all the time. Then, too, you figure that maybe some day you want to get married and you'd like to have a job where you could make a little more money after you've been at it for a while. There's no chance like that in most of the jobs we get. Like on the docks, when business gets bad nearly everybody gets laid off. So half the time you don't know whether you really got a job or not.

Well, I'm gonna cut out now. So long.

The search for acceptance, the abdication of personal responsibility, the protection of the group—these factors seem to underlie the gang delinquency found in the slums of every large American city. They also are involved in other deviant behavior. Take prostitution, for example. Nearly all prostitutes have pimps whom they support. Part of the prostitute's willingness to accept the degradation which her way of life entails stems from her desire to preserve what to her is a most valuable relationship. The following case history from a recent book about prostitutes operating in New York City illustrates the point.[5]

NAME: *Lee Balish*
AGE: *29*
MARITAL STATUS: *Single*
EDUCATION: *Ungraded (feeble-minded)*

"The Blonde Hippo," as Lee Balish has come to be known, is huge-hipped and big-bosomed, with blue eyes, round and

[5] With permission of McGraw-Hill Book Company, Inc., New York, from *Cast the First Stone* by John M. Murtagh and Sara Harris, pp. 63–67, 72–76, Pocket Book Edition, Copyright © 1957 by John M Murtagh and Sara Harris.

wondering as a baby's, and long hair, light and stiff and straight as straw. She is a money-maker, and Big Bill Bloom, the pimp, is more pleased with her than he is with either of her wives-in-law, skinny little twin redheads who call themselves Brenda and Frenchy Love.

All four of them, Brenda and Frenchy, the Blonde Hippo, and Big Bill himself, live in a two-bedroom apartment on 28th Street. Brenda and Frenchy have the big bedroom and the Blonde Hippo, a come-lately, has the tiny hall bedroom containing nothing but an oversized double bed. Big Bill divides his nights, turn and turn about, between Frenchy and Brenda, who share him, and the Blonde Hippo.

Big Bill and the Blonde Hippo play games on the nights they spend together, all kinds of games with hands and feet and faces. First off, they get in bed and see who can look wickeder. Big Bill, tall and stout, with a large-pored pasty face and squinting blue eyes, would seem to have the natural advantage, but the Blonde Hippo can bring into the combat all her long years of practice, years when she used to stand at the mirror and make faces at herself for hours on end.

She began making the faces when she was a little girl. Sometimes they'd be droll and convivial, so that she would have to laugh with pleasure at the sight of them. They were, however, abhorrent more often than nice. Her moods determined the kinds of faces she made at herself, and they were always influenced by whether on one day or another her family showed her the love and affection she craved. Oh, the jolly, jolly faces she could devise on the days Ma, Pa, and Lila Mae seemed to love her. If only they had been able to love her more. If only they had been able to keep her from knowing how she saddened and shamed them.

Lee was a comely infant and she grew into a healthy, strapping child. It was not until she was three years old, and still not talking like other children, that her parents, both schoolteachers, began to grow anxious about her. Why wasn't she talking? What was wrong with her? They asked each other, but did not answer, with the truth both of them suspected deep in their hearts.

Different children, they assured each other, developed differently. . . .

Finally the mother, wounded beyond endurance, sat down with the father and told him the plain facts.

"We've got to be honest," she said, "at least with each other. Oh, darling. . . ."

And he, imperturbable and distant, a blond giant she felt she had never really known, said, "Very strange. Here all these years, I've been operating under the delusion that we have been honest with each other."

"No," she said, "no. We've been scarced, you and I. And we've got to be brave. We owe it to the child. If she's a moron. . . ."

"You're the moron," he said shortly. "You, not Lee."

She said, "Oh, my God."

He said, "Please, I'm sorry," but was impelled to add, "Damn it, my family's healthy on both sides."

She drew herself up. "My family, too."

"Yes, yes," he said, "I know. I didn't say it wasn't."

She said, "I can take a hint. You don't have to say things in so many words. I happen not to *be* a moron, even though my husband thinks I'm one. You consider my family. . . ."

"Look," he said, "I don't think anything except what I've told you. If the shoe fits, wear it—you and your family."

And then he came back and begged her pardon over and over again. She told him she forgave him but she remained bitter toward him, not alone for what he had said, but also because she blamed him for the child. Deep in her heart she felt, your fault, your fault. In the future, the mother and father would quarrel from reversed vantage points. He would be the one to face reality and she would run and hide from it. He would talk about mental deficiency, struggling to break through the barriers she set up, and she would laugh in his face and say, "Don't be silly, dear. The child's just slow and needs a little help."

She devoted her whole life to giving Lee the help she thought she needed, working with her from morning till night, and in the process repudiating her home and her husband. She spent hours teaching Lee to say words and to dress herself. The little girl, anxious for affection and eager to please, tried to do right. She tried with everything in her, trying, trying until she became hot and perspired so that her mother, watching, had, perforce, to pity and bid her stop. Once in a while, Lee experienced a small victory, learning, for instance, to put her shoes and socks on frontwards instead of backwards, but most of the time, for all her fine intentions, she could not master the simplest tasks.

Then it was, during the lame times, the impotent times, that the mother saw her child as her cross. Then it was that the mother, despite all the love she had in her, despite neverending patience, had to look at Lee without joy and without pride. Strangely, the child knew the meaning of her mother's look. Or, if she did not know it, she felt it. And since there is more to a person than intellect, and since Lee was and still is today good and kind inside, she went on trying for her mother's sake to overcome the insuperable obstacles.

But it seemed that the older Lee grew, the harder it became to please her mother. Naturally, the mother, spending all her time with the child and having no other life of her own, had to keep on rationalizing Lee's handicaps. After a while she succeeded in persuading herself that the child was uncooperative, not unintelligent. And so she treated her failings with severity. She often slapped her for her mistakes. Of course she was sorry afterward. Lee forgave her each time, just as today she forgives Big Bill Bloom when he slaps her around. As she does with Big Bill now, so she did with her mother then—waited until the spleen had spent itself and then came round with smiles and pats and kisses. . . .

. . . [When] Lee was twenty-four years old . . . she needed to go with men and boys. She liked having them make love to her and they treated her nicely when they were with her. Some of them brought her presents, dime-store jewelry, bottles of toilet water, and the varicolored ribbons in which she still delighted. After a while she began to ask for gifts from all who wanted her, and she hoarded what she got so that her room was turned into a veritable treasure trove. Of course, her family, knowing nothing about how she came to accumulate it, ridiculed the treasure trove. Mama called it a "pile of junk," and stuck-up

Lila said, "Hey, Lee, what'll you charge to haunt a garbage pail?"

Oh, that stuck-up Lila Mae. If she only knew what Lee knew—that her dear boy friend, Hal Burton, had made numerous contributions to Lee's treasure trove. True, he spent his evenings with Lila Mae, sitting in the living room and singing sentimental songs while Lila played them on the piano. But there were plenty of afternoons when he met Lee and went with her either in the alley which she had come to call hers or in somebody's hallway. He told her not to tell Lila Mae about their afternoons. He said he would stop liking her if she did. She couldn't have borne Hal's dislike, not Hal's or anyone's, and so she kept the secret.

She never told about the other boys either. It felt so good to have them like her so much. Sometimes she'd go with one boy and the others would stand around waiting their turns. And once in a while, a man would fondle her. That always made her feel fine. Then, too, men would whistle when Lee passed them in the street. She was flattered, but Mama, who heard them once in a while, became angry and walked along muttering: "Like an animal. Like an animal." Lucky for Lee, the mother was busy with private students these days or she would have spent all her time supervising her daughter. Doubtless she would not even have permitted Lee to take lone walks if she had been able to help herself. But because the father was no longer sending money home and it was up to her to support the family, she had to spend all her free time working and had to let Lee go more or less her own way.

So Lee went her way, seeing the men and the boys who wanted her, and happy because she could oblige them. But there was a great hurt mixed in with the happiness, a great hurt and a great melancholy. For out of all the men and boys she went with, there was not one she could call her friend, not one who would take her to a dance or to a movie, not one who would come and sit at home with her, as Hal Burton came and sat with Lila Mae.

Then one day she met Big Bill Bloom and everything changed. She was first attracted by his squinting blue eyes and his hair that was as straight and blond as hers. Somehow the hair and eyes seemed a bond between them. She could not cease pointing out the resemblance. Over and over she said, "Your hair's like mine. Your eyes are like mine."

He laughed each time she told him and when she stopped, he told her, "Your hair's like mine. Your eyes are like mine." And when it came time for the two of them to go together and she offered him a choice between the alley and a hallway, he said he didn't want to go to either one and took her home to his apartment instead. What a fine time they had, too, drinking whisky, playing records, playing games, and then getting into bed together. It was a wondrous evening in spite of the two girls, Frenchy and Brenda Love, who lived with Big Bill and seemed to hate the sight of her. She didn't know why they should hate her, but Big Bill said not to mind. He said they'd grow to like her after they got to know her better.

Lee went home at midnight. Big Bill took her and on the way he asked her for a movie date. Naturally, Lila Mae and the mother could not believe in the date when she told them about it the next morning. Lila mocked and the mother looked pitying and told her not to be too disappointed if Mr. Bloom didn't show up. But Lee knew he just had to come. He couldn't let her down.

Well, Lee, all washed, dressed, and inspected for the cleanliness of neck, ears, and fingernails, sat waiting for the bell to ring. But it didn't ring. And now it was eight o'clock. Lila Mae announced the time.

"Eight o'clock, Lee."

Eight o'clock and no Bill Bloom. He had promised to come at eight. He had promised faithfully.

"Eight-o-five, Lee," Lila Mae said.

Where was Bill Bloom? Where was he? And now it was eight-fifteen. And eight-thirty. Still no Bill. At a quarter to nine Lee's eyes were full of tears. Then the doorbell rang and the mother, some of the old-time tenderness back in her voice, said, "Honey, baby, it may be somebody else. But God, how I hope it's Bill."

And, of course, it was Big Bill. True to his promise. And

with an orchid for Lee. The mother pinned it on her while Lila Mae watched with shocked, unbelieving eyes.

Lee had many dates with Big Bill after that. They went to the movies and to dances and always ended up going to bed at his apartment. One night he told her he loved her and she asked what about Frenchy and Brenda. Then he said he didn't love them as much as he did her, but they worked for him and so he was loyal to them. He also told her that if she would work for him, she would always be his favorite. So she began to go to his apartment every day and to sleep with the men he brought for her. Sometimes there were only a few, but sometimes there were so many that they had to sit around waiting for her, taking turns the way they used to do. Each man, when he finished with her, paid Big Bill ten dollars. It made her very happy to be helping him out this way and he always told her how much he loved her for doing it.

A little more than a year after Lee and Big Bill had met, Lee's mother died of a heart attack. Lila Mae, Hal Burton, Big Bill, and Lee were the only ones who went to her funeral. Lee cried and cried and only stopped when Big Bill told her that, from now on, she could come and live with him and the two Love girls. She has been there for four years now and when you ask her how it is, she looks at you with her baby-blue eyes and tells you that it's wonderful when she makes lots of money, because then Big Bill loves and cherishes her. And as you must know, she lives for his love and affection and will die if he ever withdraws it.

The rejection of self-reliance on the part of the gang member and the prostitute is relatively crude. Middle-class people have more genteel ways of escaping the danger of being on their own. According to David Riesman (*The Lonely Crowd*), being "other-directed" is becoming more usual than being "inner-directed." This means that the promptings of the conscience are less important nowadays compared with harmonious relations with other members of the group. People worry less about "doing the right thing" and more about not "rocking the boat." David Riesman, Erich Fromm, and other students of the American scene are concerned about the trend toward conformity. Can a democracy remain healthy when citizens lack convictions, when they try to think the way everybody else is thinking?

William H. Whyte, Jr., the assistant managing editor of *Fortune,* argues that "groupthink" has penetrated even that stronghold of rugged individualism, the business community. Under the banners of "human relations," "communications skills," and "team play," large corporations have been cultivating mediocre yes-men instead of creative innovators. The following is a review of Whyte's recent book analyzing this trend, *The Organization Man.*[6]

. . . William H. Whyte, Jr. marshals evidence brilliantly for his thesis that ". . . the dominant ideological drift in organization life is toward (1) idolatry of the system and (2) the misuse of science to achieve this." . . .

. . . Let us assume for the time being that his description of Organization Men is valid. They not only work for The Organization but deify it as well. They have "taken the vows." Whyte bridles at this worship of the Golden Corporation because he believes it threatens the dignity of the individual. For example, although he does not believe that personality tests can select with any precision persons to work harmoniously with others, his objection to such tests is not their failure to pry open more efficiently the minds of applicants for jobs. "Were the tests truly scientific, their effectiveness would make the ultimate questions more pressing, not less. Is the individual's innermost self any business of the organization's? . . . The Bill of Rights should not stop at organization's edge." Whyte apparently would oppose wiretapping and private detectives for precisely the same reason—and regardless of efficacy in evaluating executives. This concern with the dignity of the individual explains why he condemns other attempts on the part of corporations to influence the private lives of their executives, e.g., the pressure to take work home, ". . . the growing domination of the family by the corporation and the active 'wife programs' some large corporations were instituting to make the domination more absolute." But what discourages Whyte is that executives don't mind

⁶ Jackson Toby, "Review of *The Organization Man* by William H. Whyte, Jr.," *Public Opinion Quarterly,* Vol. 21 (Fall, 1957), pp. 395–396.

being pushed around this way. They accept this new tyranny and, what is more, they fail to recognize it as tyranny. How come?

Whyte maintains that they have been seduced by the "human relations" ideology. All this talk about teamwork, getting along with people, group dynamics, harmony, group creativity, morale, conference sense, communication, has made the possessiveness of the company seem benevolent. "Held up as the end-all of organization leadership, the skills of human relations can easily tempt the new administrator into a tyranny more subtle and more pervasive than that which he means to supplant. No one wants to see the old authoritarian return, but at least it could be said of him that what he wanted primarily from you was your sweat. The new man wants your soul." And it is not that the new man deliberately enslaves his subordinates; on the contrary, he is dangerous because he is so well meaning. "It is easy to fight obvious tyranny; it is not easy to fight benevolence, and few things are more calculated to rob the individual of his defenses than the idea that his interests and those of society can be wholly compatible." Whyte's recommendation: The Organization Man should ". . . fight the Organization. Not stupidly, or selfishly, for the defects of individual self-regard are no more to be venerated than the defects of co-operation. But fight he must, for the demands for his surrender are constant and powerful, and the more he has come to like the life of the organization the more difficult does he find it to resist these demands, or even to recognize them."

Whyte extends this fascinating polemic into other areas. Just as "human relations" has provided the ideology for a new corporate tyranny, the "life adjustment" educational philosophy has justified a sacrifice of intellectual training in the schools. Children ". . . do not have to be taught to shake hands with other people; society will attend to this lesson. They have to be taught to reach. All of them. Some will be outstanding, some not, but the few will never flourish where the values of the many are against them." Similarly, he argues that the emphasis on sociability, outgoingness, and *Gemütlichkeit* in suburbia is a kind of benevolent straitjacket. "The group is a jealous master. It encourages participation, indeed, demands it, but it demands one kind of participation—its own kind—and the better integrated with it a member becomes the less free he is to express himself in other ways." The individual must avoid submerging himself in the group—whether the group be a neighborhood, a school, or a corporation.

SUMMARY

In the *psychological* sense, individuals are necessarily self-reliant: Each individual has a unique awareness of his own needs and problems and a unique perception of the alternative modes of adaptation available to him. However, no society can institutionalize in any thorough-going way this trait of self-reliance because everyone is dependent on other people for the satisfaction of his needs and even for the very definition of most of them.

In America, the institutionalization of self-reliance has gone about as far as it can go. It demands that the individual find satisfaction of his own needs with his own resources, cutting his dependence on others to an absolute minimum. But this requirement is inherently unstable. If it is not to be relentlessly obeyed in the ways shown in the previous chapter, which turn self-reliance into ruthless egocentricity or self-defeating failure, it is likely to be *dis*obeyed in the ways shown in this chapter which represent escape from self-reliance into group dependency.

Pearl and Jim Elno and Ruth found refuge in the protective solidarity of relatives and friends; and the middle-class whip of self-reliance lost its power to drive them. The young gang members whose cases were reported in this chapter abandoned their independence for the sake of sheer survival and found security in gang loyalty. Lee Balish's use of what limited resources she had led her to adapt to the rule of self-reliance by becoming pathetically dependent on Big Bill Bloom, her pimp. Ambitious employees of modern organizations are sometimes led by the demands of self-reliance to submerge themselves in a deified organization.

ANNOTATED BIBLIOGRAPHY

Cantril, Hadley, *The Psychology of Social Movements* (New York: John Wiley & Sons, Inc., 1941). ¶ An analysis of the motivations for joining organizations dedicated to changing some aspect of society. Among the movements discussed are those associated with Father Divine and Dr. Townsend. In each case, there is almost by definition, a rejection of an individual solution of the problem which the movement attempts to deal with.

Cohen, Albert K., *Delinquent Boys: The Culture of the Gang* (Glencoe, Illinois: The Free Press, 1955). ⟨ An important contribution to the theory of subcultural differentiation. The author explains the delinquent gang as a structure which serves to cope with the status problems of lower-class boys, problems they feel incapable of dealing with as isolated individuals.

Ferguson, Charles W., *Fifty Million Brothers: a Panorama of American Lodges and Clubs* (New York: Rinehart & Company, 1937). ⟨ A study of the "joining" propensities of Americans. Ferguson argues that the proliferation of lodges and clubs in the United States is at least partly to be understood as an effort to escape from the loneliness and isolation of "self-reliance."

Fromm, Erich, *Escape from Freedom* (New York: Rinehart & Company, 1941). ⟨ A famous psychoanalyst's analysis of the psychological sources of the Protestant Reformation and of the rise of totalitarianism in Germany. Fromm argues that the burden of freedom—in the sense of total self-reliance—has proved too much for modern man, who seeks to escape from it through surrender either to totalitarian decision-makers or to the "herd."

LeBon, Gustave, *The Crowd* (New York: The Macmillan Company, 1896). ⟨ The classic work on the surrender of individual self-control to the sway of the crowd. Many of LeBon's theories are no longer credible, but his vivid descriptions of individual abandonment to crowd or mass influence are worthwhile illustrations of the "rejection of self-reliance."

Riesman, David, *The Lonely Crowd* (New Haven: Yale University Press, 1950). (Paperback edition, abridged by the author, published by Doubleday Anchor Books.) ⟨ A wide-ranging, impressionistic "study of the changing American character," in the tradition of de Tocqueville and Bryce. Riesman's portrait of the "other-directed character," whose "self-reliance" consists chiefly of sensitizing himself to the directives of others, is now close to a classic.

CHAPTER ELEVEN

The refusal to accept defeat:

Relentless bargaining

The principle of negotiated exchange means that, once having found someone in a position to meet your needs, you must persuade him to do so by making it "worth his while." What do you have that *he* wants? How much of it are you prepared to give him? Bargaining is most fully institutionalized in the economic system, and its operation in this sphere of American life is usually considered desirable. Even in the market place, however, negotiated exchange can be carried too far. When it becomes sufficiently relentless, social problems ensue, especially when one of the bargainers is weaker or more ignorant than the other. Consumers, for example, are ordinarily in a poor position to evaluate the claims of competing advertisers—or even to avoid products containing harmful ingredients.[1] The Pure Food and Drug Administration and the Federal Trade Commission are Federal agencies which operate to counteract an adage of the market place, *caveat emptor* (let the buyer beware). There are also state and municipal agencies which protect the consumer in various ways. The bargaining principle, strictly construed, commands that you give him as little as possible and try to get as much as possible. As you saw in Chapter 6, of course, this principle is not usually *strictly* construed; it is often tempered by other considerations, such as the *needs* of the person with whom you are bargaining, or some other principle of "fairness." For example, during World War II, sellers of gasoline, meat, and other scarce goods were expected *not* to sell their supplies to the highest bidder, but rather to ration them in accordance with *equally* distributed ration books. For peacetime examples: If you are a shoe salesman, you are expected to exert some effort to make sure that the shoes you exchange for your customer's money really fit him. Women are not expected to sell their sexual services to the highest bidder. Physicians are, at least by some interpretations of the Hippocratic Oath, not supposed to refuse to treat patients because the patients cannot pay enough. And so on.

When, however, the principle of negotiated exchange is so widely and deeply institutionalized as we saw it to be in Chapter 6, and when individuals feel themselves threatened by their inability to obtain what they need, those tempering values may be discarded. This is what we mean by *"relentless"* bargaining: Whatever it is you have to sell, sell it to the highest bidder— and make him bid as high as possible.

The process by which an individual with the normal amount of commitment to such tempering values as "fairness" and "decency" can, under pressure, be led to suppress them and engage in relentless bargaining is illustrated in the following case histories.[2]

[1] See Arthur Kallet and F. J. Schlink, *100,000,000 Guinea Pigs* (New York: Vanguard Press, 1933). See also the magazine, *Consumer Reports*.

[2] From Edwin H. Sutherland, *White Collar Crime* (New York: Dryden Press, 1949), pp. 235–239. Reprinted by permission of Mrs. Myrtle C. Sutherland.

When I graduated from college I had plenty of ideals of honesty, fair play, and cooperation which I had acquired at home, in school, and from literature. My first job after graduation was selling typewriters. During the first day I learned that these machines were not sold at a uniform price but that a person who higgled and waited could get a machine at about half the list price. I felt that this was unfair to the customer who paid the list price. The other salesmen laughed at me and could not understand my silly attitude. They told me to forget the things I had learned in school, and that you couldn't earn a pile of money by being strictly honest. When I replied that money wasn't everything they mocked at me: "Oh! No? Well, it helps." I had ideals and I resigned.

My next job was selling sewing machines. I was informed that one machine, which cost the company $18, was to be sold for $40 and another machine, which cost the company $19, was to be sold for $70, and that I was to sell the de luxe model whenever possible in preference to the cheaper model, and was given a list of the reasons why it was a better buy. When I told the sales manager that the business was dishonest and I was quitting right then, he looked at me as if he thought I was crazy and said angrily: "There's not a cleaner business in the country."

It was quite a time before I could find another job. During this time I occasionally met some of my classmates and they related experiences similar to mine. They said they would starve if they were rigidly honest. All of them had girls and were looking forward to marriage and a comfortable standard of living, and they said they did not see how they could afford to be rigidly honest. My own feelings became less determined than they had been when I quit my first job.

Then I got an opportunity in the used-car business. I learned that this business had more tricks for fleecing customers than either of those I had tried previously. Cars with cracked cylinders, with half the teeth missing from the fly wheel, with everything wrong, were sold as "guaranteed." When the customer returned and demanded his guarantee, he had to sue to get it and very few went to that trouble and expense: the boss said you could depend on human nature. If hot cars could be taken in and sold safely, the boss did not hesitate. When I learned these things I did not quit as I had previously. I sometimes felt disgusted and wanted to quit, but I argued that I did not have much chance to find a legitimate firm. I knew that the game was rotten but it had to be played—the law of the jungle and that sort of thing. I knew that I was dishonest and to that extent felt that I was more honest than my fellows. The thing that struck me as strange was that all these people were proud of their ability to fleece customers. They boasted of their crookedness and were admired by their friends and enemies in proportion to their ability to get away with a crooked deal: it was called shrewdness. Another thing was that these people were unanimous in their denunciation of gangsters, robbers, burglars, and petty thieves. They never regarded themselves as in the same class and were bitterly indignant if accused of dishonesty: it was just good business. . . .

. . . .

A graduate student in an urban university, in order to supplement his income, took a job as an extra salesman in a shoe store on Saturdays and other rush days. He had no previous experience as a shoe salesman or in any other regular business. He described his experience in this store thus:

One day I was standing in the front part of the store, waiting for the next customer. A man came in and asked if we had any high, tan button shoes. I had told him that we had no shoes of that style. He thanked me and walked out of the store. The floor-walker came up to me and asked me what the man wanted. I told him what the man asked for and what I replied. The floor-walker said angrily: "Damn it! We're not here to sell what they want. We're here to sell what we've got." He went on to instruct me that when a customer came into the store, the first thing to do was to get him to sit down and take off his shoe so that he couldn't get out of the store. "If we don't have what he wants," he said, "bring him something else and try to interest him in that style. If he is still uninterested, inform the floor-walker and he will send one of the regular salesmen, and if that doesn't work, a third salesman will be sent to him. Our policy is that no cus-

tomer gets out of the store without a sale until at least three
salesmen have worked on him. By that time he feels that he
must be a crank and will generally buy something whether he
wants it or not."

I learned from other clerks that if a customer needed a 7-B
shoe and we did not have that size in the style he desired, I
should try on an 8-A or 7-C or some other size. The sizes were
marked in code so that the customer did not know what the
size was, and it might be necessary to lie to him about the size;
also his foot might be injured by the misfit. But the rule was to
sell him a pair of shoes, preferably a pair that fit but some other
pair if necessary.

I learned also that the clerks received an extra commission
if they sold the out-of-style shoes left over from earlier seasons,
which were called "spiffs." The regular salesmen made a practice
of selling spiffs to anyone who appeared gullible and generally
had to claim either that this was the latest style or that it had
been the style earlier and was coming back this season, or that it
was an old style but much better quality than present styles. The
clerk had to size up the customer and determine which one of
these lies would be most likely to result in a sale.

Several years later I became acquainted with a man who
worked for several years as a regular salesman in shoe stores in
Seattle. When I described to him the methods I had learned in
the shoe store where I worked, he said: "Every shoe store in
Seattle except one does exactly the same things and I learned
to be a shoe salesman in exactly the same manner you did." . . .

. . . .

The following statement was made by a young man who had
graduated from a recognized school of business, had become a
certified public accountant, and had been employed for several
years in a respected firm of public accountants in a large city:

While I was a student in the school of business I learned the
principles of accounting. After I had worked for a time for an
accounting firm I found that I had failed to learn many important things about accounting. An accounting firm gets its work
from business firms and, within limits, must make the reports

which those business firms desire. The accounting firm for which I work is respected and there is none better in the city. On my first assignment I discovered some irregularities in the books of the firm and these would lead anyone to question the financial policies of that firm. When I showed my report to the manager of our accounting firm, he said that was not a part of my assignment and I should leave it out. Although I was confident that the business firm was dishonest, I had to conceal this information. Again and again I have been compelled to do the same thing in other assignments. I get so disgusted with things of this sort that I wish I could leave the profession. I guess I must stick to it, for it is the only occupation for which I have training.

Most consumers are aware that the salesman is not always looking out for the best interests of the customer. As a result, they are distrustful of people who want to sell something, especially when that something appears on the surface to be a bargain. The practical joker who offered to sell genuine $5 bills for $1 could not find customers because Americans are afraid of being "played for a sucker" (outnegotiated). It may be that the mutual distrust aroused by relentless adherence to the bargaining principle is more harmful to American society than the losses of those who are cheated.

Sharp practice in business leads to social problems in another way. The line between relentless bargaining and illegal transactions is sometimes so thin that businessmen move quite easily from one to the other. Thus, studies of the black market during World War II show that neither unassimilated immigrants nor hoodlums ran the black markets. The black marketeers were the legitimate businessmen of prewar days.[3] Apparently, many businessmen were so accustomed to driving the best bargain they could that they were unable to reconcile themselves to selling for less than the market would pay—even though price and other controls were necessitated by the war emergency.

Another consequence of the principle of negotiated exchange for industrial societies, namely, divisive conflicts, is analyzed in the following remarks of a British historian.[4]

[3] See Marshall B. Clinard, *The Black Market* (New York: Rinehart & Company, 1952), pp. 285–329.

[4] From *The Acquisitive Society* by R. H. Tawney, pp. 40–43, copyright 1920, by Harcourt, Brace and Company, Inc., New York; renewed 1948, by R. H. Tawney. Reprinted by permission of the publishers.

. . . Social life is turned into a scene of fierce antagonisms and . . . a considerable part of industry is carried on in the intervals of a disguised social war. The idea that industrial peace can be secured merely by the exercise of tact and forbearance is based on the idea that there is a fundamental identity of interest between the different groups engaged in it, which is occasionally interrupted by regrettable misunderstandings. Both the one idea and the other are an illusion. The disputes which matter are not caused by a misunderstanding of identity of interests, but by a better understanding of diversity of interests. Though a formal declaration of war is an episode, the conditions which issue in a declaration of war are permanent; and what makes them permanent is the . . . denial that industry has any end or purpose other than the satisfaction of those engaged in it.

That motive produces industrial warfare, not as a regrettable incident, but as an inevitable result. It produces industrial war, because its teaching is that each individual or group has a right to what they can get, and denies that there is any principle, other than the mechanism of the market, which determines what they ought to get. . . . Self-interest, indeed, may cause them to refrain from using their full strength to enforce their claims, and, in so far as this happens, peace is secured in industry, as men have attempted to secure it in international affairs, by a balance of power. But the maintenance of such a peace is contingent upon the estimate of the parties to it that they have more to lose than to gain by an overt struggle, and is not the result of their acceptance of any standard of remuneration as an equitable settlement of their claims. Hence it is precarious, insincere and short. It is without finality, because there can be no finality in the mere addition of increments of income, any more than in the gratification of any other desire for material goods. When demands are conceded the old struggle recommences upon a new level, and will always recommence as long as men seek to end it merely by increasing remuneration, not by finding a principle upon which all remuneration, whether large or small, should be based.

. . . The true cause of industrial warfare is as simple as the true cause of international warfare. It is that if men recognize no law superior to their desires, then they must fight when their desires collide. For though groups or nations which are at issue with each other may be willing to submit to a principle which is superior to them both, there is no reason why they should submit to each other.

Hence, the idea . . . that industrial disputes would disappear if only the output of wealth were doubled, and every one were twice as well off, not only is refuted by all practical experience, but is in its very nature founded upon an illusion. For the question is one not of amounts but of proportions; and men will fight to be paid $120 a week, instead of $80, as readily as they will fight to be paid $20 instead of $16, as long as there is no reason why they should be paid $80 instead of $120. . . . The naive complaint, that workmen are never satisfied, is, therefore, strictly true. It is true, not only of workmen, but of all classes in a society which conducts its affairs on the principle that wealth . . . belongs to those who can get it. They are never satisfied, nor can they be satisfied. For as long as they make that principle the guide of their individual lives and of their social order, nothing short of infinity could bring them satisfaction.

The force of Professor Tawney's argument may be illustrated by a report on an American strike, which for more than three years brought violence and hatred to a small town.[5]

An enormous mess, not just an everyday, run-of-the-mine botch, requires good, strong men to produce. Weak men lack the courage and tenacity of purpose, the dignity and above all the individualism to produce a well-nigh hopeless shambles. Consequently what is happening in Sheboygan County, Wis., and radiating outward from there to all corners of the nation is a rare thing. Let there be no doubt about it: these men are the salt of the earth, the backbone of America, and the mess is a large one.

[5] Reprinted from an article entitled "A Long Strike's Human Damage" by Robert F. Wallace as it appeared in *Life* magazine, May 20, 1957, pp. 146–164. Copyright © 1957, Time, Inc.; reprinted by permission of *Life* magazine.

The mess is a labor dispute involving the wealthy, family-owned Kohler Company, second largest manufacturer of plumbing ware in the U. S., and the United Automobile Workers, the second largest union. The U.A.W.'s Local 833 has been on strike against Kohler for more than three years, having begun the fourth year on April 5. This is by far the longest and bitterest major strike in the nation, and there is still no indication as to how, when, or whether it may ever end.

What makes the strike so prolonged and so difficult to settle is the fact that it is not about wages or hours or pensions or hospitalization plans or any other issue that lends itself to arithmetical compromise. It is about principles. And they are not the tepid, flaccid principles so frequently encountered today but good old-fashioned ones involving no less than human rights and dignity. . . .

There are no Communists in Sheboygan, although the accusation is sometimes laid on the strikers by people who have no sympathy for them. Take the case of Mrs. Ethel Fesing. Mrs. Fesing was having a beer not long ago in Christ & Elly's Oui Oui Bar, one of the 155 taverns, and talking casually about the strike. Her husband is a striker. As it happened, a non-striker came into the tavern and made what both Mrs. Fesing and her husband, who was present, considered an untoward remark.

"I'll beat his brains out," said Mr. Fesing.

"Oh, no, you won't," said Mrs. Fesing. "I will."

And with that Mrs. Fesing, a lady of considerable muscle, picked up the non-striker, to whom she referred in loud tones as an indelicate scab, and threw him through a screen door. This was done with such violence that although the non-striker landed outside the tavern, his shoes remained inside. Mrs. Fesing is not a Communist. She was just sore.

Stubborn independence, perhaps a little slow to be asserted but asserted with emphasis when at last it is, is a prime ingredient in the Sheboygan personality—which is to say, in the personalities of the Kohler strikers. But the identical ingredient is also prominent in the personality of the strikers' arch opponent, Herbert V. Kohler, president and board chairman of the company. He too stems from the rugged Teutonic stock and he too, even at the age of 65, is as tough as an oak post. There may be minor differences in education and other matters, but the principal difference between Herbert V. Kohler and the strikers is that Herbert V. Kohler has all the money. Exactly how much money he has is no one's business, but his personal wealth runs well into the millions and the tangible net worth of his company is about $40 million.

The Kohler family has been prominent in Wisconsin politics, two Kohlers having held the governorship—Walter J. Kohler, Herbert's half-brother, in 1929–30, and Walter J. Kohler, Jr., Herbert's half-nephew, in 1951–56. The Kohler Company has also done its part in philanthropies, having given large sums to Sheboygan churches over the years and having donated so much to the local hospital that a new wing was named Kohler Pavilion. "Nobody says Herb is a bad-hearted man," one of the strikers observes. "He's not mean. He just tromps on us out of habit."

For many years the Kohlers, in running their family business, have been sedulous practitioners of old-fashioned paternalism, or father-knows-bestism. The union sometimes refers to this as "benevolent dictatorship," but more often omits the "benevolent." In reply, Herbert V. Kohler stoutly maintains that it is the union which practices dictatorship, the union which tries to tell him how to operate, and that this is a damnable outrage. . . .

The one old-world condition that the Kohler workers at last found intolerable was the Prussian variety of discipline maintained in the factory. It was discipline based on fear, demanding a sacrifice of personal dignity that finally became too great. There are no Patrick Henrys or Tom Paines in Sheboygan. To the question, "Why are you striking?" man after man shrugs, reddens and says, "Well, I got sick of kissing the foreman's elbow," or, "Well, I wanted them to treat me decent, like a man," or, "It was—well, I don't know how you put it, but it got so I couldn't breathe."

None of the strikers questions the necessity for discipline or the right of the management to enforce it; it is only the manner of enforcement that rankles. "They keep books on us like FBI files," a striker says. "I'm not kidding, I mean real books. John

Smith spent six minutes in the washroom. Bill Green made a dirty crack about the second supervisor in the pottery. Everything you do or say goes down in the books, even loud talking or laughing too much. The way the company punishes you is by transferring you."

"Suppose you've got a nice clean daytime job at high pay. I mean high for Kohler, maybe $2.30 an hour. You tell a joke the foreman doesn't think is funny, and all of a sudden you're on the night shift, and you've got a black mark on you, they're gunning for you. Next thing you know you're working in the foundry at a worse job, maybe $2.00 an hour. It's hotter than hell in the foundry, but not hot enough, so they put you in the pottery. Did you ever work around a kiln at 2,400°, Buster? For maybe $1.85 an hour? Then they pull you off that and make you a sweeper, $1.30 an hour—you can't do a thing about it, except quit. A young guy, he can quit, but I've seen men way past 60, guys who used to have good jobs, pushing brooms on the night shift. They can't quit because nobody else will hire them."

In almost all of U. S. industry today, grievances arising from disciplinary transfers and the downgrading of elderly men are submitted to arbitration. There are clauses providing for arbitration, not only of transfer cases but of various other grievances, in approximately 93% of the labor contracts now in force. The Kohler Company, however, will not agree to arbitration. Herbert V. Kohler takes the view that arbitration is a surrender of management's function.

The Kohler workers have been trying for more than 25 years to force some sort of satisfactory grievance-arbitration mechanism on the management. In the early 1930's many of them joined an A.F.L. union which recruited in the plant, hoping to achieve a position of strength from which to negotiate. The management opposed the union; a strike and a bloody battle ensued. In July 1934 there was a riot outside the gates of the plant which was quelled with tear gas and gunfire, resulting in the death of two men and the wounding of 28 others, all strikers or spectators. The A.F.L. union was broken.

In the middle 1930's a "company union," the Kohler Workers Association, was formed with the encouragement of the management. The KWA had no affiliation with any outside group. It also had no strength.

In 1952 the U.A.W. began to organize the plant, and after several months of furtive work succeeded in enlisting a majority of the production workers.

The motivation of the Kohler workers in joining the U.A.W. cannot be overstressed. It was not because they were interested in advanced politico-economic theories; the phrase "class struggle" to them was something that might be applied to a high school ball game. It was not because they were greedy for more money; their pay was not high by the standards of Detroit or Gary, but it was good for the Sheboygan area and they were reasonably content with it. All they wanted to do was to get the foremen off their backs. This required that they go out and get a big, husky friend to help them. If the big, husky friend had some advanced ideas, the workers were not concerned. They just wanted muscles.

The first contract negotiated between the Kohler Company and U.A.W. Local 833, as the new union was numbered, ran for a period of one year and expired early in 1954. It did not have an arbitration clause that satisfied the union members, having been negotiated rather gingerly. Neither side was anxious, at the outset, to provoke a fight. But before the contract expired both sides served notice that they would not renew it, and the lines of battle began to form.

The executives of the Kohler Company, including Herbert V. Kohler and his chief attorney and negotiator, Lyman Conger, have a great deal in common with the executives of the international U.A.W., including President Walter Reuther and Secretary-Treasurer Emil Mazey. The remark may cause them to choke on their cigars but it is nonetheless true. Politically and in economic theory, needless to say, they have basic differences. But they are all good citizens of the republic, honorable men, and they are nearly identical in matters of courage, stubbornness and the willingness to fight for a cause. It is a pity that the four men, as a team, cannot go and negotiate something with the

Russians, as they would doubtless come back with Bulganin's goatee. And it is a pity that the four men, as two teams, had to square off against each other.

Herbert V. Kohler approached the battle determined not only to hold his ground but, if he could, to smash the union. He made no bones about it. In reference to the fact that the Taft-Hartley law requires employers, as well as employes, to bargain, he agreed that he did have to bargain with them but was heard to say, "You don't have to give them anything to bargain."

The executives of the international U.A.W.—they, rather than the local's executives, are the ones who call the shots—approached the battle determined to make Kohler yield or to leave him dead in the market place as an example to any other employers who might try to go back to 1928. And so the ultra-conservative employer and the ultraliberal union took each other by the throat.

Although the principle of negotiated exchange is most relevant to economic activities, it infiltrates every area of American life. Political corruption, for instance, requires not only a public official who is overly self-reliant; persons or organizations must be willing to bribe him in order to drive a more advantageous bargain with the government. As Harold Ickes, Secretary of the Interior in the Roosevelt Administration, put it, "I have never known a public official to corrupt himself." The following article entitled, "The Anatomy of Graft," is a rather sympathetic account of the seduction of a politician.[6]

Victor Martin was in grammar and high school during the confident years before 1914. His father had done well as a city contractor and Victor went on to college, taking a sort of common denominator course and specializing in nothing because he had no idea of what kind of career he wanted. But World War I, a year in the Army, a commission as second lieutenant of infantry, and a chance afterward to help organize a local post of the American Legion, bent him toward politics.

[6] Joseph F. Dinneen, "The Anatomy of Graft," *Harper's Magazine,* July, 1952, pp. 38–41. Reprinted by permission of the author. Copyright © 1952 by Harper & Brothers, New York.

What he knew about it then he had learned chiefly from observation. His father, he was well aware, had paid graft to city councilors, state representatives, and senators: had contributed to mayors' campaign funds and had delivered the votes of those who worked for him. Victor knew this was wrong. He felt he had ideals and principles. He had seen some politicians who didn't seem to work that way, and he was determined that he wouldn't.

Victor's father, interested in his ambition, spoke to a state senator. Victor was appointed executive secretary to a joint recess committee investigating electric light and power rates. When the hearings ended, he could hardly recognize his report after members tore it apart, amended, rewrote, and distorted it; but as he was Mike Martin's boy, the committee praised his work elaborately and he was taken over by the Public Utilities Commission as an assistant secretary. During the next three years he became an active member of every fraternal, service, and civic organization open to him, and managed to stand before the news camera at outings, clambakes, and celebrations. So when he became a candidate for the City Council his name was fairly well known.

This candidacy of his was a carefully planned move. He had thought it out, talked it over with his father. He got heavy assists from the political friends to whom his father had paid graft for contracts, and the fact that he was engaged to Jean Tarbi, daughter of another contractor, did not hurt in a ward with a heavy Italian vote. In a nonpartisan election he won handily.

Thus Victor Martin, at the age of twenty-five, took the first step up the political spiral stairs. He was loyal, dependable, a good campaigner, a hard worker for the party; he went down the line regularly at every primary and election. And he was ambitious. Victor Martin does not, of course, exist under that name, but almost every political reporter knows a dozen or more Victor Martins; they are to be found in every rank of government.

Soon after his first election to the Council, Victor faced a decision he had long contemplated and never quite resolved. He had resigned his $4,500-a-year job in the Public Utilities Com-

mission because the law forbade elected officials to hold ap-
pointive office. As a councilor he would receive $2,500 a year,
hardly enough to support himself, let alone a wife and possibly
family. He had four choices of means to amplify that salary.

He could get a job with a public utility, always eager to hire
a councilor and thus control his vote. If he did so he would be
forever hamstrung politically as a "tool of the vested interests."

He could take a job with a private employer or corporation
remote from politics; but such jobs were not easy to find.

He could make a profession of politics in the same manner
as some of his associates, milking all comers who needed his
vote and trading with other councilors and the mayors for salable legal privileges.

Or he could accept the apparently genuine, harmless kudos
that came his way merely because of his political position, and
hope that this would somehow augment his income in time. He
wanted no financial help from his father or Jean's father. He
wanted to be independent.

Joe Barron, owner of the Gamecock Cafe, posed the question first. He stopped in at Victor's house soon after dinner one
night. "Vic," he began, "I want a swinging overhead sign outside my place." It was a simple request. Vic was surprised.

"What's stopping you from getting it?" Vic asked. "All you
have to do is drop in at the street department at City Hall, fill
out an application, pay $25 for a permit, and put up your sign."

Joe Barron shook his head, threw six fifty-dollar bills on the
table beside Victor, and said: "Not me! You do it, Vic."

"Don't be silly, Joe," Vic said. "You're entitled to that permit. Nobody can stop you from getting it. Put that money back
in your pocket. You don't need me for that."

Joe shook his head. "You get it," he insisted. "If $300 isn't
enough, say so. I've paid a lot more than that for less; and when
it comes time for me to renew my liquor license, I'll want you to
look after that, too."

Vic shook his head. "Don't be childish. Anybody can get a
permit for a swinging sign in your neighborhood. It's zoned for
business. Go into City Hall tomorrow, ask for it, pay for it, and
get it."

"Suppose they refuse me?" Joe said.

"They won't. If they do, I'll go in there and raise hell and you'll still get your permit for $25."

Joe shook his head. "I don't want any trouble. You get it."

Victor tossed the money back. "I'll tell you what I'll do, Joe," he said. "I'll be your errand boy. I'll drop in at City Hall, pick up the application, and deliver it to you. You fill it out and I'll file it. It will cost $25 and that's all."

"No dice, Vic," he said. "If I go to a doctor—a specialist— and his charge is $500, I pay it. If I go to a lawyer, I pay his fee, and lawyers don't work cheap. Same way with anybody. If I pay I get my money's worth."

Vic was losing patience. "I don't charge money to do a friend a thing he can do for himself for nothing." He leaned over and stuffed the money in Joe's breast pocket.

Joe . . . put it on the table beside Victor. "Look, Victor," he said. "You've just been elected. You don't know your way around very well yet. You've taken Tom Drennan's place in the Council. He goes upstairs to the House of Representatives where the picking is better maybe. I've always paid Tom. I like it that way and he liked it that way."

Vic shook his head. "But I'm not Tom Drennan," he said. "I don't take bribes and I don't take graft—and I don't take money for doing a favor."

Joe bristled, "Am I bribing you?" His eyes snapped. "Do you call that three hundred bucks graft? I'm not trying to buy you for three hundred smackers. Show me how I'm breaking any law—or how you are, either, by taking that dough."

Vic was momentarily frustrated. "Why do you want to pay money like that? You're entitled to the permit."

"Right," Joe agreed. "The only trouble is: if I go in and get an application and file it with the clerk, he'll tell me to come back in five days after it is investigated. The precinct police lieutenant will come by and decide that the sign is an obstruction. The traffic commission inspector will rule that it blocks a signal light that nobody can see from that angle, anyway. A sidewalk inspector will rule that it's an accident hazard. I may even find that the abutters are organized against me and they may ask for a hearing. Before I'm through sugaring everybody up a $30 sign may cost me $900 instead of $300."

Victor's eyes narrowed. "Have you tried to get a sign before? Are any of these things true? Is it an obstruction? Will it block off a light? Is it a hazard?"

"The answer is no to everything," Joe said. "If I ask for it they'll all wonder why I didn't ask you to get it for me. They'll figure either you're sore at me; that I can't ask you; or that you're not interested, and they'll all collect. It isn't worth that to me. It's worth $300—no more."

"You go in and get that application," Victor directed. "If the city clerk holds up the permit or holds you up for dough, let me know, and maybe we'll have a new city clerk; if a sergeant or cop or anybody else puts the bite on you, tell me and there'll be a showdown on that too."

Joe held up his hand for silence. "Wait a minute, Vic. That's courageous talk but you're not going to make a hero of yourself by making a stool pigeon out of me. I've got a good business and I don't want any trouble. If you don't take the money, I'd rather pay a higher price to somebody else. I'll have plenty of trouble for you to iron out during the next two years—with the licensing board, the Alcoholic Beverages Commission, the cops, the Board of Health, and people like that. If you're being paid for it you'll do a good job. I never deal with people who work for nothing. The way I figure it, a guy gets what he pays for."

Joe got up to leave. "I'm not going to take that dough back, Vic," he said. "Think it over. Talk it over with your old man. He's paid plenty to politicians over the years; so has Jean's father. You know that as well as I do. They got what they paid for; and they'd be the first to tell you so. You're a politician now. Be one. If you're going to be a reformer, you'll be just a flash in the pan, good for one term."

He left. Vic looked at the money for a long time; finally put it in his pocket. He decided to talk it over with his father and Jean.

He had an uncomfortable feeling that he had surrendered something that he could retrieve only by giving the money back,

even though it meant in the end making a cold friend or outright enemy of Joe Barron and in any case sacrificing his political support. He knew without even discussing it with him how
his father felt about it, but he brought it up just the same.

"Why not?" his father said. "You're not in the business for
your health. You can't live on a councilor's salary. If I hadn't
been paying politicians ever since I've been in business I
wouldn't have been making money enough to own a nice house
and send you through college."

"What do you think of it?" he asked Jean after giving her a
full account. "Shall I keep the money or give it back?"

The pattern was not unfamiliar to her. She knew how her
father operated.

"Precisely what is wrong about it, Victor?" she asked. "Is it
a bribe? Is he paying you money to influence your vote or to
persuade you to act illegally in his favor?"

Victor shook his head. "He's paying me to be an errand
boy."

"Why?"

"Because he feels sure that a political errand boy can do for
him a job he can't do for himself."

"You didn't solicit money from him. He is making you a
voluntary gift. Isn't that so?" Victor nodded. "Is there any
fraud involved? Does it require you to do anything dishonest
or illegal?"

"Not at all," he said. "I'm merely acting as his agent."

"The city is not deprived of any money it is entitled to?"

"Right," he agreed.

"Then, who loses?" she asked.

"As Joe Barron sees it," he said, "the only persons who lose
are officials who would put the bite on him like the police sergeant, a sidewalk inspector, or a traffic commission agent."

"But," she protested, "they're losing dishonest money. They
have no right to ask it. You're really preventing them from
breaking the law."

He nodded again. "Their function is to investigate honestly
and recommend for or against. If the prestige of a councilor

is behind the application, these investigations are perfunctory. They wouldn't want to tangle with the councilor. Otherwise they can victimize the applicant."

"If they were honest," she went on, "and discovered any reason why he should not have a simple unimportant thing like a swinging sign, any one of them still could recommend against it in spite of the councilor?"

"That's right," he agreed.

"Do you think that Joe Barron wants to put you under an obligation to him, so that you would have to take orders from him in the future?"

"Not at all," Victor answered. "Actually he is under an obligation to me. The shoe is on the other foot. Even if he asks me to do something for him again—and there is no doubt that he will—I still can refuse if his proposal is dishonest or I don't like it for any other reason."

"Let's face it, Victor," she said. "Is this $300 graft?"

He shook his head. "Not within the meaning of the term as it is commonly understood. Graft is a politician's participation in the profit he has made possible for any person or partnership or corporation doing business with or working for any government. There's no profit involved in displaying a sign."

"Then if it isn't dishonest, and it isn't graft, and you're not selling out to him, I can't see anything wrong about taking it. Why are you so reluctant?"

"I can't define the reason, except to say that it doesn't seem quite right to me. I wasn't elected to accept gratuities; and that's what it comes down to."

"Aren't you being a little too stuffy and scrupulous about it, Vic?" she asked.

It was not a pleasant subject. They were anxious to decide it and dispose of it forever, and they had explored it enough now to know what was in each other's mind. Victor was still inwardly uncomfortable, but he decided not to return Joe Barron's money.

"I won't sell jobs or promotions or cut myself in on any political melons," he said. "I won't take graft as such. But if this is the way to play the game, I'll play it according to the rules."

He told Joe Barron much the same thing. It did not take Joe long to publish it throughout the ward to all and sundry who wanted to do business with the new councilor.

What Victor Martin, with his talk of graft "as such" did not realize was that although he had indeed done nothing illegal, and nothing which he would define as dishonest, he had nevertheless taken the first step on a very long path. For by accepting money from an interested party in even so small a matter as permission to erect a swinging sign—a permission which pretty surely should have been granted anyhow—he was undercutting the principle of fair play before the law, a basic principle of democratic government. He was giving to one man an advantage to which others might not have access. How about the next man who wanted a sign and was entitled to one and might not have $300? How would this other man make out with the inspectors? Furthermore, in taking Joe's word that the sign would not be a menace, he was circumventing the judgment of the officials who were called upon by the law to determine these matters disinterestedly after impartial investigation. How carefully would the next inspector, when asked whether or not a sign should be put up, use his best judgment to protect the public safety?

If there are degrees of graft, Victor had been engaged in a very minor and apparently innocent sort. Yet his inability to detect the fine distinctions which separate one sort of favor from another was destined to affect his future in ways which he could not then foresee.

During his first term Victor did a better than average business with petitioners for legal rights, licenses, and privileges. His traffic with city employees, police, firemen, skilled and unskilled workers looking for jobs, promotions, or changes in civil-service ratings was phenomenal. Usually they offered him money either before or after they got what they wanted. He always refused it. They would pay off in votes, support, and campaign work in the future.

He was given $500 on three occasions for negotiating permits for tank storage of gasoline; $1,000 twice for filling-station licenses. Liquor and alcohol licenses accounted for $5,000; permits to open streets for various private purposes, chiefly among apartment house owners for central heating plants, $3,000. His total income during his first year was $11,000—of which $2,500 was salary. Halfway through the term he and Jean were married.

Actually, outright bribery is less common today than it was a hundred years ago and more unusual in state and federal agencies than in municipal governments. However, lobbyists are still active, and, if they do not bribe, they make campaign contributions; they hold cocktail parties; they give Christmas gifts. In short, they strive to influence the negotiations between their clients and government agencies by placing the relevant officials under obligation to them. Consider the following account of gift-giving and gift-taking in Washington, where having a friend in power may be worth a million dollars or more.[7]

Almost any discussion of the Washington gift problem comes back to the 12-pound ham. A member of the Reconstruction Finance Corporation told a Senate subcommittee in 1948 that he would accept a 12-pound ham as a gift but not a 13-pound ham. Some scoffed, but others felt this got to the heart of the matter. It expressed the vital thought that wherever personal morality draws the line it will probably appear ridiculous but that, ridiculous or not, some line must be drawn. Senator Paul Douglas, for example, draws the line for personal gifts at a value of $2.50. If the gift is worth $2.60—back to the donor it goes, collect.

This was really what President Eisenhower meant in his statement on the Sherman Adams case. He told his press conference on June 18: "All of us in America should be aware of one truth—a gift is not necessarily a bribe. One is evil; the other is a tangible expression of friendship."

Yet the problem of what is evil and what is friendship persists, and, like the size of the ham, continues to trouble Washington. Improper gifts and favors, or suspicions of them, have probably caused more political stories out of the capital than

[7] Richard L. Strout, "Washington Gifts, or the 12-Pound Ham," *New York Times Magazine,* June 29, 1958, pp. 8–44. Reprinted by permission of Richard L. Strout and *The New York Times.*

any other subject. Gift-giving and influence-peddling are important in Washington because this is the city where the Fat Contract and the Avid Contractor meet—not to mention the Regulator and the Regulated. Scandals seem to arise most conspicuously after wars or when some neglected area of government is suddenly rediscovered.

That is happening now in the regulatory agencies. The fact that so many people almost automatically accept the theory that a mere call from the White House would throw one of these independent, quasi-judicial agencies off balance is a measure of the national distrust. For the first time in history, Congress is making an investigation of them—with an appropriation of $250,-000 to do so. The preliminary inquiry has indicated some sleazy conditions.

What form does Washington gift-giving take? The problem is really the gift with strings, the two-way favor, the reciprocal good deed. By this is meant the gratuity of an interested party generating an obligation for something in return. It is the gift that weans the recipient away from dedication to public duties and tempts him to be a servant to private interests. Most gift-giving in Washington is innocent enough—the Christmas calendar, the pencil stamped, "Jones Hardware," the modest lunch for a busy official to continue a legitimate business discussion. But these prosaic amenities shade gradually into other phases: the loan of a nice TV color set; the social obligation fostered at a cocktail party or a champagne dinner; the junket, the tip on the stock market; the dangled hope of a fat outside job. . . .

As the center of government, Washington has three characteristics affecting the problem of gifts: (1) it is full of politicians who take for granted the desirability and necessity of accepting campaign gifts, though some of them boggle at the size; (2) it has an equal or larger population of businessmen and lobbyists, all of whom know exactly what they want and who bring to the capital a quite different attitude toward gift-giving and commercial favors than that of civil servants, and (3) Washington has a lively social life in which the trophies dangled before inexperienced eyes may be social advancement, publicity and the heady gratification of knowing celebrities—while the celebrities themselves face the insidious hazards of the corrupting sense of power.

The story can best be told, perhaps, by actual examples.

SEA TRIPS

The King subcommittee in the Truman Administration disclosed that Theron Lamar Caudle, Assistant Attorney General in charge of the Tax Division, and Charles Oliphant, a Treasury attorney, took deep-sea fishing trips as the guests of a man under investigation for possible tax fraud.

MIAMI VACATION

Donald Dawson, White House administrative assistant, spent twenty-two days in a $30-a-day room at a Miami Beach hotel in the spring of 1950. When he left, he was told the "bill was already paid." Dawson had been connected with the R. F. C., which had given the hotel a loan.

PERSONAL LOANS

Richard A. Mack, before resigning from the Federal Communications Commission in February, 1958, acknowledged receiving several thousand dollars—in loans—from a representative of a company whose subsidiary received Miami TV Channel 10. Mack had voted for the award.

JOB TRANSFER

The Fulbright Committee found that the Boston manager of the R. F. C., drawing a $10,000 annual salary, reversed the unfavorable recommendation of a loan examiner and recommended a $9-million loan to the Waltham Watch Company. A month after approval of the loan, the manager resigned and became an executive of the company at $30,000 a year.

CAMERAS

The American Lithofold Company of St. Louis, which prints business forms and wanted an R. F. C. loan, had a motto in 1948—*A Government employe is a company's best friend*. It distributed gifts lavishly but selectively in the capital; these included, for example, twenty-six Polaroid cameras costing $150 each. One went to a White House secretary, another to the general counsel of the Internal Revenue Bureau.

THE LITTLE WOMAN

Lauretta Young, White House stenographer and wife of Merle Young, the dazzling Washington influence-peddler, got her famous "natural royal pastel mink coat" ($8,540 less 10 per cent discount) from the head of the Washington law firm with which her husband teamed up. Young, whose fantastic career at one time included holding simultaneous jobs with two R. F. C. debtors, each unknown to the other, was ultimately jailed.

DEEP FREEZERS

In this famous episode, a Chicago business man showed his appreciation of favors bestowed by jovial White House Military Aide Harry H. Vaughan by sending four war-scarce freezers, costing $390 each, to Vaughan and his friends in June, 1945, and later, when caught in a tax investigation, sending three more, costing $420 each—this time to top Treasury officials.

EXPENSE MONEY

The current House investigation of regulatory agencies disclosed that members of the F. C. C. have frequently (and probably legally) accepted speaking honorariums, expense money and other favors from the warm-hearted members of the industry which they regulate.

JUNKETS

The initial run of the new Grace liner, Santa Rosa, this June took along half a dozen Government officials and thirteen Congressmen who deal with ship subsidies. It was an all-expense-paid pleasure voyage—wives included. As to junkets in general, a compilation by the Congressional Quarterly shows that forty-six Senators and 176 Representatives took Government trips abroad in 1957. ("Junket" comes from the Latin *juncus,* or reed, from which baskets are made; hence, food carried in baskets; hence, banquets and feasting; hence—U. S.—an outing at public cost, principally for officials.)

.   .   .   .

These examples raise all sorts of questions. Should the donors be punished as well as the receivers of expensive gifts? ("I have never known a public official to corrupt himself," said Harold Ickes.) Where to draw the line? How big the ham? Again, what should be the attitude of top officials? When the magazine, *U. S. News & World Report,* asked in 1955 about the Eisenhower gift policy, it was told by a White House official that "the office of the President is too big to be influenced by any gift." This is doubtless true, yet the question arises, how about the example set for lesser officials?

The normal Government executive who sees a social amenity offered to him does not want to seem stuffy and priggish by rejecting it; on the other hand, he does not want to be compromised. He has to draw the line somewhere. Almost every Federal agency has its own code of rules and regulations to help him with the answer, but these are not definitive. In an issue of good taste, there is always some discretion.

Senator Douglas in his book, "Ethics in Government," noted how the primrose path opens for some workers. He observed:

"The steps in the process of seducing public officials are indeed very similar to those which were chronicled in paperbound novels and melodramas forty years ago, describing how the mustached villain sought to conquer the virtue of the poor working girl."

The penalties for getting caught need hardly be stressed. A number of officials in the instances above ended in jail. Besides the personal tragedies, the loss of political prestige, and, worse, of public morale, was shattering. . . .

One specific proposal would require a two-year interval before Government officials could practice before their old agencies or take employment with firms which had benefitted by their official acts.

After all the codes of ethics and procedure are written, however, the question of attitude still remains. Nobody sends deep freezers to the Supreme Court. Why? It would be unthinkable. "It just isn't done." It is part of our unwritten constitution. The British have raised their Government standards to this point all around. America has a long way to go, and yet, judging by the remarkable progress since Webster's day, it may not take as long as we think.

There is evidently an invisible line somewhere between gifts that are proper and those that are improper. Perhaps the best rule of thumb is that offered by the Senate subcommittee on Ethical Standards of Government (1951) for the Federal worker:

"At the moment a doubt arises as to propriety, the line should be drawn. Innocence is perhaps lost when one is conscious that it exists." . . .

"Appearance as well as reality must be considered. Even though a public official is not influenced by favors in his attitude toward the donor's official business, if it might seem to an observer that the recipient would be influenced, the gift becomes improper. It is not to the public interest that the integrity of officials should be suspected. The effect of the example on other employes and on other members of the public is also to be considered. Will one man's acceptance of a gift lead others to do so, who may be more easily influenced? Will it lead other businessmen to believe that they must give presents to public officials, and so create a larger problem where a smaller one exists today?

"If we are to build higher standards in the community, public officials should avoid the appearance as well as the reality of evil."

The principle of negotiated exchange leads to other political problems akin to corruption. Consider the obligations incurred by the Democratic and Republican parties in soliciting campaign contributions. Isn't it reasonable, in the light of the principle of negotiated exchange, for contributors to expect a *quid pro quo?* (Theodore Roosevelt and, more recently, Senator Neuberger have suggested that Federal subsidy of political parties is necessary.[8]) Political corruption also derives from the bargaining principle indirectly. Consider how the overrepresentation of rural areas in state legislatures and even in Congress tempts rural representatives to sell their votes.[9]

[8] See Richard L. Neuberger, "Who Should Pay for Political Campaigns?", *New York Times Magazine,* June 3, 1956, pp. 25–66.

[9] From *Morality In American Politics,* by George A. Graham, pp. 104–105. Copyright 1952, by George A. Graham. Reprinted by permission of Random House, Inc., New York.

The disproportionate power of rural representatives in state legislatures is . . . a major cause of personal corruption. The over-weighted legislators are inherently vulnerable, for they have votes which can be used to defeat measures which may little concern their own constituents but which are of great concern to the urban or industrial sections of the state. These votes have great market value, and they can frequently be bought in one way or another. Hence the alliance so frequently observed between conservative business interests, which are located in urban sections of a state, and the rural politicians. One group has money; the other has votes.

The disproportionate power of rural politicians contributes greatly to pork-barrel politics. If they are a majority of one house of the legislature, they can very nearly demand what they want, and get it, in public works, highways, contracts, and jobs. They have to be appeased. They are also in a position to engage in blackmail. At every session of many state legislatures, measures are introduced which are not meant to pass, but which move along in the legislative mill until their sponsors are bought off in one way or another. The interests (usually business interests) that would be injured if such bills should pass know what they are expected to do and come across.

Great power brings its temptations inevitably, and the temptations of irresponsible power are well-nigh irresistible. The power of representatives of a minority of a state's population to pass legislation, or to block it, is the most dangerous sort of irresponsible power.

The intrusion of negotiated exchange into areas of American life where law and custom suggest other means of working out relationships can be illustrated also in the sale of sexual services. As Kingsley Davis points out in his classic article, "The Sociology of Prostitution," prostitution arouses public indignation because it substitutes the mechanism of the market place for direct institutional controls over erotic gratification.[10]

[10] Kingsley Davis, "The Sociology of Prostitution," *American Sociological Review,* Vol. 2 (1937), pp. 744–755. Reprinted by permission of Kingsley Davis and The American Sociological Society.

Since prostitution is a contractual relation in which services are traded (usually in terms of an exchange medium) and sex is placed in an economic context, it is strange that modern writers have made so much of the fact that the "social evil" has economic causes. One might as well say, with equal perspicacity, that retail merchandising has economic causes. Prostitution embraces an economic relation, and is naturally connected with the entire system of economic forces. But to jump from this truism to the conclusion that prostitution can be abolished by eliminating its economic causes is erroneous. Economic causes seldom act alone, and hence their removal is seldom a panacea.

The causal ramifications of commercial coitus extend beyond the economic sphere. At least three separable but related problems must be recognized: (1) the causes of the existence of prostitution; (2) the causes of the *rate* or *amount* of prostitution; and (3) the causes of *any particular individual's entrance into, or patronage of,* prostitution. The existence of prostitution seems related both to the physiological nature of man and to the inherent character of society, both of which include more than the sheer economic element. These basic factors, constantly operative, account for the ubiquity of prostitution, but not for the variations in its rate. This second problem must be dealt with in terms of the specific institutional configuration existing at the time, in which economic factors are highly but not exclusively important. Finally, any particular person's connection with prostitution is a result of his or her own unique life-history, into which an infinite variety of strands, some economic and some not economic, are woven. The factors in (1) and (2) are operative in the individual's life, but are never sufficient in themselves to explain his or her behavior.

These issues are generally confused by those who believe that by removing alleged economic causes one can abolish prostitution. Let us follow their arguments further, considering first the removal of economic causes within the capitalist system, and second the removal of them in a noncapitalist system.

1. A frequent proposal for abolition under capitalism is that the salaries of working girls be raised. This proposal, which ignores the demand side, assumes that girls enter prostitution

through economic necessity—a paradoxical assumption, for if it is true it indicates that prostitution must have other than economic causes and remedies, while if it is untrue this particular proposal is fallacious.

Why should a girl enter prostitution *only* through economic necessity? Is the occupation so arduous? On the contrary, we often speak as if harlots "would rather prostitute themselves than work." It is even true that some women enjoy the intercourse they sell. From a purely economic point of view prostitution comes perilously near the situation of getting something for nothing. The woman may suffer no loss at all, yet receive a generous reward, resembling the artist who, though paid for his work, loves it so well that he would paint anyway. Purely from the angle of economic return, the hard question is not why so many woman become prostitutes, but why so few of them do. The harlot's return is not primarily a reward for abstinence, labor, or rent. It is primarily a reward for loss of social standing. She loses social esteem because our moral system condemns the commercialization of intercourse. If, then, she refuses to enter the profession until forced by sheer want, the basic cause of her hesitation is not economic but moral. Only when the moral condition is assumed, do wages or economic want take on any importance. Prostitution, therefore, is not purely a matter of economic factors alone.

We have taken for granted that in the face of moral condemnation, only starvation wages can drive girls into prostitution. Actually this is only partly true. But even if it were, the proposal to eliminate prostitution by raising wages would not work. In a competitive system as soon as the salaries of working girls are increased, the supply of prostitutes diminishes. The resulting scarcity increases the effective demand, in the form of price, which rises as the supply diminishes. (The demand rests upon a constant imperative need, not always conveniently satisfiable by substitutes.) With the rise in price, working girls even with good salaries will be tempted into the profession. Moreover, it will be possible for more women to live on the proceeds of prostitution alone—without performing arduous labor in store or restaurant. The net result will be as much prostitution as before, and in terms of actual money invested and changing hands, there may be more. The facts seem to bear out these theoretical propositions, for apparently prostitution does not increase greatly with low wages for women nor decrease with high, although other factors, such as the correlation between men's wages and women's wages, must be considered in working out the relationship.

Finally, this proposal does not touch the demand for prostitution. To touch demand requires more than economic changes; for even less than the woman who sells herself, is the man who buys guided by economic motives. His motivation, as we shall see later, springs from bio-social forces for which the economic are simply instrumental.

2. In her book, *Red Virtue,* Ella Winter has a chapter entitled "Ending Prostitution," at the head of which stands a quotation from a Soviet physician: "Soviet life does not permit of prostitution." Widely accepted and frequently repeated, this belief is taken for granted as one of the main values of a communist as against a capitalist system.

There can be little doubt, I think, that in Soviet cities prostitution has diminished in the last few years, but there can be grave doubt that it has been ended or that the diminution has resulted solely from the abolition of private property. Not only did prostitution exist before capitalism arose, but capitalist countries themselves have frequently tried to stop private ownership of prostitutes for purposes of profit. They have consistently legislated against third parties—pimps, real estate owners, bookers—only to find that none of these measures succeed. In short, capitalism, like communism, has tried in the case of prostitution to negate the basic capitalistic principle.

Doubtless it is harder to eliminate the business aspect of prostitution (organized syndicates operated by third parties) in a capitalist system where business prevails anyway, than it is in a communist system where all business is frowned upon. In the latter, profit-making organizations possess high visibility, are easily hunted down. But this does not mean that unorganized prostitution, in which seller, manager, and worker are all rolled into the same person, cannot thrive.

Payment for prostitution need not be in terms of money. It may be in terms of privilege, power, food, clothing, almost any form of exchangeable value. These exchangeable commodities (and some medium of exchange) must exist in any complex society, no matter what the system of political control, because the specialized producers must mutually exchange their surpluses. At the same time there is, in any society, a system of privilege, authority, and dominance. Some have rights, belongings, and talents that others lack. Soviet Russia may have abolished the capitalistic alignment of classes, but it has not abolished social class; the class principle is inherent in the nature of social organization. In the Soviet system, as in any other social structure, there lies the external possibility and the eternal incentive to trade sexual favor for non-sexual advantage. This becomes clearer after analyzing the demand side of prostitution.

When outlawed, prostitution falls into one peculiar category of crime—a type exceedingly hard to deal with—in which one of the willful parties is the ordinary law-abiding citizen. This kind of crime, of which bootlegging is the archetype, is supported by the money and behavior of a sizable portion of the citizenry, because in it the citizen receives a service. Though the service is illegitimate, the citizen cannot be held guilty, for it is both impossible and inadvisable to punish half the populace for a crime. Each citizen participates in vital institutional relationships—family, business, church, and state. To disrupt all of these by throwing him in jail for a mere vice would be, on a large scale, to disrupt society. But the eagerness of otherwise decent citizens to receive the illicit service attests powerful forces behind the demand element.

On the one hand, the demand is the result of a simple biological appetite. When all other sources of gratification fail, due to defects of person or circumstance, prostitution can be relied upon to furnish relief. None of the exacting requirements of sex attraction and courtship are necessary. All that is needed is the cash, and this can be obtained in a thousand ways. Prostitution is the most malleable, the most uninvolved form of physical release.

But in addition to the sheer desire for sexual satisfaction, there is the desire for satisfaction in a particular (often an unsanctioned) way.

The common and ignorant assumption that prostitution exists to satisfy the gross sensuality of the young unmarried man, and that if he is taught to bridle gross sexual impulse or induced to marry early the prostitute must be idle, is altogether incorrect . . . The prostitute is something more than a channel to drain off superfluous sexual energy, and her attraction by no means ceases when men are married, for a large number of men who visit prostitutes, if not the majority, are married. And alike whether they are married or unmarried the motive is not one of uncomplicated lust.[11]

The craving for variety, for perverse gratification, for mysterious and provocative surroundings, for intercourse free from entangling cares and civilized pretense, all play their part.

Prostitution, again by its very nature, is aptly suited to satisfy this second side of demand. The family, an institution of status rather than contract, limits the variety, amount, and nature of a person's satisfactions. But since with the prostitute the person is paying for the privilege, he is in a position to demand almost anything he wants. The sole limitation on his satisfactions is not morality or convention, but his ability to pay the price. This is an advantage which commercial recreation generally has over kinds handled by other institutional channels.

There is no reason to believe that a change in the economic system will eliminate either side of demand. In any system the effective demand as expressed by price will vary with current economic and moral forces, but the underlying desire both for sheer gratification and for gratification in particular ways will remain impregnable.

We can imagine a social system in which the motive for prostitution would be completely absent, but we cannot imagine that the system could ever come to pass. It would be a regime of absolute sexual freedom, wherein intercourse were practiced solely for the pleasure of it, by both parties. This would entail at least two conditions: *First,* there could be no institutional con-

[11] From *Studies in the Psychology of Sex,* Vol. 6, by Havelock Ellis, pp. 295–296.

trol of sexual expression. Marriage, with its concomitants of engagement, jealousy, divorce, and legitimacy, could not exist. Such an institution builds upon and limits the sexual urge, making sex expression contingent upon non-sexual factors, and thereby paving the way for intercourse against one's physical inclination. *Second,* all sexual desire would have to be mutually complementary. One person could not be erotically attracted to a non-responsive person, because such a situation would inevitably involve frustration and give a motive for using force, fraud, authority, or money to induce the unwilling person to co-operate.

Neither of these conditions can in the nature of things come to pass. As we have seen, every society attempts to control, and for its own survival must control, the sexual impulse in the interest of social order, procreation, and socialization. Moreover, all men are not born handsome nor all women beautiful. Instead there is a perfect gradation from extremely attractive to extremely unattractive, with an unfavorable balance of the old and ugly. This being the case, the persons at the wrong end of the scale must, and inevitably will, use extraneous means to obtain gratification.

While neither the scale of attractiveness nor the institutionalization of sex are likely to disappear, it is possible that the *particular form of institutionalization* may change. The change may be in the direction of greater sex freedom. Such a change must inevitably affect prostitution, because the greater the proportion of free, mutually pleasurable intercourse, the lesser is the demand for prostitution. This, it seems, is the true explanation of the diminution of prostitution in Soviet Russia.

The conclusion that free intercourse for pleasure and friendship rather than for profit is the greatest enemy of prostitution emerges logically from our statement that a basic trait of prostitution is the use of sex for an ulterior purpose. Should one wish to abolish commercial coitus, one would have to eliminate this trait. This proposition however, is unacceptable to moralists, because, as we saw, the underlying trait of prostitution is also a fundamental feature of reputable sexual institutions, and intercourse for sheer pleasure is as inimical to our sacred institutions as it is to the profane one of mercenary love. Though Lecky's suggestion that harlotry sustains the family is perhaps indefensible, it seems true that prostitution is not so great a danger to the family as complete liberty.

Where the family is strong, there tends to be a well-defined system of prostitution and the social regime is one of status. Women are either part of the family system, or they are definitely not a part of it. In the latter case they are prostitutes, members of a caste set apart. There are few intermediate groups, and there is little mobility. This enables the two opposite types of institutions to function side by side without confusion; they are each staffed by a different personnel, humanly as well as functionally distinct. But where familial controls are weak, the system of prostitution tends to be poorly defined. Not only is it more nearly permissible to satisfy one's desire outside the family, but also it is easier to find a respectable member of society willing to act as partner. This is why a decline of the family and a decline of prostitution are both associated with a rise of sex freedom. Women, released from close family supervision, are freer to seek gratification outside it. The more such women, the easier it is for men to find in intimate relations with them the satisfactions formerly supplied by harlots. This is why the unrestricted indulgence in sex for the fun of it by both sexes is the greatest enemy, not only of the family, but also of prostitution.

Not only in Soviet Russia has pleasurable sex freedom invaded and reduced prostitution, but also in America and England, where "amateur competition" is reputedly ruining the business of street-walkers and call girls. This indicates that independently of communism or capitalism, due to factors more profound than mere economic organization, sex freedom can arise and, having arisen, can contribute to the decline of prostitution. Its rise seems correlated with the growth of individualization in an increasingly complex society where specialization, urbanism, and anonymity prevail—factors which are also inimical to reproductive institutions of the familial type.

But even if present trends continue, there is no likelihood

that sex freedom will ever displace prostitution. Not only will there always be a set of reproductive institutions which place a check upon sexual liberty, a system of social dominance which gives a motive for selling sexual favors, and a scale of attractiveness which creates the need for buying these favors, but prostitution is, in the last analysis, economical. Enabling a small number of women to take care of the needs of a large number of men, it is the most convenient sexual outlet for an army, and for the legions of strangers, perverts, and physically repulsive in our midst. It performs a function, apparently, which no other institution fully performs.

Still another deviant application of the negotiated exchange principle is the commerce in infants. Unmarried mothers give up their babies to "baby brokers," who sell the infants to married couples who want children but are not able to conceive them. No doubt, the bulk of illegitimate infants are placed through legitimate social work agencies, but the commerce in babies is a thriving one; some American baby brokers get infants from as far away as Canada. If it were automobiles that were being allocated in this manner, nobody would argue that social workers could make fairer allocations. But babies are human beings —potentially anyway—and Americans have not been willing to buy and sell human beings since the Emancipation Proclamation of 1863.

SUMMARY

Relentless bargaining, in short, is a technique of adjusting to the potential insecurity involved in negotiated exchange by all-out conformity to this principle. The resulting behavior may be perceived as a social problem because, in the course of relentless bargaining, cherished values may be violated. Three such values have been illustrated in this chapter:

1. The notion that some things should not be exchanged at all. The girl who sells sexual charms or the mother who sells her unwanted baby is permitting the commercial principle of the market place to intrude into relationships where law or custom requires a less calculating attitude.

2. The notion that crucial roles must continue to be played lest society disintegrate. Thus, labor disputes, in which a power struggle determines the terms of exchange regardless of the

disruptive consequences for the rest of society, jeopardize the production and distribution of important goods and services.

3. The notion that "fair" exchange requires approximate equality of bargaining power. When high pressure salesmanship exploits the ignorance of consumers, this seems suspiciously like matching a lion against a mouse. Moreover, although the *motivation* of the relentless negotiation is quite different, it resembles in *behavior* the mode of adjustment to which we turn in the next chapter.

ANNOTATED BIBLIOGRAPHY

Bolles, Blair, *How to Get Rich in Washington* (New York: W. W. Norton & Company, 1952). ([A journalistic account of corruption and favoritism in the Federal government. The author demonstrates through dozens of examples how business firms tempt government officials to bargain in their own behalf rather than in the public interest.

Galbraith, John Kenneth, *The Affluent Society* (Boston: The Houghton Mifflin Company, 1958). ([Chapter 7, "Inequality," is a stimulating discussion of the problem of income distribution, and contains recent data on the distribution of incomes in the United States.

Galbraith, John Kenneth, *American Capitalism; the Concept of Countervailing Power* (Boston: The Houghton Mifflin Company, 1956, rev. ed.). ([An important contribution to understanding of the "bargaining" process, by a stimulating economist, who knows how to write. Galbraith's thesis—that what we have called the bargaining process functions in lieu of "competition" to preserve freedom—is different from the perspective taken in the present text (though not incompatible) and deserves attention from readers interested in pursuing this theme.

Kallet, Arthur, and Schlink, F. J., *100,000,000 Guinea Pigs* (New York: Vanguard Press, 1933). ([A popular and influential book documenting the weakness of consumers—due to technical ignorance—in purchasing goods from manufacturers. Partly as a result of this book, consumer research organizations were established which improve the bargaining power of consumers by increasing their comparative knowledge of product quality.

Key, Jr., V. O., *Politics, Parties, and Pressure Groups* (New York: The Thomas Y. Crowell Company, 1942). ([A leading political scientist's analysis of just what the title indicates: politics, parties, and pressure groups. Key describes with scholarly precision the role of bargaining in American politics.

Warner, W. Lloyd, Haringhurst, Robert J., and Loeb, Martin B., *Who Shall Be Educated?* (New York: Harper & Brothers, 1944). ([A good report on the extent to which educational opportunities are distributed according to class position.

Wilson, H. H., *Congress: Corruption and Compromise* (New York: Rinehart & Company, 1951). ⟨ A well-documented and interestingly
written set of case studies of "corruption and compromise" in Congress by a political scientist. The author also develops a comparison
between Congress and Parliament in his analysis of the reasons for
the corruption he reports.

CHAPTER TWELVE

The refusal to accept defeat:

Rejection of negotiated exchange

In order to bargain successfully, it is necessary to have *something* that other people want: professional training, good looks, money, charm. Those who do not have anything that commands attention in the market place have nothing to negotiate about. They may reject the principle of negotiated exchange and struggle for a place in the sun in some other way. In the United States, stealing is the main "other way" that this mode of adjust-

287

ment takes. (Begging is not as common here as it is in European and Asiatic countries.) The annual total of robberies, ~~burglaries,~~ larcenies, and auto thefts tops the two million mark each year. Most of these crimes are committed by unskilled hoodlums. The predatory motivation, however, is similar for an impulsive holdup and a carefully planned confidence game. The selection to follow reports the *modus operandi* of that highly skilled professional thief, the con-man.[1]

The modern wire store is operated by one regular insideman who poses as a Western Union official, a variable staff of shills, and a staff of several outsidemen or ropers. These ropers travel the country over looking for victims who have money and can be played for the wire. Some ropers depend largely on luck to enable them to find a mark and do very well by this haphazard method; others are more systematic, resorting to advertisements for "business opportunities" inserted in metropolitan newspapers, and carefully interviewing and sifting out the resulting clientele; the most enterprising have agents who locate prospective marks, investigate their financial standing, and compile a list from which the roper can select the fattest and juiciest. There is one restriction which, though it was formerly ignored especially in New York, is now rigidly observed: the mark must not be a resident of the city where he is to be trimmed.

Wherever the roper finds his mark, he knows that each one is an individual problem and that the play must be varied somewhat for each victim. Consequently, in an account of the wire it has seemed best to simplify it in order to present the general principles of the game without confusing the reader by the infinite possible variations in the play.

In order to visualize the wire in operation, let us assume that a roper whom we shall christen Louis Sanborn has been told that one John Bates, owner of a small department store in Providence, is a prospect for the wire. So Mr. Sanborn visits Mr. Bates, represents himself as the agent for a large corporation which is buying up small stores, and gets his victim's confidence.

[1] From *The Big Con* by David W. Maurer, Pocket Book edition, pp. 33–52, copyright 1940; used by special permission of the publishers, The Bobbs-Merrill Company, Inc., Indianapolis, Indiana.

Mr. Bates is pleased to find a buyer for the business because it has not been too profitable. The two spend several days going over the matter. Sanborn blows hot and cold, then finally decides to buy and makes Bates a very generous tentative offer, subject to the final approval of his superiors. Mr. Bates snaps it up. So Mr. Sanborn takes an option on the business and invites Bates down to New York to consummate the deal.

They arrive in New York around noon and take up quarters at the Fairdale. Mr. Sanborn phones his "main office" and reports that their attorneys are occupied with another deal and will not be available until the following day. Then he excuses himself and makes a private call from a phone booth to his insideman, whom we shall call Charley Maxwell.

"I have a businessman from Providence," he says. "What time can we play for him?"

Maxwell consults his appointment book. "How about half past two this afternoon?" he asks.

"Fine," says Sanborn. "We'll be there."

When he returns to the room he finds his victim ready for lunch. They go down to the dining room. There, during luncheon, Sanborn plants the first seeds for the play to come. He casually mentions the fact that his cousin is manager of the central office of the Western Union here in New York.

"On my way up I tried to locate a friend in New London," he explains. "Charley wanted to see him about some kind of deal, but he was out of town."

Luncheon progresses. They talk of the pending sale of Mr. Bates' business. When it is time to depart, Sanborn picks up the check and again brings up his cousin. "We aren't in any hurry," he says, "and Charley's office is just around the corner from here. Would you mind walking around that way with me? I think you'll like Charley."

And Mr. Bates does like cousin Charley, for he has a dignified and attractive personality which puts Bates immediately at his ease. He is one of the best insidemen in New York. When they arrive, he is very busy directing the activities of a staff of telegraphers. In the midst of this wholesome hum and clatter the introduction is made.

"Where are you staying, Louis?" asks Charley.

"Over at the Fairdale," says Louis. "Mr. Bates is here on business with me and he is over there too."

"Why, you're just around the corner," observes Charley. "What about our man in New London? Have you talked to him?"

"Not yet," says Louis. "He was out of town."

Cousin Charley rolls up his sleeves another notch and adjusts his green eyeshade. "I want to talk to you about him later, but I can't entertain you here. The inspectors will be around any minute now and it wouldn't look good to have a couple of strangers loafing in the office. I think you understand the situation. Now you two go on down to the hotel and as soon as inspection is over I'll join you there in the lobby. It won't take long. Good-by."

Little does Mr. Bates suspect that the Western Union office he has just been in is entirely fake, that the energetic whir of teletypes was for his benefit only, that as soon as he left, it ceased entirely, the Western Union sign came down, and that cousin Charley put on his coat and dropped his manner of dignified, conscientious executive. The outward appearances have been so convincing, the stage set with such precision, that it does not occur to him to question its authenticity.

Half an hour later, in street clothes, Charley meets Mr. Bates and Mr. Sanborn in the hotel lobby. "It's all over," he remarks, "and they're gone. Now, Louis, how about Brown? You said that you'd find him and bring him along."

Louis explains that he learned that Brown is out of town for two weeks. He ventures to suggest tentatively that perhaps his friend here, Mr. Bates, could be persuaded to fill in on the deal. Cousin Charley looks somewhat shocked at this suggestion and gives Mr. Bates an appraising look.

"How long have you known this gentleman, Louis?" he asks.

"Not very long," answers Louis, "but long enough to know that he is a responsible man, with his own business in Providence. He is O.K. I feel sure that you can depend on him."

Mr. Bates' very natural discomfort in this situation is quickly allayed by cousin Charley, who turns upon him full force the benign rays of his personality and suggests that they talk the matter over confidentially. Mr. Bates begins to feel that he likes Mr. Maxwell even better than he does Mr. Sanborn. Charley Maxwell already "has his con."

They go up to Sanborn's suite and relax. Mr. Maxwell rises to the occasion and "tells the tale" with such dignified sincerity that even the cynical Mr. Sanborn is touched by his fine acting. He explains to Mr. Bates that he has worked for a heartless corporation for years; that he has had advancement, but never what he had been promised and assured; that the company has neglected him when it should have promoted him, and that he has decided to resign.

We must not assume that Mr. Bates is a fool. He has been about a bit himself, he manages his own business and he flatters himself that he knows a good deal about people. If he ever saw character, there it is in Charley Maxwell. He is not so much touched by the facts which Maxwell has outlined, but by the manner in which they are presented. Instead of a dissatisfied, disgruntled employee, he begins to see before him a man with the makings of a fine executive who has been neglected and wronged.

"And," Mr. Maxwell adds, "I have decided that when I resign, I will not be poor. I know how to swing a deal by which I can make a very good profit without hurting my company in the least. But I must have the assistance of an honest and dependable man, one who is able to put up some funds in return for a share of the profits. Louis' friend, Mr. Brown, was the man I had in mind. Now he cannot be located. I must act quickly, for I may not have the opportunity a second time. Are you interested?"

Mr. Bates is chary. Is Maxwell trying to make a touch? What is this deal? Is it legitimate? How much would he have to invest? And, though he does not say so, the really serious question: *How much is the profit involved?* He stalls for more information.

Mr. Maxwell drops the question of financing and tells him about the deal. He explains that through his central office pass the race results for all the bookmakers in the city, that the horse-poolrooms are growing fat on the profits from gambling on races, that rich men with inside information can win through the bookmakers, but that the poor fellow with only a form-sheet to guide him always loses more than he makes. He says that he has worked out a system whereby he can beat the bookmakers at their own game by delaying the results long enough to phone them to his assistants who are to be stationed next door to the poolroom and who will bet on the races after they are run. Then the results will be released, and of course their bets will pay a very neat profit. And no one will suffer but the rich and dishonest bookmakers.

Once the mark has gone this far, he seldom backs out. If he does, further pressure may be put on him or he may be dropped altogether. But we will assume that Maxwell's smooth voice and sincere manner have had their effect. Bates likes the proposition and sees in it a high profit with no risk. It is a sure thing.

"Now," says Mr. Maxwell, aside to Mr. Bates, "Louis doesn't understand much about this business and I will count on you to take the responsibility of seeing that everything goes all right. You and he go on down to this address on 48th Street and look the place over. Then go into the drugstore next door and wait for a call from me at three sharp. I'll give you the name of the winner and hold up the results just long enough for you to go next door and place your bet. I can't hold them for more than three or four minutes. That way we can see whether or not our system will work, and of course you and Louis can keep anything you win for yourselves. If it works out, we will want to try something bigger."

Mr. Bates and Louis follow the instructions they have received. They visit the poolroom and find there all the paraphernalia that go with a booking establishment. Races are chalked on the blackboard. The ticker is thrumming merrily. Prosperous gentlemen are winning and losing large bets nonchalantly. The caller calls the races with great zest. Bets of $10,000 to $20,000 are laid casually. Very large amounts of cash are changing hands like nickels in a crap game. Everywhere there is cash. The patrons peel off large bets from fat bank rolls or from bulging wallets. The cashier counts out $40,000 winnings without batting an eye. Louis and Mr. Bates are much impressed. A little of the fever of that atmosphere has worked its way into Mr. Bates' blood.

Three o'clock approaches. They return to the drugstore. Maxwell gives them, shall we say, Seabiscuit as winner. They hasten back and plunge into the thick and throbbing atmosphere. Both Mr. Bates and Louis put a ten-dollar bill on Seabiscuit to win. Mr. Bates feels a queer sensation of mingled guilt and triumph. It is a wonderful feeling to bet on a sure thing, even for ten dollars. They have hardly placed their bets when the caller says the magic words, "They're off!" Then he calls the race. Seabiscuit wins, at 4–1. Our pair of innocents collect fifty dollars each. The larceny in Mr. Bates' veins begins to percolate. He can already see a fortune stretching out ahead of him. Why, there is no limit—except the resources of the bookmaker—to what one could make out of this thing. And there are thousands of bookmakers.

They look about them while they await the next race. The same air of dignified, restrained feverishness prevails. No one seems to notice them. Mr. Bates looks the crowd over. It is not large, but it is sporty. Brokers with pasty faces. Sportsmen, tanned and casual. A financier with a Vandyke and highly tailored clothes. The thick blue haze wherein mingle the thin silver streams from a dozen fine cigars. They are betting, joking, absorbed in themselves.

Mr. Bates is a little taken aback at the nonchalant way in which these men handle money. He likes it, and would like to feel that he is a part of it. But he knows that he isn't. He turns to his friend Sanborn. The next race is coming up. They retire to the 'phone for more information. Then they bet fifty dollars each on War Admiral to win at 4–1. He does.

This nets them $250 apiece. "I think I'll shoot the works on the next race," says Mr. Bates. Sanborn counsels caution. After all, this thing is just starting. This is only an experiment to see if their plan will work. Charley knows what he is about, and perhaps they had better do as he says and place only small bets. But Mr. Bates is hooked. He returns to the telephone, awaits a horse, and comes back with the firm intention of placing the

$250 on his nose. Louis cautiously refrains from betting this time.

Mr. Bates hurries to the window to place his bet. He has the $250 in his pocket, ready to be laid. But there are several men just ahead of him. They are laying down very big bets. He cannot help noticing the fat, sleek piles of fives, tens, twenties, fifties and hundreds in the cashier's drawer. He sees the piles of bills on the shelf behind the cashier. He sees the deft hands swiftly paying out and taking in thousands of dollars. He grows impatient. Time is short. The race will be called any moment now. He pushes the line along, but it doesn't seem to move fast enough. He shifts his weight from one foot to the other and peers ahead. Only one man, now. Laying a fifteen thousand dollar bet. Will he never get that money counted down? The man moves casually away, biting the end off a heavy cigar. Mr. Bates removes the wadded bills from his pocket. Challedon. Charley said Challedon to win.

"They're off!" shouts the caller.

Mr. Bates stands there, futilely fingering his money. Betting is closed. Challedon. . . . Where is Challedon? He lags to the rear. He is under wraps. The caller reads off the ticker with such animation that he might as well have been an eyewitness. Will Challedon never make his move? Here it is. They enter the stretch with Challedon moving up. He is booted home a winner. And 6–1. Mr. Bates does a little sketchy mental arithmetic and wonders why he wasn't just one ahead in the line at the window.

He doesn't know it, but he has been given the "shut-out" or the "prat-out," a clever method of stepping up the larceny in the veins of a mark when the manager feels that he is not entering into the play enthusiastically enough. It may be repeated several times so that the mark is fully impressed with what he has missed. The shills who surround the mark at the window usually play for more than the mark is being played for; if the mark is being played for $25,000, the air is full of $50,000 bets; thus the mark always feels like a piker instead of a plunger. Furthermore, ambitious marks must not be allowed to get too much of the store's cash into their pockets.

Mr. Bates returns to Louis. "Tough luck," says Louis.

A suave-looking gentleman approaches them. He is quiet, polite, but authoritative. And just a little condescending. Mr. Bates doesn't know just why, but he feels embarrassed.

"Are you the gentlemen who have been placing these small bets?" he asks, waving a pair of slips.

"We just made a fifty-dollar bet, if you call that small," says Louis.

The manager looks at them with patronizing good nature. "Well, I'll have to ask you not to place any more small bets here," he says. "We have other poolrooms for working men. Small bets make too much bookkeeping for us." He smiles and gently starts them toward the door. Mr. Bates feels patronized. He doesn't like it.

"How much does a man have to bet here?" asks Louis.

"A thousand dollars is usually the lower limit," answers the manager, smiling. "Beyond that, you can go as high as you like. Come back, gentlemen, some other time."

As they pass the doorman, they see Maxwell coming down the street. "Did it work?" asks cousin Charley. "If it did, we can all make a fortune."

"We won a couple of hundred dollars apiece on two bets," volunteers Louis. "But we never got any further. They called us pikers because we didn't bet high enough."

"Never mind that, my boy," answers Charley. "When the time comes we will arrange to bet high enough to suit them. Let's go over to the hotel. I want to discuss this thing further with you in private."

Up in the suite at the Fairdale Mr. Bates hears what he wants to hear.

"This particular poolroom," says cousin Charley, "is the one that I have marked to work on. I know that they have very extensive financial backing. Their volume of business must be tremendous."

Mr. Bates, with a mind full of greenbacks, reflects that it certainly must be.

"They can lose a million and never miss it," continues Charley. "My plan is to take eight or nine hundred thousand in four or five days, then quit. What do you gentlemen say?"

Mr. Bates and Louis agree that it would indeed be a desirable course of action.

"But we have to have cash to finance it," says Charley. "That is why I was so concerned about Brown. He could dig up the cash we need. Let's see, I believe you were thinking that you might raise some for us?"

"How much would you need?" asks Mr. Bates, fearful of appearing too anxious.

"Do you think you would be willing to finance it?" asks Charley. "After all, you know, I haven't much except my salary and Louis here is just getting a start. How much can you raise?"

Mr. Bates studies. He figures on an envelope. His mind is a whirl of mortgages, real estate, government bonds. It may take a couple of weeks to sell his business. Bonds would be the quickest. Government bonds.

"I think I could pick up twenty-five thousand within the next couple of days. Or maybe sooner," he adds, mindful of the potential Mr. Brown. "Is your friend definitely out?"

Mr. Maxwell is very cool and practical. "I hate to let Brown down," he muses. "But I think this arrangement will be fine. How much did you say you could raise? Twenty-five thousand? How is this money? In cash?"

"No, no," says Mr. Bates, "in bonds. Government bonds. I'll have to have my banker sell them and forward me a draft for the proceeds."

"That would be fine," says Charley.

"Now," says Mr. Bates, "how do you intend to split the profits? I would want to pay you whatever is right, but if I put up the money, I ought to get a good share of the profits. Otherwise it wouldn't pay me to get into it."

Mr. Bates suddenly feels important. All he needs is the information. He has the cash. That is the important thing. These men can be paid off at his own price if he finances it now, quickly, before someone else is cut in.

"I have thought that over," says cousin Charley. "Since the plan is mine, I think I ought to have at least fifty per cent. And we should cut Louis in for about twenty per cent for his cooperation. That would leave you thirty per cent which would make you a very good return on your investment."

Mr. Bates doesn't like that arrangement. He wants to cut those men out of all he can. Of course they must have something, but why let Louis in on it at all? And Maxwell. Why, he would go to prison if this thing ever became known. He schemes and argues. As they dicker, Maxwell humors him by working out a compromise whereby he and Bates will split ninety per cent of the profit, and Louis will get the remaining ten. Mr. Bates still feels that they have been too generous with Louis. He moves immediately to phone his banker in Providence. But Maxwell interposes.

"This deal must be kept absolutely secret," he argues. "If you phone in for money in a hurry, your banker may become suspicious. You know how bankers are. He may feel that you are making a mistake to dump a block of bonds like that on the market right now. It will be a little more expensive, but much safer if you catch a train out of here this afternoon and talk to your banker personally tomorrow. Explain that you are buying some real estate here in the city and want to pay down that much cash."

"But," interposes Bates, turning to Louis, "what about that appointment with your lawyers?"

"Don't worry about that," says Louis. "I'll take care of everything for you. Just send me a telegram as soon as you know when you'll be back and I'll fix things up at the office."

"That's right," says Charley. "And you'd better add a note in that telegram which will let me know how much money you are bringing. But we don't want anyone to suspect you are bringing it. So let a thousand dollars equal, say, one 'bushel.' Then you can say, 'Bringing twenty-five bushels' and I'll know you are prepared to go right ahead with the deal."

This stage of the game is known as "the send." It is a strange fact that, once a good insideman "tightens up" a mark, he can be sent anywhere for his money and will usually return despite all obstacles. For example, during the week of July 3, 1939, the metropolitan papers carried stories on the case of Mr. Leonard

B. Reel, a public accountant of Beach Haven, New Jersey, who, with his wife, was put on the send from Mexico City. The couple flew to Philadelphia and brought back $74,000 which they lost on the rag to the Velvet Kid. They reported that they made the trip with some difficulty, having been forced down en route by storms four different times. If the con men think that they can get away with using the mails, they may not use "the send."

Mr. Bates agrees that it will be best to make the trip. There must be no slips. For a moment he fears what might happen if this scheme came to light. Then he remembers that he is only financing it. He feels better. Also, the $250 in his wallet will more than cover his expenses on the trip home. Mr. Bates watches his pennies. But on the other hand, is it safe to leave the deal open here? Suppose Brown—or someone else—turned up with the ready cash?

"You have decided definitely that I am to finance it?" he asks.

"Yes, indeed," says Charley. "Here is my hand on it. We'll shake hands all the way around. That swears us all to keep this deal absolutely secret."

They all shake hands, though having Louis cut in on the deal still sticks in Bates' crop. After all ten per cent isn't much, and Louis still holds the key to the sale of his store. Well, he'll get that ten per cent back and more when Louis' company takes up that option.

Three days later he is back in New York with a draft for $25,000. He is at a high pitch of excitement. This business turns over a profit quicker than anything he has ever seen. And he gets a strange sense of elation—the same feeling, magnified a thousand times, that he felt when he had that first ten dollars on Seabiscuit and watched him romp home. He has a sure thing.

Maxwell takes him to a bank which has been fixed. Mr. John Bates endorses the check, and now has $25,000 in cash. It burns holes in his pockets.

"This afternoon I think we can work," says Charley. "I'll find out what the best odds are, you stay near the 'phone booth, and I'll tell you what to bet just before each race. I'll get any last-minute change in odds as they come through over the wire, and we'll take all that into consideration. We'll work the same as we did the other day. Now hold on tight to that money." Then he goes back to directing the destinies of a minor province in the great empire of the Western Union.

The next few hours are critical ones for the con men. Between now and post-time the mark is most likely to have a "brain-blow" and lose his head. Marks have been known to go to the police with the whole story right at this point, and a "wrong" copper might lay a trap for the con men and get the mark to co-operate. Or the mark might worry about so large a gamble and look up some friend or acquaintance to consult about the matter; of course any of these might tip the whole thing off. Occasionally the victim insists on seeking the advice of his wife, in which case wiser con mobs encourage such a move, for they have learned that such a consultation usually works in their favor. Some marks simply get cold feet at the last moment and go on about their business, or return home.

So a "tailer" is put on Mr. Bates during all the time that he is not with either of the con men. The tailer, a man of ample experience in such matters, can tell immediately by the mark's actions how he is getting along. If he consults the police, the tailer reports back immediately and the con men may simply not see him any more, or they may phone him and tell him that the Western Union has become suspicious and that the deal must be postponed. However, if he has consulted a "right" copper or detective, the con men know that they are safe, for they can pay their way as soon as the score comes off. They go right ahead and play for him knowing that the police will not "knock" him or tip him off to what is happening. If it seems necessary, the insideman himself or his fixer will go down and have a chat with the officer in order to be sure there will be no slips. Meanwhile, Mr. Bates, if he has had any traffic with police, feels better in the knowledge that the officers of the law are not suspicious of the men with whom he is dealing or of the deal (if he lets that out) which he is contemplating.

Meanwhile, Louis stalls the victim along with the pending sale of his store, which, during the play, fades into the background. Some marks become so feverish that, during the period

of the tie-up, they apparently forget all about the original reason for their coming to the city where the big store is located,
or resent the roper's attempts to continue negotiations for the
business while this big deal is in the air.

Post-time finds Mr. Bates and Louis haunting the phone
booth, awaiting the call which will come sometime during the
afternoon. Bates hugs his $25,000. Louis handles his quarry
skillfully, knowing just how to arouse his anticipations and how
far to go in quieting the doubts which may be troubling his
mind.

At last the phone jangles. Mr. Bates rushes into the booth.
It is Maxwell.

"Hello," he says, "is that you Louis?"

"No, this is John Bates."

"Well, I've got the winner. Hurry right on over and place
the money on Flying Lill. Call Louis to the phone, will you?"

Louis talks briefly to Charley. "O.K.," he says. "I understand. Place it all on Flying Lill. Good-by, Charley."

They hurry over to the poolroom and plunge into the atmosphere of synthetic excitement. There on the odds-board is Flying
Lill, 5–1. Mr. Bates feels a momentary sinking in the pit of his
stomach. His mouth is dry and his hands tremble. Louis takes
the bills from his hands and pushes them through the cashier's
window. "Flying Lill to win," he says. "Twenty-five thousand."

The cashier gives him his slip and begins to count the money.
"They're off!" calls the announcer, and the next two minutes are
hectic ones. It is Unerring by a length. Flying Lill second. Lady
Maryland third.

Mr. Bates is stunned. *Unerring won.*

"Wait a minute," says Louis, "there must be something
wrong. It isn't official yet." He looks with mingled sympathy and
anxiety into Mr. Bates' ashen face.

But it is official. The announcement cuts through the smoke
and clatter like a great somber gong. It is official.

"We've lost," says Louis, and they go out into the street.

It may occur to Mr. Bates that he has been betrayed. His
mind is probably such a chaos that he cannot think at all. He
may break into sobs immediately, and wildly tear his hair. But

we will assume that he is a gentleman and that he restrains his emotions and reserves his judgments until he learns what has happened. Louis has already solicitously begun the "cooling-out" process which will pave the way for Maxwell's smooth patter.

They meet Charley, who can only partly conceal his jubilation, a short distance from the Western Union office. He is talking in terms of winning $125,000. Mr. Bates tells him that Louis bet the horse to win, but that it placed and they lost. Charley turns on Louis in a fury. "Don't you know what the word *place* means?" he roars. Louis tries to justify his mistake on the basis of their misunderstanding of the word *place*. But Maxwell will have none of it. He rakes that young man over the coals until he hangs his head in red-faced shame and humiliation. Mr. Bates is very likely to come to Louis' defense, on the grounds that he, too, misunderstood. Then Mr. Maxwell turns on him and gives him also a piece of his mind. But finally he cools off.

"Well," he says, "we'll never make that mistake again." Then he takes Mr. Bates in hand in such a way that the "cooling-out" process is perfect and Mr. Bates lives only until he can raise enough money to give the plan a second trial. When Charley Maxwell cools a mark out, he stays cooled out. And if he has decided that the mark is good for another play—as about fifty per cent of them are—he will "feel him out" to see whether or not he can raise more cash; some marks have been beaten four or five times on the same racket. If he knows he has been swindled, or if he cannot raise any more money, he is "blown off" and disposed of as quietly as possible. Let us assume that Mr. Bates, being the perfect mark, is good for another play. Mr. Maxwell retains his confidence to such an uncanny extent that he will do almost anything he is told to do. So he is "put on the send" again for $20,000, which he borrows, using real estate as collateral.

The second play takes up just where the first left off. The only delay is caused by obtaining Mr. Bates' money. Louis knows how to handle the deal regarding Mr. Bates' business and assures him that everything is going along fine, but that his corporation is going to investigate the department store further before they sign the final papers. Usually, if the mark is good for a second play, he is by this time so wrapped up in the wire that he has practically dropped the legitimate deal. Some con mobs will send a tailer along home with the mark to see if he consults the police before returning. The tailer may pose as an agent for the corporation which is interested in the mark's business.

The big store, the boost, and all the necessary stage-settings are again called into play. When the time comes to make the big bet, the sting is put in a little differently. Over the phone Mr. Maxwell gives the mark Johnny J. at 6–1 to win. Mr. Bates and Louis bet the $20,000, making sure that there is no misunderstanding this time regarding that tricky word *place*. The betting is heavy all around them, though Mr. Bates does not realize that those bank rolls have seen much service as props. The $50,000 in cold cash laid down by the better just ahead of him is real money; it makes an impression.

"They're off!" says the caller. The room quiets. The smoke drifts in swirls. The gamblers listen with polite eagerness. It is Johnny J. by a neck.

Mr. Bates feels a great exhilaration; his fingers and toes tingle; a warm wave of relief sweeps over him. His horse has won $140,000. Now to take his share and build it up into a fortune.

"Let's cash it right away," urges Louis, "before something happens to it."

Mr. Bates waves the ticket before the impassive cashier, who is imperturbably stacking big bills; Mr. Bates has never seen so much loose cash. It is everywhere. The cashier looks at him with polite indifference.

"Cash this, cash this, please," says Mr. Bates, pushing the ticket under the grating.

"Just a minute, sir," says the cashier. "I'm sorry, but those results are not yet official. Wait just a minute."

"Flash!" says the caller. "Flash! A mistake in colors. It was Silverette by a neck, Johnny J. second, Technician is third. This is official."

Mr. Bates vaguely hears a man beside him say to his friend, "I'm very glad that horse disqualified. I had $7,000 on Silverette."

"I'm not," says his friend. "That damned Johnny J. cost me just twenty thousand. . . ."

Mr. Bates is dazed. He remonstrates with the manager. He cries and curses his luck. He suspects that he has been swindled but doesn't know how. The manager is polite, firm and impersonal. The heavy play goes right on for the next race. Louis, crying and complaining as if it were his $20,000 which went glimmering, leads him out into the street. The outside air only intensifies the terrible feeling of loss and despair in Mr. Bates' heart. To him money is a sacred thing. This is terrible.

Outside on the street they meet Charley. He looks tired and worried. He is nervous and distraught. He listens absently to the tale of woe. "Yes, that is terrible," he agrees. "But right now I am in terrible trouble myself. The Western Union detectives have been investigating the delay in race results and I'll be lucky if I only lose my job. If they pin anything on me, I'll go to prison. Maybe all three of us."

Mr. Bates hasn't thought of this angle since Charley first explained the deal to him. Fear now adds its agony to despair. They talk over the possibilities of arrest. Maxwell advises that Bates and Louis leave town as quickly and quietly as possible. They return to the hotel. Louis obligingly gets the time for the next train to Providence. It leaves at 10:00 P.M. Mr. Bates, worried, nervous, broken, agrees to take it. Charley promises that, if this thing blows over, he himself will raise enough money to play the game again and will give Mr. Bates all his money back, and some profit to boot. Then he leaves, so that he may not be picked up. Louis draws Mr. Bates aside.

"How much money do you have?" he asks.

Mr. Bates looks in his wallet. "Less than fifty dollars," he answers. "And I have to pay my hotel bill."

"Well," offers Louis, "I have nearly a hundred and fifty. You have had a bad break and I hate to see you stranded. You have been a fine sport to take it the way you do. Here, let me lend you seventy-five to get home on. You can pay it back any time. And remember," he adds, "our auditors will be at your place next week. Then I'll have everything in good shape at this end and we'll close the deal."

Mr. Bates takes the money which is pressed on him. He is surprised. Louis is a pretty nice fellow after all. He is ashamed of the way he has felt about him recently. Still in a daze, he shakes the proffered hand and Louis departs. "I'll be back about nine-thirty," he says, "to see that you get to the train safely. Wait for me in the lobby."

From now on, it is up to a local tailer to keep close tab on Mr. Bates to see what he may do, reporting any tendency he may show to consult the police. Mr. Maxwell may have him paged to the telephone and continue the cooling process by phone. The tailer watches closely; if, after this conversation Mr. Bates consults the house detective or a detective he has stationed in the lobby, the tailer reports immediately to Maxwell, who puts the machinery of the fix into operation. Or, Louis may deliberately delay his arrival at the hotel to see his victim off. As the time for departure approaches and Louis fails to appear, Mr. Bates may get nervous and make a phone call to the police, or consult a detective already stationed in the hotel. The tailer can predict the mark's reactions with a good deal of accuracy, for he has had ample opportunity to study at first hand the psychology of the trimmed mark.

Just before ten, at the tailer's signal, Louis appears with a good excuse for lateness, bundles Mr. Bates carefully into a cab, hurries him to the station, buys his ticket for Providence, and puts him on the train. He waits solicitously until the train pulls out.

As soon as the mark is safely on his way, Mr. Maxwell meets his roper, the manager and the boost at the hangout. He is a meticulous bookkeeper. He gives each one a plain envelope containing his share of the score, and drops a word about an appointment for eleven-thirty on Wednesday. And so the big store goes on.

In one sense, the con-man has not completely abandoned negotiated exchange. He pretends to be a negotiator, albeit a poor one. Certainly, the mark (victim) thinks of himself as a hard bargainer. It is only later that he realizes he gave something for nothing. Part of the reason victims of con-men often do not lodge complaints with the police is that they are ashamed to be outwitted in bargaining. Con-men have a proverb, "You can't cheat an honest man." The armed robber, on the other hand, has broken with the negotiated exchange principle completely. He does not even *pretend* to give something for what he takes. As shown in the following description of the holdup—written by a professional armed robber during the enforced leisure of a prison sentence—there is little room for negotiation during a properly planned "heist." [2]

The holdup was a relatively rare form of crime forty or fifty years ago, though well publicized even then. Nowadays it is the most common form of serious crime. It would be interesting to know the reasons for this sudden rise in popularity. No doubt the ever-increasing complexity of our way of life has had something to do with it. Psychologists declare that excessive discipline is likely to result in impulses of cruelty and destruction, and it seems probable that the innumerable social pressures to which the individual is subjected in our society give rise to aggressive feelings ultimately requiring outlets—certainly our preoccupation with bloodthirsty comics, movies, radio programs, and mystery and detective fiction is not accidental. And certainly the stickup is an aggressive action of classic directness and simplicity.

Such an explanation may account in part for the innumerable holdups of drug stores and filling stations, the frequent heists pulled with glass pistols, cap pistols, water pistols, air guns; the haberdasheries and cigar stores stuck up as Jesse James might have stuck up banks; the sadistic little jobs whose main purpose seems to be maltreatment of the victims: the Lovers Lane holdups, the cab-drivers robbed of fares and tips. Such holdups undoubtedly have a large emotional, or neurotic, component. Obviously, the motivation is not a rational weighing of risks against possible gain, for banks might be robbed almost as cheaply—not that bank robbery is lightly punished, but that we punish robbery of any type more severely than several varieties of murder (in some states by death), a lesson in applied Chris-

[2] From "The Heist: the Theory and Practice of Armed Robbery" by Everett DeBaun from the February, 1950, issue of *Harper's Magazine,* pp. 69–77. Copyright 1950, by Harper & Brothers, New York. Reprinted by permission of Harper & Brothers.

tianity as pointed, in its way, as our custom of requisitioning
lives though not money in time of war, or the size of the vote
polled by Norman Thomas.

There are more tangible reasons for the emergence of the
holdup as a *professional* technique, though here too emotional
and social factors of course are present. Technological change
occurs in the underworld, as elsewhere. During the past few
generations several ancient and dishonorable professions have
given way to others better suited to the times. In comparison
with the burgeoning of the holdup, the decline of the box-busting
racket is a case in point. Forty or fifty years ago, the safe-cracker
was considered the prince of thieves. Though the best of the
modern boxmen can open modern safes as efficiently as the
petermen of half a century ago could open those of that day, the
profession is fast on the down-grade. Cash simply is not kept
in safes as it was. For the most part, business is carried on by
check, and checks are worthless as loot. Similarly, securities are
now seldom readily negotiable, stamps are giving way to postage
meters, jewelry is a drug on the market—"slum," as it is familiarly called, brings but from 15 to 20 per cent of the replacement value at fence, while silver is hardly worth carrying off,
and watches can be disposed of for no more than a portion of the
value of the metal in the cases. Furthermore, that infallible
source of cash in large amounts, the bank, is no longer vulnerable to the safe-cracker, thanks chiefly to the time lock, a device
which may be set to jam the bolt mechanism for a period during
which a vault may not be opened even by some one possessing
the combination. Consequently, the Max Shinburnes, Leonidas
Leslies, Chauncy Johnsons, Adam Worths, Bob Scotts, and
Jimmy Hopes who during the last quarter of the past century
burglarized banks of sums said to total close to a hundred million dollars—a number of the individual "scores" were for more
than a million—have gone the way of the horse and buggy.
Their present-day counterparts are top-grade holdup-men—
"heist-men" in the underworld argot. . . .

A seventeenth-century cookbook advises those who would
prepare jugged hare first to catch their hare. To pull a heist, first
find your "mark." A mark may be any considerable sum of

money or the equivalent in readily convertible swag. Professional heist-men judge marks in terms of the probable cash return relative to the risks involved.

Marks are either dug up or tipped off. When a heist-man says that he has dug one up, he means that he has found it himself. He may have sought it out, tailing ladies who appear in public festooned like Christmas trees with jewels, or armored cars making deliveries of payrolls, for instance. Or he may just have stumbled upon it, like one who was introduced by a casual resort acquaintance into a private poker game in which some $12,000 was in play, or another who noticed that the proprietor of a saloon where he occasionally stopped for a beer made a practice of cashing pay-checks for employees of a nearby refinery. Marks that have been tipped off are those that have been pointed out by others. One who tips off marks is called a fingerman or tipster; he may or may not be of the underworld. Sometimes pickpockets, gamblers, and other footloose grifters tip marks off to heist-men as a side-line. The standard remuneration for this service is 10 per cent of the gross score. A surprisingly large number of marks are tipped off by legit, or ostensibly honest, people, and no few are put up (whence, incidentally, the colloquial expression "put-up job") or prearranged: a truck driver would like a share of the value of the load of cigarettes or whiskey he will be carrying; a jeweler wants to beat his insurance company; a bank manager wishes to cover his embezzlements. As the police are well aware of this, many heist-men fight shy of such tips, for the legit citizen, having odd notions of honor by the thief's standards, is likely to break down under close questioning, and promises of immunity for himself, and finger his partners as thoroughly as he formerly fingered the mark.

Other things being equal, the cash mark is always preferable. There is nothing like a bank for cold cash in large amounts, and until recently the "jug" was beyond argument the best type of mark by professional criteria. It is true that for many years banks of any size have had what looks to be formidable protection, but in robbery as in warfare of other types the aggressor has a heavy advantage. Armed guards, vaults with walls of steel

and concrete several feet in thickness, and elaborate alarm systems did not prevent heist-mobs from knocking over an average
of about two banks a day during the early thirties. In 1934, however, Congress passed an act making bank robbery a federal
offense and bringing it under the jurisdiction of the FBI, a police
organization having almost unlimited funds and unique facilities,
the most important of these being a corps of stool-pigeons probably as extensive as any outside Russia. Simultaneously, the flat
twenty-five-year sentence for bank robbery became mandatory,
and the government established a special prison for "jug-heists"
(the species populates Alcatraz almost 100 per cent), operated
on principles that would turn the stomach of a Turk. These additional risks require that others be at a minimum if a bank is to
be marked nowadays, and the same is true of the mails. . . .

Given a mark, the next step is mobbing up, or getting together the men who will work the job. A working unit of underworld professionals of any type is called a mob. There are
"single-o" heist-men, such as the one known in the papers as
Slick Willie, who has robbed large and well-protected banks
single-handed, but the vast majority of the brotherhood work
in mobs. A heist-mob may comprise from two to six or eight
members—the type of mark is usually the determining factor.
Thus, the "same" mob—*i.e.,* several of a group of stickup-men
who sometimes work together—may be five-handed for a jug-
heist and three-handed for a payroll job. There are excellent
reasons why the mob is generally of the minimum size compatible with efficient operation. One is selfish: "The smaller the
mob, the bigger the cut." The other is protective: each additional
member adds to the risk of a fall, paradoxical as this may seem.
The answer is that the professional runs little danger of falling
either *en flagrante* or, despite the highly imaginative information
ladled out for popular consumption along this line, as a result
of acute detective work. Almost always he is caught because
of information given to police.

Eddie suddenly squares his debts and springs with a new car,
for instance, or begins shooting high craps and buying drinks
for the house, or buys a fur coat for Marge, who cannot resist
throwing the needles to that catty Doris, who puts two and two

together and confides the result to Nettie, whose husband Louie peddles dope or does a bit of pimping or wants to get City Hall's okay to book numbers or horses in his cigar store. In every city, police permit numerous Louies to operate in consideration for periodical cash donations, plus just such favors as the one Louie is now in a position to confer. If Eddie cannot stand up under the beatings he will now undergo as a matter of police routine, or if Marge knows who his partners are and can be talked or frightened into trading the information for a lighter sentence for him, the whole mob may fall.

Popular notions notwithstanding, the basic units of a heist-mob are not a "mastermind" and some servile morons who carry out his orders. As a matter of fact, among "heavy" thieves no one gives orders for the good reason that no one takes them— the heavy is as independent a character as walks the earth. Within the mob, equality reigns. All share equally in risk and gain. All have equal authority. This is not to imply that the members of a mob simply behave as they please on the job. There a rather rigid discipline prevails, but all have had a voice in the plan being carried out and authority has been delegated willingly.

The true essentials of a heist-mob are a wheel-man and a rod-man. The former is a skilled driver, often a specialist who takes no other part (this is preferred practice). Yet if the mob is short-handed or somewhat slipshod in operation he may work the inside with the others. The rod-man's title is self-explanatory. A rod is a gun. Since most holdups involve the close control of a number of people during the course of the actual robbery, most mobs have two or more gun-wielding members. In special cases, a mob may use a man on the outside in addition to the man on the wheel. For example, the getaway route for a job located in the business section of a city may begin with a run down a narrow alley or a one-way street, in which case a tail, a car or truck which cuts in behind the getaway car and blocks the way long enough for the former to get a sufficient jump, may be used. But the great majority of heist-mobs work with a single man on the wheel and either two or three on the inside.

A mob forms rather casually. Eddie, let us say, has a promising mark. He decides that it can "go" three-handed. Thinking over the experienced men of his acquaintance who are out for action he fixes on Big Pete. His choice is based upon several considerations. Pete has a rep as a good man, which means that he is known to be trustworthy, dependable, and resourceful. When he makes a meet, or engagement, he keeps it. He has plenty of belly, or courage. He has shown that he is a sticker who will not panic and leave the others to shift for themselves in the event of trouble, and he has repeatedly stood up, or kept his mouth shut, under police questioning—American police question prisoners; only foreigners torture them. Furthermore, he will not burn, or cheat, his partners; he does not flash, or make a show of his money; and he has an air of calm authority which is valuable on the job: he can control a whole roomful of people without frightening them so that someone may do something foolish.

Eddie and Pete talk the job over—"cut it up," they say. If a tip is involved, Eddie lets Pete know that there will be a tipster's end (10 per cent) to come off the top, or before any deductions have been made, but without telling him who the tipster is, just as he will not tell the latter who will work the job, for by his code anyone who deals with him is entitled to full protection, and he considers them bound by the same standard. Other details are discussed. Yes, between them, the two can handle the inside without trouble. Probably they could handle the whole thing, but to be on the safe side they had better have a man on the wheel.

Since the mark is Eddie's, he is boss in this respect. He "owns" the job; it is therefore his right to select those who are to participate. Anyone who does not wish to work with any of the others may pull out, or withdraw. If one who pulls out should thereupon get his own mob together and take the job, Eddie would feel morally justified in shooting him, though if another mob working independently happened to beat Eddie to the job he would not consider himself wronged. If something happened to prevent him from taking part in the touch and Pete filled in another man and took it, Eddie would be entitled to half an end, or share, even though he was in prison when the job came off.

In this case, there is no trouble in filling the mob. Both Eddie and Pete are friendly with Bangs, so called from his habit of causing his car to backfire during chases to the end of instilling a proper caution in amateur pursuers, who seldom require much encouragement to imagine they are being shot at. One of them looks him up and inquires casually if he wants "a little action on the wheel." Bangs asks questions: what kind of action? what's in it? who is working? If the answers, which are given in general terms, are to his liking, he says, "Okay, I'm in," and the mob is complete. Only then is he given specific details.

The detailed planning and preparation which constitutes the next stage is the most important part of the heist. If this layout is done well, the mark is in the bag. The robbery itself becomes a simple transaction lasting but a few moments—sometimes less than thirty seconds.

Professionals agree that casing is far and away the most important part of laying out a heist. This word, which like many others of underworld origin is coming into popular use, is from the argot of faro, once as popular a betting game as craps is today. It originally referred to a record of the cards played as kept on an abacus-like contraption called a "case." As used in the underworld, the word means gathering information from observation.

Even when the tip includes detailed information, a good mob cases its marks with care. Tipsters often err. One mob, whose tipster worked in the place to be taken, was furnished with a layout-chart so complete that they did not bother casing the inside, to their subsequent sorrow, for the tipster had neglected to indicate that the partitions setting off the office they were to rob did not extend to the ceiling, and police were waiting for them when they came out.

Several matters are cased with particular care. The size of the score is checked in advance whenever possible—tipsters are likely to be very optimistic about the size of a prospective touch. If the mark is a bank, checking may involve little more than a glance at the quarterly statement, available at the local library or Chamber of Commerce, and the size of payrolls may be estimated satisfactorily from the number of employees, but most other kinds of mark are difficult to case accurately for size. A knowledge of the floor plan, arrangement of furniture, placement of doors and windows, and so forth, is essential to a fast, smooth piece of work.

On the theory that it helps to know where trouble is likely to come from, some heist-men like to get an advance look at the people on the inside as well. Impressionable young squirts who attend the movies too often and an occasional old towser who has had his job for thirty years—"heroes," the heist-man calls them sardonically—may, if not closely watched, rise in defense of the insurance company's stockholders, especially if women or big bosses are present. It is always well to know how many women must be dealt with, since they are an occupational hazard of the first order which I will describe later on. Armed guards are of course cased with care, though unless ensconced in a protective cage or turret they represent a threat more apparent than real, since they cannot go about with cocked pistols. A well-executed job takes so little time that alarm systems call for little or no attention, unless the mark is a bank. Bank heists usually take several minutes.

Sometimes ingenuity is required to case a job without attracting attention. Unless there is heavy pedestrian traffic, outside casing is usually done from a car or the window of a nearby building. Various ruses are resorted to in casing the inside, the commonest being the pose of having business to transact. This can be excellent vocational training—at least, it proved to be in the case of Keister (Suitcase) John, an old-timer who came by his moniker in honor of a battered salesman's case full of janitor supplies which he used as a prop, religiously charging off the full original cost of the outfit, some forty dollars, against the nut, or expense, of every job he worked. A time came when jokes about his "ten grand" suitcase circulating in the hangouts came to the ears of police, and John went to stir. There he came to the conclusion that he was becoming too old and too well-known to continue in his wicked ways, so upon release he set up in the building maintenance business, in which he prospered.

Generally speaking, casing is the job of the inside-men. The wheel-man has work of his own. The procurement of the getaway car is one of his responsibilities. There are many car-thieves who will deliver to specifications of year and make for moderate fee, but heist-men seldom patronize them for reasons of security. The simple job of stealing a car may be considerably complicated by the wheel-man's personal predilections. Most of them have strong convictions concerning various makes of car for this particular kind of service. Certain makes, widely known as "dogs on the get-out," which is to say that they accelerate slowly from a standing start, automatically are ruled out. In general, a small, fast car of common make is preferred for work in city traffic, but a heavy one where the get-away entails a long run over country roads. Having procured a suitable car, the wheel-man provides it with license plates which are not hot and plants it, or places it somewhere out of harm's way, until it is needed.

The wheel-man's other major responsibility is the layout of the get, or getaway route, a simple matter if the job is in a city and the mob intends to piece up there but complicated if a run to another locality is in prospect, as is usually the case if the mark is located in a small community. In the latter event, he must cruise back roads and country lanes until he has pieced together a route which by-passes towns, main highways, and, so far as is possible, roads followed by telephone lines. He runs this route until thoroughly familiar with it, and may even chart it in detail:

> L over bridge
> 40 for S-bend mi. 4
> R fork Bull sign mi. 6½
> weaves over 55 gravel. . . .

Such a chart is called a "running get." The back-country get-away—the idea of a specific route, which was once a close professional secret—is said to have been tipped off to the FBI by Brown Derby Bentz, a bank robber until recently in Alcatraz and there for this reason shunned by many of his professional brethren. Whether or not the rap is a right one for Bentz, the principle of the get is now so well known that a movie glorifying the G-men has been based upon it.

There will be other details requiring attention. Perhaps the job is located in a town whose approaches may quickly be blocked off. If so, the mob may want to hide out in town until the heat has somewhat subsided, in which case a suitable plant, or hideout, will be required. There will have to be bags for the money—the paper shopping bags used by housewives are as good as any. And there is the matter of guns.

Mobs composed of men who often work together may have a small armory of weapons belonging to the mob as a whole, but as a general thing each man furnishes his own weapon, usually a pistol. Revolvers are preferred to automatics, for many of the Colt .45's circulating in the underworld came originally from army or other federal sources, and if one is used on a job the G-heat may assume it has been stolen and enter the case on that basis. Moreover, if the magazine clip of an automatic is kept loaded for a protracted time its spring may become "tired" and the gun may jam when used. The sub-machine guns so common in the movies are rarely used in real-life holdups. They are cumbersome, difficult to acquire, and at once bring the crime under federal jurisdiction. Sprayers, which are automatic pistols of a foreign make provided with a detachable stock and custom-made magazines holding fifty or more bullets, are sometimes used on jobs where there are a large number of people to be controlled, but sawed-off shotguns are cheaper, far easier to obtain, less lethal (except at pointblank range), and more effective in terms of shock effect upon the victims.

The job is ready to go when it has been cased and the other details have been attended to. The mob will have met several times to cut up, or talk things over, and to lay the job out, or make a detailed plan of action. The preparations in their entirety will have taken anywhere from a few hours to several weeks, depending upon the mark and the class, or quality, of the mob—the better the mob, the more thorough the layout.

As has been intimated, there is not much to the holdup itself if the layout has been well done. Each man knows just what to do on the job, when to do it, and what to expect of the others. Unforeseeable complications aside, the actual robbery is largely a matter of going through the motions on schedule. The term "schedule" is used advisedly, for the time element is important—so important that the time taken to "get in, get it, and get out" is a good measure of professional competence. It is not unusual for a class mob to carry out a run-of-the-mill holdup in half a minute. . . .

In working a heist, the mob usually goes out from a meet, or appointment held a short time before the job is to go. Here the layout is gone over again, clothes are changed—if the mark is in a factory district the mob may work in coveralls, if in a business district in business suits; the idea is to remain as inconspicuous as possible—and other last-minute details are attended to. The members of the mob leave singly and go to the mark by separate routes in order to avoid the possibility of being seen together by coppers to whom they may be known. Possibly they do not rod up, or arm themelves, until they reach the job, just in case one of them might be stopped and searched. The wheel-man brings the guns in the car.

The mob meet the car a block or so from the mark and rod themselves up. They walk to the job; the wheel-man pulls ahead and parks near the entrance in such a way that he can swing out from the curb in a hurry. If possible, the inside-men work covered, or masked. This usually can be managed without difficulty unless the place must be entered directly from the street, and even then if scarves fastened with pins so that they may quickly be twitched up over the mouth and chin are used—the lower part of the face is the most easily identifiable.

Covered or bald, the mob enters as casually as any other visitors. Melodramatics are for the movies. One man does the talking: "All right, folks, stay where you're at! Keep quiet! Keep your hands where I can see them! Nobody but the insurance company is gonna get hurt, so take it easy." Generally this fellow stands near the door where he can keep the whole room under observation as well as intercept anyone who may come in while the robbery is in progress. He is an authoritative figure, the center of attention. Most witnesses hardly notice the other insidemen, who go about their job of collecting the score as quickly and with as little fuss as possible.

So far as may be, the mob are calm and polite on the job.

"Cowboying," or the wild brandishing of pistols and shouting
of orders in all directions is frowned upon; fear has made more
heroes than courage ever has. People will not be gratuitously
abused. The professional does not become so tensed up by fear
and excitement that he strikes out blindly upon insignificant
provocation. As one puts it: "When you're out on a heist you're
out to get the dough and keep out of trouble. Halloween's the
night for scaring people." However, courtesy on the job does
not include softness or indecision. A holdup may easily become
a shambles if the people under the gun think they detect nervousness or hesitation on the part of the man behind it.

The boys are particularly careful if women are present. Nobody can tell how women will react—at least, such is the considered opinion of the heist-men with whom I have cut up this
situation. Looks tell nothing. One who has all the earmarks of a
lady pipefitter may just roll her eyes and swoon, while the little
mouse who looks so scared a man itches to pat her on the head
and say something soothing is really coolly examining the mob
for warts or moles or counting the hairs on their knuckles as a
means of future identification. Guns or no guns, some women
will give out large pieces of their minds, and the less of this commodity they have to spare the more generous they appear to be
with it. There are old ladies—one heist mob had a harrowing
experience at the hands of a motherly soul who got into the middle of a loan-office heist before she realized what was going on.
Then she was horrified and spoke severely to the mob. They
should be ashamed, for she could tell that they were good boys
at heart who had got off on the wrong foot. Since this was precisely what the boys secretly thought of themselves, they were
moved; they ordered one of the clerks to destroy the record of
the old lady's loan at once. This intended kindness only shocked
her more, and she began to pray for them. The boys sweated
copiously and might even have left if the manager, who had the
combination to the safe, had not been due at that moment. . . .

Sometimes screamers can be a real hazard on the job, as
when the mob must be inside for several minutes, but on the
ordinary job they are more bothersome than dangerous and the
mob ignores them. In some circumstances, as when there is a

safe which must be opened, it may take the mob several minutes to get the score, but usually it is merely a matter of picking it up and carrying it out. The man on the door remains a few seconds to give the others time to get to the car, for despite his warning someone will probably throw up a window and begin yelling as soon as he leaves. As he comes out, the car already is inching ahead.

It is off the instant his foot touches the running board. Unless a policeman is where he cannot avoid responding to the cries coming from the window—policemen on a beat are seldom eager to career along in chase of someone who may shoot back; they are not paid or very well trained for that kind of work and are likely to shoot their revolvers on double action, to the peril of spectators in upstairs windows—or unless some civilian in search of excitement gives chase, reckless driving is not indulged in. The car whisks around the first corner, takes several others in quick succession, then straightens out for a run of two or three blocks down a street having little traffic.

If no chase car shows up behind, the getaway car heads for wherever the front car—one legitimately owned by one of the mob—is parked. Meanwhile, the inside-men may have gotten into or out of coveralls and transferred the money into the receptacle provided: where there is no pedestrian traffic outside, the mob may not take time on the job to put the loot into bags but carry it out in a wastepaper basket or any other handy container. One of the mob takes the score and pistols in the front car to the place prearranged for the meet. The other insidemen may accompany him, or, if they want to play it safe all the way, go separately. The wheel-man continues in the getaway car to another part of the city, where, having wiped down the interior to remove fingerprints, he ditches it.

By the time he arrives at the meet, the money probably already has been pieced up into as many piles as there are members of the mob. "There she is," one of the others says. "Latch onto one."

Stealing might be described as the lower-class technique for rejecting the principle of negotiated exchange. There is also a more genteel middle-class technique. Instead of negotiating directly, some people feign personal interest or friendship in the other party so as to make him less wary. This kind of manipulation—called by Professor Robert K. Merton "pseudo-*gemeinschaft*"—is a close relative of the kind of chicanery practiced by unethical businessmen (and described in Chapter 11). Exploitative manipulation is not confined to business transactions. As Willard Waller suggests in his analysis of dating practices at a state university, exploitation can be a more serious problem during courtship than mutual thrill-seeking.[3]

The emergence of thrill-seeking furthers the development of exploitative relationships. As long as an association is founded on a frank and admitted barter in thrills, nothing that can be called exploitative arises. But the old mores of progressive commitment exist, along with the new customs, and peculiar relationships arise from this confusion of moralities. According to the old morality a kiss means something, a declaration of love means something, a number of Sunday evening dates in succession means something, and these meanings are enforced by the customary law, while under the new morality such things may mean nothing at all—that is, they may imply no commitment of the total personality whatsoever. So it comes about that one of the persons may exploit the other for thrills on the pretense of emotional involvement and its implied commitment. When a woman exploits, it is usually for the sake of presents and expensive amusements—the common pattern of "gold-digging." The male exploiter usually seeks thrills from the body of the woman. The fact that thrills cost money, usually the man's money, often operates to introduce strong elements of suspicion and antagonism into the relationship.

SUMMARY

Confronted with the principle that others will give him what he wants only if it is worth their while to do so; confronted with the fact that it is apparently *not* worth their while; resolved not to accept defeat—the individual has only one avenue left: To *take* what he needs and give *nothing* in return. He can take it by

[3] Willard Waller, "The Rating and Dating Complex," *American Sociological Review*, Vol. 2 (1937), pp. 727–734.

elaborately manipulating the other person's own readiness to get something for nothing (the con game); or he can take it more directly (the heist). And "it" need not be money: The con game may be played with the coin of symbols of affection as well as with dollars. The principle is: When others have what would make your life meaningful, when they won't share it with you, and when you refuse to do without it, you seize it. This is the principle which results in such social problems as rape, theft, fraud, school cheating, adulteration of food, misleading advertising, and the political con game of demogoguery.

ANNOTATED BIBLIOGRAPHY

Kefauver, Estes, *Crime in America* (New York: Doubleday & Company, Inc., 1951). ⟨ An abridged account of the report of a Senate Committee which investigated organized crime in the United States.

McKelway, St. Clair, "The Wily Wilby," *True Tales from the Annals of Crime and Rascality* (New York: Random House, Inc., 1957). ⟨ A true story of an engaging rascal who devoted his considerable talents to embezzling money from his employers. His second wife said, when she learned about his illegal hobby, "Well, he's a very fine man except for that one quirk. . . ."

Shaw, Clifford R., *The Jack-Roller* (Chicago: University of Chicago Press, 1930). ⟨ The true story of a young boy who took up robbing drunks as a criminal specialty.

Sutherland, Edwin H., *The Professional Thief* (Chicago: University of Chicago Press, 1937). ⟨ The autobiographical account of a craftsman in predatory crime. Chic Conwell showed remarkable self-reliance in his chosen career.

Turkis, Burton B., and Feder, Sid, *Murder, Inc.: The Story of "The Syndicate"* (New York: Farrar, 1951). ⟨ A horrifying exposition of the consequences of the rejection of negotiated exchange by organized crime. Murder becomes one of the techniques of conducting business.

CHAPTER THIRTEEN

The refusal to accept defeat:
Relentless competition

The governing principles of American society are inter-related. The self-reliance principle counsels the individual to depend on himself alone; the negotiated exchange principle tells him that he must induce people to give him what he wants through bargaining. The competitive principle looks sideways at other self-reliant negotiators and tells the individual that these are his enemies. He must outperform them or undercut them, or

320

they will secure life's satisfactions instead of *him*. Sometimes the competitive principle is interpreted to mean that winning is all that counts, that it doesn't matter *how* victory is secured. When this happens, when no holds are barred, a defeated competitor is all but destroyed. As an illustration of relentless competition, consider the ruthless techniques employed by segments of the American railroad industry in fighting competition from truckers. What follows are parts of the official court record in the United States District Court for the Eastern District of Pennsylvania.[1]

    . . . the use of long-haul trucks for interstate hauling of freight had increased so enormously by May of 1949 that it was a matter of immediate and vital self-interest to the railroads to do something about the erosion of what had been up to this time almost an exclusive monopoly of long-haul freight transportation. At first blush, to the ordinary person it would appear that the primary concern of the railroads might have been directed to improving service and to attempt to meet by more flexibility and speedy delivery the growing competition of the truckers. The evidence in this case has disclosed there were certain areas wherein the trucks could not compete. It was testified that the trucks would not compete with the railroads in taking the coal out of the mountains of West Virginia since one diesel engine could take a great number of cars on the downgrade of the West Virginia mines to the Norfolk breakwater. That the railroads would continue to enjoy this type of business was completely self-evident. On the other hand, the greater flexibility of the truck and the speedier delivery of goods were elements in the competitive market which the railroads might themselves have attempted to meet by the use of trucks or otherwise. The door-to-door feature of truck delivery was also important. However, the record in this case is barren of any attempt on the part of the railroads to adjust their thinking and their actions to meet this definite threat to a segment of business theretofore enjoyed by them. They engaged in what has been termed throughout the trial of this case as a "concert of action" to "improve their posi-

[1] *Noerr Motor Freight, Inc., et al., v. Eastern Railroad Presidents' Conference, et al.,* 113 Fed. Supp. 737.

tion" in the long-haul freight competitive market. And here is how they did it.

In May of 1949 the evidence discloses that the top executives of the Pennsylvania Railroad, before attending the May 19th, 1949, meeting of the [Eastern Railroads Presidents] Conference, were considering a campaign for Federal and State taxes against users of highways, waterways, etc. The recommendation which came out of this consideration was that they should explore the possibility of organizing private motorists and other groups to be held out to the public as completely non-railroad inspired for the sole purpose of restricting the truckers by making their operations so expensive that they could not operate at a profit. The obvious corollary is that the railroads would be the beneficiaries of these restrictions. On May 19th, 1949, at a meeting of the Conference, there was appointed a Competitive Transportation Committee with Subcommittees designated Legal, Research, and Public Relations. David I. Mackie, then vice-president of the Delaware & Lackawanna Railroad, was made Chairman of the Legal Committee. Raymond J. Littlefield, tax agent and later general agent of the Pennsylvania Railroad, was made Chairman of the Research Committee. Thomas J. Deegan, Jr., then executive vice-president of the Chesapeake & Ohio Railroad, later staff vice-president of the Allegheny Corporation, operators of the New York Central Lines, was made Chairman of the very important Public Relations Subcommittee. While these three subcommittees maintained an effective liaison, the most active and most potent of the committees was the Committee on Public Relations. Deegan and his subcommittee determined on a plan of operation. The single objective of the campaign was harassment of the long-haul truckers. One of the objectives was the enactment of legislation, not under the sponsorship of the railroads but by others acting on their behalf, by what was called in inoffensive and pleasing language, "The third-party technique."

The campaign was to begin in New York, New Jersey and Ohio, and other states were to be brought in later as the program developed, consistent with the degree of success of the program. It was also determined that the campaign should be handled through an independent public relations firm. A number of public relations firms were interviewed and of the four or five selected for interview, all were leaders in that particular field. It may be noted in passing that of those interviewed and who submitted proposals, about which proposals testimony was given at the trial, each and every one of the suggested programs provided for a campaign of publicity to put the truckers in a bad light with the public; to encourage normal public resentment of the motoring public to the operation of big trucks on the highways; to secure the assistance of organizations which were apparently "independent and public spirited" in the campaign against the truckers, and to create a demand for legislation penalizing the truckers either by limitation of size and weight or the imposition of user taxes which would make their operation unprofitable.

A presentation was made by the defendant-Byoir firm prior to the execution of the contract on August 15, 1949. Byoir's presentation laid great stress on the success of that firm in prior legislative campaigns, particularly its success before the Louisiana Legislature in reducing a tax on sulphur; in the spring of 1938 before the New York Legislature in opposing a chain store tax; in connection with A & P activities which will be discussed later in the opinion; in 1948 before the Congress of the United States in connection with the distilling industry, and finally in connection with the maufacturers of floor and wall tile with regard to building code changes which Byoir claimed his firm had secured for that industry in some two thousand cities. After the contract was awarded a memorandum of agreement was executed providing for payment to Byoir of $75,000 a year, plus reimbursement of each and every expense of any sort involved in the campaign. Byoir immediately organized a staff to put the program into effect and execution. The understanding of the Byoir organization as to its duties in connection with the campaign, set forth in extenso in Exhibit P5, is entitled "The Objectives."

While the ultimate objective is shrewdly set forth as legislation affecting the truckers, the intermediate goals are also set forth, all designed and aimed at injury to the truckers. These objectives, including the crystalization of motorist resentment arising from commercial heavy truck operations over the roads, were designed to arouse the public generally of the need to obtain new methods of financing public highways and by methods which would not appear to emanate from railroad sources. The total objectives were ostensibly set forth in a memorandum to the Department Heads of Byoir by Reynolds Girdler, Account Executive of the ERPC Account, dated September 13, 1949, in which he paraphrased the National Transportation Policy of Congress to suit his own needs, interpreting it for the purposes of the campaign as a National Legislative Policy and that (1) airlines should be used for speed; (2) trucks for short hauls and (3) only railroads for long hauls. He pointed out that if this program could be made effective through public relations the railroads' financial troubles would be at an end. He also pointed out that "our" newspaper stories, magazines articles, pictures and radio programs will be concerned with what the national transportation policy should be, dramatizing highways and heavy trucks in the following particulars: (1) highway construction costs; (2) highway safety and the part trucks play in lack of safety on the highways; (3) highway damages by trucks; (4) state revenue and expenditures; (5) general taxation stories; all geared to reflect discredit upon the heavy truck industry and all to be done without attribution to the railroads. The magazine department of Byoir was directed to "plant" stories in magazines for later use in the campaign as authoritative sources of factual information. More will be said of this later in the opinion. . . .

MAGAZINE ACTIVITIES

One of the most unusual of Byoir's employees, the head of the Magazine Department, was Patricia Lochridge Hartwell. Mrs. Hartwell, whose professional name while she was with Byoir was Patricia Lochridge, joined the Byoir organization in November of 1949 and was assigned to the ERPC account. She thereupon set out to develop magazine articles which would portray the railroads' point of view and would be unfavorable to the trucking interest. Her method of operation was to interest an editor of a magazine in a story and if the editor thought it had sufficient merit he might assign one of his staff writers or editors to do the piece. In that event Mrs. Hartwell would furnish the writer with the data which Byoir had compiled, which data of course was always slanted against the truckers. She also made use of free-lance writers. She would interest them in a particular story and pay them while they researched the proposed story at Byoir's or at other places, which amounts in many instances ran into several hundreds of dollars. Since the ultimate aim was to hurt the truckers, any such payments were reimbursed by the railroads, and should the free-lance writer be able to sell the article to a magazine the entire fee went to the writer. In other words, Byoir paid the writer during the preparation of the article and the magazine paid him for writing it. In the extremely limited number of instances that a writer contemplated an article which would be favorable to the railroads' point of view with respect to the truckers, Byoir extended every facility it possessed for use of the writer and at no cost to the writer.

The worth of such a project in the attainment of the ERPC goal cannot be minimized. In addition to the ordinary extensive circulation which the magazines themselves possessed, it was possible, at railroad expense, to circulate reprints of the articles widely to civic organizations, state, city and government officials, as well as to legislators and other individuals who were concerned with public opinion. While it is true that her efforts in every case did not meet with complete success, she was successful in having enough magazine articles released to make an important contribution to the railroads' antitruck campaign. Without attempting to individuate the details of each article, it will be sufficient to recount some of the articles published and Byoir's connection with them.

The first article, "The Giants Wreck Highways" with a subtitle "Heavy Trucks Are Making Their Runs On Your Tax Dollars," appeared in the April, 1950 issue of *Everybody's Digest*. It was based almost completely upon Byoir's research and development. In the same month Byoir claimed credit for having furnished minor research and comment for an article by Senator

Joseph C. O'Mahoney entitled, "What Bad Roads Are Costing Us," which appeared in the April, 1950 issue of the *American Magazine*.

Early in 1950 Mrs. Hartwell presented an outline of a story about truck damage to roads to the editor of *Harper's Magazine*. This outline was very extensive and *Harper's* evinced interest in it. Thereafter Mrs. Hartwell contacted Myron Stearn, an independent free-lance writer, interested him in the story, furnished him with all the Byoir data on the trucks, and the completed product appeared in the September, 1950 issue of *Harper's Magazine* under the caption, "Our Roads Are Going To Pot." At approximately the same time an article entiled, "The Rape Of Our Roads," by Frederick Brownell, a Byoir protégé, appeared in the *Reader's Digest*. This article was condensed from a Buffalo *Evening News* story. These two articles became the first authoritative sources of so-called independent public attacks upon the trucking industry.

Through the good efforts of Clinton Johnson, Director of Publicity for the Maryland Roads Commission, and a close associate of the Byoir organization, David G. Wittels, an outstanding writer for the *Saturday Evening Post,* in the September 16th, 1950 issue of that magazine wrote a very critical article entitled, "Are Trucks Destroying Our Highways?" Byoir furnished extensive national research in a five thousand word background memorandum to round out his story on the Maryland State Highway Commission Program. It was the same Clinton Johnson who persuaded Mr. Wittels to go to Maryland and actually research the story in the field; live with the highway crew, meet the highway commissioner, and find out what the problems were for himself. While the article justifiably was critical of a certain class of truckers, it must be realized that the initiative for the article stemmed from railroad-inspired sources and portrayed a particularly venal type of trucker as representative of the entire trucking industry. The distortion, however, was so skillfully done and so subtly written as to make a profound impression upon a casual reader of the article. Again, it is a variation of third-party technique approach, which technique in its application to this case will receive further attention.

Hardy Burt, "a sometime employee of Byoir" and a some-time independent free-lance writer, wrote an article in the April, 1952 issue of the *National Grange Monthly* entitled, "History, Trucks and Money." This article was actually authored by a Byoir ghost writer, James Miller, and according to Mrs. Hartwell "skillfully developed all the major points in the ERPC campaign." This article, which pictorially highlighted the collapse of a bridge due to an overladen truck attempting to escape a weighing station on a main highway and the destruction of a detour on a main highway over a country road, was skillfully designed to arouse the farmers in opposition to the trucks.

Again, in the August, 1951, Sunday issue of *Parade* magazine, which is a supplement to hundreds of Sunday newspapers throughout the country, Clinton Johnson assisted Byoir in obtaining the insert of an article entitled, "Trucks: Help Or Headache?" This article, completely critical of trucks, contained the words and pictures of the Byoir organization.

In the July 30th, 1952 issue of *People* magazine appeared an article entitled, "Trucks Wreck Your Roads." This article again critical of the trucking industry was not only "planted" by Byoir but extensive circulation of reprints was made with the article appearing as the lead article on the cover of the reprint whereas the original magazine cover contained no such reference.

An article which represented an extremely important item in the railroads' campaign against the truckers was that which appeared in the April, 1952 issue of the *Country Gentleman*. This article by Emilie Hall, described as "You Can Have Better Roads" was referred to by the magazine as a "new chapter in the farm roads story." The writer was discovered by Horace Lyon, a Byoir employee assigned to the ERPC account, and Mrs. Hartwell did most of the research and editing for the article, with Jim Miller and Dick Strouse of Byoir helping in some last minute rewrites. Quoting Mrs. Hartwell's appraisal of the publication of this article: "This was a difficult job to put across, entailing two complete rewrites of the article to satisfy both a pixie author and a difficult editor. This was accomplished without too much pain and the underlying philosophy of the ERPC

account came through in the final draft." After various complications Lyon and Lochridge were able to get the article endorsed
in a box which appeared on the first page of the article by the
president of the all-important Association of American State
Highway Officials. This article received widespread distribution
at the hands of Byoir but more importantly a motion picture
based on this article was made for distribution to farm groups
throughout the country. The story of how this motion picture
came into existence, the purpose behind the picture, and the
ultimate success of the endeavor is significantly interesting.

For some seventeen years one Fred O. Bailey had served as
reporter and farm editor of the United Press Association. During the years 1945, 1946 and 1947 he had served as Legislative Counsel of the National Grange. Subsequent to 1947 he
served a number of national magazines in the farm field as a
reporter and columnist. According to the testimony of David I.
Mackie, one of those magazines served was the *Country Gentleman*. During the year 1951 Bailey had discussed the formation
of a Farm Roads Foundation but nothing came of it during that
year. However, the general idea of such a Foundation was to
cooperate with and assist farm organizations and farm groups
in planning for an adequate balanced roads program to serve
their needs. The first and only function of the Farm Roads
Foundation up until May of 1953, the date of Mr. Bailey's de-
position in this case, was the distribution of a film, "Highways
and Byways, U. S. A.," based upon the story in the *Country
Gentleman* magazine, "You Can Have Better Roads." The evidence in this case discloses beyond peradventure of doubt that
the moving force in the making of this film was the Western Association of Railroads. Bailey was approached by representatives
of that association and offered an outright grant of a picture for
distribution. It was not until this offer had been made that the
Farm Roads Foundation was incorporated and came into being.
The evidence is also crystal clear that Byoir, in conjunction with
representatives of the Western Railroads Association, had been
working on a script for this picture. In fact, Byoir edited the
script. Dudley Pictures of Hollywood were commissioned by the
association of railroads to make the picture and the cost of mak-

ing the picture was divided between the Eastern, Western and Southern railroads on a basis of 18% to the Southern railroads and 41% each to the Eastern and Western railroads. The assessment to the Eastern railroads was $62,500. Based on the above percentages of assessment it would appear, therefore, that the cost of the film to the three railroad associations exceeded $150,000. This film, the cost of the public distribution of which (and it was most extensive) has always been borne through a grant by the railroads, was exhibited at the trial of this case and the film and a transcript thereof have been filed of record. The film is professional and skillfully done. It demonstrates clearly the needs of the farmers for auxiliary roads and suggests united, combined, intelligent community efforts to obtain the necessary funds to bring about this very desirable result. The lasting impression, however, created by the picture is contained in a very few sentences of the dialogue and as the picture concludes; the lasting impact of the film is that big trucks do not pay their fair share of highway construction and maintenance. While extremely expensive it constituted a very important piece of propaganda carrying a terrific impact upon its viewers. Mr. Bailey, whose cooperation had been sought in the editing of the script, was completely unaware of the very important role played by Byoir. He had no idea of the cost of the film nor of the cost of distribution which was borne by the railroads. Two distribution companies were employed to distribute the film through their regular agencies to farm groups and other interested parties. It was distributed free of charge for showing in regular moving picture houses. 186 colored prints were made in 16 millimeter size and 10 black and white 16 millimeter size copies were made for showing on TV. The testimony indicates that considerable use was made of the film on TV. Four 35 millimeter copies were made for showing in regular motion picture theaters. To a viewer of the picture it would appear that the sponsors were the *Country Gentleman* and the Farm Roads Foundation. No suggestion either in the title, dialogue or screen credits indicated the connection of the railroads with this film. Viewed as it was by millions, the effect was most certainly to build up prejudice in the public mind against the trucking industry. . . .

ROAD TEST ONE—MARYLAND

In 1949 the Governors Conference requested the Council of State Governments to study and report upon the matter of reasonable and uniform standards of motor-vehicle maximum-size-and-weight limitations. At the call of Governor Lausche of Ohio and cosponsored by highway officials from 14 midwestern and eastern states, a conference was held at Columbus, Ohio, on December 5 and 6, 1949, to consider the size and weight problem as a matter of interregional concern. Early in the deliberations of the conference, it became apparent that an objective determination of the effects of *axle loads* of various magnitudes would afford the only possibility of eventual agreement of the entire membership on the important question of axle-load limitations.

The conference formed itself into the Interregional Council on Highway Transportation and appointed a Committee on Test Roads. This special committee met in Baltimore, Maryland, on January 9 and 10, 1950, to inspect a test-road location proposed by representatives of the Maryland State Roads Commission. After visiting the site of the proposed test road, the committee decided that the project identified as Road Test One—Maryland was feasible and recommended that tests be conducted at the joint expense of the participating state highway departments and with Highway Research Board direction of the project. The highway departments of the following states: Connecticut, Delaware, Illinois, Kentucky, Maryland, Michigan, New Jersey, Ohio, Pennsylvania, Virginia, Wisconsin and the District of Columbia, executed contracts with the National Academy of Sciences, of which the Highway Research Board was a component part, agreeing to participate financially in the cooperative venture. The project was administered and supervised by the said Highway Research Board through a small Project Executive Committee and an Advisory Committee. The Advisory Committee included one representative from each participating state, the Bureau of Public Roads, the Automobile Manufacturers Association, the Petroleum Industry, the American Trucking Association, and the Department of the Army. The Bureau of Public Roads provided personnel and instruments for measurements of surface roughness, slab strains and deflections caused by the test loads, soil surveys, and other necessary instrumentation and testing services, and also provided the services of the project engineer and three assistants.

The principal object of the test was to determine the relative effects on a particular concrete pavement of four different *axle loadings* on two vehicle types. The loads employed were 18,000 and 22,400 pounds per single axle, and 32,000 and 44,800 pounds per tandem axle. The tests were conducted on a 1.1-mile section of Portland cement-concrete pavement constructed in 1941 on U. S. 301 approximately 9 miles south of La Plata, Maryland. The pavement consisted of two 12 ft. lanes, each having a 9–7–9 in. cross-section and reinforced with wire mesh. The road at the beginning of the test was in fairly good condition and insofar as the records of the Maryland Road Commission could determine the entire length of the test site was constructed on good granular subbase material.

There were four separate test sections. The first, which was the west lane of the southern half mile of the pavement under test, was subject to 18,000 lbs. single axle load; the second, which was the east lane of the southern half mile, was subject to 22,400 lbs. single axle load; the third, which was the west lane of the northern 0.6 mile, was subject to 32,000 lbs. tandem axle load; and the fourth, which was the east lane of the northern 0.6 mile, was subject to 44,800 lbs. tandem axle load.

The test truck operations began on June 12, 1950, for Sections 1 and 2, single axle loads, and the tandem heavier trucks on the eastern end began operation on June 23, 1950. Operations of all test trucks were continuous, on a 24-hour day, seven-day week basis, except when necessary to interrupt operations for vehicle and pavement maintenance and service, meals and rest stops for drivers, and special tests, such as strain and deflections. In addition, operations were suspended for 24 hours for three holidays during 1950: July 4, Labor Day and Thanksgiving Day. The drivers worked three 8-hour shifts and were allowed a 10-minute rest period each hour and 30 minutes for a meal in the middle of the shift. The 18,000 lb. axle load totaled 111,889 miles; the 22,400 lb. axle load totaled 111,792 miles; the 32,000 lb. tandem axle load totaled 106,668 miles; and the 44,800 lb. tandem axle load totaled 59,256 miles due to cessation of operations during the month of November occasioned by excessive damage to that part of the test highway.

This was to be, and was, insofar as the Highway Research Board was concerned, a completely objective test. Mr. Herbert S. Fairbanks, Deputy Commissioner of the Bureau of Public Roads and Chairman of the Highway Research Board, estimated in his testimony in this case that the stress placed on the road during the pendency of this test would approximate 40 years of normal usage of the same road. Contrary to the general understanding of the content of the subsoil of the road, it became very evident as the test progressed that certain portions of the road, particularly that over which the heavier trucks ran, had a subgrade which consisted in great part of fine grain soil. When water permeated the fine grain soil the deflection caused by the weight of the trucks would push the water and solid matter from the subbase of the road and eventually this would create a hole or pocket under the road. The weight of the truck would then crack the concrete immediately over the hole or pocket. The water which would lodge in these pockets or holes would be "pumped" up through the expansion joints of the road. While test procedures might have allowed normal maintenance of the roads, such as filling in and reinforcing these cavities under the road, deliberately and in the interest of scientific knowledge minimal maintenance was indulged in throughout the entire period of the test. Naturally this resulted in much faster deterioration than would be the case had normal maintenance been carried out.

It will be recognized that the impetus for this test came from Governor Lausche of Ohio. His Director of the Ohio Department of Highways, T. J. Kauer, Chairman of the Interregional Council on Highway Transportation, as such, had extremely close contacts with all features of the test. It will also be recalled that Harold Cohen, Chief of Public Relations of the Ohio Department of Highways, was a very close associate of Stull, Byoir's representative in Ohio. The purpose of this test was a scientific determination of what a road of this character could carry safely. The distortion of this aim and purpose, and the peculiar conduct of Messrs. Kauer, Cohen and Clinton Johnson, Director of Publicity for the Maryland Roads Commissions, makes an interesting chapter in the Byoir-railroad antitruck campaign. It was the purpose of Byoir to obtain as early as possible any information from this test which would support their theory that the *gross weight* of the truck (whereas the test was an examination of the effects of *axle-load weights*) was alone responsible for breaking up roads. With this in mind close liaison was kept with Kauer, Cohen and Johnson. The records of the Byoir organization show that Johnson during the course of this test was a frequent visitor at the Byoir offices in New York and that the expenses of his visits were borne by Byoir and reimbursed by the railroads. There also appear in the evidence many vouchers which indicate that the railroads reimbursed Byoir for entertainment of Johnson and his wife. Ultimately he became an employee of the ERPC, receiving $1,000 per month plus expenses from December of 1952 through September of 1953. A further inference may be drawn from the fact that in an undated memorandum (P–121) from Hardy, Byoir's New Jersey and Pennsylvania agent, to Mr. Deegan, Hardy noted that in checking over the agenda of an ERPC meeting it occurred to him that Deegan might not want to discuss Johnson at the open meeting. He further mentioned that he talked to Littlefield about this and that he was interested in Deegan's idea. Hardy's explanation that the reason they might not want to discuss Johnson at the open meeting was because it was a mere matter of slight detail does not satisfy the Court. (R.745) While out-and-out bribery of Mr. Johnson has not been proven by a preponderance of evidence, the Court is satisfied that the plaintiffs have proved that Mr. Johnson, because of the above-mentioned factors, was not an objective public employee, but rather was working for the interests of the railroads in order to further his own personal goal of obtaining a lucrative position with the ERPC.

There is no doubt and the record abundantly proves that Byoir actually did get information about the test as it progressed. It was the purpose of Mr. Fairbanks and his associates that no conclusion be published until the full committee had time for a mature consideration of all of the factors involved in the test. From time to time, however, Byoir put out releases which indicated that big trucks, in the sense of gross weights rather than axle loads, were the primary factor in destroying the roads and highways of this country. Byoir even released pictures terming the Maryland Road Test as a "Crackathon"; pictures which showed the pumping action when heavy trucks ran over joints where the subsoil was of fine grain sand rather than the granular subsurface which withstood the test of all of the weights with remarkable durability. If a "Crackathon" is a highly technical and scientifically controlled attempt to crowd into a period of several months the effect of roughly four decades of road use in order to determine what factors ultimately result in the break up of roads, Byoir used the proper appellation in describing the Maryland Road Test. But this Court finds that Byoir meant, and the reading public so interpreted it as meaning, that a "Crackathon" was the result which invariably followed from the use of heavy trucks on concrete roads. In a word—big trucks are the sole procuring cause of road destruction, rather than the true nature of the test which was to crack the road under controlled conditions.

Mrs. Hartwell likewise entered into this picture. She spent about a week at the site of the test, taking notes and watching the progress of the test, and did her best to get releases which would favor the railroads. She also sent a woman free-lance writer to the scene with instructions to represent herself as an editor of *Colliers,* which she was not. As such purported editor she was well received by all at the site including representatives of the American Trucking Association and she was accorded every courtesy possible. Her report to Mrs. Hartwell is a masterpiece of the venomous approach which any one connected with Byoir took toward the heavy trucks.

One particular feature of the test and Byoir's approach to it deserves special mention. A running motion picture of the test at selected times was made for the Bureau of Public Roads. At the conclusion of the test and with the approval of Mr. Fairbanks, this motion picture was edited and narrated by a competent Washington, D. C. news commentator. The original so-called "long version" of the motion picture was shown at the trial of the case and the Court was impressed with the completely objective approach to the problem and the fair comments of the narrator. Viewing the motion picture at the end of one day's session, the Court felt that the picture clearly demonstrated that the most important cause of cracking of concrete highways was the presence of a fine grain silty or clay soil subgrade. One important statement was made in the long version of the film:

"The test shows conclusively that a concrete pavement, of the strength and dimensions of the test road, will support indefinitely, without structural failure, single-axle loads as great as 22,400 pounds—*if* there is a subgrade, of adequate thickness, of non-plastic, granular soil. The equivalent of such support must be supplied by the design of roads *in the future*."

Among others, this important statement was carefully removed from the later shortened version of the film.

The film was in three parts. The first part showed pictures at the actual site with the narrator explaining methods of operation, the purpose, and some of the results. The second part was devoted almost entirely to a precise engineering explanation of the test and its purpose, illustrated by model trucks and drawings. The third part was the conclusion in which the narrator summarized the test, its purpose, and results. It was at this point that Byoir directly entered the scene. One of the Byoir representatives in Washington called upon Mr. Fairbanks and told him that the Byoir organization representing the railroads would like to have a copy of the film for distribution and showing to selected groups. Mr. Fairbanks demurred at the suggestion of Byoir that a shortened version of the film would be adequate to show the purpose and results of the test. Under considerable pressing by Byoir, Mr. Fairbanks said he would consider a shortened version of the film, if it could be demonstrated to him that it did not distort in any way the purpose of the test and the results obtained therefrom. Byoir then suggested that certain portions of the film be shown consisting of the first part of the film and the last part of the narrator's summary. The shortened version of the film was thereafter shown to Mr. Fairbanks and his associates and after one viewing Fairbanks approved the release of the shortened version of the film to Byoir for the railroads. It was only when Mr. Fairbanks received a proposed brochure from Mackie, representing the railroads, which brochure was intended to be sent out with the film, that he realized there might be possible distortion. His statement in a letter dated April 3, 1953 to Mr. Mackie makes that extremely clear:

> "However, we do not regard the film as an indictment of large or even heavy trucks *per se;* and certainly, it would be foreign to our purpose were the film in any way to become an instrument of partisan attack upon highway transportation or the trucking industry."

In addition, he suggested that the Bureau of Public Roads should not appear as the sponsor of the picture, if such use was intended to be made of it. Mackie thereupon agreed not to distribute it with the brochure and asked permission to exhibit the shortened version of the film already purchased by Byoir on behalf of the railroads. Since Mr. Fairbanks was honestly of the opinion at that time that the film did not distort the purpose and the results of the test he agreed that they might retain the copies and exhibit them.

As stated above, the long version of the film was exhibited on one of the trial days. On the next day the shortened version of the film was exhibited. The profound impact on the Court of the short film was that big trucks *per se* were the sole cause of damage to the highways. Important language which would have made clear the results of the test, particularly with respect to bad subgrade soil and pumping, were entirely eliminated. The impression left with the Court at the conclusion of the short film disagreed entirely with the sworn statements of Mr. Fairbanks regarding the results of the test. His statements agreed with those made in the long version of the film as previously set forth. That the distortion was intentional as well as effective is clearly evident from an overall reading of this record. Mr. Fairbanks viewed the exhibition of both films in the courtroom. On the basis of his sworn testimony the Court finds that Mr. Fairbanks was fooled by Byoir and tricked into approving a distorted film. This particular episode in the Byoir-railroad anti-truck campaign is a classic example of the "use" of public officials by the Byoir organization in furtherance of its campaign. Such was an everyday occurrence in the Byoir approach to public officials in this case, and I have particular reference to the above situation as well as the "use" of Governor Lausche and Messrs. Taft, Manning, Dimit and Schmidt; the latter two being referred to under "Pennsylvania Activities." On the other hand, any "use" of individuals such as Clinton Johnson, Menzie, Kauer, Cohen and "Cappy" Thompson (of Pennsylvania) was with their complete knowledge and for the purpose of advancing their own personal interests rather than those of the public that they represented. These and other instances will be referred to in more detail in other headings of this opinion. It is only fair to Mr. Fairbanks at this point to say that the Court considered him a fine, honorable and dedicated public servant, who in giving permission for the shortened version of the film never contemplated that it would be used for the very purpose which he decried in his letter of April 3, 1953 as "an instrument of partisan attack upon highway transportation or the trucking industry."

Needless to say Byoir made full use of its publicity outlets to tell the world that big trucks crack roads. It was a complete distortion not only of the test but of Mr. Fairbanks' opinion that the road tested could carry gross weights without danger as high as 73,280 pounds (R.3318).

On or about January 8 of 1951 there was distributed to the members of the Advisory Committee a proposed copy of the findings or in other words the tentative committee report of Road Test One—Maryland. Kauer's copy was in the hands of Byoir within a remarkably short time after its receipt by him despite the Advisory Board's decision that the data was not to be issued to the general public at that time. Byoir summarized the tentative findings and gave them to *Newsweek,* where they appeared as completed studies, although the final report was not approved until May of 1951 and the printed copies not available until sometime after October of 1951 (R.3322–3326). The results as given to *Newsweek* and printed in a box in that magazine completely distorted the purpose and results of the test and attributed all road damage to big trucks, the position taken by Byoir from the outset and entirely false insofar as the objective findings of the test are concerned.

It might be well at this point to set out what the actual conclusions of the officials in charge of the test were as officially reported in Publication 227 of the National Research Council. There were 19 technical findings which are carefully set out in technical engineering language. Briefly stated with respect to the point under discussion in this case that big trucks break roads, they are as follows: (1) That where the road was built on granular soil very little damage occurred no matter what type of vehicle was used; (2) That where the test road was built on fine grain soil, there was no damage until the fine grain soil became permeated with water; (3) That in the presence of water, the subsoil was pumped from under the concrete slab through joints in the road; (4) That the degree of pumping was faster and the amount greater upon the application of the heavier vehicles; (5) That with the subsoil removed the concrete would and did crack, with the heavier vehicles doing the greater and quicker damage.

As publicized by Byoir, both in its releases and in the shortened version of the film, one conclusion was bound to be reached by the ordinary observer from the reading of the releases or viewing of the short film—that only big trucks did damage to the highways and that without regard to any other contributing factor. . . .

When competition is carried on so relentlessly, it becomes a social problem. The railroad-trucking struggle appears to have reached this stage since World War II. Other industries reached it earlier. Competition in the lumber industry threatened to destroy every timber stand on the American continent until President Theodore Roosevelt intervened on behalf of conservation. Competition among farmers has been a chronic problem for decades, producing overproduction on the one hand, and erosion of irreplaceable topsoil on the other. Competition among manufacturers led to the well-known industrial abuses of the nineteenth century: child labor, excessive hours of work (sweatshops), preventable accidents, starvation wages, unhealthy working conditions (and, more specifically, occupational diseases).

Frequently, competitors are aware of the social problem they are creating; they do not wish to create it but they feel helpless to stop the practice unilaterally. They cannot afford to assume costs that are not a similar burden on their competitors. For example, consider the problem of air pollution.[2]

In contrast to the widespread recognition of the losses caused by the impairment of the human factor, the social costs of air and water pollution have attracted much less attention. This is probably due to the fact that the causal relation between productive activities and air and water pollution is more complex and less easily seen than the relatively clear connection that exists between private production and, say, industrial accidents. Moreover, whereas the impairment of human health by industrial accidents and occupational diseases tends to affect a relatively well-organized group of persons all of whom have a strong interest in the prevention of the risks and dangers to which they are exposed in their daily work, the harmful consequences of the pollution of the atmosphere and the contamination of water by various kinds of industrial waste products are usually felt by a highly heterogeneous, unorganized group of persons. Their reaction is, therefore, less articulate than that of injured workers in the case of industrial accidents and occupational diseases. Nevertheless, there can be no doubt that the social costs of air and water pollution are considerable. In the United States these costs may well reach several billion dollars annually. The present . . . [discussion] is devoted to a study of the social costs of air pollution . . .

. . . While the domestic use of coal continues to be a contributing cause of atmospheric pollution, it is primarily the emanations of smoke and gas from industrial establishments, railroads and large heating plants which, at present, cause most of the prevailing air pollution. Indeed, the large-scale replacement of man and horse power by such energy resources as bituminous coal and oil has made air pollution a common and

[2] Reprinted by permission of the publishers, Harvard University Press, Cambridge, Massachusetts, from Karl William Kapp, *The Social Costs of Private Enterprise*, pp. 67–74, 76–78. Copyright 1950, by the President and Fellows of Harvard College.

characteristic phenomenon around many industrial centers. Nor can it be assumed that the replacement of coal and oil by atomic energy may one day eliminate the pollution of the atmosphere. On the contrary, recent experiments with radioactive disposal systems seem to indicate that radioactive waste materials— solids, liquids and gases—may get into the air and represent not only short-lived but long-lived risks for neighboring cities and countries. In fact, if not properly controlled, the problem of air pollution in the atomic age may well become world-wide.

The manner in which present industrial production tends to give rise to air pollution need not occupy us to any great extent. Suffice it to point out that the formation of smoke and other gaseous emanations is almost invariably a sign of improper and incomplete combustion of fuels; in other words, the existence of smoke is always indicative of technical inefficiencies in the use of energy resources. Such inefficiencies fail to be eliminated whenever the private returns (or savings) obtainable from their elimination are not high enough to cover the private costs involved. The fact that the resulting pollution of the atmosphere may cause substantial losses to other people will not and cannot normally be considered in the cost-return calculations of private enterprise. . . .

The most obvious of the ill effects of smoke are those evidenced in the progressive destruction and premature deterioration of building materials, metals, paint coatings, merchandise, etc. Thus the various sulphur compounds contained in smoke have a destructive effect on stone and metals, corroding or disintegrating "practically all kinds of building materials (slate and granite possibly excepted); marble tends first to turn green and then black, limestone deteriorates very rapidly, turning to gypsum owing to its great affinity for sulphur. The absorption of sulphur causes the stone to expand, thus rendering it soluble and powdery so that particles are constantly washed or blown away." Materials such as stone, mortar, concrete, etc., are "soiled by soot and the necessary cleaning by wire brush and detergent chemicals, a sandblast or other drastic methods, is not only costly, but injures the stone itself." Metals, if exposed to smoke-polluted air, suffer not only from soot and tar but also from the presence of obnoxious gases and acid vapors. While "the destruction of iron is most noticeable, for it is the metal in most common use and it is more readily corroded than the majority of metals," there is hardly any metal which is not susceptible to the corrosive action of smoke. In fact, "the sulphuretted hydrogen in smoke blackens, disfigures or tarnishes nearly all metals. Copper and bronze rapidly darken . . . aluminum is affected by vapors and acids, many metals become pitted from electrochemical action and even gold and gilded articles become dull."

Protective paint coatings applied to metallic surfaces and other materials are subject to contamination by atmospheric carbon and dust which tends to reduce their protective efficiency and makes necessary frequent washing. . . .

Furthermore, smoke-polluted air affects the interior of buildings and interior decorations. Air-conditioning and ventilating equipment in particular are subject to corrosion and have been seen to fail within a period of three months owing to smoke-polluted air. Similarly, factory smoke is responsible for the deterioration of the quality and value of all kinds of merchandise, causing substantial losses to wholesale and retail businesses. In addition, air pollution causes social losses as a result of the necessity of more frequent household cleaning and washing.

The social costs of atmospheric pollution go far beyond the losses resulting from the more rapid deterioration of building materials, metals, and paint coatings. Several students of the problem of air pollution have pointed to the injurious effects which the loss of daylight and of ultraviolet light may have upon human health. The most important damages to persons seem to be caused by the inhalation of smoke-polluted air. The poisonous compounds and soot particles contained in smoke-polluted air may serve "as carriers of the obnoxious products of human fatigue which irritate the sensitive membranes of the eyes, nose, throat, lungs, and gastro-intestinal tract, increase the susceptibility to gastro-intestinal, pulmonary and nasopharyngeal disorders, diminish the potential reserve, working capacity, and well-being of the individual, increase fatigue, irritability and malcontent, and may tend to hasten premature decay."

Other less direct effects of air pollution on human health are revealed by the following brief analysis of the influence which factory smoke may have upon weather and general meteorological conditions. To be exact, air pollution and weather conditions influence each other. The presence of smoke in the atmosphere tends to increase the relative humidity and affects adversely the character of daylight; and similarly, high temperatures, low winds and high relative humidity add to the intensity of air pollution in any given locality. In particular, it was found that "smoke lessens the duration and intensity of sunshine; reduces the intensity of daylight, the limit of visibility and the diurnal winter temperature; increases humidity, mists, the frequency and duration of fogs and possibly alters the electrical potential." Moreover, "fogs may become mixed with smoke to such an extent that their color is changed from white to brown, or even black, and prevent sunlight from penetrating to the level of the street. Heat rays as well as light rays are thus stopped so that evaporation of the fog is retarded." . . .

Investigations of the smoke nuisance and its effects on light in the United States established the fact that "city fogs are more persistent than country fogs, principally because of their increased density due to the smoke that accumulates in them." This, in turn, leads to less intense sunshine as well as to "fewer hours of sunshine in the cities than in the surrounding country."

A special study of the loss of light due to smoke on Manhattan Island emphasizes that "in some cases the average hourly or daily percentage loss was greater than 50. The average percentage loss for the whole year was 16.6 for clear days, 34.6 for cloudy days, and 21.5 for all days. The percentage loss on cloudy days was, therefore, about twice as great as on clear days."

In the light of these findings it is not difficult to understand why a smoke-filled atmosphere may have far-reaching effects upon human health and all animal and plant life. The loss of sunshine and the exclusion of ultraviolet radiation reduces physical vitality and makes the human body more susceptible to colds and other bacterial infections. Moreover, humidity intensified by smoke increases the solid poisonous contents of the air, aggravates various pathological conditions of the body, reduces the sensibility of some organs and depletes the vital potential. Fogs likewise "increase the prevalence of diseases and augment the death rate." Still other disadvantages accrue from the fact that artificial light made necessary by the loss of sunshine has injurious effects on human health inasmuch as colorless daylight is superior for visual efficiency and optical health.

It must be noted, however, that the gradual absorption by the human system of the poisonous products of imperfect combustion does not necessarily "give rise to any definitely recognizable acute disorder or specific disabilities. But the process of slow poisoning may insidiously eat away like a mild cancer at vital tissues and thus in time deplete our potential reserve . . ."

Numerous investigations by private and public agencies have yielded a wealth of evidence and quantitative estimates of the social losses caused by air pollution in different industrial localities. Careful studies have been made with a view to measuring the amount of carbon, ash, tar, iron oxide and sulphur dioxide in the air which in the form of dust settles in and around industrial communities. For example, it has been found that 1,800 tons of dust settle per square mile per year in the center of the city of Baltimore, while three miles from the center only 800 tons of settled dust were recorded, and ten miles out in the country the settled dust was 340 tons per square mile per year.

Several monetary estimates of the social costs of air pollution have been made; the earliest and most detailed of these estimates are those of the Mellon Institute of Industrial Research of the University of Pittsburgh in 1913. According to the Smoke Investigation of the Mellon Institute, the smoke nuisance costs the people of Pittsburgh approximately $9,944,740 per annum. This figure applies to conditions prevailing in 1913. More recent estimates place the losses caused by smoke in Pittsburgh at $9.36 per person per year. Later investigations in Pittsburgh convinced the Institute "that we were safe in estimating the cost to each man, woman and child in the city at about $15 each year." Studies made in other places, among them New York, Chicago, Cincinnati, Salt Lake City, Boston and Baltimore have revealed losses amounting to "from $10 to $30 per capita." Estimates for Cleveland range as high as $80 for each family.

The total costs of the smoke nuisance in New York City are placed at about $100,000,000 per year. For the country as a whole "the annual bill for smoke . . . lies in the neighborhood of $500,000,000, of which $140,000,000 is said to represent the cost of spoiled merchandise and of building cleaning." H. W. Wilson of the U. S. Geological Survey likewise placed the loss which the country as a whole suffers as a result of smoke at over $500,000,000 "in damage done to merchandise, defacement on buildings, tarnishing of metals, injury to human life and to plant life, the greatly increased labor and the cost of housekeeping and the losses of the manufacturers due to imperfect combustion of coal."

Air pollution has become a problem because business firms do not wish to incur the expense of installing smoke traps on their chimneys unless their competitors are forced to assume the same obligation.[3] Water pollution, like air pollution, is largely the result of competitive pressures. Proper treatment of industrial waste is expensive. Unless all firms are compelled by law to do so, economic prudence counsels the producer of untreated waste to go right on dumping it into rivers and streams. This kills the fish, makes it more costly for the people downstream to obtain drinking water, and, of course, prevents use of the stream for swimming.

The list of natural resources wasted as a result of competition is long. The same economist who reported on air pollution analyzes waste of petroleum.[4]

Like wildlife, petroleum and natural gas are "migrating" resources in the sense that they are capable of changing their location. Crude oil tends to flow "toward any point where the pressure is reduced below the equalized natural pressure throughout the reservoir. This means it flows toward any well that penetrates the structure." Moreover, crude oil and natural gas are also "free" resources, inasmuch as property rights to these resources

[3] The latest type of air pollution—radioactive fallout resulting from the testing of atomic weapons—can be attributed to international military competition rather than to conventional economic competition.

[4] Karl William Kapp, op. cit., pp. 108–109, 117–118.

are recognized only after their "capture." Just as game belongs to the hunter who kills it, crude oil belongs to the owner of the oil well from which it is produced, regardless of whether or not the oil migrated from beneath land to which some one else had title. "Consequently, when a new pool is discovered, each operator races to drain the field before the oil migrates and is produced through a neighboring well." Even if an individual owner should prefer to postpone production in anticipation of higher prices in the future, he is unable to do so "because postponement of capture means loss of the resource altogether."

It is, therefore, not surprising that the discovery of new reserves usually gives rise to a competitive drilling campaign in the course of which wells tend to be drilled and spaced in such a manner as to maximize their offsetting effect upon each other. In other words, not only will an excessive number of wells be drilled in each newly discovered dome but the position and spacing of these wells will be governed by the desire of each operator to capture as much oil as possible. As a matter of fact, the more the ownership of the surface land is scattered, the more accentuated will be the general rush to withdraw oil from as many "offset" wells as possible. This practice of draining oil pools as rapidly as possible receives adidtional impetus from the fact that oil wells are often operated under a leasing system. In the majority of cases the owner of the oil-bearing tract receives a royalty on the oil produced and therefore is materially interested in the technique and volume of oil recovery from his property. Not infrequently, special stipulations in the leasing contract compel the operating company to produce and to drill offset wells. In other words, if the lessee decided to retard production he would not only "suffer . . . the loss of oil captured from him, but also forfeit the lease itself for neglecting the interests of the lessor." . . .

. . . As already pointed out, the competitive exploitation of petroleum reservoirs is bound up with the drilling of wells far in excess of the number necessary for the recovery of the oil underground. These "unnecessary wells" constitute duplications of capital outlays, which from the point of view of society must be regarded as social losses. Estimates of the magnitude of these losses have been advanced by the oil industry itself as well as by independent investigators. Thus, after careful investigation of the matter, the Independent Petroleum Association of America placed the total number of unnecessary wells in the East Texas field "conservatively" at 12,500 up to 1936. Assuming "that the average cost of drilling a well in the East Texas field over a three-year period is $13,000 . . . the total unnecessary expense merely for the drilling of the 12,500 unnecessary wells is in round figures $162,000,000." Since 1936 more than 4,000 additional wells are reported (by the U. S. Bureau of Mines) to have been drilled in the East Texas field "so that the expenditure for unnecessary wells drilled in that field to date likely exceeds $200,000,000." More recently, Professor McLaughlin, in his testimony before the Temporary National Economic Committee, referred to estimates that "3,000 wells [in the East Texas field] would have been sufficient for production and that in the drilling of 21,000 additional wells perhaps $300,000,000 has been wasted up to the middle of 1937. Moreover, new and unnecessary wells are being added to the field at an additional cost of about $13,-000,000 to $20,000,000 per year." In the Oklahoma City field it was estimated that 360 instead of 677 actually drilled wells would have been ample to recover the oil. At an average cost of $100,000 the total unnecessary expenditures for the 317 wells amounted to $31,700,000.

Sometimes wasteful competition is not based on economic considerations. Thus, important as is the role of commercial fisheries in "mining" streams of salmon and shad, the amateur fisherman contributes his share. In his zeal to catch more fish than his rivals, he may take (a) more than his limit under the fish and game laws or (b) smaller fish than he is allowed. Sportsmen have become so unsporting about it that most states have to stock streams with fish raised specially for this purpose. Still the spirit of competition drives the sportsmen on. They follow the trucks which stock the streams, giving the fish hardly a chance to hit the water before they start casting.

Sometimes the competition that occurs in the context of economic activities is motivated by prestige considerations rather

than money. Consider the following example of relentless competition in a public employment agency.[5]

This paper discusses performance and variations in competitiveness among twelve interviewers in two small sections of
a public employment agency. The duties of the interviewers in
both sections were essentially alike. They received requests for
workers over the phone. The order forms on which job openings
were described were filed in a common pool in each section.
Most of the official's time was spent interviewing applicants for
jobs. After ascertaining the client's qualifications, the interviewer
searched the sectional files for suitable vacancies. If an acceptable job was found, he referred the client to it and later phoned
the employer to determine whether the client had been hired.

"The statistics which show how many interviews and how
many placements each person in the section did are passed
around to all interviewers. Of course, you look at them and see
how you compare with others. This creates a competitive spirit,"
said one of the interviewers, voicing the sentiments of most of
his fellows. In a period of job shortages, competition took the
form of trying to utilize job openings before anybody else did.
Interviewers were so anxious to make placements that they even
resorted to illicit methods. Said one:

When you take an order, instead of putting it in the box,
you leave it on your desk. There was so much hiding of
orders under the blotter that we used to ask, "Do you have
anything under your rug?" when we looked for an order.
You might leave an order you took on the desk, or you might
leave it on the desk after you made no referral. . . . Or,
you might take an order only partially; you write the firm's
name, and a few things; the others you remember. And you
leave it on the pad [of order blanks]. You keep on doing
this, and all these orders are not in the box.

You can do some wrong filling out. For instance, for a
rather low-salary job, you fill out "experience required." Nobody can make a placement on that except you, because you,

[5] Reprinted from "Co-operation and Competition in a Bureaucracy," by
Peter M. Blau, which was published in the *American Journal of Sociology*,
Vol. 59 (1954), pp. 530–535, by permission of The University of Chicago
Press, Chicago, Illinois. Copyright 1954, by The University of Chicago Press.

alone, know that experience isn't required. Or, if there are several openings [on one order], you put the order into "referrals" [file category for *filled* job openings] after you make one placement. You're supposed to put it into "referrals" but stand it up, so that the others can see it. If you don't, you have a better chance of making the next placement than somebody else. And time and again you see four, five openings on one order filled by the same person. [In one case on file eight out of nine openings on one order had been filled by the same interviewer.]

The major opportunity for competitive monopolization of job openings occurred when they were received from employers. Since illicit practices were concealed from the observer, the extent of competition could not be determined through questioning or direct observation but was betrayed by the record of official transactions. The extent to which an interviewer filled the vacancies he had received over the phone with his own clients in excess of chance expectations furnishes an index of competitiveness. . . .

The interviewers in *both* sections disliked working in a competitive atmosphere. A member of Section A said: "If I see that an interviewer keeps orders on her desk, I take them and put them in the box. . . . Of course, you don't make friends that way." Since the majority in this section, including its most popular members, were highly competitive, to antagonize them was to threaten one's own standing in the group. This deterred interviewers from discouraging competitive practices. Antagonizing a deviant, however, does not endanger one's status. Consequently, since a striver was unpopular in Section B, its members could use sanctions freely to combat competitive practices and enforce co-operative norms. . . .

To maximize his placements, the interviewer in Section A hoarded jobs and simultaneously tried to prevent others from doing so, thereby antagonizing his co-workers, whose co-operation he needed if he was to do well. The members of this section therefore attempted to conciliate colleagues whom their competitive practices had alienated. Often, shortly after having interfered with her operations, an interviewer paid another a compliment about her work or her apparel. The most competitive interviewer was in the habit of taking time out to joke with her co-workers and was proud of making more placements than anybody else, "nevertheless." Actually, this compensating friendliness, which made her popular despite her competitiveness, helped her to be productive.

In Section A, interviewers had to make special efforts at conciliation in order to make placements, but this was not necessary in Section B. At least, this impression is corroborated by the finding that frequency of private contacts with others was also related to productivity in Section A (rank correlation $= +.84$) but not in Section B (rank correlation $= +.13$). The members of the cohesive group, whose operating practices did not put colleagues at a disadvantage, did not have to devote time and energy to solicit and encourage co-operation, since it was not extended reluctantly. Their spontaneous co-operation improved operating efficiency.

Social cohesion also lessened the status anxiety generated by the evaluation system. Such anxiety is most acute in the individual who does not feel integrated in his work group and therefore seeks to derive social recognition from excelling at his task and from approval of superiors. Friendly relations with co-workers made the standing of the individual in the cohesive group independent of his productivity, particularly since fast work was disparaged as a sign of superficial service. The consequent reduction of anxiety in the antiproductivity-oriented group actually raised its productivity.

SUMMARY

Competition—the principle of allocating roles on the basis of who can surpass the other aspirants to the role—has been a major spur to diligent role performance and to efficient use of resources in American society. There is little question that it has resulted in strenuous effort and a high rate of innovation. But it has been a costly spur, being the direct source of many *in*efficiencies and casualties.

Its weakness as a source of productive effort lies in the fact that the pressure it places on people is pressure to *get into* and *hold onto* a role, not, except accidentally, pressure to be productive or to insure that efficiency is maximized. Thus the railroads, faced with competition from the trucking industry, were not pressured thereby into increasing their efficiency. They were pressured to hold onto their role of "transportation-provider" by attempting to discredit truckers. Another example is the case of air pollution: Competitive pressure works against, not for, the efficient burning of fuel. Competition also has made it inefficient, from the individual's point of view, to drill the proper number of oil wells. In an employment agency, it resulted in practices which are competitively efficient for the individual interviewer, but inefficient for the function the agency was supposed to perform.

ANNOTATED BIBLIOGRAPHY

Chase, Stuart, *The Tragedy of Waste* (New York: The Macmillan Company, 1937). ❡ A skillful and highly readable popular account of wasted resources in America. The author discusses wastes, traceable in large part to the pressures of competition, in consumption, manpower and natural resources.

Kapp, Karl William, *The Social Costs of Private Enterprise* (Cambridge: Harvard University Press, 1950). ❡ An economist's attempt to focus attention on a variety of "costs" of doing business in a competitive structure that do not show up in corporate balance sheets. Kapp shows how the pressures of competition make it impossible for any single firm to reckon with such costs as air and water pollution, soil erosion, unemployment, and so on, even if it wanted to.

Loomis, Stuart D., and Green, Arnold, "The Pattern of Mental Conflict in a Typical State University," *Journal of Abnormal and Social Psychology,* Vol. 42 (1947), pp. 342–355. ❡ An analysis of the competitive stresses on a college campus through the clinical investigation of students with psychological problems. According to the authors, many of the mentally ill students were casualties of a competitive social system.

Packard, Vance, *The Hidden Persuaders* (New York: David McKay, 1957). ❡ A somewhat naive and therefore alarming account of the manipulation of the consumer's subconscious mind by advertising agencies and public relations firms. The implicit villain of the book is "relentless competition."

Ross, Ralph, and Van Den Haag, Ernest, *The Fabric of Society* (New York: Harcourt, Brace and Company, Inc., 1957). ❡ A stimulating basic text in sociology, unusual for its urbane, literate, and generally civilized style and the authors' unabashed weaving of their personal convictions into the threads of their exposition. Chapter 7, "Competition and Conflict," is a good discussion of the differences between those two forms of interpersonal relations, and the bases on which they are distinguished.

CHAPTER FOURTEEN

The refusal to accept defeat:

Rejection of competition

Adherence to the competitive principle requires fortitude. In almost any competition, there are few winners and many losers. The disgruntled freshmen who describe a mixer dance as a "rat race" are reacting to the strains of competition. Rejection of competition as the guiding principle for allocating roles does not necessarily produce social problems. On the contrary, co-operative arrangements are often brought into being when it

351

becomes evident that competition produces too many casualties. Thus, the National Safety Council continues to plead for a mitigation of the competitive spirit on the nation's highways. Unfortunately, the rejection of competition does not always result in socially desirable "cooperation." Sometimes erstwhile competitors combine in an alliance so as to exploit bargaining opponents, for example, customers, suppliers, employers. This is especially common in economic activities. The Sherman Anti-Trust Act, which Congress passed in 1890, implicitly assumes that social problems result from such collusion: "Every contract, combination in the form of trust or otherwise, or conspiracy in restraint of trade or commerce among the several States or with foreign nations, is hereby declared to be illegal." Despite the Sherman Act and the Clayton Anti-Trust Act, passed in 1914, monopolistic practices continue. The following selection summarizes some of the relevant findings of a Congressional investigation of such practices.[1]

"Monopoly," of course, is not a precise word; it is subject to many interpretations and may thus provoke many misunderstandings and much needless quibbling. There are degrees of monopoly, varying from no control to complete domination. Moreover, domination may be achieved by one producer or by a combination of producers. Combination may be overt and tangible, or it may represent subtle and intangible alliances and understandings unrecognized by the consuming public and unreached by the monopoly laws. "Monopoly" is used here in its broadest sense and is intended to embrace all arrangements by which producers effect varying degrees of market control and by which they succeed in obtaining for themselves some of the benefits of monopoly price. Variations from pure monopoly have been discussed in recent years under more precise terms, which include "monopolistic competition," "duopoly," "oligopoly," and "imperfect competition."

One of the most prominent types of monopolistic combination today is the loose, but effective, practice which has come to

[1] From *The Concentration of Economic Power* by David Lynch, pp. 195–198, copyright 1946. Reprinted by permission of the Columbia University Press, New York.

be known as "price leadership." Unlike the trust, the pool, the holding company, the merger, and other methods of combination prevalent at the turn of the century, price leadership is inconspicuous and offers little tangible evidence of collusion or conspiracy, however obvious its results may be. The practice is similar to the price pool, but there is no overt evidence of its existence, and it often represents nothing more than a tacit understanding among producers to "follow the leader" in price policy.

Price leadership may become operative in a number of ways. Sometimes it results from an unwritten agreement among producers, arrived at after deliberation and consultation. At times it occurs when one producing unit is so large and possesses such industrial strength that it dominates the field, with the result that lesser firms, guided by prudence and experience, indicate their willingness to follow the policies of the leader. It may develop in an industry where there are a few giant firms of approximately equal strength, each with a healthy respect for the power of the others and each reluctant to engage them in all-out competition. The result, therefore, may be a "live-and-let-live," "follow-a-leader" truce. Other instances have occurred in which militant and aggressive producers in a given field have employed duress to whip competitors into a price leadership program.

Price leadership commends itself to those seeking to control the market not only because it is effective but also because it is beyond the reach of the law. When no agreement exists and when there is no formal organization, it is quite impossible to show collusion or conspiracy. In fact, the defenders of price leadership have asserted that the very existence of the end product—uniform price—is in itself proof of effective competition, since in a regime of free competition all producers sell at one price—market price.

Prices determined under the price leadership regime probably constitute the most common form of controlled prices in the American market. Though relatively unknown a few decades ago, price leadership was described to the TNEC as one of the most dominant of prevalent types of monopoly. In recent years this method of control has been common in the following industries: crackers, newsprint, steel, anthracite, gasoline, flour, corn syrup, stoves, tin plate, cigarettes, and milk bottles.

It should not be concluded from these remarks that the price leader policy is clandestine or that its existence is denied by industrialists with guilty consciences. On the contrary, the practice is openly referred to and discussed with frankness and candor. A few remarks by industrialists are illustrative. One corporation president said, "We generally make the prices"; another told the TNEC, "I was very glad . . . of the opportunity to follow the Corporation's lead"; others indicated that it was their practice never to initiate price changes but to meet them and to follow a policy of "live-and-let-live." One executive described the position of his firm thus: "We are too small to lead," while another more supinely said, "We have to follow." One industrialist testified that price leadership had been an established practice in his industry as far back as he could remember: "It is the custom of the industry. We have always done it."

Marketing Gasoline. The instructions sent by its executive to the members of the National Association of Petroleum Retailers vividly describe the operation of price leadership. After setting forth the intent of initiating a series of price increases for retail gasoline, the writer turned to the mehod by which uniform increased prices might be obtained. He proposed to emulate the example of the distributors.

> The answer has been before our eyes for many years. . . . In each territory there has been a supplier that was recognized as the market leader and other suppliers have merely met the competition set by the leader. . . . The dealers can do the same thing. . . . The leader must be a petroleum retailer and he must be followed by all other retailers in the territory.

That such price control is a violation of the spirit and the purpose of the monopoly laws and constitutes a carefully implemented method of circumventing those statutes is emphasized by the care with which the trade association advised its members; concert, collusion, and "conspiracy against the public" was the aim and the purpose of the policy proposed, but all tangible evidence of such intrigue was to be avoided with meticulous care. The members of the trade association were told:

> By this time you should be in a position to select your "market leader" who has the courage and those qualities of leadership that others recognize and will follow. After he is selected, give him your whole-hearted support. Remember to not agree upon a price, but each individual has the right to determine what he wants to do and to announce it, thus avoiding any conspiracy. Your "market leader" can set a price and the organization can send out a notice.

Many independent retail gasoline dealers or their representatives testified that price leadership is a common practice at the filling stations. Usually the pace is set by one of the large integrated companies who, because of their oligopolistic positions, adopt the same policies and follow the same procedures. When one company posts a price cut, they all follow suit; when one posts a price raise, they fall in line. Usually the market leader in a given area is the company which sells the largest gallonage

TABLE 1. *Market Leadership in the Petroleum Industry, 1939*

Area	Price Leader
New York and New England	Socony-Vacuum Oil Corp.
Pennsylvania and Delaware	Atlantic Refining Co.
New Jersey, Maryland, District of Columbia, Virginia, North Carolina, and South Carolina	Standard Oil Co. of New Jersey
Ohio	Standard Oil Co. of Ohio
Kentucky, Mississippi, Alabama, Georgia, and Florida	Standard Oil Co. of Kentucky
Tennessee, Louisiana, and Arkansas	Standard Oil Co. of Louisiana
Michigan, Indiana, Wisconsin, Illinois, Iowa, Missouri, North Dakota, South Dakota, Nebraska, Kansas, and Minnesota	Standard Oil Co. of Indiana
Montana, Wyoming, Colorado, New Mexico, Idaho, and Utah	Continental Oil Co.
Washington, Oregon, California, Nevada, and Arizona	Standard Oil Co. of California
Oklahoma	Magnolia (subsidiary of Socony)
Texas	Magnolia or Texas Corp.

in that area. Thus, the leader almost always is one of the great integrated companies and more often than not a member of the original Standard Oil group. Table 1 lists the market leaders for various areas in 1939.

An interesting illustration of the *modus operandi* employed to implement price leadership came to light in the Ohio area. The Pennzoil Company regularly required its retailers to market its product at prices established by the Standard Oil Company. Frequently retailers of Pennzoil products knew as far as a day in advance the nature of price changes announced by Standard. Mimeographed price notices published by Standard Oil were distributed by the Pennzoil Company to its dealers. A formal pool or a trust arrangement could scarcely have been more effective.

The Steel Industry. In 1936 the president of the United States Steel Corporation testified before a Senate committee that price leadership was characteristic of the steel industry. The following testimony is pertinent:

MR. IRVIN. I would say we generally make the prices.
THE CHAIRMAN. You generally make the prices?
MR. IRVIN. Yes, sir; we generally make the prices, unless some of the other members of the industry think that that price may be too high and they make the price.
THE CHAIRMAN. You lead off, then, with a price charged, either up or down, at Gary, is that correct?
MR. IRVIN. Yes, sir. . . . We always notify the trade papers . . . and others interested as to what our prices are.
THE CHAIRMAN. Then the rest of them follow that?
MR. IRVIN. I think they do. That is, I say they generally do. They may quote the same price, but maybe they need some business and make a better price. We do not always know that until it is over.

In the steel industry both the leader and those who were led freely acknowledged that this practice was customary. Mr. Eugene C. Grace, representing the Bethlehem Steel Corporation, preferred to designate it as "meeting a competitive situation" when his company adopted pricing policies in concert with the United States Steel Corporation. Whatever the lead of the latter, whether the price change was up or down, the Bethlehem

Steel Corporation followed. Mr. Grace appeared to be unable to cite any important instance in recent years when his company had taken the initiative or had been aggressive in quoting prices. He paid frequent tribute to the price leadership system and to the direction given it by the United States Steel Corporation. Some of his tributes were as follows: "It is a good guide for us"; "We welcomed the opportunity"; "We needed it and we followed it"; "I was very glad then of the opportunity to follow the Corporation's lead."

Similarly, representatives of other steel companies indicated that they adhered to the policy fixed by the United States Steel Corporation. The president of the National Steel Corporation testified that his company never initiated a price and always met whatever price was established. He preferred to call this "meeting competition" rather than to recognize it for what it was— monopoly price through price leadership. Obviously, when no one cuts the base price established by the leader and all meet that price simultaneously, that is not competition. This concept of competition was more realistically acknowledged by some to be a policy of "live-and-let-live."

The flight from the rigors of competition occurs among small firms as well as large. But we know much more about the monopolistic practices of giant corporations because the Anti-Trust Division of the Department of Justice does not concern itself with trifles. When competition is perceived as too threatening, business firms devise monopolistic practices. For essentially the same reasons, workers who feel insecure in their relations with the employer establish informal norms restricting production. Donald Roy shows some of the control mechanisms, by means of which these norms are enforced, in his article, "Quota Restriction and Goldbricking in a Machine Shop." [2]

I here report and analyze observations of restriction made during eleven months of work as a radial-drill operator in the machine shop of a steel-processing plant in 1944 and 1945. For

[2] Reprinted from an article entitled "Quota Restriction and Goldbricking in a Machine Shop," by Donald Roy, which was published in the *American Journal of Sociology,* Vol. 57 (1952), pp. 427–438, by permission of the University of Chicago Press, Chicago, Illinois.

ten months I kept a daily record of my feelings, thoughts, experiences, and observations and of conversations with my fel-
low-workers. I noted down the data from memory at the end of
each workday, only occasionally making surreptitious notes on
the job. I recorded my own production openly in the shop. I
did not reveal my research interests to either management or
workers. I remained "one of the boys on the line," sharing the
practices and confidences of my fellows and joining them in their
ceaseless war with management, rather indifferently at first, but
later wholeheartedly. . . .

From November 9, 1944, to August 30, 1945, I worked
1,850.5 hours. 1,350.9 (73 per cent) were "production-piecework" hours. The remaining 499.6 hours were taken up with
time study, rework, and set-up. In 669.4 (49.6 per cent) of the
production-piecework hours, I "made out." That is, I produced
enough pieces of work to "earn," at the piece rates for the kinds
of work done, the 85-cent-per-hour "base rate" which we received for every hour spent on the job. I thus "earned" my 85
cents in about half the hours when there was opportunity—
through completing more pieces—to earn more than that. Ob-
versely, about half the time my "turn in" (work done and turned
in) fell below the base-rate standard.

My hourly earnings on production piecework varied from
$0.09 to $1.66, a range of $1.57. Table 2 shows that the spread
of hourly earnings for the various jobs, or "operations" performed, was bimodal; this distribution suggests two major types
of output behavior.

About one-half of my hours of piecework "earnings" fell on
either side of the 85-cent-an-hour "day-rate" and "make-out"
point, indicating 85 cents as an approximate median. However,
this distribution by no means forms a bell-shaped curve, with 85
cents as a modal point. "Make-out" and "non-make-out"—
piecework hours form two almost separate distributions, with
74.1 per cent of the 669.4 "make-out" hours concentrated in the
$1.25–$1.34 interval, and 43.2 per cent of the 681.5 "non-
make-out" hours clustered in two adjacent intervals, $0.35–
$0.54. Concentration of "make-out" hours is even more marked,

for 82.8 per cent fall within three 5-cent intervals, $1.20–$1.34, and 64.1 per cent fall within the one 5-cent interval, $1.25–$1.29.

TABLE 2. *Production Piecework Hours Worked by Ten-Cent Earning Intervals*

Earnings per Hour (in cents)	Hours Worked		Per Cent	
Unknown*	103.9		7.7	
5–14	3.0		0.2	
15–24	51.0		3.8	
25–34	49.8		3.7	
35–44	150.1		11.1	
45–54	144.5		10.7	
55–64	57.7		4.3	
65–74	63.8		4.7	
75–84	57.7		4.3	
Total under 85 cents		681.5		50.4
85–94	51.2		3.8	
95–104	19.5		1.5	
105–114	17.9		1.3	
115–124	83.0		6.1	
125–134	496.3		36.7	
165–174	1.5		0.1	
Total 85 cents or more		669.4		49.6
Total		1,350.9		100.0

* All "unknown" hourly earnings fell below the base-rate level of 85 cents per hour.

That this bimodal pattern of hourly earnings for the ten-month period does not represent the joining of the "tails" of two temporal distributions—i.e., one for an initial learning period and the other showing completely different production behavior with the acquisition of skill—is indicated by a comparison of earning distributions for two periods of four and six months, respectively. In this comparison (Table 3) the period from November through February represents one level of skill; that from March through August, a higher level. Although the proportion of make-out hours for the second period was more than double that of the first and although concentration of make-out hours in modal earning intervals increased, the pattern was clearly bimodal in both periods. Both "levels of skill" show the same modal earning interval of $1.25–$1.34 for make-out hours. The modal earning interval for non-make-out hours advanced but one notch, from $0.35 to $0.44 to $0.45 to $0.54.

TABLE 3. *Production-Piecework Hours Worked, by Ten-Cent Earning Intervals, per Two Diary Periods*

| Earnings per Hour (in Cents) | PERIOD 1 (NOVEMBER THROUGH FEBRUARY) | | PERIOD 2 (MARCH THROUGH AUGUST) | |
	Hours Worked	Per Cent	Hours Worked	Per Cent
Unknown*	66.4	11.4	37.5	4.9
5–14	3.0	0.5	. . . .	. . . .
15–24	13.5	2.3	37.5	4.9
25–34	37.8	6.5	12.0	1.6
35–44	93.0	16.0	57.1	7.4
45–54	74.0	12.8	70.5	9.1
55–64	43.1	7.4	14.6	1.9
65–74	36.8	6.3	27.0	3.5
75–84	49.0	8.5	8.7	1.1
Total under 85 cents	416.6	71.7	264.9	34.4
85–94	39.1	6.7	12.1	1.6
95–104	9.7	1.7	9.8	1.3
105–114	3.8	0.7	14.1	1.8
115–124	18.0	3.1	65.0	8.4
125–134	93.2	16.1	403.1	52.3
165–174	. . . .	. . . .	1.5	0.2
Total 85 cents or over	163.8	28.3	505.6	65.6
Total	580.4	100.0	770.5	100.0

* All "unknown" hourly earnings fell below the base-rate level of 85 cents per hour.

While I did not keep a complete record of the hourly earnings of my "day man" on the radial drill (I worked a "second" shift), I frequently jotted down his day's run. His figures were roughly correlative with my own. References to the diary will be made to show that I was not out of line with other operators in the shop.

The bimodal pattern was the rule of the shop. An outsider might believe that it reflects the struggle of workers with two kinds of jobs, hard and easy. He might then posit any number of reasons why the jobs fall into two piles rather than into one bell-shaped heap: some peculiarity of time-study men or some change of company policy. It would indeed be difficult so to set piece rates that it would be equally easy to "make out" on all kinds of work. But one sophisticated in shop ways and aware of all the devices of time-study men would hardly credit them with either the ability or the will to turn up "tight" and "loose" piece rates in other than a single bell-shaped distribution. He would not attribute the bimodal distortion of hourly earnings to anything so improbable as bimodal distribution of hard and easy jobs. It could be that the operators, ignoring finer distinctions in job timing, sort jobs into two bins, one for "gravy" jobs, the other for "stinkers."

Let us assume that the average of worker effort will be constant from job to job. Job A might be rated as 5 cents an hour "harder" than Job B. But Job A turns out to yield 75 cents an hour less than Job B instead of the expected 5 cents an hour less. One suspects that effort has not been constant. When an operator discovers that he can earn $1.00 an hour on Job B, he will then put forth extra effort and ingenuity to make it $1.25. When, however, he finds that he can earn only 95 cents an hour on Job A, he rejects that amount and drops to a level of effort that earns only 50 cents an hour and relies upon his 85-cent base-pay rate for "take home." Job B has therefore become the "gravy" job, and Job A the "stinker." Into the "stinker" bin goes A, along with 90-cent jobs, 85-cent jobs, and 60-cent jobs.

The pronounced dichotomy in the production behavior of the machine operator suggests that restriction might be classified into two major types, "quota restriction" and "goldbricking." The heavy concentration of hours at the $1.25–$1.34 level with no spilling-over to the next level makes "quota restriction" appear as a limitation of effort on "gravy" jobs in order not to exceed set maximums. It could also be inferred that "gold-bricking" appears as a "holding-back," or failure to release effort, when a close approach to the quota seems unattainable. . . .

When I was hired, a personnel department clerk assured me that the radial-drill operators were averaging $1.25 an hour on piecework. He was using a liberal definition of the term "averaging." Since I had had no previous machine-shop experience and since a machine would not be available for a few days, I was advised to spend some time watching Jack Starkey, a radial-drill man of high rank in seniority and skill.

One of Starkey's first questions was, "What have you been doing?" When I said I had worked in a Pacific Coast shipyard at a rate of pay over $1.00 an hour, Starkey exclaimed, "Then what are you doing in this place?" When I replied that averaging $1.25 an hour wasn't bad, he exploded:

"Averaging, you say! Averaging?"

"Yeah, on the average. I'm an average guy; so I ought to make my buck and a quarter. That is, after I get onto it."

"Don't you know," cried Starkey angrily, "that $1.25 an hour is the *most* we can make even when we *can* make more! And most of the time we can't even make that! Have you ever worked on piecework before?"

"No."

"I can see that! Well, what do you suppose would happen if I turned in $1.25 an hour on these pump bodies?"

"Turned in? You mean if you actually did the work?"

"I mean if I actually did the work and turned it in!"

"They'd have to pay you, wouldn't they? Isn't that the agreement?"

"Yes! They'd pay me—once! Don't you know that if I turned in $1.50 an hour on these pump bodies tonight, the whole God-damned Methods Department would be down here tomorrow? And they'd retime this job so quick it would make your head swim! And when they retimed it, they'd cut the price in half! And I'd be working for 85 cents an hour instead of $1.25!"

From this initial exposition of Starkey's to my last day at the plant I was subject to warnings and predictions concerning price cuts. Pressure was the heaviest from Joe Mucha, day man on my machine, who shared my job repertoire and kept a close eye on my production. On November 14, the day after my first attained quota, Mucha advised:

"Don't let it go over $1.25 an hour, or the time-study man will be right down here! And they don't waste time, either! They watch the records like a hawk! I got ahead, so I took it easy for a couple of hours."

Joe told me that I had made $10.01 yesterday and warned me not to go over $1.25 an hour. He told me to figure the set-ups and the time on each operation very carefully so that I would not total over $10.25 in any one day.

Jack Starkey defined the quota carefully but forcefully when I turned in $10.50 for one day, or $1.31 an hour.

Jack Starkey spoke to me after Joe left. "What's the matter? Are you trying to upset the apple cart?"

Jack explained in a friendly manner that $10.50 was too much to turn in, even on an old job.

"The turret-lathe men can turn in $1.35," said Jack, "but their rate is 90 cents, and ours 85 cents."

Jack warned me that the Methods Department could lower their prices on any job, old or new, by changing the fixture slightly, or changing the size of drill. According to Jack, a couple of operators (first and second shift on the same drill) got to competing with each other to see how much they could turn in. They go up to $1.65 an hour, and the price was cut in half. And from then on they had to run that job themselves, as none of the other operators would accept the job.

According to Jack, it would be all right for us to turn in $1.28 or $1.29 an hour, when it figured out that way, but it was not all right to turn in $1.30 an hour.

Well, now I know where the maximum is—$1.29 an hour.

Starkey's beliefs concerning techniques of price-cutting were those of the shop. Leonard Bricker, an old-timer in the shop, and Willie, the stock-chaser, both affirmed that management, once bent on slashing a piecework price, would stop at nothing.

"Take these $1.25 jobs. One guy will turn in $1.30 an hour one day. Then another fellow will turn in, say, $1.31 or $1.32. Then the first fellow will go up to $1.35. First thing you know they'll be up to $1.50, and bang! They'll tear a machine to pieces to change something to cut a price!"

In the washroom, before I started work, Willie commented on my gravy job, the pedestals.

"The Methods Department is going to lower the price," he said. "There was some talk today about it."

"I hope they don't cut it too much," I said. "I suppose they'll make some change in the jigs?"

"They'll change the tooling in some way. Don't worry, when they make up their minds to lower a price, they'll find a way to do it!"

The association of quota behavior with such expressions about price-cutting does not prove a causal connection. Such a connection could be determined only by instituting changes in the work situation that would effect a substantial reduction of "price-cut fear" and by observing the results of such changes. . . .

Whatever its causes, such restriction resulted in appreciable losses of time in the shop. I have evidence of it from observation of the work behavior and talk of fellow-operators and from my own work behavior. Since ability to "make out" early was related to skill and experience, it was some time before I found enough time wasted on quota restriction to record. But I discovered early that other operators had time to burn.

One evening Ed Sokolsky, onetime second-shift operator on Jack Starkey's drill, commented on a job that Jack was running:

"That's gravy! I worked on those, and I could turn out nine an hour. I timed myself at six minutes."

I was surprised.

"At 35 cents apiece, that's over $3.00 an hour!"

"And I got ten hours," said Ed. "I used to make out in four hours and fool around the rest of the night."

If Sokolsky reported accurately, he was "wasting" six hours per day.

Ed claimed that he could make over $3.00 an hour on the two machines he was running, but he could turn in only

$1.40 an hour or, occasionally, $1.45 or $1.50 for the two machines together. Ed said that he always makes out for ten hours by eleven o'clock, that he has nothing to do from 11:00 to 3:00, and has even left early, getting someone to punch his timecard for him.

"That's the advantage of working nights," said Ed. "You can make out in a hurry and sit around, and nobody says anything. But you can't get away with it on day shift with all the big shots around. Jack has to take it easy on these housings to make them last eight hours, and that must be tough.

"Old Pete," another "old-timer" confided in me:

"Another time when they timed me on some connecting rods, I could have made $20.00 a day, easy. I had to run them at the lowest speed on the machine to keep from making too much. I had a lot of trouble once when I was being timed, and they gave me $35.00 a hundred. Later they cut it to $19.50 a hundred, and I still made $9.50 a day."

If Old Pete could have made $20.00 a day, he was "wasting" four hours a day.

My own first "spare time" came on November 18.

Today I made out with such ease on the pedestals that I had an hour to spare. To cover the hour I had to poke along on the last operation, taking twice as much time to do 43 pieces as I ordinarily would.

But it wasn't until March, when I experienced a sudden increase in skill, that I was capable of making out early on any job but the pedestals. With this increase in skill I found the pedestals quickly fading as the supreme distributors of "gravy." One and one-half hours of loafing recorded on March 22 was a portent of things to come.

I stalled along tonight, turning out only 89 pieces, adding in my kitty of 40 pieces for a turn-in of 129. Joe had a kitty of 13, and I figured that the 116 pieces left would just do him tomorrow. I finished my last piece about 9:30 and started cleaning up the machine about ten o'clock. I noticed that Tony was also through early, standing around his machine.

"This is the earliest you've made out, isn't it?" he asked.

Dick Smith remarked to me, "That's the kind of job I like. Then I can go at it and enjoy it."

On April 7 I was able to enjoy four hours of "free time."

I turned out 43 pieces in the four hours from three to seven, averaging nearly 11 an hour (or $2.085 per hour). At seven o'clock there were only 23 pieces left in the lot, and I knew there would be no point in building up a kitty for Monday if Joe punched off the job before I got to work. I could not go ahead with the next order (also a load of connecting rods) because the new ruling made presentation of a work order to the stock-chaser necessary before material could be brought up. So I was stymied and could do nothing the rest of the day. I had 43 pieces plus 11 from yesterday's kitty to turn in for a total 54.

I sat around the rest of the evening, and none of the bosses seemed to mind.

By August I was more sophisticated in the art of loafing, and complaints of being "stymied" were not recorded.

I had good luck with the reamers and had my needed 26 pieces by six o'clock. I did 10 more for a kitty for Monday and wound up the evening's work at seven o'clock. The last four hours I sat around and talked to various operators.

I reached my peak in quota restriction on June 27, with but three and a half hours of productive work out of the eight. . . .

On "gravy jobs" the operators earned a quota, then knocked off. On "stinkers" they put forth only minimal effort; either they did not try to achieve a turn-in equal to the base wage rate or they deliberately slowed down. Jobs were defined as "good" and "bad" jobs, not in terms of the effort or skill necessary to making out at a bare base-rate level, but of the felt attainability of a substantial premium, i.e., 15 cents an hour or more. Earnings of $1.00 an hour in relation to a $1.25 quota and an 85-cent base rate were considered worth the effort, while earnings of 95 cents an hour were not.

The attitude basic to the goldbricking type of restriction was expressed succinctly thus: "They're not going to get much work out of me for this pay!"

Complaints about low piecework prices were chronic and universal in the shop.

The turret lathe men discussed the matter of making out, one man stating that only half the time could a man make 84 cents day rate on a machine. It was agreed: "What's the use of pushing when it's hard even to make day rate?"

His 50–50 estimate was almost equal to my own experience of 49.6–50.4. Pessimistic though it was, it was less so than usual statements on the subject:

I asked Jackson if he was making out, and he gave me the usual answer, "No!"

"They ask me how I'm making out, and I always say, 'O.K.' As far as I'm concerned, I'm making out O.K. If they start asking me further, I'll tell them that this place stinks."

"The day man isn't making out either. We get a lot of little jobs, small lots. It's impossible to make out when you're getting small jobs all the time."

Joe was working on a new job, time study on some small pieces tonight. I asked him, "Something good?" and he replied, "Nothing is good any more!"

There seemed to be no relation between a man's ability to earn and his behavior on a "stinker." That the men who most frequently earned the quota goldbricked like the rest on poor jobs appears in the following extracts:

Al McCann (the man who made quota most often) said that he gives a job a trial, and if it is no good he takes his time. He didn't try to make out on the chucks tonight.

Joe Mucha, my day man, said of a certain job: "I did just one more than you did. If they don't like it they can do them themselves. To hell with them. I'm not going to bust my ass on stuff like this."

Old Peter, the multiple drill man, said, "I ran some pieces for 25 minutes to see how many I could turn out. I turned out 20 at 1½ cents apiece (72 cents an hour). So I smoke and take it easy. I can't make out; so —————— it."

I notice that when Ed Sokolsky, one of the better operators on the line, is working on an operation he cannot make out on, he does not go at his task with vigor. He either pokes around or leaves his machine for long periods of time; and Paul (set-up man) seems always to be looking for him. Steve (supt.) is always bellowing, "Where in hell is Ed?" or "Come on, Ed, let's have some production around here!" Tonight I heard him admonishing Ed again, "Now I want you to work at that machine till three o'clock, do you understand?"

Mike Koszyk, regarded as a crack operator: The price was a poor one (a few cents a hundred) and the job tough. Mike had turned out only 9 pieces in 3 hours. When Mike takes his time, he really takes his time!

According to Al, Jack Starkey turned in 40 cents an hour today on his chuck parts. Al laughed, saying, "I guess Jack didn't like this job."

Gus Schmidt, regarded as the best speed-drill operator on the second shift, was timed early in the evening on a job, and given a price of $1.00 per 100 for reaming one hole, chamfering both sides of three holes, and filing burrs on one end of one hole. All that for one cent!

"To hell with them," said Gus.

He did not try to make out.

The possibility of covering "day rate" was ordinarily no spur to the machine operator to bestir himself on a job. A remark of Mucha's was characteristic: "I could have made out," he said, "but why kill yourself for day rate?"

Average hourly earnings of less or even a little more than $1.00 an hour were usually thrown into the "day-rate" category.

Joe Mucha drilled 36 of the bases (at $8.80 per 100) today. "The most I'll ever do until they retime this job is 40," he said. "Do you know, they expect us to do 100? Why, I wouldn't bust my ass to do 50, for $8.00, when day rate is almost that!"

McCann was put to drilling some pieces at $6.50 per 100. I noticed him working furiously and walked over to see what he was doing. He asked me to figure out how many pieces at 6½ cents he had to turn out per hour to make $1.20. When I told him 18 or 19 he said, "I give up," and immediately slowed down.

A few minutes later I met him in the washroom, and he said, "I wouldn't work that hard for eight or ten hours even if I could make out. I thought I'd try it for an hour or so and see what I could do."

He figures that he was making 95 cents an hour. At lunch time he said that he had averaged $1.00 an hour for the two hours and thought maybe he would try to make out.

Resentment against piecework prices that were considered too low to offer possibilities of quota earnings often resulted in deliberate attempts to produce at lower rates than mere "dogging it along" would bring. This kind of goldbricking was particularly noticeable on jobs that came relatively often and in large lots. Toward a short order of poor price that was assigned to his machine but once or twice a year, the operator's attitude was likely to be one of "I don't give a damn," and the result would be production below "standard." But toward a low-priced order assigned every month or two and in amounts that would take several shifts to a week to process, i.e., jobs that played a major part in the operator's repertoire, the attitude was likely to be, "Just for that, you'll get as little as I can turn out and still be operating this machine!"

The hinge-base fight is an example of deliberate restriction on a major job that was regarded as poorly priced. This fight went on for at least nine months at the machine operated by Jack Starkey. During this period three men worked second shift on Jack's machine in the following sequence: Ed Sokolsky, Dooley, and Al McCann.

December 19. Ed Sokolsky and Jack Starkey have not been doing well. Ed cusses intermittently and leaves his machine for long periods of time. The foremen find the machine idle, and Steve bellows about it. Ed calls the piece he is working on a "stinker." I know it is, because Ed is free with his advertising of the "gravy" he finds.

Ed seems to have constant trouble with his jig, a revolving piece attached to the side of the table. Two disks seem to stick together, and Ed is constantly (every day or so) using the crane to dismantle the jig (a very heavy one). He sands the disks and oils them, taking several hours for the cleaning operation. Steve saw the dismantled jig again tonight and bellowed, "Again?" Steve does not like it.

Paul, the set-up man, gets concerned, too, when he finds the jig torn down and Ed away somewhere. He says, "Where the hell's Ed?" in a provoked manner.

February. I noticed that Ed was poking along and asked him if he had a good job. He shook his head, saying that he was making but 46 cents an hour, turning out 2 pieces an hour that paid 23 cents each.

February 26. Jack Starkey told me tonight that although his job on the hinge bases was retimed, there was no raise in price. The price is still 23 cents.

I said, "All you've got to turn out is 5 an hour to make $1.15."

"I'd just like to see anybody turn out 5 of these an hour," said Jack, "with a tolerance of 0.0005!"

Later, Ed Sokolsky said that he and Jack were turning out about 24 pieces in a ten-hour period (2.4 an hour), that the job had been retimed several times, but no raise in price had been given.

Ed and Jack asked for a price of 38 cents. Ed said that they could turn out 3 an hour, but, until they got a decent price, they were turning out 2 an hour.

Toward the end of the evening I noticed that Ed's machine was idle, and Ed was sitting on a box, doing nothing.

"What's the matter, did they stop the job on you?" I asked.

"I stopped it," said Ed. "I don't feel like running it."

March. Dooley worked on the hinge bases again tonight. He admitted that he could barely make out on the job, but "Why bust my ass for day rate? We're doing 3 an hour or less until we get a better price!"

This 3-an-hour-or-less business has been going on several months. The price is 23 cents; so Dooley and Jack turn in 69 cents an hour (or less).

May. McCann said that Starkey was arguing all day over the price of the hinge bases. The methods men maintain that they can't raise the price "because the jacks that the parts go on sell for $14.00 apiece." They plan to retool the job and lower the price. According to McCann, Jack told them that if he didn't get a decent price he was going to make out on the job but scrap every one of the pieces.

"Jack fights it out with them," said McCann. "He'll stay right with the machine and argue. I get disgusted and walk away.

"Jack turned out 28 today," McCann went on. "That's too many, nearly 3 an hour. He'll have to watch himself if he expects to get a raise in price."

Starkey was running the hinge bases again tonight. I remarked, "I see you're in the gravy again."

His reply was, "Yeah! 69 cents an hour!"

McCann did not seem to enjoy the hinge bases either. He looked bored, tired, and disgusted all evening. His ten hours is a long stretch at day work. He cannot make out early and rest after 11 o'clock (for four hours), but has to keep on the machine until three.

August 14. Al McCann was working on the hinge bases tonight, one of the jobs that he and Jack are protesting as to price. Gil (the foreman) sat and stood behind Al for at least an hour, and I could see that Al did not like it. He worked steadily, but with deliberate slowness, and did not look at Gil or speak to him. Al and Jack have agreed to restrict production on the hinge bases until they get a better price, and Gil was probably there to see what Al could really do. I think that Al and Jack could make out on the job, but not at $1.25 an hour, and they cut production to less than 80 cents an hour.

August 16. Al told me that they had won a price raise on the hinge bases, from 23 to 28 cents, and another raise to 31 cents.

"But it's still not high enough. As it is now we can make exactly 94 cents an hour. We're trying to get 35 cents. We can turn out 1 in exactly 16 minutes. That's not 4 an hour. We've been giving them 3 an hour."

One of the reasons American workers join unions is that a strong union greatly reduces the competition among workers vis-a-vis the employer. This reason is usually phrased in terms of the elimination of favoritism and discrimination.[3]

Another potent motive for joining a union is the worker's interest in eliminating favoritism by management. The insistence with which the union representative normally puts forth the claim for a seniority system in a newly organized plant reflects the high value workers place on seniority as a method of insuring understandable objectivity in layoffs and rehiring. Golden and Ruttenberg, with much experience in organizing steel workers, observe that the appeal against favoritism is "perhaps the organizer's strongest appeal."

Join the union so you can get a square deal. When you get a contract with seniority protection you don't have to worry every morning when you get to work whether you'll have a job when you come home at night; you won't have to worry about the boss firing you because he don't like the

[3] From *Labor Unions in Action* by Jack Barbash, pp. 8–12. Copyright 1948 by Harper & Brothers, New York. Reprinted by permission of Harper & Brothers.

color of your hair, or of promoting a younger man to the
job you should have because he is a member of the same
fraternal order as the boss; and you won't have to shine the
foreman's shoes [or some other colloquialism] to get a nickel
raise or a better job—it'll be yours if you have the years of
service to get it and can do the job.

The antifavoritism motivation is set in another context by the
Marine Firemen:

> . . . prior to the unionization of the industry, you hunted
> your jobs on the docks and ships. You stood around in the
> rain and the snow when a ship came in, and waited for an
> opportunity to ship. When your chance finally did come, some
> contemptuous shipping master crooked his finger with a
> "Hey, you!"
> You got pushed around plenty, brother. You stood
> around, and saw the guys with pull and drag get the jobs.
> Guys from college making a trip for fun and getting on a ship
> because they knew the port captain or the chief engineer or a
> big stockholder in the company. You wore out plenty of shoe
> leather prowling from ship to ship and dock to dock.
> The cards were stacked against you! Favoritism was rife!
> The guy that was the lackey got the first preference. You got
> shoved around in an atmosphere of uplifted noses and su-
> periority complexes, for you were "the crew." Focsle hands.
> Trash! Tripe! Scum of the universe, and devoid of humane
> consideration. . . .

Even though there may be no *formal* closed shop prevailing
in a plant where union membership predominates, the new
worker, even if he is so disposed, cannot long persist in a refusal
to join the union, against the social and other kinds of pressures
exerted on him by his fellow workers. A steel shop steward says,
"When a new man comes into our shop he has twenty days to
qualify. . . . If that man . . . gets close to qualifying it is the
duty of the office and the shop steward to inform that man that
there is a union in the shop and that he is expected to join. We are
not asking him to join, we expect him to join." On the railroads the
closed shop is forbidden by law. As a matter of practice, however, it
is difficult for a worker to remain in the good graces of fellow employees on organized roads if he holds out against joining the
union. The nonunion worker in these situations finds it ex-

tremely hard to get adequate handling of his grievances. This fact the union members on the job are at great pains to point out to him. In extreme cases the organized workers will refuse to work with "free riders."

Even if there is no favoritism, even if the employer is capable of evaluating the performance of workers with Olympic detachment, the employee becomes anxious when he believes that his job tenure depends on outperforming the worker alongside him as well as all the potential employees whom the employer *might* hire.

Competition for roles in the economic system is a special case of competition for interpersonal status. In this broader context, the rejection of competition also takes the form of preventing some potential competitors from competing on equal terms. Consider race prejudice from this viewpoint. The doctrine of White Supremacy relegates Negroes to inferior roles in Southern society; conversely, it means that white persons who would lose out in fair competition with Negroes attain a superior status automatically. This *function* of the White Supremacy concept may not be consciously understood by its partisans, but, as Ruth Benedict, the anthropologist, has suggested, racism is a remarkably effective formula for quelling doubts about competitive adequacy.[4]

Racism is essentially a pretentious way of saying that "I" belong to the Best People. For such a conviction it is the most gratifying formula that has ever been discovered, for neither my own unworthiness nor the accusations of others can ever dislodge me from my position—a position which was determined in the womb of my mother at conception. It avoids all embarrassing questions about my conduct of life and nullifies all embarrassing claims by "inferior" groups about their own achievements and ethical standards.

It has also the advantage of great simplicity. It avoids any of the actual complexities of human nature and of human history and sets up a five-word proposition which the most uneducated can remember and glory in: "I belong to the Elect." For political purposes the racist formula has no rival.

[4] See Ruth Benedict, *Race: Science and Politics* (New York: Viking Press, rev. ed., 1945), p. 99.

This formula in its modern guise would have been impossible before the days of Darwin and of anthropomorphic measurements. It appeals to evolution and to anthropometry. It claims that the Elect to whom I racially belong are *biologically* destined to lead human destiny and that in destroying others they achieve the survival of the fittest. These Elect, moreover, can be identified by measurements of the body. These refinements could not have arisen in the world before the nineteenth century.

Interviews with Southern whites on the subject of Negroes seem to confirm Dr. Benedict's functional interpretation of prejudice.[5]

Leslie Needham is fifty years old and lives in Atlanta. He was a brakeman but is now a watchman on WPA. He was graduated from high school and spent about a year in a business college.

They are all right if you keep them in their place. But they must be kept in their place. I don't approve of associating with them myself. These WPA jobs are full of Negroes. If everybody was the way I am with them, it would be all right; for example, some men will drink out of the same cup after a Negro—but I'd never do that. Give 'em a separate bucket and cup. *I am not prejudiced against them.* We have plenty of 'em in Atlanta—when you go downtown to a market on Saturday night they are everywhere. I don't believe in stepping aside for a Negro, I just shove 'em out of the way . . . They are treated too well. They get too much pay for what they do . . . I used to be an agent (selling) and traveled quite a bit. Most maids and butlers and help in the home was colored. They work cheaper and will do things that a white person wouldn't . . . If I had my way they'd be put in a section by themselves and keep them there. They shouldn't be allowed to move into white neighborhoods. There are lots of houses they are now tearing down that are good enough for Negroes . . . Oh yes, they are gettin' an education. They'll keep on improving, sure. But they won't improve so much

[5] Reprinted with permission from Hadley Cantril, *The Psychology of Social Movements,* pp. 87–91, 92–93, 115; copyright 1941, John Wiley & Sons, Inc., New York.

that we can respect 'em. Some people will respect 'em. But
I don't care who they are or how much education they have,
I wouldn't. They are black to me. I am afraid that the white
people are not going to take this serious enough in time.
They shouldn't have let the Negroes get as far as they have.

Ella Ferguson is a house servant in Alabama. She is in her
early thirties, was raised on a farm, and had a high-school
education.

I think their mentality is low, I do . . . Niggers oughta
have their own social life like the whites—among themselves, but they oughta stay with their kind. They are beings
like us but their skin is a different color and they oughta
stay to themselves. I don't think much about it myself. They
oughta have their own schools and churches, yes sir, their
own churches and schools. They can do the same work as the
whites—laboring work—if they provide their own labor. The
better jobs though should be kept for the whites. I want a better job myself and maybe that's why I say that. I don't know.
Some folks would say that I'm doing nigger work myself, but
that ain't so. I think that the good jobs oughta be for the
whites. If they can't have busses and street cars for the niggers
and one for the whites, they oughta have a place in 'em for
the niggers. But they oughta have busses and cars for both.
I was on a bus one time that had niggers on it and we put 'em
in the back. I don't know how they do in the North or other
places, but that's the way it oughta be.

Sarah Lee is a middle-aged housewife living in a small town
in Arkansas. Her husband is unemployed. She is slouchy and
uneducated.

I was about thirteen when we come to Arkansas. That
was the first time I'd ever lived 'mongst niggers and had any
dealin's with 'em. Oh my goodness! I jest couldn't git used to
'em. They've got a funny turn and funny ways. A lotta niggers
down here don't stay in a nigger's place. One of the agents at
the depot and his wife used to "mister" the niggers. They'd
call us by our first names and call the niggers Mr. and Mrs.
We thought that was awful. Mrs. Goodman ask my daughter
to help her teach a nigger Sunday school class. It jest *killed*
Marie. She never *did* like Mrs. Goodman after that . . .
Since I moved to the South, I went through Illinois and had
to set in the train with 'em. I didn't have to set right in the

same seat but we was in the same car together. It embarrassed me. Yessum. I never had seen it done before and I
jest thought it was the terriblest thing I ever heard of . . .
I've had some niggers be mighty nice to me . . . I think
there's some niggers as good as white people, but you jest
can't class youself with 'em . . . I think the niggers oughta
be sent back to where they come from or git a big plantation
and make 'em stay on there. You take the old generation of
niggers, they're not so bad, but these young 'uns comin' on,
they're so biggety. I know people git along with those that
are uneducated better than those educated . . . Another
thing, a nigger keeps the white men out of work. They'll
work for cheaper wages. Look at Mr. Flore and Mr. Woodfin.
They'll keep niggers on their place if they can git 'em . . . If
niggers had the same chance as white people they'd be about
the same. There's a better class of niggers just like there's a
better class of white folks. Just like the little boy said,
"There's a little bad in all of us." I don't know what it'd *be*
you'd admire about 'em. The young generation jest think
they're jest as good as white folks. You notice on the streets
of Brinkley. They won't give you one inch to pass 'em. You
take these *old* African niggers, they know their place, but
'chew jest take this young generation comin' up! . . . The
younger generation hasn't any ambition, you can jest figger it
any way you wanta. No'um, I don't think they're as clean
as white people. You take Lillie, she's *clean,* and she's a
good cook. Seems like niggers is more gifted in their music
than white people are . . . A nigger can git work when a
white man can't in the South . . . They're not as trustworthy as a white person. I jest think they're fitted for the
plantation. You take *one nigger woman* can chop more cotton
than *three* white women. They're gifted with that hoe. No'um,
they shouldn't be allowed to take all kinds of jobs. That's
jest what's knocked out the white people. You take these
porters on these trains, a white man could do that job jest as
well. I don't think they should work together, but how you
gonna help yourself down here? Jest like this WPA, niggers
and whites work all together. I guess they have to live jest
like the white people, but they oughta be separated. This
WPA is the unfairest thing I ever heard of . . . I'm gonna
tell you my honest opinion. I don't think they *should* vote,
but they pay poll taxes and there's no way in the world to
keep 'em from it. Some of 'em think they can't vote in the
primary, but if it was taken to a test they could . . . I don't

really think they have the same privileges as other citizens. We're in Arkansas now, that's all I'm speakin' for. As the boy said, "When you're in Rome do as Rome." No'um, I don't really think they *should* have the same privileges as white people.

These are specific reflections of the general frame of reference that Negroes are inferior and destined forever to play a servile role in a world primarily meant for white men. The popular stereotypes of the Negro are systematically, perhaps quite unconsciously, perpetuated. In the white man's vaudeville, radio programs, or joke books, the Negro appears as a happy-go-lucky, harmless, ignorant soul; in the white man's moving pictures or advertisements, the Negro is represented as the humble, faithful, God-fearing servant. And the Negro is popular and tolerated to the extent that he conforms to some similar stereotypes. Even the higher education that may be provided for him in the South has a strong vocational tinge—to teach him how to be a better shoemaker, servant, or mechanic for the white man. Other stereotypes, portraying the Negro as a potentially sensuous criminal, a danger to white womanhood, are sustained by the widespread, distorted publicity of rape as the cause of mob violence and by gossip concerning the Negro's sexual prowess. All presuppose a lower standard of living for the colored man. Also, if one suggests that Negroes may not be happy the way they are, the answer is either a flat denial of the possibility or the retort that what they have is good enough for them.

The southerner who has this frame of reference toward the Negro as part of his mental context is likely to be extremely sensitive about it. He knows that the standards of judgment which he accepts as the basis of his point of view are not completely shared by the majority of the people in the whole nation. He is nostalgic for the days before the Civil War when his values were accepted as an intrinsic part of the whole culture. He realizes that he has been unable to defend his standards by force of arms, by law, or by ethical considerations. Yet because he feels that these standards still are a part of him, because they involve his personal pride and status, he is still very much on the defensive. And he must now defend himself in other than legal ways or in a second resort to civil war. He does this by his racial discrimination, the perpetuation of his standards from generation to generation, and, when necessary, by demonstrations of his dominance, demonstrations which are overt in local areas but covert from the point of view of the legally and ethically accepted standards of the national majority. . . .

This deliberate perpetuation and enforcement of an accepted frame of reference which is strongly felt because of its ego involvement means that other frames of reference, with their consequently different attitudes, will encounter enormous difficulty. Divergent frames will be accepted gradually only by small minorities of the population who have somehow from education and experience interiorized different standards of judgment upon which they can base different frames of reference and attitudes. It means, furthermore, that since one psychological problem of southern whites is to maintain their status relative to the Negro, they cannot allow an improvement in the conditions and opportunities of Negroes unless their own conditions and opportunities are proportionately increased. And since the collapse of the economy based on slavery, the southern landowner has felt himself steadily sinking, while today he sees no bright and permanent prospects for rehabilitating himself to a commanding economic position. The small landowner, the small merchant, and the white tenant farmer likewise see little chance for them to increase their economic and social positions. Hence, as the individual approaches closer to the Negro's cultural level, overt persecution remains the only available method of avoiding his own fear of inferiority.

The discrepancy between the status of the white and of the colored man can obviously be reduced not only by a decline in the position of the former but also by a rise in the position of the latter. Increased education and opportunity have enormously developed the latent talents so long submerged in the Negro race. The Negro is improving his position economically, politically, and culturally even in the face of great odds. This, too, often produces greater discrimination, segregation, and persecution. The Negro who dresses as well as a white man is an unwelcome person in most southern white communities; the able Negro doctor must be careful not to let his professional success beguile him into thinking that he can mix equally with his professional white colleagues or that his wife and children can live on the same plane as the wives and children of the white colleagues; the skilled or unskilled colored worker who has a job that a white man would like is, as we have seen above, a renegade. The situation is aggravated in many areas because of the fact that Negroes will work for lower wages largely because of the standards of living they are used to and, in some instances, because white workers are more conscious of the power of labor organization and hence refuse to undercut their fellows.

Since the position of the white southerner is so dependent upon the labor and status of the Negro, the more he keeps the colored man "in his place," the lower becomes his own cultural standard. He is forced by the logic of his own frames of reference to oppose general improvements in housing, methods of farming, and education. For, in the process, his position relative to the Negro might be threatened even though on an absolute and objective basis his condition might be improved.

The conditions which create a lynching mob are, therefore, deeply interwoven with the whole social context surrounding individual mob members. The norms of the culture and the possibilities the culture provides for the satisfaction of needs largely determine what things people take for granted, what obstacles cause their frustrations, what roles they regard as suitable for persons of their status. Just as an explanation of why a gun shoots a bullet is inadequate if one simply learns that it is because the trigger is pulled, so any explanation of mob action which begins merely with the commission of a specific crime and ends with the final gasp of the victim isolates the phenomenon and obscures understanding. . . .

I reckon folks from the North think we're hard on niggers, but they just don't know what would happen to the white people if the niggers ran wild like they would if we didn't show them who's boss. If I was you, I wouldn't go back up North and say you saw us down here trying to catch a nigger to lynch. It just wouldn't sound right saying it up there, because people would get the idea that we're just naturally hard on all niggers all the time. There's a lot of fine ones in this country, but they're the ones who know how to keep their place, and they don't make trouble. This nigger that raped that white girl is a mean one. Of course, that girl is a whore, and everybody knows it, and for all I know she led him on, but just the same she was a white girl, and he was a nigger, and it just wouldn't do to let him go. That's why we're out here trying to jump him in the woods. Maybe the sheriff will get him before we do, but it's going to be a race, and whoever gets him first is going to keep him. I reckon you understand how it is now, and if I was you I wouldn't go back up north and say you came down here and saw us trying to lynch a nigger. If you say something like that, people will think we're hard on niggers. I've got niggers workin' for me, and I get along the best way with them, because they know how to keep their place. If that nigger out there in the woods gets jumped before the sheriff finds him, it will all be over and done with by sundown, and everybody will be satisfied.

Needless to say, prejudice is not confined to the South. Nor are Negroes the only victims. The most virulent expression of race prejudice in recent history occurred in Europe during World War II. The Nazis systematically incinerated—in specially built crematoria located in concentration camps—millions of men, women, and children. The purpose of this unbelievable brutality was to exterminate nationalities that the Nazis considered inferior: Jews, gypsies, Poles, Russians. Prejudice is rarely carried to its ultimate implication: Beat competition by killing your competitors. In the following selection, written after the world learned of the Nazi horrors, Carey McWilliams analyzes the motivations underlying prejudice against Jews.[6]

In the summer of 1877, Joseph Seligman, the New York banker, was bluntly and noisily refused accommodations for himself and his family at the Grand Union Hotel at Saratoga Springs. Here, simply stated, was one of the first major overt manifestations of anti-Semitism in the United States. This is not to say, of course, that minor incidents had not previously oc-

[6] From *A Mask for Privilege: Anti-Semitism in America* by Carey McWilliams, pp. 3; 4–6; 8; 11–13; 18–20, by permission of Little, Brown & Company, Boston, Massachusetts. Copyright 1947, 1948 by Carey McWilliams.

curred; nor would it be accurate to say that Jews were everywhere treated with perfect equality prior to 1877. But by and large, the record up to this point had been largely free of overt or significant manifestations of anti-Semitism. . . .

To appreciate the significance of the Saratoga Springs incident, however, the principals must be identified. Joseph Seligman had emigrated from Bavaria in 1837 because, so his biographer states, "he had become dissatisfied with the lack of opportunities for Jews in Germany." With his brothers, he had founded the well-known banking firm of Seligman Brothers in New York. Although they had arrived as penniless immigrants, the Seligmans were well-educated and cultured men and could hardly be regarded as *nouveaux riches*. Henry Ward Beecher, who had summered with the Seligmans for several seasons prior to 1877, said that they had "behaved in a manner that ought to put to shame many Christian ladies and gentlemen." During one of the darkest hours of the Civil War, Joseph Seligman had undertaken, at his own suggestion, to dispose of a large government bond issue in Europe. The historian William E. Dodd has characterized the successful fulfillment of this mission as scarcely less important to the Union cause than the Battle of Gettysburg. Largely in recognition of these services, Seligman had been offered the post of Secretary of the Treasury by President Grant.

In 1877 the Grand Union Hotel was owned by Judge Hilton, a prominent New York politician, and A. T. Stewart, the well-known New York merchant. Born in Ireland, Stewart had arrived in America as penniless as the Seligmans and, like them, had risen to a position of great wealth and prominence. A notice in the *Dictionary of American Biography* points out that Stewart was notoriously penurious, a shrewd, harsh disciplinarian whose wage policies had once aroused widespread criticism. Legend has it that the coffin containing his remains was stolen and held for ransom by persons who had resented his dictatorial manner. Clearly personifying the new forces that had come to dominate the American scene after the Civil War, it was Stewart, not the Seligmans, who belonged in the *nouveau riche* category. The locale of the incident is also important. The Grand Union Hotel epitomized the parvenu splendor of the gilded age. Through its

luxurious grounds strolled the millionaries who had emerged
with such abundance in the postwar period.

On June 24, 1877, Henry Ward Beecher preached a famous
sermon on the Saratoga Springs incident at Plymouth Church.
"What have the Jews," he said, "of which they need be ashamed,
in a Christian Republic where all men are declared to be free
and equal? . . . Is it that they are excessively industrious? Let
the Yankee cast the first stone. Is it that they are inordinately
keen in bargaining? Have they ever stolen ten millions of dollars
at a pinch from a city? Are our courts bailing out Jews, or com-
promising with Jews? Are there Jews lying in our jails, and
waiting for mercy, and dispossessing themselves slowly of the
enormous wealth which they have stolen? You cannot find one
criminal Jew in the whole catalogue. It is said that the Jews are
crafty and cunning, and sometimes dishonest in their dealings.
Ah! What a phenomenon dishonesty must be in New York! Do
they not pay their debts when it is inconvenient? Hear it, O ye
Yankees!" . . .

What Charles Beard has called "the second American Revolution"—the revolution that assured the triumph of the business enterprise—had been fought and largely won by 1877. "In
1865," writes Matthew Josephson, "three-quarters of the American people set to work instinctively, planlessly, to build a heavy
industry where there had been almost nothing of the sort, and
to produce twice as much goods, food, and wealth of all kinds, as
they had produced in 1860." In four great lines of endeavor—
manufacturing, extractive industries, transportation, and finance
—business marched from one swift triumph to another. In 1860
about a billion dollars was invested in manufacturing plants
which employed 1,500,000 workers; but in less than fifty years
the investment had risen to 12 billions and the number of workers to 5,500,000. The output of American iron and steel—true
measures of industrial power—had been far below the tonnage
of England and France in 1870; but within twenty years the
United States had outdistanced both nations. Even in retrospect,
it is difficult to measure the swiftness and the magnitude of the
transformation which the second American Revolution worked
in American life. . . .

The nature of the cultural transformation that accompanied the second American Revolution has never been more graphically described than in a passage from Thorstein Veblen's *The Theory of the Leisure Class* (emphasis added). "The wave of revulsion," he wrote, "seems to have received its initial impulse in the psychologically disintegrating effects of the Civil War. Habituation to war entails a body of predatory habits of thought, *whereby clannishness* in some measure *replaces the sense of solidarity,* and a sense of invidious distinction supplants the impulse to equitable, everyday serviceability. As an outcome of the cumulative action of these factors, the generation which follows a season of war is apt to witness *a rehabilitation* of elements *of status* both in its social life and in its scheme of devout observances and other symbolic and ceremonial forms. Throughout the eighties, and less plainly traceable in the seventies, also, there was perceptible a gradually advancing wave of sentiment favoring quasi-predatory business habits, *insistence on status,* anthropomorphism, and conservatism generally."

One of the ways in which this new clannishness and insistence on status expressed itself at the expense of the older solidarity was in an effort to achieve unity, out of the chaos of the times, by the negative device of opposing something—the Negroes, the Chinese, the Indians, the foreigners. For these outsiders furnished a counterconception upon which, as Oscar Handlin has noted, "all the qualities the community feared and disliked could be ascribed and around opposition to which it could unite."

In 1879 about 177,000 immigrants had arrived in America; but by 1882 the annual influx had risen to 788,000. Faced with a growing competition for place and power, their security threatened by the forces of a rampant industrialism, the groups identifying themselves with the dominant cultural pattern sought to maintain that pattern at all costs. For it was in part through such dominance that they hoped to retain their status. After the Civil War, status lines were drawn more sharply than ever before and the struggle for status became one of the major motivations in American culture. There is, therefore, much meaning in the opening sentence of Booth Tarkington's *The Magnificent Am-*

bersons: "Major Amberson had 'made a fortune' in 1873, when other people were losing fortunes, and the magnificence of the Ambersons began then." Feeling the pinch of the new economic dispensation, the native Americans and the older immigrant groups sought to exclude first one group and then another from identification with the dominant cultural symbols. A remarkable correlation developed between nationality and status; between race and status; and, to a lesser degree, between religion and status. In an increasingly insecure world, the maintenance of status distinctions created the illusion of security and group differences of all kinds suddenly acquired a new meaning. "In spite of the magnificent dimensions of our continent," wrote Hjalmar H. Boyesen in 1887, "we are beginning to feel crowded." In view of these tendencies—all too briefly sketched here—it is not surprising that the first overt manifestation of anti-Semitism should have occurred in the summer of 1877. . . .

The tycoons that rose to power with the triumph of the second American Revolution were, as Charles Beard has pointed out, largely of North European stock, mainly English and Scotch Irish, and of Protestant background, as a roll call will readily confirm: Gould, Vanderbilt, Huntington, Hill, Harriman, Rockefeller, Carnegie, Cooke, Morgan, Armour. Only Gould, in the characteristic phrase of Henry Adams, "showed a trace of Jewish origin." The first threat to the unchallenged dominance of these industrial tycoons came from German-Jewish immigrants in the United States.

At the time of the first census in 1790, there were only about 2000 Jews in the United States in a population of approximately 2,000,000. From this figure the number increased to about 250,000 in 1880. This increase was largely made up of German Jews who, like the Seligmans, had been discouraged by the wave of reaction which had engulfed Europe in the wake of the Napoleonic Wars. Swept immediately into the current of westward expansion, the German Jews were carried far from the ports of entry. In the rapidly growing communities of the Middle West, the Far West, and the South, many of these immigrants made the transition from peddler to prosperous merchant with extraordinary swiftness. In such cities as Cincinnati, Chicago,

Louisville, St. Paul, Dallas, San Francisco, and Los Angeles, German Jews were accorded a high status based upon priority of settlement—they were among the "first families"—and the wealth and distinction which they had achieved. The mention of such names as Straus, Rosenwald, Seligman, Warburg, Schiff, Morgenthau, Sloss, Sutro, and Lubin is alone sufficient to indicate this amazing upward mobility.

That the first overt manifestation of anti-Semitism in the United States took place in 1877 is to be explained in terms of the corrosion which the industrial revolution had brought about in the American scheme of values and the revolutionary democratic culture and its traditions. But that this initial act should have taken place in the upper reaches of society, and that it should have assumed the form of social discrimination is to be explained by the rapid rise of German Jews in the new social and economic hierarchy. As prosperous and successful merchants, bankers, and traders, the German Jews could not be altogether excluded from the civic and social life of the communities in which they had settled; but they could be made to feel a subtle sense of rejection, and limitations could be imposed against their further encroachment on the citadels of power. The erection of these invisible barriers at the top levels of society was largely prompted by the feeling that, at this level, they were to be regarded as serious competitors for place and power. While the non-Jewish tycoons were prone to war among themselves, they were quick to protect their social power and dominant position in American industry by the exclusion of these agile newcomers. In the period from 1840 to 1880, when the bulk of the German Jews arrived, some 10,189,429 immigrants entered the United States. Lost in this avalanche of peoples, the German Jews were numerically insignificant and aroused almost nothing in the way of popular antagonism or hostility. It was only in the upper reaches of society that their remarkable success excited feelings of envy and disdain.

According to McWilliams, American anti-Semitism developed first among the business and industrial elite where it manifested itself in social discrimination. Only later did it percolate down to the lower classes and manifest itself in other forms. Historical reconstruction is always difficult; other students of prejudice disagree with McWilliams' emphasis on the priority of *social* over *economic* discrimination. But his insistence that discrimination is motivated, consciously or unconsciously, by fear of competitors is widely accepted. In a dynamic society, the uncertainties of status competition are reduced somewhat by prejudice. A Christian has only to capitalize on his gentileness to feel superior to all Jews. And the less confident he is that he can survive in the flux of status competition, the more he is tempted to rig the competition by demanding automatic superiority.

A similar analysis has recently been applied to political behavior. As Professor Richard Hofstadter of Columbia University put it, "Political life is not simply an arena in which the conflicting interests of various social groups in concrete material gains are fought out; it is also an arena into which status aspirations and frustrations are . . . projected." That is to say, political affiliation may be used to assert one's status credentials. Thus, certain right-wing groups, by asserting a monopoly on patriotism, lay a claim to high status which might otherwise be dubious. The following article is from a symposium devoted to an analysis of status politics in general and "the new American right" in particular.[7]

Who is the pseudo-conservative, and what does he want? It is impossible to identify him by class, for the pseudo-conservative impulse can be found in practically all classes in society, although its power probably rests largely upon its appeal to the less educated members of the middle classes. The ideology of pseudo-conservatism can be characterized but not defined, because the pseudo-conservative tends to be more than ordinarily incoherent about politics. The lady who, when General Eisenhower's victory over Senator Taft had finally become official, stalked out of the Hilton Hotel declaiming, "This means eight more years of socialism" was probably a fairly good representative of the pseudo-conservative mentality. So also were the gentlemen who, at the Freedom Congress held at Omaha over a year ago by some "patriotic" organizations, objected to Earl

[7] From "The Pseudo-Conservative Revolt" by Richard Hofstadter, originally published in the Winter, 1954–55 issue of *The American Scholar*. Copyright 1954, by *The American Scholar*. Reprinted by permission of Richard Hofstadter and *The American Scholar*.

Warren's appointment to the Supreme Court with the assertion: "Middle-of-the-road thinking can and will destroy us"; the general who spoke to the same group, demanding "an Air Force capable of wiping out the Russian Air Force and industry in one sweep," but also "a material reduction in military expenditures"; the people who a few years ago believed simultaneously that we had no business to be fighting communism in Korea, but that the war should immediately be extended to an Asia-wide crusade against communism; and the most ardent supporters of the Bricker Amendment. Many of the most zealous followers of Senator McCarthy are also pseudo-conservatives, although there are presumably a great many others who are not.

The restlessness, suspicion and fear manifested in various phases of the pseudo-conservative revolt give evidence of the real suffering which the pseudo-conservative experiences in his capacity as a citizen. He believes himself to be living in a world in which he is spied upon, plotted against, betrayed, and very likely destined for total ruin. He feels that his liberties have been arbitrarily and outrageously invaded. He is opposed to almost everything that has happened in American politics for the past twenty years. He hates the very thought of Franklin D. Roosevelt. He is disturbed deeply by American participation in the United Nations, which he can see only as a sinister organization. He sees his own country as being so weak that it is constantly about to fall victim to subversion; and yet he feels that it is so all-powerful that any failure it may experience in getting its way in the world—for instance, in the Orient—cannot possibly be due to its limitations but must be attributed to its having been betrayed. He is the most bitter of all our citizens about our involvement in the wars of the past, but seems the least concerned about avoiding the next one. While he naturally does not like Soviet communism, what distinguishes him from the rest of us who also dislike it is that he shows little interest in, is often indeed bitterly hostile, to such realistic measures as might actually strengthen the United States vis-a-vis Russia. He would much rather concern himself with the domestic scene, where communism is weak, than with those areas of the world where it is really strong and threatening. He wants to have nothing to do with the democratic nations of Western Europe, which seem to draw more of his ire than the Soviet Communists, and he is opposed to all "give-away programs" designed to aid and strengthen these nations. Indeed, he is likely to be antagonistic to most of the operations of our federal government except Congressional investigations, and to almost all of its expenditures. Not always, however, does he go so far as the speaker at the Freedom Congress who attributed the greater part of our national difficulties to "this nasty, stinking 16th [income tax] Amendment." . . .

All of us have reason to fear the power of international communism, and all our lives are profoundly affected by it. Why do some Americans try to face this threat for what it is, a problem that exists in a world-wide theater of action, while others try to reduce it largely to a matter of domestic conformity? Why do some of us prefer to look for allies in the democratic world, while others seem to prefer authoritarian allies or none at all? Why do the pseudo-conservatives express such a persistent fear and suspicion of *their own government,* whether its leadership rests in the hands of Roosevelt, Truman or Eisenhower? Why is the pseudo-conservative impelled to go beyond the more or less routine partisan argument that we have been the victims of considerable misgovernment during the past twenty years to the disquieting accusation that we have actually been the victims of persistent conspiracy and betrayal—"twenty years of treason"? Is it not true, moreover, that political types very similar to the pseudo-conservative have had a long history in the United States, and that this history goes back to a time when the Soviet power did not loom nearly so large on our mental horizons? Was the Ku Klux Klan, for instance, which was responsibly estimated to have had a membership of from 4,000,000 to 4,500,000 persons at its peak in the 1920's, a phenomenon totally dissimilar to the pseudo-conservative revolt?

What I wish to suggest—and I do so in the spirit of one setting forth nothing more than a speculative hypothesis—is that pseudo-conservatism is in good part a product of the rootlessness and heterogeneity of American life, and *above all, of its peculiar scramble for status and its peculiar search for secure identity.*[8]

[8] Italics added by Bredemeier and Toby.

Normally there is a world of difference between one's sense of national identity or cultural belonging and one's social status. However, in American historical development, these two things, so easily distinguishable in analysis, have been jumbled together in reality, and it is precisely this that has given such a special poignancy and urgency to our status-strivings. In this country a person's status—that is, his relative place in the prestige hierarchy of his community—and his rudimentary sense of belonging to the community—that is, what we call his "Americanism" —have been intimately joined. Because, as a people extremely democratic in our social institutions, we have had no clear, consistent and recognizable system of status, our personal status problems have an unusual intensity. Because we no longer have the relative ethnic homogeneity we had up to about eighty years ago, our sense of belonging has long had about it a high degree of uncertainty. We boast of "the melting pot," but we are not quite sure what it is that will remain when we have been melted down.

We have always been proud of the high degree of occupational mobility in our country—of the greater readiness, as compared with other countries, with which a person starting in a very humble place in our social structure could rise to a position of moderate wealth and status, and with which a person starting with a middling position could rise to great eminence. We have looked upon this as laudable in principle, for it is democratic, and as pragmatically desirable, for it has served many a man as a stimulus to effort and has, no doubt, a great deal to do with the energetic and effectual tone of our economic life. The American pattern of occupational mobility, while often much exaggerated, as in the Horatio Alger stories and a great deal of the rest of our mythology, may properly be credited with many of the virtues and beneficial effects that are usually attributed to it. But this occupational and social mobility, compounded by our extraordinary mobility from place to place, has also had its less frequently recognized drawbacks. Not the least of them is that this has become a country in which so many people do not know who they are or what they are or what they belong to or what belongs to them. It is a country of people whose status ex-

pectations are random and uncertain, and yet whose status aspirations have been whipped up to a high pitch by our democratic ethos and our rags-to-riches mythology.

In a country where physical needs have been, by the scale
of the world's living standards, on the whole well met, the luxury of questing after status has assumed an unusually prominent
place in our civic consciousness. *Political life is not simply an
arena in which the conflicting interests of various social groups
in concrete material gains are fought out; it is also an arena into
which status aspirations and frustrations are,* as the psychologists
would say, *projected.*[9] It is at this point that the issues of politics,
or the pretended issues of politics, become interwoven with and
dependent upon the personal problems of individuals. We have,
at all times, two kinds of processes going on in inextricable connection with each other: *interest politics,* the clash of material
aims and needs among various groups and blocs; and *status
politics,* the clash of various projective rationalizations arising
from status aspirations and other personal motives. In times of
depression and economic discontent—and by and large in times
of acute national emergency—politics is more clearly a matter
of interests, although of course status considerations are still
present. In times of prosperity and general well-being on the
material plane, status considerations among the masses can
become much more influential in our politics. The two periods
in our recent history in which status politics has been particularly prominent, the present era and the 1920's, have both
been periods of prosperity.

During depressions, the dominant motif in dissent takes expression in proposals for reform or in panaceas. Dissent then
tends to be highly programmatic—that is, it gets itself embodied
in many kinds of concrete legislative proposals. It is also future-
oriented and forward-looking, in the sense that it looks to a time
when the adoption of this or that program will materially alleviate or eliminate certain discontents. In prosperity, however,
when status politics becomes relatively more important, there is
a tendency to embody discontent not so much in legislative proposals as in grousing. For the basic aspirations that underlie

[9] Italics added by Bredemeier and Toby.

status discontent are only partially conscious; and, even so far as they are conscious, it is difficult to give them a programmatic expression. It is more difficult for the old lady who belongs to the D.A.R. and who sees her ancestral home swamped by new working-class dwellings to express her animus in concrete proposals of any degree of reality than it is, say, for the jobless worker during a slump to rally to a relief program. Therefore, it is the tendency of status politics to be expressed more in vindictiveness, in sour memories, in the search for scapegoats, than in realistic proposals for positive action.

Paradoxically the intense status concerns of present-day politics are shared by two types of persons who arrive at them, in a sense, from opposite directions. The first are found among some types of old-family, Anglo-Saxon Protestants, and the second are found among many types of immigrant families, most notably among the Germans and Irish, who are very frequently Catholic. The Anglo-Saxons are most disposed toward pseudo-conservatism when they are losing caste, the immigrants when they are gaining.

Consider first the old-family Americans. These people, whose stocks were once far more unequivocally dominant in America than they are today, feel that their ancestors made and settled and fought for this country. They have a certain inherited sense of proprietorship in it. Since America has always accorded a certain special deference to old families—so many of our families are *new*—these people have considerable claims to status by descent, which they celebrate by membership in such organizations as the D.A.R. and the S.A.R. But large numbers of them are actually losing their other claims to status. For there are among them a considerable number of the shabby genteel, of those who for one reason or another have lost their old objective positions in the life of business and politics and the professions, and who therefore cling with exceptional desperation to such remnants of their prestige as they can muster from their ancestors. These people, although very often quite well-to-do, feel that they have been pushed out of their rightful place in American life, even out of their neighborhoods. Most of them have been traditional Republicans by family inheritance, and they have felt themselves edged aside by the immigrants, the trade unions, and the urban machines in the past thirty years. When the immigrants were weak, these native elements used to indulge themselves in ethnic and religious snobberies at their expense. Now the immigrant groups have developed ample means, political and economic, of self-defense, and the second and third generations have become considerably more capable of looking out for themselves. Some of the old-family Americans have turned to find new objects for their resentment among liberals, left-wingers, intellectuals and the like—for in true pseudo-conservative fashion they relish weak victims and shrink from asserting themselves against the strong.

New-family Americans have had their own peculiar status problem. From 1881 to 1900 over 8,800,000 immigrants came here, during the next twenty years another 14,500,000. These immigrants, together with their descendants, constitute such a large portion of the population that Margaret Mead, in a stimulating analysis of our national character, has persuasively urged that the characteristic American outlook is now a third-generation point of view. In their search for new lives and new nationality, these immigrants have suffered much, and they have been rebuffed and made to feel inferior by the "native stock," commonly being excluded from the better occupations and even from what has bitterly been called "first-class citizenship." Insecurity over social status has thus been mixed with insecurity over one's very identity and sense of belonging. Achieving a better type of job or a better social status and becoming "more American" have become practically synonymous, and the passions that ordinarily attach to social position have been vastly heightened by being associated with the need to belong. . . .

Status problems take on a special importance in American life because a very large part of the population suffers from one of the most troublesome of all status questions: unable to enjoy the simple luxury of assuming their own nationality as a natural event, they are tormented by a nagging doubt as to whether they are really and truly and fully American. Since their forebears voluntarily left one country and embraced another, they cannot, as people do elsewhere, think of nationality as something that comes with birth; for them it is a matter of *choice,* and an object of striving. This is one reason why problems of "loyalty" arouse such an emotional response in many Americans and why it is so hard in the American climate of opinion to make any clear distinction between the problem of national security and the question of personal loyalty. Of course there is no real reason to doubt the loyalty to America of the immigrants and their descendants, or their willingness to serve the country as fully as if their ancestors had lived here for three centuries. None the less, they have been thrown on the defensive by those who have in the past cast doubts upon the fullness of their Americanism. Possibly they are also, consciously or unconsciously, troubled by the thought that since their forebears have already abandoned one country, one allegiance, their own national allegiance might be considered fickle. For this I believe there is some evidence in our national practices. What other country finds it so necessary to create institutional rituals for the sole purpose of guaranteeing to its people the genuineness of their nationality? Does the Frenchman or the Englishman or the Italian find it necessary to speak of himself as "one hundred per cent" English, French or Italian? Do they find it necessary to have their equivalents of "I Am an American Day"? When they disagree with one another over national policies, do they find it necessary to call one another un-English, un-French or un-Italian? No doubt they too are troubled by subversive activities and espionage, but are their countermeasures taken under the name of committees on un-English, un-French or un-Italian activities? . . .

Both the displaced old-American type and the new ethnic elements that are so desperately eager for reassurance of their fundamental Americanism can conveniently converge upon liberals, critics, and nonconformists of various sorts, as well as Communists and suspected Communists. To proclaim themselves vigilant in the pursuit of those who are even so much as accused of "disloyalty" to the United States is a way not only of reasserting but of advertising their own loyalty—and one of the chief characteristics of American super-patriotism is its constant inner urge toward self-advertisement. One notable quality in this new wave of conformism is that its advocates are much happier to have as their objects of hatred the Anglo-Saxon, Eastern, Ivy League intellectual gentlemen than they are with such bedraggled souls as, say, the Rosenbergs. The reason, I believe, is that in the minds of the status-driven it is no special virtue to be more American than the Rosenbergs, but it is really something to be more American than Dean Acheson or John Foster Dulles—or Franklin Delano Roosevelt. The status aspirations of some of the ethnic groups are actually higher than they were twenty years ago—which suggests one reason (there are others) why, in the ideology of the authoritarian right-wing, anti-Semitism and such blatant forms of prejudice have recently been soft-pedaled. Anti-Semitism, it has been said, is the poor man's snobbery. We Americans are always trying to raise the standard of living, and the same principle now seems to apply to standards of hating. So during the past fifteen years or so, the authoritarians have moved on from anti-Negroism and anti-Semitism to anti-Achesonianism, anti-intellectualism, anti-nonconformism, and other variants of the same idea, much in the same way as the average American, if he can manage it, will move on from a Ford to a Buick.

Such status-strivings may help us to understand some of the otherwise unintelligible figments of the pseudo-conservative ideology—the incredibly bitter feeling against the United Nations, for instance. Is it not understandable that such a feeling might be, paradoxically, shared at one and the same time by an old Yankee-Protestant American, who feels that his social position is not what it ought to be and that these foreigners are crowding in on his country and diluting its sovereignty just as "foreigners" have crowded into his neighborhood, and by a second- or third-generation immigrant who has been trying so hard to de-Europeanize himself, to get Europe out of his personal heritage, and who finds his own government mocking him by its complicity in these Old-World schemes?

To sum up, the rejection of the competitive principle occurs in the context of economic activities as well as in the broader sphere of interpersonal and group relations. Status monopolies and economic monopolies create similar problems: reduction in the efficiency with which social roles are performed and hostility between marginal and full-fledged competitors.

SUMMARY

When individuals, groups, or companies feel too weak to respond to competitive pressures by redoubling their competitive efforts, they may respond by agreeing among themselves not to compete. Business concerns follow this mode of adjustment in many ways, among them, "price leadership." Workers informally, but nonetheless effectively, protect themselves against the rigors of competition in similar ways, by agreeing among themselves on the rate at which they will work. On a formal level, workers accomplish the same end by substituting collective action for competitive action when dealing with an employer.

On a less-consciously-thought-out level, the anxieties resulting from competitive pressures may also be reduced by the simple expedient of not permitting entire categories of people to enter the competition for prestige, income, housing, women, or anything else; hence, the powerful hold of racial, ethnic, and religious prejudice on the minds of many who feel themselves competitively threatened. In the same way, the basing of self-respect on invidious comparisons may lead to compulsive efforts to deny legitimacy to the politically different as well as to the racially or religiously different.

ANNOTATED BIBLIOGRAPHY

Golden, Clinton S., and Ruttenberg, Harold J., *Dynamics of Industrial Democracy* (New York: Harper & Brothers, 1942). (⟦ The case for unions expounded by a veteran labor leader (United Steelworkers of America) and a professional economist. In essence, they argue that a job market in which workers compete with one another freely provides no protection against tyrannical or arbitrary employers.

Myrdal, Gunnar, *An American Dilemma* (New York: Harper & Brothers, 1944). (⟦ The monumental survey and analysis of "The Negro Problem and Modern Democracy," by a well-known Swedish social scientist. Throughout the book are to be found numberless examples of the use by whites of racial discrimination to reduce competition for scarce means and ends. In Appendix 5 (pp. 1073–1079), there is a little-noticed essay on the similar exclusion of women from competitive equality with men.

National Resources Committee, *The Structure of the American Economy* (Washington: Government Printing Office, 1939). (⟦ A remarkable documentation of the extent to which the American economic system limits the free play of market forces. So-called nonmarket controls include interlocking corporate directorships, price "leadership" by the largest firm in an industry, alliances established by banks and other leading institutions, and the solicitation of government intervention.

Roethlisberger, F. J., and Dickson, William J., *Management and the Worker* (Cambridge, Massachusetts: Harvard University Press, 1946). ¶ The classic account of informal worker organization in industry. As a result of a research program at the Hawthorne works of the Western Electric Company, industrial sociologists began to understand how and why workers rejected competitive incentive plans.

Simpson, George E., and Yinger, J. Milton, *Racial and Cultural Minorities* (New York: Harper & Brothers, rev. ed., 1958). ¶ An outstanding and well-written text. Chapters 3–5, 9, and 10 especially are important for the student interested in pursuing the "rejection of competition." The authors describe the personality functions of prejudice and the use of prejudice as a weapon in group conflict and present a detailed analysis of anti-Semitism.

CHAPTER FIFTEEN

The refusal to accept defeat:
Relentless materialism

In Chapter 3, it was suggested that Americans are materialistic by default, that we try to use "things" to express our search
for the meaning of existence. In an age of anxiety, we hope that
science can save us. In an age which has lost its faith, we turn to
tangible reality—to stall showers, air-conditioned cars, frozen
foods, television, jet airplanes—and try to forget that the basic
questions remain unanswered. When satisfactions are not forth-

coming, when the individual finds himself failing to live up to the adequacy, worthiness, gratification, or security standards of American society, one possible response is to emphasize "things" even more relentlessly. Americans buy bigger and better things even when they do not have the money to pay for them. The following case study shows why installment credit in the United States topped thirty billion dollars in 1957.[1]

I'll never forget the day we stopped kidding ourselves and realized what a terrible fix we had got into by trying to keep up with all of our neighbors.

It had started when we looked around and told ourselves that if other people could keep up all those payments, we could do it too. When we couldn't make it, we got desperate and tried to borrow money. Then we sold our new home, figuring that ought to pull us out. Next we tried to turn some things back for the amounts we still owed on them, but even that didn't work. Then came that day when I reached the airline shops to go to work as usual, and my supervisor called me aside.

"Marion, what's this all about?" he asked. "A Palo Alto firm has attached your pay."

His tone was kindly enough, but I can remember only one other time in my life that I ever came so close to real panic— the day during the war when our bomber was so badly shot up we thought she'd crash.

I knew the company fired employees who didn't pay their bills. Our nice new suburban home was already gone, our new car, our fancy food freezer and our TV set were gone, we still owed more than we could possibly pay, and now it seemed that my job was gone. . . .

It was in February, 1953, when we all piled into our old 1941 car for the trip out of the snow to California—Bernice and I and our three children. Our oldest, Mary Florence, was only seven then; Aleta Fern was five, and Daniel Floyd was three. The car was bulging and the kids were yipping, but we didn't

[1] From "We Couldn't Pay Our Bills" by Marion F. Rairigh as told to Elmont Waite. First published in the *Saturday Evening Post*. Copyright 1958 by The Curtis Publishing Company. Reprinted by permission of Brandt & Brandt, New York, agents for Marion F. Rairigh.

mind. We were sure things were going our way at last. I was going to be making nearly seventy-five dollars a week, and to us that seemed a fortune.

We were practically broke when we got to Palo Alto and moved into a motel. It was cheap, as motels go—twenty dollars a week for two little rooms. Even so, it didn't take us long to persuade ourselves that it would be only good business to buy a new house.

I would come back in the evenings to our crowded, hot little motel unit, and Bernice would be looking pretty tired and harassed, handling three children in that cluttered little space.

"Look, honey, I don't see why we don't go ahead and buy a house," I said. "You know my mother told us she would give us five hundred dollars any time we were ready to get a home of our own, and that would cover the whole down payment, the way they're selling these places in California. Monthly payments couldn't be more than this dump, we know that."

We hadn't found any bargains in rentals either—not with three small children. So we looked around at new homes for sale and found a three-bedroom, ranch-style house in a new sub-division in Sunnyvale. It cost $11,500, but the down payment was only $500, plus $250 in closing costs. After a month on my new job, I figured I could scrape up the $250. Payments would be only seventy-two dollars a month, including taxes and insurance.

I remember the day we paid our little deposit to hold the place, standing in the middle of that bare living room, with the kids scooting around, laughing and giggling. We were feeling a little frightened and a little proud of ourselves, and tremendously excited. This was a palace!

We passed two more danger signs right there, without even opening our eyes. In the first place, I was a brand-new employee with the airline and if there were any cutback at all I'd be out of work. This problem of job security never entered my mind. Fortunately, I never was laid off, but the big risk was certainly there.

In the second place, neither Bernice nor I had any idea what a new house costs after you've bought it.

One extra cost we hadn't anticipated didn't really hurt; it was more of an annoyance than a problem. Taxes and insurance promptly rose, so that our seventy-two-dollar monthly payment became seventy-eight dollars.

"But what are we going to use for furniture?" Bernice asked. That did hurt us.

We bought the house in March, 1953, and didn't get possession until May first, so we had a little time to save a few dollars. But we didn't save enough to pay cash for furniture—even secondhand furniture. We did buy a used stove for cash, and we made a $100 down payment on a lot of new furniture. We got only what we thought we had to have, but the total bill was nearly $1000, so we owed $900—agreeing to pay it at $40.49 a month. No matter what kind of a rose-colored pencil you use to add that to a seventy-eight-dollar house payment, the total still comes out $118.49 every month.

Another cost we hadn't figured at all was landscaping. The subdivision homes had no lawns. We had thought we'd wait a while for ours, but one day I heard a couple of our neighbors talking. They didn't see me.

"I don't see why some people around here don't get their lawns in," one of them said. "The dust is terrible. How long do we have to put up with this?"

I walked quietly away and went down to price some grass seed. I figured maybe forty dollars, but, including a few garden tools, the bill came to nearly $100, and I had to borrow the $100. So there was fourteen dollars a month to be paid on that loan, raising our monthly total to $132.

Early that summer, too, the heat coming through our uninsulated roof made the house almost unbearable in the afternoons. So a salesman didn't have much trouble persuading me that insulating the ceilings would be a fine investment. Of course, he was right. It would make the house worth more—and think how much cooler it would be! Well, that job cost $200 and the payments were twelve dollars a month. That made our monthly debt payments total $144, but I don't believe I ever bothered to add them up.

That's another danger sign I'd like to point out. When you

buy things on credit, always keep track of how much you are committed to pay every month. Hardly anyone seems to know how much money he owes nowadays or even how much he must pay every month and how long it will take to get out of debt. You don't need elaborate bookkeeping. You can add the figures on a scrap from a grocery sack, jotting the answers on a calendar—but do it! It may well keep you from getting in too deep, the way we did.

I'm certain I never realized how much I already owed when the water-softener salesman came to our door one day.

"Could you use some extra money?" he asked.

By the time he explained that we'd have to buy a water-softener to save money on water and soap, we were hooked. Bernice was saying, "Well, our clothes did wash easier back in Colorado where we had soft water." So I wound up owing $300 more and our monthly payments rose by $14. I know now that it made our monthly installments total $158.

About that time it began to dawn on me how far our home was from my job. The old '41 car was giving out. I tried riding busses for a while; then arranged to get rides with another fellow. Finally, Bernice got a windfall—a $600 settlement as a result of an auto accident she had been in, back in Colorado. We used the check to buy a 1947 car—a pretty good one—for cash. With what little money was left, we bought a few more things for the house, including curtains. Somehow we were managing to make both ends meet, although there was no safety margin left.

Then came what we first thought was a wonderful break—although I think now it pushed us closer to the brink. I came home one hot August evening and Bernice was wearing her I've-got-a-secret look. "Guess what?" she demanded. "I've got a job too!" She was doing a little dance step around the kitchen, she was so proud of herself. I wasn't too happy about the idea, but we did need the money. The job, on the night shift in a cannery, paid fifty-five dollars a week plus frequent overtime.

I think real disaster began right then. First we bought a good used TV set for $200—at $15 per month. Our children had been everywhere except at home, because all the neighbors had television, so it was easy to talk ourselves into that one, and to ignore the fact it made our monthly installments go up to $173.

Next thing we knew, we had signed up for a bargain food-freezer deal—$500, including all kinds of food, and payments of only forty dollars a month. If I had stopped to add, I'd have known it boosted our monthly payments to a total of $213.

The last straw was something I've never been able to explain. I walked in one day to look at new automobiles in a showroom—nothing but casual curiosity.

"That old car of yours is exactly what we need for a customer of ours!" the salesman exclaimed. "I'll tell you what we'll do—"

It was, he said, a "fantastic" deal on a demonstrator. So I came out driving a new model, saddled with a new $100-a-month payment. That made our installments total $313 every month, practically my whole salary, so all our regular expenses had to come out of Bernice's earnings.

By pinching pennies, we were just able to keep our heads above water. Looking back on those days, I know neither of us was happy, in spite of all our fancy new possessions. We were trapped. We had to keep plugging away to keep up with all those bills, and we worried continually.

The crash came, finally, just as Christmas, 1953, was drawing near. I got up early one morning to get my own breakfast as usual, and there was Bernice, already putting on the coffee.

"Hey, honey, you shouldn't be up at this hour, with that night job of yours," I said.

Never one to beat around the bush, she blurted it right out, "I don't have a job. I got laid off."

I'm not a very big man, and it felt as though a huge prize fighter had just belted me in the solar plexus. I was getting the half-and-half out of the refrigerator and I must have jumped, because a slurp of cream splattered on the floor.

"Oh, no!" I said. "What are we going to do now?"

Bernice looked as though she were going to cry. I put my arm around her and told her we'd get along, and she'd probably be able to get another job.

Well, she couldn't. There were no other jobs. For the second

time we had sailed blindly past that big danger sign I mentioned
—job security. Lots of families I know seem to rely on the wife's
earnings as we did, without ever stopping to think that they may
vanish any minute. Even if the husband's job is secure, the wife
may be fired, or get sick, or have a baby, and then what?

We did the only thing we could do. We skipped the December
car payment. Then Bernice got sick and doctor's fees were
added to our pile of unpaid bills, so we missed our December
house payment.

In January, 1954, we missed a second car payment. We
knew we simply had to make the January house payment, but
Bernice telephoned me at work one day.

"I just got back from the doctor's office," she said. "Mary
Florence fell and hurt herself in the neighbor's yard; she hit a
sprinkler head in the lawn, and the X ray showed her collarbone
is broken."

That knocked out our house payment for the second month.

There was nothing I could do but get out of that car deal
somehow. I gave the car back to the dealer, but did that cancel
what we owed on it? No, sir! We still owed $600. It's legal, and
not uncommon. Models had changed and the car had depre-
ciated faster than I had been paying for it, even at $100 a
month.

So we still owed $600, and had no car at all. Other creditors
were beginning to hound us, and it got so we hated to see the
mailman coming. I had already tried to borrow enough money
to clear up all our bills and then pay at a smaller rate on the
one loan, but I couldn't. I did get one small loan that month,
however, that covered a few of our debts and let us buy an old
1941 car for $100 cash, but we were still broke, still deeply
in debt, and the loan payment itself added $21.68 a month to
our obligations.

Bernice tried place after place, but couldn't find a job anywhere.

"We might as well admit it," she said, as we sat glumly in the
living room one night. "I don't stand a chance of getting another
job, since the cannery season is over. I haven't any special
training."

We decided, then and there, that we'd have to sell the house. We even looked forward to getting rid of it, hoping we might get a little peace of mind.

But selling our house didn't clear our bills. We were three months behind in the house payments by then, and the sale price left us only $200, after paying the house loan and the water-softener and insulation bills.

We moved to a $46.50 rental unit in the Lindenville public-housing project in South San Francisco, taking nothing but our old car and our furniture—and more bills than we could possibly pay.

The firm we owed for the food freezer had taken it back, but there again I was stuck. They sold it to someone else, cheap, and I still owed for the difference, plus a second lot of food I hadn't paid for. This was the bill that brought the attachment of my pay check, in June, 1954, and by that time it amounted to more than $500—as much as the original price of the freezer.

Of course, the advertising industry reinforces the trend toward materialism, but advertising expresses materialistic values as well as reinforcing them.[2]

A century ago advertising was a very minor form of economic activity, involving relatively small sums of money and playing only a negligible part in the distribution of goods or the formation of consumer habits. It was practiced principally by retail distributors who offered items without the mention of brands. Producers, who regarded the distributors as their market and who had as yet no concept of trying to reach the ultimate consumer, did not advertise at all and did not attempt to signalize their product by a distinctive name or label. Advertising ran heavily toward short prosaic notices like the want ads of today, in which the tone was didactic rather than hortatory or inspirational, and the content was factual. But patent medicines, even at that time, were a conspicuous exception. . . .

But those days are gone forever, and no other phenomenon

[2] From David M. Potter, "Advertising; The Institution of Abundance," *Yale Review,* Vol. 43 (Autumn, 1953), pp. 51–70.

of eighty years ago is now more remote. By 1880 advertising had increased threefold since the Civil War period. By 1900 it stood at $95,000,000 a year, which marked a tenfold increase over the amount in 1865. By 1919 it exceeded half a billion dollars, and by 1929 it reached $1,120,000,000. After 1929 it declined because of the Depression, but by 1951 it had again surpassed all previous levels and stood at $6,548,000,000 a year. . . .

Inevitably a question arises: Why did this immense growth of advertising take place? To this query each of us might offer responses of his own, but perhaps the most carefully considered answer, at least in terms of economics, is provided by Neil H. Borden in his extremely thorough study of *The Economic Effects of Advertising* (1942). Borden explains this growth partly in terms of the widening economic gap between producers and consumers and the consequently increased need for a medium of communication, and he attributes the growth of large-scale national advertising, with its color, large spreads, and other expensive features, to the growth of big corporations able to pay for such publicity. But in addition to these explanations he adds another very essential one: "The quest for product differentiation became intensified as the industrial system became more mature, and as manufacturers had capacity to produce far beyond existing demand."

In other words, advertising is not badly needed in an economy of scarcity, because total demand is usually equal to or in excess of total supply, and every producer can normally sell as much as he produces. It is when potential supply outstrips demand—that is, when abundance prevails—that advertising begins to fulfill a really essential economic function. In this situation the producer knows that the limitation upon his operations and upon his growth no longer lies, as it lay historically, in his productive capacity, for he can always produce as much as the market will absorb; the limitation has shifted to the market, and it is selling capacity which controls his growth. Moreover, every other producer of the same kind of article is also in position to expand output indefinitely, and this means that the advertiser must distinguish his product, if not on essential grounds, then on trivial ones, and that he must drive home this distinction by employing a brand name and by keeping this name always before the public. In a situation of limited supply the scarcity of his product will assure his place in the market, but in a situation of indefinitely expandable supply his brand is his only means of assuring himself of such a place.

Let us consider this, however, not merely from the standpoint of the enterpriser but in terms of society as a whole. At once the vital nature of the change will be apparent: the most critical point in the functioning of society shifts from production to consumption, and, as it does so, the culture must be reoriented to convert the producer's culture into a consumer's culture. In a society of scarcity, or even of moderate abundance, the productive capacity has barely sufficed to supply the goods which people already desire and which they regard as essential to an adequate standard of living. Hence the social imperative has fallen upon increases in production. But in a society of abundance, the productive capacity can supply new kinds of goods faster than society in the mass learns to crave these goods or to regard them as necessities. If this new capacity is to be used, the imperative must fall upon consumption, and the society must be adjusted to a new set of drives and values in which consumption is paramount. . . .

In contrast with . . . [the church and the school as educational media], advertising has in its dynamics no motivation to seek the improvement of the individual or to impart qualities of social usefulness, unless conformity to material values may be so characterized. And, though it wields an immense social influence, comparable to the influence of religion and learning, it has no social goals and no social responsibility for what it does with its influence, so long as it refrains from palpable violations of truth and decency. It is this lack of institutional responsibility, this lack of inherent social purpose to balance social power, which, I would argue, is a basic cause for concern about the role of advertising. Occasional deceptions, breaches of taste, and deviations from sound ethical conduct are in a sense superficial and are not necessarily intrinsic. Equally, the high-minded types of advertising which we see more regularly than we sometimes realize are also extraneous to an analysis of the basic nature of advertising. What is basic is that advertising, as such, with all its vast power to influence values and conduct, cannot ever lose sight of the fact that it ultimately regards man as a consumer and defines its own mission as one of stimulating him to consume or to desire to consume.

If one can justifiably say that advertising has joined the charmed circle of institutions which fix the values and standards of society and that it has done this without being linked to any of the socially defined objectives which usually guide such institutions in the use of their power, then it becomes necessary to consider with special care the extent and nature of its influence —how far it extends and in what way it makes itself felt.

To do this, it may be well to begin with the budget, for the activity of all major institutions—great churches, great governments, great universities—can be measured in part by what they spend, and, though such measurements are no substitute for qualitative evaluation, they are significant. In political history the importance of the power of the purse is proverbial. I have already said that the amount spent for advertising in the United States in 1951 was $6,548,000,000. Perhaps this may be a little more meaningful if I add that the amount is equivalent to $199 per year for every separate family in the United States. Compare this with what the nation paid for primary and secondary public education in 1949, which amounted to a total expenditure of $5,010,000,000. This means that, for every household, we paid $152. Our national outlay for the education of citizens, therefore, amounted to substantially less than our expenditure for the education of consumers. It would also be interesting to compare the financial strength of advertising and of religion, but, since the churches do not publicize records of their financial operations, I can only remark that there were 180,000 gainfully employed clergymen in the United States in 1950, and most of them were men of very modest incomes. For every clergyman supported by any church, advertising spent $36,000.

Perhaps more explicit comparisons may serve to reinforce this point of the relative magnitude of advertising activities. I will mention two: In 1949–50 the operating expenses of Yale

University were $15,000,000; in 1948 the expenses, for news-paper advertising only, of two major distilleries, Schenley and National Distillers, were more than half of this amount, or $7,800,000. In 1944 the major political parties spent $23,000,-000 to win the public to the support of Mr. Roosevelt or of Governor Dewey; in 1948, Procter and Gamble, Colgate-Palm-olive-Peet, and Lever Brothers spent more than $23,000,000 to win the public to the support of one or another of their products.

With expenditures of this order of magnitude, advertising clearly thrusts with immense impact upon the mass media and, through them, upon the public. The obvious and direct impact is, of course, through the quantity of space it occupies in the newspapers and magazines and the amount of time it occupies in radio and television broadcasts. Either in space or in time the totals are impressive, and, if advertising had no influence upon the information in newspapers, the stories in magazines, and the programs in radio and television, it would still be a force worthy of major consideration because of the influence of the advertising matter itself. But it does have a profound influence upon the media, and for students of American opinion and American life it is important that this influence should be un-derstood.

To appreciate this influence, let us consider the position of most magazines a century ago, as contrasted with their position today. At that time the only financial support which a magazine could expect was from its readers. This meant that, if a person did not care to read, the magazine had no means of appealing to him and no objective in doing so. If editors worried about circulation, it was because they needed more revenue from sub-scriptions, and if they had enough subscriptions to support them on a modest scale of operations, they could safely proceed on a basis of keeping their standards high and their circulation limited. They did not worry very much about advertising, for the reason that there was not much advertising to worry about. At the time of the Civil War, for instance, it is estimated that the total income from advertising received by all newspapers and periodicals averaged about 25 cents per capita yearly for the population at that time.

Today, of course, these conditions have ceased to apply. Newspapers and magazines no longer look to their subscribers as the major source of revenue. As long ago as 1935 the revenue of all newspapers in the country was $760,000,000, of which $500,000,000 came from advertising and $260,000,000 from subscriptions. At the same time, the magazines of the United States enjoyed a revenue of $144,000,000 from subscriptions and $186,000,000 from advertising. That is, approximately two out of every three newspaper dollars came from advertising, and more than one out of every two magazine dollars came from the same source. The subscriber had been reduced to a sad position: whereas at one time periodicals had fished for subscribers, they now fished for advertisers and used subscribers as bait. Since that time, newspaper advertising has increased more than three-fold, to the total of $2,226,000,000, and magazine advertising has risen to $562,000,000, from which we may infer that the subscriber is now, more than ever before, a secondary figure. If I may express the same point in a different way, the situation is this: In 1935 American families paid an average of $6.60 a year to receive newspapers, but advertisers paid an average of $12.70 to have newspapers sent to each family, and in 1951 advertising was paying $56 a year to have newspapers delivered to each family. Clearly that was far more than the household itself could possibly be expected to pay. Similarly, with magazines, while subscribers in 1935 were paying $3.60 a year to receive them, advertisers were paying $4.70 to have them sent, and by 1951 American advertising had increased enough to pay $14 per family per year as its stake in the magazines on the living-room table of the American home. In many cases, as of magazines with large advertising sections, the real situation is that the advertiser buys the magazine for the "purchaser," and what the purchaser pays as the "price" of the magazine is really only a kind of qualifying fee to prove that he is a bona fide potential consumer and not a mere deadhead on whom this handsome advertising spread would be wasted.

If this were merely a matter of some magazines being published for consumers and other magazines being published for readers, with the public retaining a choice between the two, the result would not have been quite so sweeping; but the effect of this change has been to threaten with extinction the magazine that is published first and foremost for its readers.

The threat operates in this way: the magazine with large advertising revenue can afford to pay its contributors more, and therefore it can secure better contributors than the magazine which enjoys very little revenue of this kind. In a sense, the advertiser is prepared to buy better authors for the reader than the reader is prepared to buy for himself. But this means automatically that any magazine which wishes to secure or retain the best writers must get advertising. But to get advertising it must also get mass circulation. To get mass circulation it must publish material with a mass appeal. Also, it must keep its subscription costs low, which in turn makes it more dependent than ever upon advertising revenue. At this point a fixed cycle is virtually inescapable: millions of readers are essential to secure a large revenue from advertising, advertising is essential to enable the magazine to sell at a price that will secure millions of readers—therefore, the content of the magazine must be addressed to the millions. Thus the best writers, those who have proved able to write for the most discriminating readers, are put to work writing for consumers who may not be readers at all.

But it is even more significant to realize that other media are far more completely part of the institutional apparatus of advertising than are periodicals. Magazines and newspapers are still paid for in part by the consumer; but radio and television programs are paid for almost wholly by advertisers. In 1951 it was estimated that there were 100,000,000 radios in the United States, and radio advertising was estimated at $690,000,000. That is, advertisers were annually spending $6.90 to provide each set with programs, while the programs received by the 15,000,000 television sets were being subsidized at the rate of $32 a set.

What this means, in functional terms, it seems to me, is that the newspaper feature, the magazine article, the radio program, do not attain the dignity of being ends in themselves; they are rather means to an end: that end, of course, is to catch the reader's attention so that he will then read the advertisement or hear the commercial, and to hold his interest until these essential messages have been delivered. The program or the article becomes a kind of advertisement in itself—becomes the "pitch," in the telling language of the circus barker. Its function is to induce people to accept the commercial, just as the commercial's function is to induce them to accept the product.

A year or two ago an English critic complained of American periodical writing that it "fixes the attention but does not engage the mind." If this is true, it is not because of any intrinsic vacuity on the part of American writers but because the most important financial supporters of such writing are paying for it to do exactly what is alleged. "To fix the attention but not to engage the mind" is a precise statement of the advertiser's formula. . . .

In this discussion of the importance of advertising, the purpose has been to explore its effects upon the noneconomic phases of our culture. For that reason I have refrained from introducing some significant points in connection with the changes wrought by advertising in the economy. For instance, it is important that advertising tends less to provide the consumer with what he wants than to make him like what he gets. In this connection Richard B. Tennant, in his recent book on the American cigarette industry, shows that the American Tobacco Company, in the second decade of this century, produced at least eight different brands of cigarettes, designed to meet the diverse demands of varying smoking tastes and different purses; but after 1925 it began to concentrate its advertising upon Lucky Strike and after 1927 began to dispose of its minor brands to other companies, though it did later develop Herbert Tareyton and Pall Mall. Also, it is important that advertising tends to minimize information and maximize appeal, with the result that producers tend less to differentiate their products physically, in terms of quality, or economically, in terms of price, than to differentiate them psychologically in terms of slogan, package, or prestige. "How many advertisers," asked Walter Dill Scott in 1903, "describe an undergarment so that the reader can feel the pleasant contact with the body?" Surely this is one question to which time has given us a definite answer.

But the most important effects of this powerful institution

are not upon the economics of our distributive system; they are upon the values of our society. If the economic effect is to make the purchaser like what he buys, the social effect is, in a parallel but broader sense, to make the individual like what he gets—to enforce already existing attitudes, to diminish the range and variety of choices, and, in terms of abundance, to exalt the materialistic virtues of consumption.

Certainly it marks a profound social change that this new institution for shaping human standards should be directed, not, as are the school and the church, to the inculcation of beliefs or attitudes that are held to be of social value, but rather to the stimulation or even the exploitation of materialistic drives and emulative anxieties and then to the validation, the sanctioning, and the standardization of these drives and anxieties as accepted criteria of social value. Such a transformation, brought about by the need to stimulate desire for the goods which an abundant economy has to offer and which a scarcity economy would never have produced, offers strong justification for the view that advertising should be recognized as an important social influence and as our newest major institution—an institution peculiarly identified with one of the most pervasive forces in American life, the force of economic abundance.

A recent book by the Harvard economist, John Galbraith, *The Affluent Society,* goes even further. According to Galbraith, the emphasis on more and better gadgets every year underlies the instability of the American economy—as well as the scarcity of teachers and scientists. We pay a fearful price for our materialism. Stuart Chase summarizes Galbraith's thesis in a review entitled, "The Economic Embarrassment of America's Riches." [3]

The United States has shattered all tradition and all previous theory by providing a majority of citizens with goods well above the line of subsistence, leaving only a minority still poor—"case"

[3] From "The Economic Embarrassment of America's Riches," by Stuart Chase, as it appeared in *The Reporter,* June 26, 1958, pp. 34–36. Copyright 1958, by The Reporter Magazine Company. Reprinted by permission of Stuart Chase and the editorial department of The Reporter Magazine Company.

poverty, where the breadwinner is sick or feeble-minded or alcoholic, and "insular" poverty, as in the Ozarks.

Affluence has been won in one society at least—Canada, Australia, and western Europe are following a similar trend— but it is not to be confused with Utopia. The formula, or better the behavior pattern, by which the United States maintains its affluent supremacy is shaky; while the good life, in the sense of a balanced supply of goods and services, still eludes most of us. We are at once affluent in gross tonnage of fin-tailed cars and poverty-stricken in the more lasting forms of satisfaction—a lop-sided society in a lopsided economy. Television for everybody; inadequate schoolrooms and teaching staff for hundreds of thousands of children.

Can the balance be righted? Galbraith believes there is a possibility, not so much by virtue of reforming zeal but because trends are running in that direction. (And, I might add, because of Russian competition.) He offers some stimulating proposals to bring the economy into balance, but warns that they will be fought by the "conventional wisdom"—a spook that haunts this essay. New Dealers will combine with classicists in objecting to some of the proposals.

The study accepts no ideology, Right, Left, or Center. It cuts through the words and slogans to discover what is actually going on out there in the market place. Some such course as the book outlines may turn out to be the only possible way for an open society to keep its affluence—the only way for a modern democracy to adjust to an economy of abundance. Certainly this sort of objective examination must be made before a course can be charted. . . .

The story begins with the great traditional assumptions in economics, outlined by Adam Smith, then made precise by David Ricardo and ferocious by Herbert Spencer. It is interesting to remember that Marx built solidly on Ricardo, and was so convinced of the latter's validity that he thought the only escape from the relentless laws of capitalism was violent revolution. Ricardo and company assumed: (1) poverty for the majority; (2) inequality enforced by the iron law of wages; (3) insecurity

for both entrepreneur (the risk taker) and worker; (4) the
beneficence of private production in any amount and any
variety; (5) the insatiability of human wants; and (6) the necessity of free competition to insure maximum output, government
to act as arbiter only. Herbert Spencer even demanded that
governments get out of the business of running schools and
delivering mail.

Some of these assumptions still exist in Asia today—mass
poverty, for instance, and inequality between sheik and shepherd. In the West, however, and especially in the United States,
we have been veering away from them for a hundred years, until
now a vast gulf separates the conventional wisdom from actual
behavior. Mass poverty is gone. Inequality has been profoundly
modified, especially by the graduated income tax—a mechanism
that would make Ricardo turn in his grave and Marx refuse to
believe his eyes. Insecurity for the rank and file has been reduced by social-security legislation, fringe benefits in industry,
and the manifold provisions of the welfare state. The free market
has been profoundly altered by the administered prices of Big
Business, by the contracts of Big Unions, by subsidies to farmers,
and by increasing governmental regulations. . . .

But it is against the classical assumption of an abstract and
limitless "production" that Galbraith makes his most novel and
striking contribution. Conservatives and liberals alike, the
N.A.M. and the A.D.A., genuflect before G.N.P.—Gross National Product. "We'll hit $600 billion by 1970" seems to be all
we know, and all we need to know. The classical assumption
stands firm, but the facts of economic behavior are anything but
firm. To boost the G.N.P. every year demands that consumers
must be bludgeoned by ever more frenzied publicity, including
motivational research, into accepting the importance of the unimportant. This acceptance entails a mammoth increase in consumer credit to finance the purchase of the unimportant, at least
in the areas of planned obsolescence. Creeping inflation becomes
inevitable, together with a staggering waste of good iron, copper,
oil, and other natural resources.

But human wants are *not* insatiable. As one's income grows,
one's wants shift, and at certain limits tend to cease altogether.

Poverty-stricken societies may talk about insatiable wants; affluent societies should be more discriminating. There is a limit to what a human being can eat, a limit to the number of cars one can cram into a garage, a limit to the number of television programs that can be watched simultaneously on separate sets for each member of the family.

Veblen in 1900 could talk about conspicuous consumption, but Galbraith talks about the growing enclaves of inconspicuous consumption, where a Volkswagen is a better symbol of prestige than a Cadillac, where—heaven help Madison Avenue—one keeps down with the Joneses. Our author describes the emergence of a new social class that cares more for the interest of the job than for the pay, in which satisfactions run more in professional work well done than in gross tonnage of stuff consumed.

Another important change has occurred in the conventional wisdom since Ricardo's time, primarily as a consequence of the great depression. The goal of full employment and high wages is now supported by practically everybody in America. How else indeed can the affluent society absorb its own production? This goal entails, however, a painful side effect in the wage-price spiral and more inflation. "Where inflation is concerned," Galbraith notes, "nearly everyone finds it convenient to confine himself to conversation. All branches of the conventional wisdom are equally agreed on the undesirability of any remedies that are effective." Effective means of combating inflation conflict with the ideal of production for the sake of full employment, and a bigger G.N.P.

There is a theory that advancing the discount rate by the Federal Reserve will check inflation, but recent monetary history, alas, shows this to be an illusion. Such changes, furthermore, can be dangerous by checking business investment and encouraging unemployment, while administered prices soar majestically upward. The same attitudes that lead us to advocate full employment and the use of industrial plant at capacity "deny us the measures to prevent inflation." This is a shattering conclusion, but I am afraid it is true.

Conventional wisdom maintains that wants originate in the breast of the consumer, and that business should employ all available resources to satisfy them. Galbraith takes a close look at the advertising pages of our slick magazines and comes to the more realistic conclusion that the producer now manufactures not only the goods but the wants. Independent choice rules undefiled in the textbooks but not in the market place, and certainly not in the offices of B.B.D.O. To this method of packing goods and wants in one blunderbuss he gives the name "dependence effect," and it is cardinal in our affluent society.

As sane men, however, do become surfeited, the difficulties and costs of manufacturing the wants mount steadily. If sane men really desired unlimited production as an end in itself, the hours of labor would not have been cut in half since the Civil War. Think of all the stuff we might be able to produce on an eighty-hour week!

Our affluent society suffers from another serious malady— its neglect of what Galbraith calls "social balance." Even the sanest American is not surfeited by certain kinds of goods; as a matter of fact, he is starved for them. They lie, however, in the public rather than in the private sector. They cannot be wrapped in cellophane and sold. They include such things as schools, scholarships for bright youngsters, research in pure science, parks, playgrounds, hospitals, mental-health research, care of the aged, safer highways and airways, urban redevelopment, conservation, open spaces, clean rivers, the arts, the opportunity to relax and invite one's soul. Massive as the G.N.P. may be, it is remarkably deficient in many of the things that make life worth living.

Conventional wisdom holds that only private output constitutes wealth; public output is at best a necessary evil. So we picnic on exquisitely packaged foods, from a portable icebox, beside a polluted stream lined with empty beer cans and billboards. "The counterpart of increasing opulence will be deepening filth," of which the smog of Los Angeles is perhaps the supreme example.

If we could achieve a balance of true wealth, the range of true wants would expand, leaving less to be contrived by the higher salesmanship. Or, as Galbraith concludes, "At least this is a plausible hypothesis."

With this plausible hypothesis the book might well end. Galbraith has taken the affluent society apart, to find that it cannot continue indefinitely on its present course; inflation, unbalanced output, and consumer rebellions are becoming unmanageable, and a new formula must be found.

He then proceeds to make five suggestions for recovering balance. I did not find them as exciting as the analytical work, but I believe they indicate the sort of thing that must be done. Galbraith advocates:

A flexible system of unemployment compensation, financed outside of actuarial standards by the Federal government, on top of what the states may do. As unemployment increases, scales of compensation go up until they are just under weekly earnings. As unemployment declines, scales go down. Thus when jobs are plentiful the system will provide little incentive for malingering; when jobs are scarce, no useful distinction can be made between those who are idle voluntarily and those unable to find work. A full head of consumer demand is meanwhile maintained, and "the effect . . . is to make tolerable the unemployment which is associated with price stability." We cannot hope to check inflation without having some unemployment from time to time; this fact must be faced.

Limited price and wage controls. Not nearly so drastic as during the war, but enough to stop the wage-price spiral.

A Federal tax system that will automatically divert a share of increasing income taxes to public authority for public purposes—schools, roads, hospitals, and the rest.

An expanded sales tax for maintaining social balance in states and cities. Liberals will cry havoc. A sales tax hurts the poor! But there are no poor in affluent societies; at least almost nobody is below the line of subsistence. "A poor society rightly adjusts its fiscal policy to the poor." Wake up, friends—it isn't that kind of economy any more!

Good schools, public services, medical care, and scholarships guaranteed to the children of that minority which is still poor—the "case" poor and the "insular" poor. The children must not suffer. In Russia today, every gifted child is given all the education he can absorb. Can we do less?

These five proposals, while novel, are comfortably within the limits of an open society, far short of socialism, defined as the public ownership of the means of production.

The sober reader, while admitting that there is nothing subversive about Mr. Galbraith's program, may say the time is not ripe for such drastic changes. The sober reader should remember, however, that we are in an economic race with Russia and China for the uncommitted peoples of the world. Unless we are ready to experiment with new ideas and new machinery to preserve our open society from disastrous inflations and depressions, we shall surely lose the race, and perhaps our democracy along with it.

To put the same point another way, political apathy may result from relentless materialism. Some Americans are so busy worrying about money or about immediate personal problems that they do not have time to concern themselves with international relations or civil liberties. In the summer of 1954, for example, American television and radio networks buzzed with excitement over the "cold war" with the Soviet Union and with Senator McCarthy's investigation of Communist activity in America. Yet, two of the leading public opinion research organizations in the country, the American Institute of Public Opinion and the National Opinion Research Center, could not discover at the time a high level of interest on the part of the general public on either issue. Here is how the director of the survey, Professor Samuel A. Stouffer of Harvard's Laboratory of Social Relations, reported the interview materials bearing on this point.[4]

. . . This survey took some care to learn the context in which an individual's opinions are held. The entire first part of the interview was a quite free-flowing conversation between the interviewer and respondent. Its purpose was to find out what things were worrying people in the summer of 1954, and to find these out with a minimum of prompting. During the first part of this conversation the interviewer was not permitted to

[4] From *Communism, Conformity and Civil Liberties* by Samuel A. Stouffer, pp. 58–70. Copyright 1955, by Samuel A. Stouffer. Reprinted by permission of Doubleday & Company, Inc., Garden City, New York.

introduce on his own initiative the topic of Communism or civil liberties or any other specific issue, lest this bias the replies.

PERSONAL AND FAMILY PROBLEMS ARE OF FIRST CONCERN

After showing credentials and obtaining consent, the interviewer opened with the question:

On the whole, do you think life will be better for you or worse, in the next few years than it is now?

This was followed by:

Everybody of course has some things he worries about, more or less. Would you say you worry more now than you used to, or not as much?

And then:

What kinds of things do you worry about most?

The answers may not be surprising to the managing editor who has to know what kind of news people like to read, or to the television producer who has to know what kind of programs most closely relate to the personal concerns of viewers, or to the precinct captain who has to deliver a vote for his political party. But they possibly will be surprising to some persons whose major concern is with great issues of the day and whose occupations are somewhat remote from the rank and file—for example, to academic people, to executives in government or business, and to some professional writers concerned with analyzing public issues.

First we shall examine the national cross-section. The separate sample of leaders will come later.

The big, overwhelming response to the question, What kind of things do you worry about most? was in terms of personal and family problems. Eighty per cent of the men and women in the cross-section answered *solely* in these terms. And many of the remainder answered in the same terms but went on to express anxiety about other problems. Ten per cent professed no worries about any problems.

The number of people who said that they were worried either about the threat of Communists in the United States or about civil liberties was, even by the most generous interpretation of occasionally ambiguous responses, *less than 1%!*

Even world problems, including the shadow of war, did not evoke a spontaneous answer from more than 8%. It will be argued, of course, that some people tend to suppress or mask deep anxieties about which they can do little. Being unconscious, the anxieties cannot be reported. Even if we grant this possibility, it is still hard to argue that the American people, as of the summer of 1954, were consumed with anxieties about war, not to mention internal Communism or civil liberties. Otherwise we should have heard more frequent spontaneous comments, even if the respondent talked first of personal or domestic affairs. In the "door-opener" question, the most striking fact was the essential optimism in the American climate. Only 13% said they expected life to be worse for them in the next few years than it is now—an answer which is hardly compatible with an overwhelming concern with impending doom. This is especially significant when we note that a disproportionately large number among this 13% were people in their sixties, seventies, and older, whose answers often were couched in terms of failing health or loss of earning power.

Yet even the most optimistic tended to have some worries and talked quite freely about them to the interviewer under the pledge of anonymity. The largest single block of personal worries involved concern over personal business or family economic problems. A total of 43% volunteered anxieties in this general area. The date of the survey must be remembered—late May, June, and July 1954. As compared with previous high levels of employment, there was a mild recession involving some unemployment or limited employment, as well as reduction in overtime. How many people would make responses like this in a period of even higher or in even lower employment, we do not know. Some illustrations:

"How to make a living for my family is my biggest worry. We've got the new house now if we can ever get it paid for. I don't worry about things like politics, because we have people who are paid to do that kind of worrying."—*Furnace maker,* Michigan.

"My children. They are too ambitious for our income; takes more money than we've got. And I work too, in an office, to help out the income."—*Wife of fish-hatchery owner,* Georgia.

"Meeting payments of interest and some principal on the mortgage. But I don't really worry compared with how my folks did."—*Farm wife,* Iowa.

"Business conditions at the store worry me some. Trade isn't as good as it was."—*Grocer,* Texas.

"Mainly with my employment now. They're having a lot of shifting around and just where will I end up? They're reducing the force in my place of work. Who's going to go and who's going to stay? Wonder if I'll be one of them to go."—*Carpenter,* New Jersey.

"How I'll manage to finance my way through college. I'm working nights as a switchboard operator and have a responsibility to keep my mother and my younger brother."—*College student* (male), Pennsylvania.

"I work hard when I can. I don't see where I'm getting anywhere now. I can't get no work to do."—*Timber cutter,* Georgia.

"Paying bills. My husband has been in the hospital and may have to go back again."—*Wife of shipping clerk,* New Jersey.

"I've been laid off three months. I'm worried about making a living. Doesn't seem to be much work. I worry I may lose my job, also I might get sick."—*Employee in axle plant,* Pennsylvania.

"I've served my time on Guadalcanal and now I'm home minding my own business. I work graveyard shift and put in a crop besides. The plant has cut down to a four-day week. That's what bothers me. I don't worry about world problems. When trouble gets here I can take it. I'm paying taxes for someone to do my worrying for me."—*Textile worker,* North Carolina.

"Ever since I came home from the Army last year I have been having troubles getting a job."—*Factory worker,* Illinois.

"My job. I'm just new at managing this chain store and I'm very concerned about it."—*Grocer,* North Dakota.

"I worry about my pension. Might not have enough to eat. Hard times now and no work. I want fixings for my new house, but things cost a lot."—*Coal miner,* Pennsylvania.

"Money goes too fast. Food, it is so expensive. High rent. We are moving to California to see if we can get a better living there."—*Finisher in suit factory* (female), New York.

"It appears that I can't prosper at nothing I do."—*Farmer*, Texas.

"Security, we do not own our place. We want to and hope to. And we want to educate our children."—*Farmer*, North Carolina.

"Money to take care of children, health. I have seven children and I'm 51. I wouldn't worry if I had enough money and the kids were healthy. But one of them is sick and I am off in work now. I wish business be what it was in '50 and '51."—*Tool estimator*, Michigan.

"The financial future. How am I going to send my children to college?"—*Wife of telephone supervisor*, Indiana.

"Oh God, to find work. My man started to work four days a week. So I've tried to find work too, but it's poor—only a couple of hours a week at a dress factory."—*Wife of steelworker*, Pennsylvania.

"Trying to pay my honest and just debts."—*Truck driver*, Alabama.

"The weather and the crops. My income depends on that."—*Farmer*, Nebraska.

"Whether I'll sell enough cars to keep going, business conditions being what they are."—*Auto salesman*, Massachusetts.

"I've got to support two children. If I don't work I can't pay for them. My mother-in-law keeps them and she don't have no income. Down at my plant everybody's talking about who's going to work and who's going to be laid off—talking about borrowed money if you're laid off."—*Mixer's helper, glass factory*, Pennsylvania.

"Husband hasn't worked since January, but I really don't worry like I did when my son was missing in Burma. I depend entirely on God."—*Wife of glass blower*, Pennsylvania.

"Cattle and hogs is about the only thing I can think about right now. And the wind and the sand."—*Farmer*, Idaho.

"Business problems. Whether business will hold up and how to get more business."—*Salesman*, Virginia.

"The neighborhood worries me. We need a yard. The kids have to play on the porch. I can't let them out in this dirty neighborhood. But we can't move because we've got so many bills to pay. Doctor bills and hospital bills."—*Wife of taxi driver*, New York.

It is particularly notable that few people in the cross-section made general remarks about business conditions in the abstract. It was almost always in terms of what the situation *means to me*.

HEALTH OF SELF AND FAMILY

The second largest block of answers was in terms of health, either of oneself or of members of the family. A total of 24% in the cross-section mentioned health problems (including some who *also* mentioned family finances or other problems). As might be expected, a larger proportion of women than of men were in this category. Men were somewhat more likely than women to respond in terms of finances; women somewhat more likely than men to respond in terms of the health of the family, especially of the children. Some illustrations:

"I worry about my husband because he has tuberculosis of the spine and eventually faces surgery."—*Wife of worker in aircraft factory*, California.

"I've got a mother that isn't well and a young sister that's been in bed six years with rheumatic heart, and I don't feel so well myself."—*Wife of textile worker*, New York.

"I worry most about my sister, Edith, than anything else. She is mentally ill."—*Proprietor of soft-drink parlor*, North Carolina.

"My health. I worry most about not being able to call on the people as much as I want to. My husband is a minister and I am supposed to do a good deal of calling."—*Wife of preacher*, Oklahoma.

"I worry most about my children getting hurt someday driving in the traffic we have on the highways."—*Salesman*, Illinois.

"My health—I've got three kinds of illnesses—diabetes, cardiac, and black lumps. I've got a granddaughter paralyzed for two years and that worries me too."—*Retired cigar maker*, New York.

"Someone said worry is like a rocking chair. It gives you something to do and doesn't get you anywhere. I am not really the worrying kind, but I do worry about my mother's health right now."—*Wife of hospital orderly,* Wisconsin.

"I'm going to have a baby and I worry about if it's going to turn out all right."—*Wife of bellhop,* Indiana.

"It's the polio season at the present time [June] and that has me worried."—*Wife of furniture dealer,* Texas.

"I worry about my health. Other worries I leave to Papa. He's got the brains in the house."—*Wife of brewery bottler,* Missouri.

"Will I get sick? I worry for fear I'd have to go to the county home. I worry about other people, too."—*Widow of factory worker,* Pennsylvania.

OTHER PERSONAL PROBLEMS

Thirty per cent of the respondents mentioned personal problems not classifiable strictly under the categories of financial or health. Some of these were included in the former categories also. They cover a miscellany of personal problems. Illustrations:

"My marriage difficulties. I have just divorced my husband." —*Schoolteacher,* California.

"I worry about having the ability to raise my children to be God-fearing children. I have two boys coming up and I wonder what will become of them."—*Wife of electrician,* Georgia.

"It's the future of the children. I don't care for much in an economic way, as much as I concern myself with their contribution to society. What I'm trying to get at is that I want to provide them with a good perspective."—*Insurance salesman,* North Dakota.

"I worry about my son in the Navy. Also keep worrying about my younger son. Hope he won't get in any trouble."—*Wife of construction worker,* Indiana.

"I worry about my husband living in another city from mine." —*Wife of oil driller,* Kentucky.

"I wish my wife was a better housekeeper. When I was married I found out she was dirty and I had to come home and clean."—*Steelworker,* Pennsylvania.

"In-law troubles worry me most. Just trying to keep peace in the family and get along with my daughters-in-law. Otherwise I have no worries."—*Wife of foundry worker*, Washington.

"The draft. My husband is subject to the draft and that's the only thing I worry about."—*Wife of a college student*, New Jersey.

"My children's welfare. I work all day at an office and have two small children at home. That keeps me occupied. I am worried too about my father's health. Daddy is in the hospital now."—*Wife of grocery clerk*, Georgia.

"My 17-year-old son wants to marry and that really is bothering me."—*Wife of implement dealer*, Nevada.

"Well, you know we have a girl 13 and the way things are— my goodness, the things that happen—I'm afraid to let her out after dark."—*Wife of restaurant owner*, California.

"I worry about the care I'll get when I get older. I'd probably have to go into a home eventually."—*Widow, practical nurse*, New York.

"If things go wrong with the house I don't know how to go about repairs. Being a woman alone, employing mechanics and things I'm inclined to think they take advantage of you."—*Widow*, Connecticut.

"I worry about getting pregnant again. My doctor tells me not to worry, but I do."—*Wife of maintenance man, furniture factory*, Wisconsin.

"Living in town and I like the country but I married a town lady the second time. I need the country."—*Retired farmer*, Georgia.

"I don't have any worries except about the baby we're having. When it arrives, there will be a big difference in ages between our boy, 11, and the baby."—*Farmer's wife*, Kansas.

"I guess I worry about my people mostly. I ran away from home at 13. Never saw my family for years. Now I'm in the middle between my wife and family. They don't like each other."—*Tavern proprietor*, New Jersey.

"I worry about my grandsons. Their mother and father are divorced. The mother works and the children are in the care of others. It would be better if the mother could make a home for them."—*Wife of locomotive engineer*, Wisconsin.

"I worry about my children's future, especially about some of the playmates they have. And about their health."—*Wife of lumber estimator*, Kentucky.

"I worry about our children. Will I be able to educate them
and will they be able to grow up without getting into
trouble?"—*Farmer, Texas.*

CONCERNS ABOUT WORLD AFFAIRS, INCLUDING WAR

In interpreting the responses of those concerned about war,
one must exercise two cautions, in addition to noting the possibility that some people may be suppressing or masking their
anxiety.

On the one hand, the figure of 8%, which we have cited,
includes everybody who mentioned the international situation or
world affairs, even if he did not explicitly speak about war or
Russia or atom bombs. In fact, less than half of this 8% directly
used the word "war." Responses were quite commonly couched
in such terms as: "I don't like what is happening in Asia," or
"I worry about what Russia is up to," or "When will the international situation settle down?"

On the other hand, some people who responded in personal
terms may have been anxious about war but resisted verbalizing
their anxiety even though they were not suppressing it. If a
mother says, "I am worried about the future for my children,"
she may be thinking explicitly about war, but we cannot tell
unless she offers further information. Interviewers were carefully
instructed not to put forth suggestions of their own but rather
to probe by asking general questions like, "You say you worry
about the future of your children. What things about their future
do you worry about especially?"

Some interviewers were more skillful than others in this
difficult art of non-directive interviewing. Some tended to accept the first answer and dispense with probing. Others, to an
extent we do not know, may have been too explicit in further
probing. In any event, further probing on such questions often
made it quite clear that the respondent was thinking in terms of
family finances or risks of accident or illness, or of possible
juvenile delinquency.

Among the 8% who, by a generous interpretation of their
responses, expressed anxiety about world affairs, about one in

ten couched his or her worry explicitly in personal terms. Examples:

"The biggest worry is about our boy in R.O.T.C. We wonder if they take him in the Army, that will mean the end. Will he have any future? War would ruin his future."—*Purchasing agent,* New York.

"I can get into an awful stew about the next war. Whether my son will go to war. Russia—why do they want to control so much and not let everyone live in peace?"—*Wife of engraver,* Massachusetts.

"A son in the service. Things look bad. We can't go on forever feeding the youth of the world into wars and bloodshed." —*Teacher,* California.

"I worry about this war business because one of my grandsons just returned and another soon will be called."—*Farmer,* Indiana.

"Worry about my youngsters. One is in Korea, and I do worry about how the war will affect them all. I am afraid America is going to be drawn into another world war. We're living in fear."—*Foreman,* North Carolina.

"With a boy 15, I'm concerned about the war."—*Textile worker* (female), New Hampshire.

"I worry about war, as I'm still in the age. I don't know where I stand. I don't like wars and I wouldn't want to leave my family either."—*Milk delivery man,* Pennsylvania.

"World War III. I am of draft age and I have a wife." —*Machinist,* West Virginia.

"I am worried about my grandson going to war."—*Master mariner,* Washington.

It must be remembered, however, that such responses are not typical. They come from less than 1% of the cross-section. The more frequent comments about war were of the order: "I worry quite a bit about the atom bomb"; "I hope Eisenhower won't let us get mixed up in Indo-China"; "Oh, why can't we live in peace like we used to?"; or, as a Louisiana farm wife put it, "I hate to think about carrying off our home boys and they being slaughtered up."

OTHER LOCAL AND NATIONAL PROBLEMS

There was a miscellany of expressions of concern about other local and national problems, including the subject of Negro segregation, and including some comments about the political and economic scene, not couched in a personal reference. These are again somewhat difficult to classify, but at the most they do not aggregate more than about 6% of all responses.

COMMUNISTS AND CIVIL LIBERTIES

We come now to the truly minuscule proportion of the national cross-section which was sufficiently worried about the internal Communist threat or the threat to civil liberties to mention it.

Actually, the figure of 1% is an overstatement. From the context of the remarks, it was not always possible to separate comments about Communist aggression abroad from those about Communist infiltration in the United States. For example, such a comment as the following: "I am worried about the Communists. They are more deadly than most people think." In such a case, the interviewer should have probed further, but this was not always done. The few explicit comments about Communist infiltration can be illustrated by the following:

"I am worried most about Communism and all activities sponsored by subversives in all branches of our government and in education."—*Wife of physician,* California.

"American Communists. I am afraid we might be sold out." —*Postal clerk,* New Hampshire.

"I am 100% American. Seventh generation in America. I worry most about Communists and their influx into America —subversives in our government."—*Wife of attorney,* Indiana.

"Gradual selling out of our country to foreign ideologies following the Communist line and getting away from American individualism. The U.N. was a good idea but at present detrimental to our country. It is being run by Communists." —*Insurance man,* Texas.

"So many honest decent Americans have swallowed sugar-coated Marxism."—*Caterer,* Connecticut.

"I pray the Lord that the Communists won't get a hold of our government and our schools. I pray the Lord will strengthen our President."—*Widow of farmer,* Arkansas.

If the expressed anxieties about Communist infiltration were few, those about the threat to civil liberties were even fewer. This, like the small response on the Communist threat, is particularly surprising in view of the timing of the study. The Army-McCarthy hearings were not over when the survey went into the field and were still fresh in the minds of most respondents. Only a mere handful—not over 20 out of nearly 5000 respondents in the cross-section—volunteered a worry about civil liberties, excluding a few where the context was clearly in terms of Negro-white segregation. These comments were almost invariably personalized in terms of Senator McCarthy as a symbol. Examples:

"I am concerned about McCarthy—a potential Hitler. It's bad to have a man who gets hold of people as he does. I believe in wiping out Communism. If we can keep him from getting too much power, we wouldn't have to worry. We have to be on the job against Communism, but I think that Eisenhower and the Army, Navy, and State Department are capable."—*Wife of school superintendent,* Delaware.

"I am most worried about what McCarthy is doing to our American way of life."—*Businessman,* Georgia.

"McCarthy being allowed to do as he does concerns me greatly."—*Wife of owner of trucking business,* Iowa.

"I'm concerned about the fact that McCarthy can pull all the stuff he's pulled. All he develops is the froth on top of the glass and no beer underneath. For 14 years I said J. Parnell Thomas was a mental two-spot, not fit to be in Congress. Neither is McCarthy, though he has a little more brains."—*Newspaper editor,* New Jersey.

We have seen, then, in response to the question, What kinds of things do you worry about most? most Americans answered in terms of personal, family, or business problems. Only a small minority expressed anxiety about problems outside the orbit of their immediate personal life—even the threat of war. And in spite of all the headlines and radio and television stimuli, very few mentioned either the internal Communist threat or the threat to civil liberties.

WHAT A SECOND PROBE REVEALED

So much for a question that sought responses without suggestion or coaching. This question was followed immediately in the interview by another: Are there other problems you worry or are concerned about, especially political or world problems?

This question was designed, on the basis of careful pre-testing, to accomplish two purposes: One, to encourage responses from people who might feel "worry" to be too strong a word but who would reply in terms of "concern." Two, by suggesting non-personal problems, but not specifying them, to find out what further matters were high on the list of concerns.

Half of the people in the cross-section, 52% to be exact, said they had nothing to add.

But the additional question did succeed in raising the number who expressed a concern about world affairs from an initial 8% to 30%. In a great many cases, the concern seemed somewhat perfunctory; such as, "Oh, yes, I guess I would say I'm concerned about what's going on in world affairs." There is presumably a "prestige effect" in saying that one is concerned about world affairs, not unlike that which leads a person to say that he reads the editorial pages of a newspaper regularly, even when his usual diet is the comic strips. In view of this possible bias, it is surprising that the number is as low as 30%. Of these, about half spoke explicitly about their concern about war, and others voiced such a concern implicitly.

Stimulated by this second probe, the number speaking of the Communist threat rose from less than 1% to about 6%, including some of the same people who spoke about foreign affairs.

The number expressing concern with civil liberties (apart from the segregation question) rose from less than 1% to about 2%, certainly not a spectacular increase.

Joseph McCarthy is dead. The irrational fears of internal traitors have given way to calmer perspectives on the Communist threat. But civic apathy continues, fed as it is by a materialism that crowds out broader concerns. Public ignorance and apathy are not healthy in a democratic society. They are conducive initially to the neglect of important issues—followed by frantic "crash" programs when the consequences of neglect finally are realized. Education is a case in point. When the Soviet Union launched an earth satellite before the United States did, the horrible suspicion formed that the Soviet Union was outdistancing us in certain scientific and technological areas. This, in turn, triggered a national breast-beating contest on the subject of American education. What is wrong with our teachers? our students? our schools? As the following pre-Sputnik article makes clear, what is wrong is that education in America is a byproduct of the desire for material success rather than an end in itself.[5]

At faculty meetings and educational conferences American teachers show great distress at how little our students learn. We confess to failure and seek methods of improving instruction. We mutter about the caliber of students these days and hope for the arrival of more educable material. Specifically, the following proposals are often discussed:

1. Let us investigate the possibility of increased use of visual aids (including educational television).

2. Let us reduce teaching loads of faculty members so that we can give more attention to the individual student.

3. Let us study the curriculum with a view to reducing overlapping of courses and promoting an integrated educational experience for the student.

4. Let us set up special testing programs so that the student cannot graduate merely by accumulating credits (educational bookkeeping). Let us force him to demonstrate his grasp of large areas by comprehensive examinations.

5. Let us restrict enrollments to those who can "profit" from a college education.[6]

---

[5] Jackson Toby, "The American College Student: a Candidate for Socialization," *American Association of University Professors Bulletin,* Vol. 43 (1957), pp. 319–322. Reprinted by permission of Jackson Toby and the *American Association of University Professors Bulletin.*

[6] Sometimes this means raising admissions requirements so that students deficient in basic skills cannot lower the level of class instruction by forcing a recapitulation of high school work. At other times proponents of restrictive admissions seem to be interested less in the accomplishment level of prospective students than in their values. They want to eliminate the Joe College

6. Let us improve academic advising, especially to freshmen.

However reasonable these proposals may appear, they seem to neglect sociological aspects of student "illiteracy." Take the suggestion that enrollments be restricted to more intellectual students. The sociologist points out that students rarely come to American colleges because they hunger for knowledge. For the average student "education" means eligibility for business and professional careers. Americans are willing to devote such considerable resources to education because education is regarded as a means of socio-economic ascent, and the possibility of progressing from rags to riches is part of the American dream. If education were thought by the general public—from which student bodies are recruited—to be a means of intellectual improvement and nothing else, the American experiment with mass higher education might be abruptly discontinued. For good or for ill, college professors have been assigned a gatekeeper function by the community. Only those certified by a college degree have good chances for elite occupations. Thus, we have an opportunity to make students more thoughtful and better informed for having been exposed to us. But we are deluding ourselves if we imagine that society expects us to develop intellectuals. The students know better. They come to college to get a degree, to have a good time, to "make contacts," to play football, to meet attractive, interesting girls, and—oh, yes—to learn.

This being so, the sociologist is not surprised that colleges compete more vigorously for football players than for "grinds" and that parents are more concerned about the social reputation of a college than about its faculty. Furthermore, the sociologist knows that the colleges are not free to restrict enrollments—even if they wished to do so. While the selection criteria of colleges vary and some colleges turn away more students than others, the admissions policies of American colleges as a whole reflect the sentiments of the American people. If half of the students who wish to enter college are not admitted to *some* institution which

types and the professional athletes in order to increase the proportion of those who have a genuine interest in learning. See, for example, Van Cleve Morris, "Football and the University," *American Association of University Professors Bulletin,* Vol. 38 (1952), pp. 460–468.

they define as a college, though perhaps not to their college of first choice, the pressure to lower the barriers or to establish new colleges would become irresistible. Professors can impose their philosophy of education on admissions offices only in small, private institutions—and only if there are not too many such places.

Suggestions that we tinker with the curriculum, with advising, or with teaching methods are more sophisticated. While society controls admissions, professors have a say in policy making within the academic community. But we exaggerate our ability to motivate students by the rewards and punishments currently available to us. There are rarely discipline problems at college, but this does not mean that the faculty successfully imposes its values upon the students. By the time students reach college, they have learned the efficacy of passive resistance. They are aware that teachers cannot flunk all of them. Collectively, *they* determine what can be expected on examinations. As a result, we are not usually able to induce them to read or study more diligently than their classmates feel is legitimate. Like the workers in a modern factory, they have a concept of a fair day's work, and they oppose speed-ups. We underestimate our students when we attribute their imaginative spelling and idiosyncratic punctuation to stupidity. Compare their feats of memory on the subject of baseball with their amnesia on the subject of poetry; clearly, academic work does not call forth their maximum abilities.

To realize at the end of a semester of our inspired teaching how little students have learned wounds professorial vanity. It is especially painful because we like to think that students beat paths to our classrooms in search of our brilliant insights. In truth, many students are not eager to come to college; they are responding to the pressures of parents and neighbors. They feel compelled to register for courses and perhaps to attend class meetings, so they make the best of a bad business. They hunt for teachers who are amusing, who have a reputation for giving high grades and short assignments, whose courses are "interesting" and meet at convenient times.

Faculty members are perplexed by the existence of a gigantic educational industry in which students do not learn much. Rather inconsistently, we vacillate between confidence in our ability to motivate students, a mood in which we become interested in curriculum changes, and despair at influencing students, a mood in which we pin our hopes on raising standards of admission. The sociologist would be less prone to such ambivalence. He notes that students respond to many other influences besides professors and that these influences help to explain why students fail to write intelligent essays after we have harangued them for a semester or more. After all, the student learns a conception of the student role not only from the faculty but also from his fraternity brothers, his roommate, his girlfriend, the campus "wheels," the basketball coach, and his parents. He is not necessarily a dolt because he responds more readily to their conceptions than to ours.

SUMMARY

The identification of the meaning of life with materialism was what Emerson had in mind when he wrote:

'Tis the day of the chattel,
Web to weave, and corn to grind;
Things are in the saddle,
And ride mankind.

From the consumer's point of view, "relentless materialism" means the vision that one more gadget, one more convenience, one recent model of something, will be the thing to make life pleasant and worthwhile. From the producer's point of view, it means the devotion of more and more resources to whipping up the demand for more things, newer things, different things. From the point of view of social antics, the belief that the "good society" is the society which produces more and more "things" is reduced to an absurdity when the society is already glutted with things.

Quite apart from the human potentialities that go undeveloped as a result of exclusive preoccupation with things, critical issues are ignored by a public which is too preoccupied with meeting installment payments to notice what might be happening to civil liberties or the United Nations. Thus, education becomes one of the activities which get "ridden" when "things are in the saddle."

ANNOTATED BIBLIOGRAPHY

Galbraith, John Kenneth, *The Affluent Society* (Boston: Houghton Mifflin Company, 1958). ⟨ A creative economist's illuminating and stimulating appraisal of what he considers the obsolete American emphasis on material values.

Huxley, Aldous, *Brave New World* (New York: Doubleday, Doran & Company, 1932). ⟨ A famous English novelist's description of materialism carried to its stupefying extreme.

Lewis, Sinclair, *Babbitt* (New York: Harcourt, Brace and Company, Inc., 1922). ⟨ Lewis' pitiless caricature of American materialism has made Babbittry a part of the English language.

Mayer, Martin, *Madison Avenue, U. S. A.* (New York: Harper & Brothers, 1958). ⟨ A lively, well-documented series of case studies of the American advertising industry.

Sorokin, Pitirim, *The Crisis of our Age* (New York: E. P. Dutton & Company, Inc., 1941). ⟨ A condensation by a well-known sociologist of parts of his four-volume *Social and Cultural Dynamics*. Sorokin's argument, although not accepted in all respects by most sociologists, provides an excellent (if extreme) portrait of a materialistic culture and contrasts it with two alternative kinds of value-orientation envisaged by the author: "ideational" and "idealistic."

CHAPTER SIXTEEN

The refusal to accept defeat:
A search for new meanings

If the American preoccupation with "things" is in lieu of a
sense of direction, if we use money "as a bandage" to cover up
our suspicion that life is meaningless, then one would expect the
rejection of materialism to be a popular mode of adjustment.
The individual who, in terms of materialistic values, cannot feel
successful not only has a better chance for a favorable self-

image by rejecting materialism, but also on the positive side he may find an ideology or world view that supplies the missing "point" better than does a materialistic philosophy. One such world view, standing ready at hand in America, is the Judeo-Christian tradition, especially those factions within it that renounce the "things of this world" in favor of eternal salvation. Consider, for example, Jehovah's Witnesses, perhaps the fastest growing sect in the United States.[1]

One hundred and eighty thousand Jehovah's Witnesses, from every part of this country and about 130 other lands, recently gathered in New York for what they called a Divine Will International Assembly. It was the largest gathering of any kind ever held in the city, and it drew attention as never before to this group, which in recent years has been growing more rapidly than any other religious organization.

The Witnesses impressed New Yorkers not only with their numbers, but with their diversity (they include people from all walks of life), their racial unself-consciousness (many Witnesses are Negroes) and their quiet, orderly behavior (in contrast to the religious controversy, and hostility, they have often aroused). In streets, subways, buses, everywhere New Yorkers looked they seemed to see the Witnesses wearing their yellow and purple badges with the legend: "God's Kingdom Rules—*Is the World's End Near?*"

The Witnesses' most striking belief is that since 1914 Satan has ruled the world, but that, in the rapidly approaching Battle of Armageddon, God—whom they call Jehovah—will destroy Satan and all other evil in the world. Thereafter, they believe, God will rule the world and those who have accepted his rule will live on in life everlasting. In one of his many talks at Yankee Stadium and the Polo Grounds, both of which the Witnesses took over for eight days, their leader, Nathan H. Knorr, told them that civilization stands now "at the threshold of a peaceable, happy and life-giving world."

"This is the grandest news," he declared, "although it means

[1] Wayne Phillips, "What Impels Jehovah's Witnesses?", *New York Times Magazine,* August 10, 1958, pp. 15; 48–49. Reprinted by permission of Wayne Phillips and *The New York Times.*

that we are living at the end of this worry-filled, problem-wracked, insane, loveless old world. We want the new. We are eager to leave the old."

Jehovah's Witnesses, who take this name from Isaiah xliii, 10 ("Ye are my witnesses, saith the Lord, and my servant whom I have chosen * * *."), grew from a small Bible class organized at Alleghany, Pa., near Pittsburgh, in 1872 by Charles Taze Russell. As the movement spread, a printed course of Bible instruction was evolved and sold from door to door. The Watchtower Bible and Tract Society, which printed these courses and is the organizational form of the movement, was first incorporated in 1884. The name Jehovah's Witnesses was not formally adopted until the first international meeting at Columbus, Ohio, in 1931.

It was a small movement and most people became aware of it only obliquely—by seeing one of its members standing on a street corner offering copies of its semi-monthly publications *The Watchtower* and *Awake!* for sale at 5 cents a copy; by having one of its members call at the door and endeavor to interest them in reading the Bible; by passing the obscure Kingdom Halls that were opened in cities throughout the country, and where Bible study classes are held five days a week.

All baptized Jehovah's Witnesses regard themselves as ministers ordained to devote their lives to preaching the Bible to all men. They work at what they call "temporal jobs" only to supply their essential material needs. All their other energies are devoted to studying the Bible and the techniques of their ministry.

Repeatedly the religious beliefs of the Witnesses have involved them in controversy. They do not believe in saluting the flag, interpreting this as a form of obeisance before temporal imagery that would conflict with their spiritual loyalties. They fought a long and bitter fight up to the Supreme Court before winning the right of their children to attend schools without taking part in flag saluting ceremonies.

For somewhat the same reasons, the Witnesses do not accept military service, and during World War II draft days they claimed exemption on the ground that they were all ordained ministers preaching to the public. Draft boards sent hundreds of young men associated with the Witnesses to Federal penitentiaries.

Another Witness belief forbids blood transfusions—a position they base on the Biblical injunction against eating blood. When, as occasionally happens, one of their children lay close to death and it seemed only a transfusion could save his life, parents have firmly forbidden it, despite extreme public pressure.

The Witnesses cite references to both the Old and New Testaments for all their beliefs, using all translations of the Bible, although their interpretations of these references differ greatly from those of other faiths. They believe the true meaning of the Bible is prophetic and is constantly being unfolded to men, and they deny any possible conflicts within it. They condemn other faiths for what they consider erroneous additions to and elaborations of the teachings of the Bible. Witnesses do not believe in the immortality of the soul, or a fiery hell, or that Christ died on the cross. They believe that only 144,000 persons will go to heaven and that all but about 15,000 of them are already there; that all others who die have no hope of life hereafter or resurrection. Such teachings have brought mob violence, imprisonment, torture and death to Witnesses in countries where other faiths are officially maintained.

In 1942 when Mr. Knorr was chosen as their president, the organization had 115,240 adherents in fifty-four countries. This year, the number of ordained Witnesses reached 780,000 scattered over 164 countries and territories.

The extent of their influence, however, may better be measured by their publishing activity. The basic book expounding their doctrine, "Let God Be True," first appeared in 1946, and so far 16,167,846 copies have been published. Their magazine, *The Watchtower,* publishes 3,550,000 copies of each issue in fifty languages, including such little-known African dialects as Cinyanja, Ibo and Xhosa.

The expansion of the Witnesses has been a matter of increasing concern to other faiths. Most of their adherents are apparently being attracted from those other churches.

Following are interviews with a number of Jehovah's Witnesses who attended the International Assembly. All talked willingly and openly about their reasons for embracing what they call "The Truth," and all were apparently deeply convinced of their beliefs. . . .

Mr. and Mrs. Wilfred Childs had come to the convention from their home in the summer resort town of York Harbor, Me. In their late twenties, they have been married three years and have no children. Mr. Childs, who has trouble with his hearing and sight, never learned to read too well, and works as a mechanic on automobiles and trailer trucks. His wife augments his $40-a-week take-home pay by caring for an invalid woman.

Florence Childs came from a French Canadian family that had moved south into Maine. She was brought up as a Roman Catholic, but had never been a very regular churchgoer. Her first contact with the Witnesses came two years ago when one of them—Mrs. Norma Vigneau of Portsmouth, N. H.—called at her door.

"She got me interested in reading the Bible," Mrs. Childs said, "and I found that if you knew where to look there were many answers to the questions the priests always told me were mysteries and had to be accepted on faith."

For more than a year Mrs. Childs continued her studies under Mrs. Vigneau's direction. "I didn't dare tell my husband about it; he was death on any kind of religion," she said. "But finally I had to tell him, because I wanted to go to one of the talks at the Kingdom Hall in Portsmouth, and I couldn't get there unless he drove me."

Mr. Childs had been raised in northern Vermont as a Methodist, but long before had rejected any church. "I was shocked when my wife first asked me," he said. "But I finally agreed to take her when she told me all they did was study the Bible. I've always had a lot of respect for the Bible, but never had any use for the way the churches used it."

About a year after his wife was baptized, Mr. Childs also accepted baptism—"because I was convinced the Witnesses preached just what was in the Bible and nothing else." Although they live twelve miles from Portsmouth, they get to meetings there three times a week, work together every day on their studies of the Bible and, once a week, go out together door-to-door to try to interest others. . . .

Norma Vigneau, the 34-year-old Witness who first came to the door of Mr. and Mrs. Childs, had her first contact with the Witnesses in the same way—when a member of the Portsmouth group called on her. Mrs. Vigneau, brought up in a family of New England Unitarians and a graduate of Lasell Junior College in Auburndale, Mass., was shocked by what he preached.

"I felt sorry for him," she recalled. "I asked myself: 'How could anyone be so ignorant as to believe these things?' I felt it was my duty to invite him in, get out my college textbooks and show him why he was wrong."

To rebut his arguments, though, she found she had to delve deeper and deeper not only into her college texts but into the Bible, and over a period of months she found it was she, rather than he, who was being persuaded.

"I began to realize that in college I had been taught to think in circles," she said. "Nothing was black or white there; everything was the same neutral shade of gray. Finally I began to wonder what I was fighting against—here was something that was simple, straightforward, honest and beyond doubt."

The time came when she had to reveal her interest to her husband, Bob, who had been brought up in a Methodist family but had little use for any church. After the war, he and a partner had opened a gasoline station in Portsmouth, but he became fed up with that business, sold out to his partner, and was using the money to build an apartment house.

For quite a while he just went along, indifferently, with his wife's new ideas. But gradually he found the preachings striking a sympathetic chord.

"During the war my eyes were opened to a lot of things," he said. "I heard the politicians and preachers telling us we were fighting to create a better world. After the war I looked around and saw the United States grabbing everything she could get everywhere, and the people everywhere hating us and telling us to get out. I knew there was nothing better about the world. It became so I got sick every time I picked up a newspaper. I knew this couldn't be what God wanted in the world, and when the Witnesses got me started reading the Bible I found out it wasn't." . . .

Otto Smith, who is 33, came to the New York gathering from Anchorage, Alaska, where he has lived since the war. But he is originally from a strict Baptist family in Corpus Christi, Tex. His dissatisfaction with the faith of his parents broke into the open during the war, he recalls.

"I was a gunner on B-24's stationed in England and flying over Germany," he said. "Before every mission the Protestant, Catholic and Jewish chaplains would get us together and pray. And I kept thinking how over there on the other side the ministers and priests were doing the same thing. 'Now, how can God listen to all of them?' I kept asking myself. It wasn't until I came in contact with the Witnesses that I understood that He wasn't listening to any of them."

Otto was working as an automobile salesman in Anchorage when the first Witness he ever met came to his door and, after a talk, left a copy of "Let God Be True." Otto read it and other literature, and began studying the Bible.

"My wife was dead set against the Witnesses at first," he said. "She comes from East Texas, and they don't have much use for Witnesses down there because of the flag-saluting business before the war." But gradually, Otto said, he interested his wife also, and they were baptized together in 1952. . . .

Among the physicians who have accepted the beliefs of the Witnesses is Dr. F. D. Roylance of Haworth, N. J. Dr. Roylance, 48, is a graduate of the Columbia College of Physicians and Surgeons and is secretary of the medical executive committee of the Englewood, N. J., Hospital.

"I was baptized by my parents in the Disciples of Christ when I was 12 years old," Dr. Roylance said, "but after starting our own family my wife and I began attending the Congregational Church."

For about ten years, he said, he had been studying the Bible on his own, looking for answers to spiritual questions that puzzled him. Occasionally he listened to talks by Fundamentalist preachers on his car radio as he rode between calls on patients.

"But I first learned about the Witnesses," he said, "from a patient who started bringing me Watchtower literature. 'This makes sense,' I said after I read it, and I wrote to the Watchtower. They sent a brother to see me."

In November, 1956, Dr. Roylance was baptized and began to give all the time he could spare from his practice to study and preaching. For him it meant a severe family crisis.

"My wife is very much opposed to all this," he said. "She is Italian, but her father took the family out of the Roman Catholic Church before they came to this country. She still goes to the Congregational Church, and she resents very much the time that this takes from my work and our three children."

Professionally, he said, it had not caused the problems that others might expect. "I recognize that there are cases where a blood transfusion is the best thing that can be done to save a life," he says, "and if a patient is not a Witness and wants the transfusion I don't have any hesitation about prescribing it."

Among the Witnesses who came from foreign countries to the New York Assembly was Max Liebster, 43, born and raised in an Orthodox Jewish home at Reichenbach, near Frankfurt, Germany. Two days after the war began in 1939 he was arrested and sent to a prison at Pforzheim. "For four months I was on my knees every day all day praying for understanding," he recalls. " 'Why, why,' I asked, 'should God permit this persecution of his chosen people?' "

After four months, he was put on a prison train to be taken to the concentration camp at Oranienburg near Berlin. In the car with him was a Jehovah's Witness.

"This man was a farmer," Mr. Liebster said. "His wife had been killed, his five children taken away and sent to a Nazi training center. But he said he would go to prison rather than fight for Hitler. Never before had I seen a man who loved God's commandment more than himself or his family. For fourteen days on the train we were together and talked. He told me how Christ was proven in the Hebrew scriptures—and he quoted the scriptures to me from his head, for they had taken his Bible from him."

At Oranienburg Mr. Liebster saw this Witness tortured and

finally killed rather than consent to serving in Hitler's army. "I saw it with my own eyes," he said, "and I made up my mind that I, too, would witness to the truth with my life if I were released."

Later he was moved to a succession of other camps until he reached Buchenwald. There the Germans had confined Leon Blum, the French Socialist leader, in a house set apart from the barracks, with a Witness assigned as his orderly. On May 15, 1945, just after the liberation, Mr. Liebster and two other former Jews were baptized as Witnesses in Leon Blum's bathtub.

"Altogether 10,000 Witnesses were sent to concentration camps," Mr. Liebster said. "Eight thousand came out, but 2,000 were too crippled to work. The 6,000 who were left started preaching all over Germany. Now there are a little over 60,000 of us in West Germany and another 25,000 in East Germany." . . .

What do the varied experiences of these Witnesses add up to?

It would be wrong to make any blanket conclusions about Jehovah's Witnesses and what motivates them on the basis of a handful of interviews. But through them run certain common threads: a deep yearning for religious experience, a conviction that the world is becoming increasingly worse, a desire to find some fundamental explanation of why, a wish to escape from worldly conflict and confusion, and a prayer that, somewhere in the undefined future, things will be better. In addition, and possibly more important, it seems clear that these people—who otherwise probably would have been both alienated from and outside any religious influence—have sought and found in the Jehovah's Witnesses a framework that provides them with both the purpose and strength for the kind of personal morality all religions seek to espouse.

Whether it is fair to term Jehovah's Witnesses a social problem is debatable. Certainly, though, their radical rejection of secular society causes difficulties with their neighbors. And their refusal to bear arms or to participate in the political process would greatly weaken the American political system—if they were more numerous. Furthermore, the Witnesses are not the only religious sect which feels it must fight secular society relentlessly. Dr. Liston Pope, Dean of the Yale Divinity School, reports on the emergence of new religious sects in a mill village in North Carolina.[2]

A composite and impressionistic picture of the kind of religious service held by extreme sectarian groups may help to lay bare the roots from which they spring:

"One traverses a grassless, rutted yard, climbs precarious 2 × 6 steps into a long, bare room filled with crude pews, and takes a seat in the Church of God. It is Sunday night, and the building is filled to overflowing, with about a thousand people present. Many stand in the doors or in the front yard of the church, including a large group of young men watching the girls go in and out. An ice cream vendor has placed his portable refrigerator near the church door, and is doing a thriving business. About 65 per cent of those present are women between the ages of fourteen and fifty-five, many of whom have sleeping babies in their laps. The atmosphere is expectant and informal; members of the congregation move about at will, and talk in any tone of voice that suits their fancy.

"A crude pulpit, a piano, and a section of pews for the choir are placed at the far end of the oblong building. Back of the pulpit to the left is a homemade board on which to register weekly attendance; beneath the board, in sprawling letters, the question:

HOW WILL YOUR
REPORT IN HEAVEN BE

To the right of the pulpit is another sign:

GOD IS ABLE

A band, including three stringed instruments and a saxophone, plays occasional music.

"The service begins at eight o'clock or thereabouts. Rather, the actions of the congregation become more intense and concerted in character; there is almost nothing by way of formal announcement. The choir, in cooperation with the pastor, breaks into a rhythmic hymn, and the congregation follows suit. The hymn has an interminable number of stanzas, and a refrain, reminiscent of mountain ballads both in

[2] Liston Pope, *Millhands and Preachers*, 1942, pp. 117–140. Reprinted by permission of the publishers, The Yale University Press, New Haven, Connecticut.

music and in narrative form. The hymn looks toward a narrative climax, and the excitement of the congregation increases as the singing proceeds. The stanzas are punctuated with loud shouts of 'Hallelujah,' 'Thank you, Jesus,' 'Glory,' and the rhythmic clapping of hands and tapping of feet. Almost immediately, various members of the congregation begin to 'get the Holy Ghost' (as a teen-age boy awesomely remarks). One young woman leaves the front row of the choir and jerks about the pulpit, with motions so disconnected as to seem involuntary, weird. A man's head trembles violently from side to side. Another man, tieless and red-faced, laughs boomingly at odd moments, in a laugh resembling that of intoxication.

"Half a dozen songs follow in succession. Then comes a prayer, with everybody kneeling on the floor and praying aloud at the same time, each in his own way. Some mutter with occasional shouts; others chant, with frequent bendings backward and forward; the volume of sound rises and falls, without unified pattern or group concentration. The pastor's voice booms out occasionally above all the others. Then, as if by a prearranged but unobservable signal, the prayer abruptly ends; the onlooker is amazed to see emerging from the confusion a concerted return to a sitting position. The cacophony of prayer is ended as suddenly as it began.

"Then the pastor reads 'the Scripture,' after confessing that he 'ain't had no time to study today,' and after attempting to induce a layman in the congregation to 'say something'—without avail, because the layman confesses that he 'ain't had no time to study neither' and insists, 'you go right ahead, brother.' Reluctantly the pastor begins to read, explaining each verse with amazing exegesis and equally amazing insight. Each verse becomes the subject for a homily, and the reader works up to a climax in its exposition—a climax reflected in increase of rhythmic motions and hortatory shouts from members of the congregation. Having finished the Scripture lesson, the preacher takes up a collection, counts it, announces that he has to have 'a little more,' and runs around in the congregation to garner proffered contributions, acknowledging each with a receipt 'God bless you, brother,' and finally emptying the collection plate into his pocket.

"Then the service moves toward a climax; the taking of the collection has been an emotional interlude. The preacher begins a sermon; more precisely, he enunciates verbal symbols that arouse immediate response from the congregation.

Such motifs play through his shoutings as 'sanctification,' 'the Second Coming,' 'the world despises and misunderstands and lies about the Church of God,' 'Jesus can heal your body and soul,' 'Believe the Word,' 'follow the knee-route.' The Church of God is depicted as a remnant of those who have escaped from the 'coldness' of the Methodist and Baptist churches. Lay preaching is urged, and personal evangelistic work. Attention is called to a number of prayer meetings to be held at various houses during the subsequent week, and to persons for whom prayer is desired—especially the family of a four-year-old girl who has just died, because 'they can't hardly get over it.'

"Then there is a testimony meeting in which a large number of the more faithful testify to their personal experience and joy in religion, some mutteringly, some loudly, fervidly. One woman defends her right to wear long-sleeved, high-necked dresses in the summer time, because 'the Spirit told me to.' Nearly all say that they are proud to speak for Christ, and not ashamed to speak out for their Master in church. The man who has been indulging the intoxicated laugh defends his right to laugh in church, saying that his religion makes him feel good all over and is not like the stiff coldness of the Methodist church. Recurring phrases appear in the testimonies: 'I'm glad I got over bein' too proud to be a Holiness and get all there was of the Holy Ghost'; 'I'm a better wife and I've got a better husband because I joined the Church of God'; 'the Baptists are all right, but I wanted more of the Lord than they had.' Several testify to marvelous cures of physical illness during the past week, through prayer and the 'laying on of hands.'

"All the while waves of ecstatic rhythm have been sweeping over the congregation, with the actions of the preacher setting the pace. There are patterns to the rhythmic actions: running around the pulpit, holding trembling hands to the sky, very fast clogging of the feet, swinging the arms in sharp, staccato motions. One girl leaps from her seat as though struck by an electric shock, races four times around the aisles of the church, screaming 'O God . . . do Jesus . . . O God . . . glory, glory, glory . . . give me more . . . more . . . glory, glory, glory'; falling over backward with hands outstretched, her whole body quivering and rhythmically jerking, she collapses at last in a dull heap on the floor, and stays there in comatose condition for several minutes. Others rise and shout at the top of their lungs for five minutes, or bang

on something in staccato rhythm. The same persons respond
again and again, with perhaps seventy-five individuals represented. Each responds with an individual pattern of motions,
but all motions revolve around a few general types. The motions appear to have been culturally conditioned, whether
immediately conditioned by the agent or not. One wonders if
some form of mass hypnotism is at work.

"About ten o'clock the pastor calls for sinners to come
to the front and kneel around the altar (constructed of a
bench quickly placed before the pulpit). About ten come,
including one five-year-old boy. A hundred members of the
congregation gather about, and a tremendous tumult ensues
as they attempt to 'pray and shout the sinners through,' in-
terspersed with wild demonstrations of joy as one is 'saved.'

"It is nearly 11 p.m., but one stays and wonders. They
cry out, and cry; 'they are drunken, but not with wine; they
stagger, but not with strong drink. . . .' "

A recent interpretation . . . attributes most of the phenomena of the newer sects to the "culture shock" involved in
transition from a rural to an urban setting. The older urban
churches symbolize to the new migrant to the city his exclusion
from urban life, and he turns to the "new" churches, which seem
to represent defense of his former standards and modes of behavior. This theory is plausible but inadequate for explanation of
the growth of sects in small villages and rural areas in other sections of the South, and is in error in assuming that the newer
sects uniquely preserve traits of rural religion.

It has been popular more recently to explain emergence of
sects primarily in terms of underlying economic conditions. Ordinarily the poorest strata of the community are attracted into
membership, and it is urged that an otherworldly emphasis in
the newer sects affords compensation for poverty and transcend-
ence of poor estate. The phenomenal rate of growth during the
recent depression argues in favor of a theory of this sort; as
economic conditions grew worse, newer sects flourished increasingly.

Another credible diagnosis ascribes psychological deficien-
cies to most members of the newer sects. Frenetic religious services represent release from psychological repression, it is said,
fulfilling a need for self-expression and for identification of one's

self with a greater power. Life in a mill village is monotonous and dull; production processes in the mills are largely mechanical in character, and the worker has little opportunity for choice as to any of the basic factors that control his daily life. The new cults are notably lay movements, and the entire membership participates in most of the services and activities of a particular group. The unusually high percentage of women who belong and who appear to be the most active participants in semihysterical religious practices is also significant; of the members of one Church of God in Gaston County, 57 per cent were women, almost all of whom were between the ages of seventen and fifty-four. A psychologist observing the religious ceremonies of the Church of God might conclude that the sex factor is crucial in explanation. Certainly members of these groups are widely accused of being immoral, and a considerable degree of sexual laxity is undoubtedly a concomitant of their services. An uptown boy explained, standing outside a Church of God while a service was in progress: "It'll get hot in there pretty soon. A lot of women come over here, which is why all the boys are hanging around. I got started out late tonight and all the dates are taken, so I have to take what I can get. Mill girls are the best looking girls nowadays anyhow." Rhythmic music, supported by stringed instruments and saxophones, tendencies toward exhibitionism, and injunctions to "let yourself go" for "possession by the Spirit" are surcharged with sex stimulation.

Ministers of the emerging denominations insist that the explanation of rapid growth in their adherents must be pitched completely on the religious plane. They argue that their rigid teachings challenge people and force them to invest so much in money and in devotion that they necessarily remain interested and become propagandists. "People are gettin' disgusted with professional religion," one of them said, "and demandin' to get results in their religion—so that's why they come to us." They hasten to add that the devotion of the ministers themselves, in contrast with the professional attitudes of ministers of the older denominations, is of great importance. The type of preacher associated with the sect groups does help to explain their rapid growth, though it does not explain their appearance. Many of the preachers are mill workers who preach as an avocation. They have very little education—often no more than completion of the fourth grade in the public schools, plus a few weeks of training in a Bible school maintained by their denomination. They are, therefore, much closer to the mill workers than ministers of the older denominations. They also work for smaller compensation, living at the level of the mill workers. One sect urges its churches to pay their pastors at least $12.50 a week aside from rent, that "they may wield a better influence in their communities"—the desire to conquer culture is making itself felt. Another sect limits the salary of its ministers to $200 a month "and expenses"; it is doubtful that many receive this amount. Most of the ministers tithe rigorously, along with their members; one denomination supervises ministerial fidelity in this respect by providing "that all members of the Conference pay at least 75 per cent of their Ministerial tithes into the Conference Treasury or else give a satisfactory reason for not doing so before their character shall be passed."

All these interpretations of the rise and growth of the sects have in them valid elements, and an adequate explanation cannot afford to ignore any of them. They all are gathered up in the general statement that such groups thrive wherever a considerable portion of the population exists on the periphery of culture as organized, whether the index used be that of education, economic status, possibilities for psychological satisfaction, or religious organization. Members of the newer religions do not belong anywhere—and so they belong, and wholeheartedly, to the one type of institution which deigns to notice them. A considerable percentage of mill workers stand on the outer fringes of their communities, and they provide the invariable starting point of sect movements. The rapidity of growth of the sects is a rough indication of the degree to which mill workers recognize their cultural alienation.

The sects substitute religious status for social status, a fact which may help to account for their emphasis on varying degrees of Grace. This emphasis, indeed, forms their most distinctive theological tenet. As over against the lack of religious differentiation within older denominations, the newer sects divide their members, and people in general, into several religious classifications: saved, sanctified, baptized with the Holy Ghost, baptized with water, recipient of the first, second, or third blessing and the like. What matters it, then, if a Methodist has more money but has never been baptized with the Holy Ghost? As over against segregation from the community, the newer sects affirm separation from the world; in the face of exclusion on educational, economic, and religious grounds, they affirm exclusion from their own fellowship of those who engage in mixed bathing, dancing, card playing, bobbing the hair, gambling, baseball, county fairs, drinking, and using tobacco. Because they have no jewelry to wear, they make refusal to wear jewelry, including wedding rings, a religious requirement. They transmute poverty into a symptom of Grace. Having no money, they redeem their economic status by rigid tithing of the small income they do possess, and thus far surpass members of churches of any other type or denomination in per capita contributions, despite the fact that they stand at the bottom of the economic scale. Many of them cannot take baths at will, because of lack of facilities, but they can practice the washing of the feet of the saints, and rejoice thereby at their superiority to older denominations which have come to regard such practices as uncouth and unesthetic. Excluded from secular society, they set up a religious society of their own, in which standards of membership are more rigid than those of the general culture that has ignored them. The inspired Scriptures, rather than general cultural standards, provide the charter of their new community; without exception, the new churches accept the Bible as their sole and adequate authority (in theory), and interpret it with direct literalness. . . .

Rather than regard their new and dangerous rivals as a thoroughbred might survey a dirty mongrel pup, the Methodists and Baptists look on them with mingled fear and contempt, with ridicule rather than pity. "They practice," said one Methodist minister, "the religion of Hurrah and Take-On, of Knock-Down and Drag-Out."

The sects thrive on persecution and exult in the harassment they afford to older denominations. One Church of God preacher announced proudly: "The Baptists look down on us, but we are getting their members; why don't they get ours, if they are better than us?" It is only toward each other that the newer denominations feel real rivalry, as contrasted with their sense of religious superiority to older denominations. Most of them are essentially alike in their fundamental teachings and practices, and therefore are competitors in the religious field. They denounce each other as impostors, thieves, plagiarists, and fanatics. Remarks by a Holiness preacher typify vilification by one sect of another:

"Those so-called Holiness Churches are completely different from my kind of Holiness; they are fanatics and bring discredit on the name 'Holiness' by their handling of snakes, their offers to sacrifice their own mothers, and the like. All the preachers who handle snakes, etc., belong to the 'unknown tongues' group, as does the Church of God. A New Testament scholar went to them to preach, began speaking in Greek, and seventeen people were saved. These folks regard any kind of outward manifestation as a sign of possession by the Holy Spirit—but to live the way they do makes you wonder if they have the Spirit. Those folks have backslid from the true way." . . .

The sect, in summary, represents a reaction, cloaked at first in purely religious guise, against both religious and economic institutions. Overtly, it is a protest against the failure of religious institutions to come to grips with the needs of marginal groups, existing unnoticed on the fringes of cultural and social organization.

While it is clear that Jehovah's Witnesses and members of the Church of God repudiate materialism, it is not so obvious that the motivation to join a secular sect may be identical. Take the Communist movement. Although, on a philosophical level, Communism is both atheistic and materialistic, many converts to Communism are attracted to it because they consider it an alternative to a materialistic society. Whittaker Chambers, a Communist editor and, later, a Communist spy, gives his interpretation of the attraction of Communism.[3]

[3] From *Witness* by Whittaker Chambers, pp. 191–196. Copyright 1952, by Whittaker Chambers. Reprinted by permission of Random House, Inc., New York.

Sooner or later, one of my good friends is sure to ask me: How did it happen that a man like you became a Communist? Each time I wince, not at the personal question, but at the failure to grasp the fact that a man does not, as a rule, become a Communist because he is attracted to Communism, but because he is driven to despair by the crisis of history through which the world is passing.

I force myself to answer: In the West, all intellectuals become Communists because they are seeking the answer to one of two problems: the problem of war or the problem of economic crises.

This is not to say that personal factors play no part in making a man a Communist. Obviously, they do, if only because every man's character and experience, and therefore his biography, are different from every other man's. No two are ever the same. Hence some men will always be more susceptible to Communism than other men, just as some are less resistant to disease than other men. But whatever factors make one man more susceptible than another to Communism once he is driven to entertain it at all, it will be found that, almost without exception, the intellectuals of the West are driven to entertain it in terms of just two challenges: the problem of war and the problem of economic crisis. This is equally true, even for men of untrained minds or without the habit of reflection; men who find it difficult to explain to themselves or to others the forces that move them to Communism. For while the susceptibility to Communism varies among men, the problems of war and economic crisis do not vary. In this period of history, they are constant, and must be until, in one way or another, they are solved.

Some intellectuals are primarily moved by the problem of war. Others are first moved by the economic problem. Both crises are aspects of a greater crisis of history for which Communism offers a plausible explanation and which it promises to end. When an intellectual joins the Communist Party, he does so primarily because he sees no other way of ending the crisis of history. In effect, his act is an act of despair, regardless of whether or not that is how he thinks of it. And to the degree that it is an act of despair, he will desire the party to use him in over-coming that crisis of history which is at the root of his despair.

There is a widespread notion that men become Communists for reasons of material gain. There are always a certain number of "rice Christians" in any movement that has anything at all to offer them. Of all movements in the world, the Communist Party has the least to offer a man bent on personal advantage. For the intellectual of any ability, it has nothing whatever to offer in the way of gain. In the days when I joined the Communist Party, it could offer those who joined it only the certainty of being poor and pariahs. During the 1930's and 1940's, when Communism became intellectually fashionable, there was a time when Communist Party patronage could dispose of jobs or careers in a number of fields. But the jobs that the Communist Party could give, or the careers it could further, presupposed that the men and women in them must have some ability to hold them at all. Almost without exception such men and women could have made their careers much more profitably and com-fortably outside the Communist Party. For the party must always demand more than it gives. What material advantage, for ex-ample, could the Communist Party possibly offer an Alger Hiss, a Noel Field, a Dr. Klaus Fuchs, equal to the demands it made on him? This persistent notion that men become or remain Com-munists from motives of personal advantage constantly baffles those who hold it with the fact that Communist parties every-where are filled with talented men and women, often of good family, and that these people are precisely among the most fanatical Communists, those most likely to be found in the party's most hazardous and criminal activities.

Nor do Marxist dialectics or Marxian economic theories have much to do with the reason why men become and remain Communists. I have met few Communists who were more than fiddlers with the dialectic (the intellectual tool whereby Marxist theoreticians probe and gauge history's laws of motion). I have met few Communists who I thought knew more than the bare rudiments of Marxian economics, or cared to. But I have never known a Communist who was not acutely aware of the crisis of history, whose solution he found in Communism's practical program, its vision and its faith.

Few Communists have ever been made simply by reading the works of Marx or Lenin. The crisis of history makes Communists; Marx and Lenin merely offer them an explanation of the crisis and what to do about it. Thus a graph of Communist growth would show that its numbers and its power increased in waves roughly equivalent to each new crest of crisis. The same horror and havoc of the First World War which made the Russian Revolution possible recruited the ranks of the first Communist parties of the West. Secondary manifestations of crisis augmented them—the rise of fascism in Italy, Nazism in Germany and the Spanish Civil War. The economic crisis which reached the United States in 1929 swept thousands into the Communist Party or under its influence. The military crisis of World War II swept in millions more; for example, a third of the voting population of France and of Italy. The crisis of the Third World War is no doubt holding those millions in place and adding to them. For whatever else the rest of the world may choose to believe, it can be said without reservation that Communists believe World War III inevitable.

Under pressure of the crisis, his decision to become a Communist seems to the man who makes it as a choice between a world that is dying and a world that is coming to birth, as an effort to save by political surgery whatever is sound in the foredoomed body of a civilization which nothing less drastic can save—a civilization foredoomed first of all by its reluctance to face the fact that the crisis exists or to face it with the force and clarity necessary to overcome it.

Thus, the Communist Party presents itself as the one organization of the will to survive the crisis in a civilization where that will is elsewhere divided, wavering or absent. It is in the name of that will to survive the crisis, which is not theoretical but closes in from all sides, that the Communist first justifies the use of terror and tyranny, which are repugnant to most men by nature and which the whole tradition of the West specificially repudiates.

It is in the name of that will to survive that Communism turns to the working class as a source of unspoiled energy which may salvage the crumbling of the West. For the revolution is never stronger than the failure of civilization. Communism is never stronger than the failure of other faiths.

It is the crisis that makes men Communists and it is the crisis that keeps men Communists. For the Communist who breaks with Communism must break not only with the power of its vision and its faith. He must break in the full knowledge that he will find himself facing the crisis of history, but this time without even that solution which Communism presents, and crushed by the knowledge that the solution which he sought through Communism is evil against God and man.

I was one of those drawn to Communism by the problem of war. For me that problem began in 1923. In that year, I went to Europe with Meyer Schapiro who had been my classmate at Columbia College. He had already begun those studies that were later to make him a professor of Fine Arts at Columbia and one of the outstanding art critics in the country. We planned to spend the summer in Europe's galleries and museums.

I saw the galleries and museums. But I also saw something else. I saw for the first time the crisis of history and its dimension. It was not only that Germany was in a state of manic desperation, reeling from inflation, readying for revolution while three Allied armies occupied the Rhineland and refugees flooded back from the occupied area into the shattered country. It was not only the aftermath of the World War, the ruins of northern France or what Bernanos would presently call "those vast cemeteries in the moonlight." What moved me was the evidence that World War II was predictably certain and that it was extremely improbable that civilization could survive it. (In this I was mistaken, though, by the end of the Second World War, civilized Europe would shrink to little more than it had been in the Dark Ages.) It seemed to me that the world had reached a crisis on a scale and of a depth such as had been known only once or twice before in history. (And in that I was not mistaken at all.)

During my years at Columbia College, I had known a number of socialists, including two or three extreme left-wingers.

They had devoted a great deal of time, tact and patience to winning me to their views. They had no effect on me whatever. What their theories could not do, the crisis did. For, in searching for the answer to the crisis, I found none but socialism.

I returned to the United States and plunged into Fabian Socialism, studying as I seldom had before in my life. I abstracted and made mountainous notes on the dull dry works of the Webbs, R. H. Tawney, Hobhouse, and the endless volumes in which G. D. H. Cole urged Guild socialism. There was no life in those books. There were statistics and theories. The reek of life was missing.

I brushed them aside. Socialism was not the answer. It was perfectly clear, too, that if socialism was to stem the crisis and remake the world, socialism involved a violent struggle to get and keep political power. At some point, socialism would have to consolidate its power by force. The Webbs made no provision for getting or keeping power. Moreover, I had a profound antipathy to force. I was glad to shelve the problem.

In that disenchanted period I returned to Columbia College to major in history, attending classes by day and working at night to pay my way. History was medieval history and I rehearsed in the collapse of Rome the crisis of history in our own time.

One day, by sheer chance, there came into my hands a little pamphlet of Lenin's. It was called *A Soviet At Work*. In a simple strong prose, it described a day in the life of a local soviet. The reek of life was on it. This was not theory or statistics. This was socialism in practice. This was the thing itself. This was how it worked. . . .

One day early in 1925, I sat down on a concrete bench on the Columbia campus, facing a little Greek shrine and the statue of my old political hero, Alexander Hamilton. The sun was shining, but it was chilly, and I sat huddled in my overcoat. I was there to answer once for all two questions: Can a man go on living in a world that is dying? If he can, what should he do in the crisis of the 20th century?

There ran through my mind the only lines I remember from the history textbook of my second go at college—two lines of

Savinus', written in the fifth century when the Goths had been in Rome and the Vandals were in Carthage: "The Roman Empire is filled with misery, but is luxurious. It is dying, but it laughs."

The dying world of 1925 was without faith, hope, character, understanding of its malady or will to overcome it. It was dying but it laughed. And this laughter was not the defiance of a vigor that refuses to know when it is whipped. It was the loss, by the mind of a whole civilization, of the power to distinguish between reality and unreality, because, ultimately, though I did not know it, it had lost the power to distinguish between good and evil. This failure I, too, shared with the world of which I was a part.

The dying world had no answer at all to the crisis of the 20th century, and, when it was mentioned, and every moral voice in the Western world was shrilling crisis, it cocked an ear of complacent deafness and smiled a smile of blank senility— throughout history, the smile of those for whom the executioner waits.

Only in Communism had I found any practical answer at all to the crisis, and the will to make that answer work. It was not an attractive answer, just as the Communist Party was not an attractive party. Neither was the problem which had called it forth, and which it proposed to solve, attractive. But it had one ultimate appeal. In place of desperation, it set the word: hope. If it was the outrage, it was also the hope of the world. In the 20th century, it seemed impossible to have hope on any other terms.

When I rose from the bench, I had decided to leave college for good, and change the whole direction of my life. I had decided to join the Communist Party. The choice was not so much for a program that promised to end war, economic chaos and the moral enervation of the West. I had already said to myself what Lenin had already said better: "We do not presume to maintain that Marx or the Marxists can show us the way to socialism in perfectly concrete terms. That would be absurd. We know the direction of this road: we know which class forces lead to it.

But in actual practice, only the experience of millions of men and women can show it when they begin the actual work."

The ultimate choice I made was not for a theory or a party. It was—and I submit that this is true for almost every man and woman who has made it—a choice against death and for life. I asked only the privilege of serving humbly and selflessly that force which from death could evoke life, that might save, as I then supposed, what was savable in a society that had lost the will to save itself. I was willing to accept Communism in whatever terms it presented itself, to follow the logic of its course wherever it might lead me, and to suffer the penalties without which nothing in life can be achieved. For it offered me what nothing else in the dying world had power to offer at the same intensity—faith and a vision, something for which to live and something for which to die. It demanded of me those things which have always stirred what is best in men—courage, poverty, self-sacrifice, discipline, intelligence, my life, and, at need, my death.

Understandably, Chambers minimizes personal motivations for joining the Communist movement. Likewise, he exaggerates its attraction to others. But his thesis is difficult to refute. At the time when Chambers was recruited at any rate, the Communist appeal was couched in the language of a prophet condemning the sinful world. After describing the Communist espionage apparatus in Washington during the 1930's, Chambers goes on to comment:[4]

The first impact of this blueprint of Communist penetration is likely to be shock at the espionage revealed. That is not the important point. Espionage is always intolerable, just as it is indispensable. No government in sound political health, no government which was not subtly infected with the revolutionary virus of the age, could tolerate in its service any employe against whom there was a suspicion of Communist espionage or even of indiscretion that might serve an espionage purpose.

[4] *Ibid.,* pp. 33–34.

The important point about the Washington apparatuses is that, in the 1930's, the revolutionary mood had become so acute throughout the whole world that the Communist Party could recruit its agents, not here and there, but by scores within the Government of the United States. And they were precisely among the most literate, intellectually eager and energetic young men in a nation which by all its traditions of freedom, initiative and opportunity, its institutions and the circumstances of its geography and history, was farthest removed from the revolutionary struggles of Europe.

The deeper meaning of the Soviet underground apparatus, and all the apparatuses that clustered hidden beside it, was not so much their espionage activity. It was the fact that they were a true Fifth Column, the living evidence that henceforth in the 20th century, all wars are revolutionary wars, and are fought not only between nations, but within them.

The men and women Communists and fellow travelers who staffed this Fifth Column were dedicated revolutionists whose primary allegiance was no longer to any country—nor to those factors which give a country its binding force: tradition, family, community, soil, religious faith. Their primary allegiance was to a revolutionary faith and a vision of man and his material destiny which was given political force by international Communism, of which the American Communist Party and the Russian Communist Party (and hence the Soviet Government, which is only an administrative apparatus of the Russian Communist Party) are component sections.

No other government in the world but that of the Soviet Union could possibly have corrupted these people from their original allegiance. They were not venal. They performed their espionage services without compensation, as a party obligation. The very repugnance of the task was a witness and a sacrifice to their faith. With few exceptions, offers of money would have outraged them. With few exceptions, they cared little or nothing for money as money. It is also absurd to say, as I have often heard it said, that they were moved by a desire for power. A few may have been, and these, like their kind the world over, would have sought power in terms of any situation they were in. The

plain fact is that most of them held tangible power of some kind in the Government they were betraying, with every assurance that simply by not endangering their routine rise that power would grow. Neither power nor money moved them. Nor was adventure a factor. An incurably romantic Communist is a contradiction in terms. A romantic underground worker endangers himself and his whole apparatus. Faith moved them, as, in the final conflict, only equal faith can overcome them.

To sum up the argument of this chapter so far, we maintain that fundamentalist sects and the American Communist Party have in common a repudiation of materialism and a search for new meanings. Going still further, we may say that cults which repudiate materialism are quite common on the American scene. Consider the cult glorifying masculine strength and beauty; dozens of magazines recount the achievements of weight lifters and body builders. Certainly the values of the physique cult are not those of material success. Or consider the cults associated with particular movie stars. No doubt these are carefully nurtured by studio publicity men for materialistic reasons indeed, but an idolatrous devotion to Elvis Presley and Marilyn Monroe exists apart from the organization of fan clubs. Certainly the James Dean cult continues to flourish after the death of the actor.[5] And women have been placing flowers on the grave of Rudolph Valentino for thirty years.

Do these cults have anything in common aside from their implicit rejection of material success as the paramount goal? We suggest that most cultists—idolatrous movie fans, physical culturists, nudists, spiritualists, vegetarians—share a romantic disregard of the limitations of the human situation. They believe that certain exercises or certain foods or certain incantations will guarantee health, wealth, or happiness. Such romanticism is a problem because, for people who remain in touch with reality, it guarantees disillusionment. A case in point is a romantic manifestation so widespread in American society that the term, "cult," seems inappropriate. We refer to "romantic love"—and especially to romantic love as the basis for establishing enduring relationships between men and women.[6]

[5] See Ezra Goodman, "Delirium for a Dead Star," *Life,* September 24, 1956, pp. 75–88.

[6] Jackson Toby, "The Case against Romance," unpublished lecture delivered before the Rutgers Psychology Club, 1953.

Americans believe in romance for much the same reason as we drink Coca-Cola: because we can no more escape romantic ideas than we can avoid billboards advertising "the pause that refreshes." We read romantic stories. We see romantic movies. We dance to the tunes of romantic songs.

> I hear music and there's no one there,
> I smell blossoms and the trees are bare,
> I wonder why, I wonder why.
> I keep tossing in my sleep at night,
> And what's more I've lost my appetite. . .
> I wonder why.[7]

Far from implying that a person with these symptoms ought to consult the nearest psychiatrist, the singer claims that all is as it should be. "There is nothing you can take to relieve that pleasant ache, You're not sick, YOU'RE JUST IN LOVE." Taken literally, such songs portray love as a form of insanity. If you are in love, you should be prepared to see and hear things which are not there to be seen and heard; to fail to be aware of what is plainly going on around you; to have fevers; to stop eating; to be unable to sleep; and to be subject to moods of depression. Nonetheless, like some mental patients with benign delusions, you feel wonderful.

> Ask me how do I feel, from this chemistry lesson I'm
>   learning,
> Well sir, all I can say is if I were a bridge I'd be burning.
> Yes, I knew my morale would crack
> From the wonderful way that you looked,
> Boy, if I were a duck I'd quack,
> Or if I were a goose I'd be cooked.
> Ask me how do I feel, Ask me now that we're fondly
>   caressing,
> Pal, if I were a salad I know I'd be splashing my dressing.
> And if I were a watch I'd start popping my spring
> Or if I were a bell I'd go ding, dong, ding, dong, ding.[8]

[7] From a song by Irving Berlin, "You're Just in Love." Copyright 1950, Irving Berlin. Reprinted by permission of Irving Berlin Music Corporation.

[8] Copyright 1950 by Frank Loesser. All rights throughout the entire world controlled by Frank Music Corp., 119 West 57th St., New York.

Apparently, "anything goes" for a person in love, from hallucinations to paroxysms of happiness. Except to a trained athlete, this must sound fatiguing. Doubtless, some people have the stamina for such a workout. But what about a man who lacks the energy to go up in smoke every time he meets a pretty girl? Will he consider himself a freak? Songs, movies, television programs, and romantic novels persuade us that it is *normal,* when love "hits," to behave like a Roman candle. What about a girl who decides she is not "the marrying kind" because she fails to experience violent enough attachments? The American romantic ideal demands a kind of frenzy that can only be fulfilled by a special type of personality. The rest of us shouldn't feel we must approximate the Hollywood pattern of galloping romance to prove that ours is true love. Ralph Linton, world-renowned Yale anthropologist, had this to say:

All societies recognise that there are occasional violent emotional attachments between persons of opposite sex, but our present American culture is practically the only one which has attempted to capitalize these and make them the basis for marriage. Most groups regard them as unfortunate and point out the victims of such attachments as horrible examples. Their rarity in most societies suggests that they are psychological abnormalities to which our own culture has attached an extraordinary value just as other cultures have attached extreme value to other abnormalities. The hero of the modern American movie is always a romantic lover just as the hero of the old Arab epic is always an epileptic. A cynic might suspect that in any ordinary population the percentage of individuals with a capacity for romantic love of the Hollywood type was about as large as that of persons able to throw genuine epileptic fits. However, given a little social encouragement, either one can be adequately imitated without the performer admitting even to himself that the performance is not genuine.[9]

The American romantic ideal demands too much, not only of the lover, but also of the object of his affections. If the man expects the girl to look like Marilyn Monroe and the girl ex-

[9] Ralph Linton, *The Study of Man,* New York: Appleton-Century Company, 1936, p. 175. Reprinted by permission.

pects the man to talk like Charles Boyer, both will probably be disappointed. There are not enough movie stars to go around. The fact is that everybody is not glamorous. Searching frantically for the girl (or boy) of Hollywood's dreams, going on hundreds of dates in hope of locating her (or him) may not be a better policy than passive waiting. An assumption of the frantic search no less than of the passive wait is that you cannot fall in love unless you find a glamorpuss. And glamorpusses—girls who have "oomph," "it," "zip," "zing"; boys who are tall, smooth, clean-cut, well-muscled—are usually interested in other glamorpusses.

The notion that a few god-like creatures have a special talent for love—denied to the rest of the human race—crept into history between the 11th and 13th centuries. Medieval French and Italian troubadours introduced "romance" in the songs they composed for the entertainment of feudal nobles. Since their patrons were aristocrats, the troubadours sang of the careers of gallant knights, of their tournaments, of their chivalry, of their passions. No doubt the troubadours tried to please their customers by portraying the nobility in a flattering light. Certainly the heroes and heroines of these songs were extraordinarily brave, extraordinarily beautiful, extraordinarily chivalrous, and extraordinarily lucky. They were not everyday people, and their loves and hates were not thought of as possible for everyday people.

Aristocracy has gone out of fashion, but we still cling to the troubadour's assumption: love is a monopoly of the glamorpusses. If this assumption is correct, he who is not a glamorpuss is faced with a nasty alternative: either he gives up hope for love and marriage if he cannot find an attractive enough partner; or he accepts an unglamorous substitute, while envying the lucky ones who have the genuine article. But this painful dilemma is unnecessary because the assumption underlying it is false. Love is for everybody; it is not a monopoly of any aristocracy, whether of youth or of charm or of wealth.

It is true, of course, that love is more passionate among the young—although not necessarily more ardent. Passion has to do with sex: with hormones and physiology. Love is emotional intimacy. Physical intimacy (sex) may serve to express emotional

intimacy (love), but there is no necessary connection between the two. Petting, for example, is sometimes motivated by affection and sometimes by hormones, but often it has nothing to do with either; adolescents may pet out of curiosity, in order to brag to friends, or to establish confidence in their own physical attractiveness. Philandering can be a game played for the thrill of conquest. That is why sexual activity is a poor index of underlying feelings. What can be measured by a count of sexual strongholds besieged? Certainly not affection. A touch of the hand may express the closest intimacy and a kiss may be a meaningless gesture. In other words, there is no guarantee that a man and a woman are in love because they are sensually stimulating to one another.

Equally confusing is the romantic fiction that love just *happens*. If you are fortunate enough to find yourself in love, relax and enjoy it. If not, there is nothing to do except wait passively for it to envelop you. Love is assumed to be a divine gift—like good looks or intelligence or rich parents. Nonsense! In matters of love, as in so many other departments of life, God helps him who helps himself. Love is a domesticated plant, not a wild one, and requires cultivation. Profound emotional intimacy between a man and a woman does not spring into being full-grown— like the goddess in Greek mythology. Nor does the relationship endure forever, immutably fixed like a bronze statue, without continuing effort on both sides. But these are the expectations aroused by romance.

Romance also teaches that love, unpredictable thing that it is, may occur at first sight—between individuals without an interest in common. Infatuation, yes. Love, no. Love, like good wine, requires mellowing. Swift courtship followed by a hasty elopement: a thoroughly romantic marriage. But scientific studies show that elopements have a much higher probability of ending in divorce than conventional weddings. Why? Because excitement, interest, enthusiasm—the best that can be expected "at first sight"—only makes one a candidate for love. Eagerness to undertake a relationship is not the same as establishing it. The couple must learn to reconcile divergent interests, attitudes, goals, and this cannot be effected on the run. Common ground has to be built up on a thousand compromises. It takes time for the psychological walls between two people to crumble, for each to learn to anticipate the other's desires and hardly to distinguish them from his own.

Finally, romance teaches that marriage should be continuous ecstacy. "And they lived happily ever after." But the shrill emotions of the honeymoon have to calm down in order to leave time and energy for earning a living, cooking meals, and reading the newspaper. And anyway, an eternity of love-making ("day and night, night and day") would fray the nerves to the point of mutual loathing. If one has doubts on this score, he has only to look for couples married a dozen years or so. Perhaps their favorite song is, "Always," but most likely it isn't, "I've Got You Under My Skin."

Marriages which have passed the test of time do not conform to the torrid specifications of romance. Wives are also mothers. Husbands go to work. Responsibilities permit them only a small fraction of the day with one another, and they do not pine away. They still love each other—but quietly. Their warmth is expressed in companionship, as, for example, in revealing innermost thoughts to one another. Each has interests apart from the other. After all, marriage may be the most intimate human relationship; nevertheless two distinct personalities are involved. Probably there are activities each prefers to engage in without the other. The tendency is to be overly possessive when too many emotional eggs are in one basket. For example, a wife who has no friends or interests outside of her marriage hovers over her husband as she might over the Hope diamond. When he wants to go fishing in solitude or play poker with his cronies, her constant desire for his attention may constitute a "pain in the neck."

To put it bluntly, marriage is not romantic. Even under the most favorable circumstances, strain and pain characterize the first adjustments. Consider how different is the vantage point from which the couple sees one another before and after marriage. On dates, the fellow was dressed in his best clothes; the girl spent hours grooming herself to "go out." Both felt in top spirits because they were having "fun." After marriage she groggily crawls out of bed to turn off the alarm clock. He learns to smile when she burns his breakfast. They have less money for recreation at movies, dances, or nightclubs and more time when they must work together on serious problems. Before marriage they may have lived with parents. The girl did not need to cook or clean or shop. The fellow did not contribute substantially to the budget of the household. After the ceremony they are supposed to manage a home of their own.

Perhaps the worst jolt is that the qualities which make one attractive as a "date"—conversational poise, good looks, athletic ability, dancing skill—are not very helpful in marriage. After the ceremony it becomes important for the man to earn a good salary and the girl to know how to cook. But neither may have looked for these qualities prior to marriage. For example, a certain girl captivated a young man with her artistic temperament; she painted, composed music, and loved poetry. After they were married, she kept up her artistic interests. But somehow he was not delighted when she showed him a new painting in the evening instead of a hot supper. The music and poetry began to pall too; he would have preferred her to clean the house and mend his socks. The girl had not changed. Ironically, the same behavior which made her husband want to marry her did not make him want to stay married to her. American marriage presents a paradox: it is as though you trained to be a track star and because you become a fast runner you are put on the debating team.

There is, of course, some carry-over into married life of the good will developed in courtship days; but the more superficial the relationship, the less there is to carry over. A couple acquainted only a short time before marriage is likely to find that enjoying dates is not the same as enjoying each other. They may lack the patience to work at mutual adjustment because they don't have a reservoir of good will; they merely have pleasant memories. Romantic ideas are an obstacle to easy adjustment because they delude the couple into thinking ". . . that marriage is made on the day of the ceremony"—instead of urging caution first and patience later.

To sum up the case against romance: it portrays love as something wonderful, which is true, but also as something effortless, which is false. The world isn't divided into those with a capacity for love and those without. All of us can love and be loved because love is an achievement, not a characteristic like height or weight. But achievements require work—even for handsome, wealthy, intelligent individuals, which most of us are not. Romance is misleading because it portrays love as timeless, effortless ecstasy. Romance deludes us into sitting passively back instead of working to build a relationship. Romance would be bearable—even though it grossly misrepresents love—if only it had nothing to do with marriage. But Americans regard marriage as an outgrowth of love. Insofar as romantic ideas fail to prepare one for marriage, they threaten the foundation of the family. Obviously, if a marriage is built on mutual illusions, there is a good chance that the spell will be broken after the honeymoon. Even if the marriage does not end in divorce, an unhappy home is hardly the best soil in which to grow the next generation. Basing marriage on romance, therefore, is like basing the national economy on the operation of a gambling casino. Disillusionment with marriage occurs more often because the man and the woman went into marriage with unrealistic ideas than because they are temperamentally unsuited to one another. Perhaps a place ought to be found in the marriage ceremony for the cautious wisdom of W. Somerset Maugham: the test of a great love is not how it begins but how it ends.

Finally, we must mention a cult which reflects lower-class romanticism, the cult of the hipster. In the first of two selections dealing with this phenomenon, a Chicago sociologist reports on hipsterism among young Negro drug addicts.[10] However, the reader should bear in mind (a) that many drug addicts are withdrawing from life rather than embracing the hipster cult and (b) that hipsterism is not confined to Negroes.

The young drug user was a creature of contrasts. Playing the role of the fugitive and pariah as he was inevitably forced to do, he turned up for interviews in a uniformly ragged and dirty con-

[10] Harold Finestone, "Cats, Kicks, and Color," *Social Problems,* Vol. 5 (1957), pp. 3–10. Reprinted by permission of *Social Problems.*

dition. And yet he talked with an air of superiority derived from his identification with an elite group, the society of "cats." He came in wearing a non-functional tie clip attached to his sport shirt and an expensive hat as the only indications that he was concerned with his appearance and yet displayed in his conversation a highly developed sense of taste in men's clothing and a high valuation upon dressing well. He came from what were externally the drabbest, most overcrowded, and physically deteriorated sections of the city and yet discussed his pattern of living as though it were a consciously cultivated work of art.

Despite the location of his social world in the "asphalt jungle" of the "Blackbelt" he strictly eschewed the use of force and violence as a technique for achieving his ends or for the settling of problematic situations. He achieved his goals by indirection, relying, rather, on persuasion and on a repertoire of manipulative techniques. To deal with a variety of challenging situations, such as those arising out of his contacts with the police, with his past or potential victims, and with jilted "chicks," etc., he used his wits and his conversational ability. To be able to confront such contingencies with adequacy and without resort to violence was to be "cool." His idea was to get what he wanted through persuasion and ingratiation; to use the other fellow by deliberately outwitting him. Indeed, he regarded himself as immeasurably superior to the "gorilla," a person who resorted to force.

The image of himself as "operator" was projected onto the whole world about him and led to a complete scepticism as to other persons' motives. He could relate to people by outsmarting them, or through openhanded and often ruinous generosity, but his world seemed to preclude any relationship which was not part of a "scheme" or did not lend itself to an "angle." The most difficult puzzle for him to solve was the "square," the honest man. On the one hand the "square" was the hard-working plodder who lived by routine and who took honesty and the other virtues at their face value. As such he constituted the prize victim for the cat. On the other hand the cat harbored the sneaking suspicion that some squares were smarter than he, because they could enjoy all the forbidden pleasures which were his stock in trade and maintain a reputation for respectability in the bargain.

The cat had a large, colorful, and discriminating vocabulary which dealt with all phases of his experience with drugs. In addition, he never seemed to content himself with the conventional word for even the most commonplace objects. Thus he used "pad" for house, "pecks" for food, "flicks" for movies, "stick hall" for pool hall, "dig the scene" for observe, "box" for record player, "bread" for money, etc. In each instance the word he used was more concrete or earthier than the conventional word and such as to reveal an attitude of subtle ridicule towards the dignity and conventionality inherent in the common usage.

His soft convincing manner of speaking, the shocking earthiness and fancifulness of his vocabulary, together with the formidable gifts of charm and ingratiation which he deployed, all contributed to the dominant impression which the young drug user made as a person. Such traits would seem to have fitted naturally into a role which some cats had already played or aspired to play, that of the pimp. To be supported in idleness and luxury through the labors of one or more attractive "chicks" who shoplifted or engaged in prostitution or both and dutifully handed over the proceeds was one of his favorite fantasies. In contrast with the milieu of the white underworld, the pimp was not an object of opprobrium but of prestige.

The theme of the exploitation of the woman goes close to the heart of the cat's orientation to life, that is, his attitude towards work. Part of the cat's sense of superiority stems from his aristocratic disdain for work and for the subordination of self to superiors and to the repetitive daily routine entailed by work, which he regards as intolerable. The "square" is a person who toils for regular wages and who takes orders from his superiors without complaint.

In contrast with the "square," the cat gets by without working. Instead he keeps himself in "bread" by a set of ingenious variations on "begging, borrowing, or stealing." Each cat has his "hustle," and a "hustle" is any non-violent means of "making some bread" which does not require work. One of the legendary heroes of the cat is the man who is such a skillful con-man that he can sell "State Street" to his victim. Concretely, the cat is a petty thief, pickpocket, or pool shark, or is engaged in a variety of other illegal activities of the "conning" variety. A very few cats are actually living off the proceeds of their women "on the hustle."

The main purpose of life for the cat is to experience the "kick." Just as every cat takes pride in his "hustle," so every cat cultivates his "kick." A "kick" is any act tabooed by "squares" that heightens and intensifies the present moment of experience and differentiates it as much as possible from the humdrum routine of daily life. Sex in any of its conventional expressions is not a "kick" since this would not serve to distinguish the cat from the "square," but orgies of sex behavior and a dabbling in the various perversions and byways of sex pass muster as "kicks." Some cats are on an alcohol "kick," others on a marihuana "kick," and others on a heroin "kick." There is some interchangeability among these various "kicks" but the tendency is to select your "kick" and stay with it. Many of these young drug users, however, had progressed from the alcohol to the marihuana to the heroin "kick." Each "kick" has its own lore of appreciation and connoisseurship into which only its devotees are initiated.

In addition to his "kick" the cat sets great store on the enjoyment of music and on proper dress. To enjoy one's "kick" without a background of popular music is inconceivable. The cat's world of music has a distinctive galaxy of stars, and the brightest luminaries in his firmament are performers such as "Yardbird" (the late Charlie Parker) and disc jockeys such as Al Benson. Almost every cat is a frustrated musician who hopes some day to get his "horn" out of pawn, take lessons, and earn fame and fortune in the field of "progressive music."

The cat places a great deal of emphasis upon clothing and exercises his sartorial talents upon a skeletal base of suit, sport shirt, and hat. The suit itself must be conservative in color. Gaiety is introduced through the selection of the sport shirt and the various accessories, all so chosen and harmonized as to reveal an exquisite sense of taste. When the cat was not talking about getting his clothes out of pawn, he talked about getting them out of the cleaners. With nonchalant pride one drug user insisted that the most expensive sport shirts and hats in the city of Chicago were sold in a certain haberdashery on the South Side. The ideal cat would always appear in public impeccably dressed and be able to sport a complete change of outfit several times a day.

The cat seeks through a harmonious combination of charm, ingratiating speech, dress, music, the proper dedication to his "kick," and unrestrained generosity to make of his day-to-day life itself a gracious work of art. Everything is to be pleasant and everything he does and values is to contribute to a cultivated aesthetic approach to living. The "cool cat" exemplifies all of these elements in proper balance. He demonstrates his ability to "play it cool" in his unruffled manner of dealing with outsiders such as the police, and in the self-assurance with which he confronts emergencies in the society of cats. Moreover, the cat feels himself to be any man's equal. He is convinced that he can go anywhere and mingle easily with anyone. For example, he rejects the type of music designated "the blues" because for him it symbolizes attitudes of submission and resignation which are repugnant and alien to his customary frame of mind.

It can be seen now why heroin use should make such a powerful appeal to the cat. It was the ultimate "kick." No substance was more profoundly tabooed by conventional middle-class society. Regular heroin use provided a sense of maximal social differentiation from the "square." The cat was at last engaged, he felt, in an activity completely beyond the comprehension of the "square." No other "kick" offered such an instantaneous intensification of the immediate moment of experience and set it apart from everyday experience in such spectacular fashion. Any words used by the cat to apply to the "kick," the experience of "being high," he applied to heroin in the superlative. It was the "greatest kick of them all." . . .

It is interesting to speculate on the reasons why a type such as the cat should emerge rather than a social movement with the objective of changing the social order. The forces coercing the selective process among colored male adolescents in the direction of expressive social movements are probably to be traced to the long tradition of accommodation to a subordinate status on the part of the Negro as well as to the social climate since the Second World War, which does not seem to have been favorable to the formation of specific social movements.

The themes of the "hustle" and "kick" in the social orientation of the cat are facts which appear to be overdetermined. For example, to grasp the meaning of the "hustle" to the cat one must understand it as a rejection of the obligation of the adult male to work. When asked for the reasons underlying his rejection of work the cat did not refer to the uncongenial and relatively unskilled and low paid jobs which, in large part, were the sole types of employment available to him. He emphasized rather that the routine of a job and the demand that he should apply himself continuously to his work task were the features that made work intolerable for him. The self-constraint required by work was construed as an unwarranted damper upon his love of spontaneity. The other undesirable element from his point of view was the authoritarian setting of most types of work with which he was familiar.

There are undoubtedly many reasons for the cat's rejection of work but the reasons he actually verbalized are particularly significant when interpreted as devices for sustaining his self-conception. The cat's feeling of superiority would be openly challenged were he to confront certain of the social realities of his situation, such as the discrimination exercised against colored persons looking for work and the fact that only the lowest status jobs are available to him. He avoided any mention of these factors which would have forced him to confront his true position in society and thus posed a threat to his carefully cherished sense of superiority.

In emphasizing as he does the importance of the "kick" the cat is attacking the value our society places upon planning for the future and the responsibility of the individual for such planning. Planning always requires some subordination and disciplining of present behavior in the interest of future rewards. The individual plans to go to college, plans for his career, plans for his family and children, etc. Such an orientation on the part of the individual is merely the personal and subjective counterpart of a stable social order and of stable social institutions, which not only permit but sanction an orderly progression of expectations with reference to others and to one's self. Where such stable institutions are absent or in the inchoate stages of development, there is little social sanction for such planning in the experience of the individual. Whatever studies are available strongly suggest that such are the conditions which tend to prevail in the lower socio-economic levels of the Negro urban community. Stable family and community organization is lacking in those areas of the city where drug use is concentrated. A social milieu which does not encourage the subordination and disciplining of present conduct in the interests of future rewards tends by default to enhance the present. The "kick" appears to be a logical culmination of this emphasis.

Accepting the emergence of the self-conception of the cat as evidence of a developing expressive social movement, we may phrase the central theoretical problem as follows: What are the distinctive and generic features of the cat's social orientation? Taking a cue from the work of Huizinga as developed in *Homo Ludens,* we propose that the generic characteristics of the social type of the cat are those of play. In what follows, Huizinga's conception of play as a distinctive type of human activity will be presented and then applied as a tool of analysis for rendering intelligible the various facets of the social orientation of the cat. It is believed that the concept of play indicates accurately the type of expressive social movement which receives its embodiment in the cat.

According to Huizinga the concept of play is a primary element of human experience and as such is not susceptible to exact definition.

"The *fun* of playing resists all analysis, all logical interpretation. . . . Nevertheless it is precisely this fun-element that characterizes the essence of play." The common image of the young colored drug addict pictures him as a pitiful figure, a trapped unfortunate. There is a certain amount of truth in this image, but it does not correspond to the conception which the young colored addict has of himself or to the impression that he tries to communicate to others. If it were entirely true it would be difficult to square with the fact that substantial numbers of young colored persons continue to become drug users. The cat experiences and manifests a certain zest in his mode of life which is far from self-pity. This fun element seemed to come particularly to the fore as the cat recounted his search for "kicks," the adventure of his life on the streets, and the intensity of his contest against the whole world to maintain his supply of drugs. Early in the cycle of heroin use itself there was invariably a "honeymoon" stage when the cat abandoned himself most completely to the experience of the drug. For some cats this "honeymoon" stage, in terms of their ecstatic preoccupation with the drug, was perpetual. For others it passed, but the exigencies of an insatiable habit never seemed to destroy completely the cat's sense of excitement in his way of life. . . . To give significance to his experience, the young male addict has developed the conception of a heroic figure, the "ideal cat," a person who is completely adequate to all situations, who controls his "kick" rather than letting it control him, who has a lucrative "hustle," who has no illusions as to what makes the world "tick," who is any man's equal, who basks in the admiration of his brother cats and associated "chicks," who hob-nobs with "celebs" of the musical world, and who in time himself may become a celebrity.

The cat throws himself into his way of life with a great deal of intensity but he cannot escape completely from the perspective, the judgments, and the sanctions of the dominant social order. He has to make place in his scheme of life for police, lockups, jails, and penitentiaries, to say nothing of the agonies of withdrawal distress. He is forced eventually to confront the fact that his role as a cat with its associated attitudes is largely a pose, a form of fantasy with little basis in fact. With the realization that he is addicted he comes only too well to know that he is a "junky," and he is fully aware of the conventional attitudes towards addicts as well as of the counter-rationalizations provided by his peer group. It is possible that the cat's vacillation with regard to seeking a cure for his addiction is due to a conflict of perspectives, whether to view his habit from the cat's or the dominant social order's point of view.

It is this limited, esoteric character of heroin use which gives

to the cat the feeling of belonging to an elite. It is the restricted
extent of the distribution of drug use, the scheming and intrigue
associated with underground "connections" through which drugs
are obtained, the secret lore of the appreciation of the drug's
effects, which give the cat the exhilaration of participating in a
conspiracy. Contrary to popular conception most drug users
were not anxious to proselyte new users. Of course, spreading
the habit would have the function of increasing the possible
sources of supply. But an equally strong disposition was to keep
the knowledge of drug use secret, to impress and dazzle the
audience with one's knowledge of being "in the know." When
proselyting did occur, as in jails or lockups, it was proselyting
on the part of a devotee who condescended to share with the
uninitiated a highly prized practice and set of attitudes.

On a more philosophical level, Norman Mailer, the novelist,
provides an explanation of the hipster cult.[11]

The Second World War presented a mirror to the human
condition which blinded anyone who looked into it. For if tens of
millions were killed in concentration camps out of the inexorable
agonies and contractions of super-states founded upon the always insoluble contradictions of injustice, one was then obliged
also to see that no matter how crippled and perverted an image
of man was the society he had created, it was nonetheless his
creation, his collective creation (at least his collective creation
from the past) and if society was so murderous, then who could
ignore the most hideous of questions about his own nature? . . .
It is on this bleak scene that a phenomenon has appeared:
the American existentialist—the hipster, the man who knows
that if our collective condition is to live with instant death by
atomic war, relatively quick death by the State as *l'univers con-
centrationnaire,* or with a slow death by conformity with every
creative and rebellious instinct stifled (at what damage to the
mind and the heart and the liver and the nerves no research

[11] From "The White Negro: Superficial Reflections on the Hipster," by
Norman Mailer, as originally published in *Dissent,* Vol. 4 (1957), pp. 277–
288. Reprinted by permission of Norman Mailer and the Editors of *Dissent.*

foundation for cancer will discover in a hurry), if the fate of twentieth-century man is to live with death from adolescence to premature senescence, why then the only life-giving answer is to accept the terms of death, to live with death as immediate danger, to divorce oneself from society, to exist without roots, to set out on that uncharted journey into the rebellious imperatives of the self. In short, whether the life is criminal or not, the decision is to encourage the psychopath in oneself, to explore that domain of experience where security is boredom and therefore sickness, and one exists in the present, in that enormous present which is without past or future, memory or planned intention, the life where a man must go until he is beat, where he must gamble with his energies through all those small or large crises of courage and unforeseen situations which beset his day, where he must be with it or doomed not to swing. The unstated essence of Hip, its psychopathic brilliance, quivers with the knowledge that new kinds of victories increase one's power for new kinds of perception; and defeats, the wrong kind of defeats, attack the body and imprison one's energy until one is jailed in the prison air of other people's habits, other people's defeats, boredom, quiet desperation, and muted icy self-destroying rage. One is Hip or one is Square (the alternative which each new generation coming into American life is beginning to feel), one is a rebel or one conforms, one is a frontiersman in the Wild West of American night life, or else a Square cell, trapped in the totalitarian tissues of American society, doomed willy-nilly to conform if one is to succeed. . . .

Like children, hipsters are fighting for the sweet, and their language is a set of subtle indications of their success or failure in the competition for pleasure. Unstated but obvious is the social sense that there is not nearly enough sweet for everyone. And so the sweet goes only to the victor, the best, the most, the man who knows the most about how to find his energy and how not to lose it. The emphasis is on energy because the psychopath and the hipster are nothing without it since they do not have the protection of a position or a class to rely on when they have overextended themselves. So the language of Hip is a language of energy, how it is found, how it is lost.

But let us see. I have jotted down perhaps a dozen words, the Hip perhaps most in use and most likely to last with the minimum of variation. The words are man, go, putdown, make, beat, cool, swing, with it, crazy, dig, flip, creep, hip, square. They serve a variety of purposes, and the nuance of the voice uses the nuance of the situation to convey the subtle contextual difference. If the hipster moves through his night and through his life on a constant search with glimpses of Mecca in many a turn of his experience . . . the faces of experience which life presents to him each day are engaged, dismissed or avoided as his need directs and his lifemanship makes possible. For life is a contest between people in which the victor generally recuperates quickly and the loser takes long to mend, a perpetual competition of colliding explorers in which one must grow or else pay more for remaining the same (pay in sickness, or depression, or anguish for the lost opportunity), but pay or grow.

Therefore one finds words like go, and make it, and with it, and swing: "Go" with its sense that after hours or days or months or years of monotony, boredom, and depression one finally has one's chance, one has amassed enough energy to meet an exciting opportunity with all one's present talents for the flip (up or down) and so one is ready to go, ready to gamble. Movement is always to be preferred to inaction. In motion a man has a chance, his body is warm, his instincts are quick, and when the crisis comes, whether of love or violence, he can "make it," he can win, he can release a little more energy for himself since he hates himself a little less, he can make a little better nervous system, make it a little more possible to go again, to go faster next time and so make more and thus find more people with whom he can "swing." For to swing is to communicate, is to convey the rhythms of one's own being to a lover, a friend, or an audience, and—equally necessary—be able to feel the rhythms of their response. To swing with the rhythms of another is to enrich oneself—the conception of the learning process as dug by Hip is that one cannot really learn until one contains within oneself the implicit rhythm of the subject or the person. As an example, I remember once hearing a Negro friend have an intellectual discussion at a party for half an hour with a white girl who was a few years out of college. The Negro literally could not read or write, but he had an extraordinary ear and a fine sense of mimicry. So as the girl spoke, he would detect the particular formal uncertainties in her argument, and in a pleasant (if slightly Southern) English accent, he would respond to one or another facet of her doubts. When she would finish what she felt was a particularly well-articulated idea, he would smile privately and say, "Other-direction . . . do you really believe in that?"

"Well . . . No," the girl would stammer, "now that you get down to it, there is something disgusting about it to me," and she would be off again for five more minutes.

Of course the Negro was not learning anything about the merits and demerits of the argument, but he was learning a great deal about a type of girl he had never met before, and that was what he wanted. Being unable to read or write, he could hardly be interested in ideas nearly as much as in lifemanship, and so he eschewed any attempt to obey the precision or lack of precision in the girl's language, and instead sensed her character (and the values of her social type) by swinging with the nuances of her voice.

So to swing is to be able to learn, and by learning take a step toward making it, toward creating. What is to be created is not nearly so important as the hipster's belief that when he really makes it, he will be able to turn his hand to anything, even to self-discipline. What he must do before that is find his courage at the moment of violence, or equally make it in the act of love, find a little more of himself, create a little more between his woman and himself, or indeed between his mate and himself (since many hipsters are bisexual), but paramount, imperative, is the necessity to make it because in making it, one is making the new habit, unearthing the new talent which the old frustration denied.

Whereas if you goof (the ugliest word in Hip), if you lapse back into being a frightened stupid child, or if you flip, if you lose your control, reveal the buried, weaker, more feminine part of your nature, then it is more difficult to swing the next time, your ear is less alive, your bad and energy-wasting habits are further confirmed, you are farther away from being with it. But to be with it is to have grace, is to be closer to the secrets of that inner unconscious life which will nourish you if you can hear it, for you are then nearer to that God which every hipster believes is located in the senses of his body, that trapped, mutilated and nonetheless megalomaniacal God who is It, who is energy, life, sex, force, the Yoga's *prana,* the Reichian's orgone, Lawrence's "blood," Hemingway's "good," the Shavian life-force; "It"; God; not the God of the churches but the unachievable whisper of mystery within the sex, the paradise of limitless energy and perception just beyond the next wave of the next orgasm.

To which a cool cat might reply, "Crazy, man!"

Because, after all, what I have offered above is an hypothesis, no more, and there is not the hipster alive who is not absorbed in his own tumultuous hypotheses. Mine is interesting, mine is way out (on the avenue of the mystery along the road to "It") but still I am just one cat in a world of cool cats, and everything interesting is crazy, or at least so the Squares who do not know how to swing would say. . . .

If, however, you agree with my hypothesis, if you as a cat are way out too, and we are in the same groove (the universe now being glimpsed as a series of ever-extending radii from the center) why then you say simply, "I dig," because neither knowledge nor imagination comes easily, it is buried in the pain of one's forgotten experience, and so one must work to find it, one must occasionally exhaust oneself by digging into the self in order to perceive the outside. And indeed it is essential to dig the most, for if you do not dig you lose your superiority over the Square, and so you are less likely to be cool (to be in control of a situation because you have swung where the Square has not, or because you have allowed to come to consciousness a pain, a guilt, a shame or a desire which the other has not had the courage to face). To be cool is to be equipped, and if you are equipped it is more difficult for the next cat who comes along to put you down. And of course one can hardly afford to be put down too often, or one is beat, one has lost one's confidence, one has lost one's will, one is impotent in the world of action and so closer to the demeaning flip of becoming a queer, or indeed closer to dying, and therefore it is even more difficult to recover enough energy to try to make it again, because once a cat is beat he has nothing to give, and no one is interested any longer in making it with him. . . .

To be beat is therefore a flip, it is a situation beyond one's experience, impossible to anticipate—which indeed in the circular vocabulary of Hip is still another meaning for flip, but then I have given just a few of the connotations of these words. Like most primitive vocabularies each word is a prime symbol and serves a dozen or a hundred functions of communication in the instinctive dialectic through which the hipster perceives his experience, that dialectic of the instantaneous differentials of existence in which one is forever moving forward into more or retreating into less.

SUMMARY

For many people the dominant materialistic answer to the quest for meaning is not satisfactory, sometimes because they have failed to get material rewards, sometimes for other reasons. Whatever the reason, there are many who search for new meanings. Religion offers a fertile source of alternative meanings and sometimes leads to actions which we might well have interpreted as "withdrawal" in Chapter 7.

Withdrawal is less evident in secular searches for meaning, as in the Communistic effort to transform *this* world into a less materialistic place. Withdrawal of a different kind—almost a denial of reality—is to be observed in the effort to find meaning in romantic love and sensual ecstasy. Closely related to romantic withdrawal is the hipster's search for meaning in new "kicks," new ways to "swing" and "go," which implicitly challenge the materialism of "squares."

ANNOTATED BIBLIOGRAPHY

Adams, Henry, *The Education of Henry Adams* (New York: Random House, Inc., The Modern Library, 1931). ¶ The autobiographical commentary on America's industrialization by the noted historian great-grandson of the second President, grandson of the sixth, and son of one of America's ablest diplomats. The pain Adams felt upon viewing the increasing materialism of America is expressed in the famous closing lines of the autobiography, referring to himself and his friends: "Perhaps some day—say 1938, their centenary—they might be allowed to return together for a holiday; . . . and perhaps then . . . they would find a world that sensitive and timid natures could regard without a shudder."

Davis, Kingsley, Bredemeier, H. C., and Levy, Jr., Marion J., (eds.), *Modern American Society* (New York: Rinehart & Company, Inc., 1949). ⟨[Chapters 16–18 present a well-rounded account of several important religious issues in the United States.

Gitlow, Benjamin, *I Confess* (New York: E. P. Dutton & Company, Inc., 1940). ⟨[An early analogue to Whittaker Chambers' *Witness*. Gitlow, Communist candidate for Vice President in 1924 and 1928, describes here the idealism that led him to the Communist Party, and the later disenchantment with its ruthless materialism that led him out.

Maurois, André, *Seven Faces of Love* (New York: Didier, 1944). ⟨[An investigation of the meaning of love to human beings through an analysis of the literary treatment of "love" by seven famous writers.

Pope, Liston, *Millhands and Preachers* (New Haven: Yale University Press, 1942). ⟨[The study from which the excerpt included in the present chapter was taken. Pope's analysis and description of the dialectic between industrial materialism and religious rejection of materialism are well worth the interested student's close attention.

Stroup, Herbert H., *The Jehovah's Witnesses* (New York: Columbia University Press, 1945). ⟨[A sociological analysis of a large and growing religious sect that repudiates the materialistic values of American society. Members of the sect refuse to salute the American flag or to serve in the Armed Forces because they consider all governments tools of the devil.

CHAPTER SEVENTEEN

The prospects for reducing casualties

Are the casualties and social costs of American society inevitable? Not if our analysis of social problems in America is correct. Recall the introduction to Part Three. There we pointed out how a major emphasis on acquiring goods and services of a tangible sort leads to frustration and efforts to avoid frustration. Material things are inherently distributive; they cannot be given to everybody to the same extent. The principles governing their

distribution in America—predominantly self-reliance, negotiated exchange, and competition—become (derivatively) criteria of self-assessment. Americans evaluate one another's
adequacy and worthiness in terms of their ability to be successful in self-reliant competition for the prizes of the market place.
Thus, ultimately, it is the stress on material goals that makes
the distributive process in America the focus of such anxiety and
the generator of so many casualties. Every society must distribute goods and services; but this does not mean that every
society must permit their distribution to become a major axis for
evaluation.

Some critics of American society are pessimistic about the
future. However *possible* a less materialistic orientation may be,
they perceive American society headed toward more rather than
less concern with the tangible. Although we recognize the
strength of the materialistic preoccupation, we take comfort
from our analysis of the *source* of American materialism (Chapter 3). We assume that Americans pursue tangible goods and
services because they have lost faith in other goals. It is materialism *by default,* the filling of a value vacuum. Faced with an
erosion of faith which threatened to create a socio-cultural chaos
in which all goals seem equally worthless, Americans turn toward the aspect of reality which science seems to stress: the
tangible. Looking at American materialism in this light makes us
suspect that a de-emphasis of material values is feasible provided
that new goals can be found which fill the value vacuum equally
well or better. World War II illustrates this possibility. The goal
of winning the war against Germany and Japan temporarily
took precedence for many Americans over acquisitive triumphs
or failures. Did there result a decreased tendency of American
society to generate the kinds of casualties we have been talking
about in this book? It is difficult to speak with assurance. It is a
fact, however, that the suicide rate during World War II years
1943 and 1944 was only two-thirds the suicide rate during the
three years preceding Pearl Harbor.[1] A reasonable interpretation
of this decrease is to attribute it to the change in goals.

Certainly, we are not advocating war as a solution of America's social problems. This would be equivalent to curing a
headache by blowing off the head. But, if belligerency seems
capable of giving a nonmaterialistic meaning to life to broad
segments of the American population, perhaps there are other

[1] U. S. Bureau of the Census, *Statistical Abstract of the United States,*
various years (Washington: Government Printing Office).

goals that are equally effective in enlisting support and, at the same time, do not entail the dreadful consequences of modern warfare. Can a functional equivalent of war be found? The authors do not believe that an unequivocal answer to this question is possible in the present state of knowledge. However, we note with satisfaction that material goals, while more obvious than the values we shall mention, have real competition. Consider the growth of professionalization, which tends to change the emphasis of the economic system. By professionalization, we do not refer merely to the proportion of the labor force who are teachers, engineers, or the like—although the growth in the professional category from census to census is certainly noteworthy. We refer to the shift in values. The professional person is more likely to regard his occupation as an activity gratifying in its own right rather than as a means of obtaining the rewards of the market place. Thus, a college professor is usually more concerned with the evaluation of his colleagues as to how he rates as a scholar and a teacher than he is with maximizing his annual income. This does not mean that college professors are more altruistic than businessmen.[2] It means rather that success for the businessman is measured by the size of his income, whereas success for the college professor is institutionally defined as achievement in his vocation. One consequence of this difference is that the college professor's self-assessment is not contingent on his driving a shiny new car. Another is that he spends his time on activities which he knows in advance will be profitless from a financial point of view: writing books only a handful of people will buy, accepting unpaid speaking engagements, studying to keep up with the latest developments in his field. The economist, Thorstein Veblen, talked about "the instinct of workmanship," and he associated this so-called instinct with skilled craftsmen and with the professions, especially engineering.[3] Another economist, Thomas Nixon Carver, contrasted the "pig-trough philosophy" with the "workbench philosophy," and he recognized that it was the "pig-trough philosophy" which generated social problems.[4]

[2] See Talcott Parsons, "The Motivation of Economic Activities," *Essays in Sociological Theory* (Glencoe, Illinois: The Free Press, 1949), pp. 200–217.

[3] See Thorstein Veblen, *The Instinct of Workmanship* (New York: The Macmillan Company, 1914).

[4] Reprinted by permission of the publishers, Harvard University Press, Cambridge, Massachusetts, from Thomas Nixon Carver, *Essays in Social Justice,* 1915, pp. 126–129, by the President and Fellows of Harvard College.

. . . if there is one desire of my heart in terms of which everything else is evaluated, then everything which interferes with that desire I shall consider as a positive injury to myself. Everything which will contribute to that single and overmastering desire has a positive value to me. This rule applies to every form of competition or rivalry, whether it be sport, love, war, or business.

If the prize of success in business, say money, is the one desire of my heart, in terms of which everything else is evaluated, then everything which interferes with the fulfillment of that one desire is to me hateful. He who stands between me and the fulfillment of that desire is my enemy. On the other hand, where I engage in a game for the sake of the game and not for the sake of the prize, then he who plays the game against me and does his best to beat me, is not my enemy but my friend. Similarly in business competition, if I am animated by the spirit of the productive life, if my desire is for production rather than consumption, if I am "playing the game" not for the sole purpose of accumulating certain prizes of success, namely, consumers' goods, then he who plays the game against me and tries to beat me is my friend and not my enemy. My feelings towards him will not be unethical and unchristian. If, however, I am playing the game for the sake of the prize, for the sake of consumption, he becomes my enemy and not my friend and my feelings toward him are eminently unethical and unchristian.

From this point of view it will be perfectly clear that the evil is not to be found in competition itself, but the spirit which dominates it. This spirit in turn is determined by the philosophy of life of the competitors. They who regard the possession or consumption of wealth as the great end of life and industry will necessarily appraise everything in terms of its effect upon their possession and consumption. Anything which, or any person who interferes with or reduces their possession or consumption will be hated. Any person who promotes that possession and consumption will be prized or possibly loved. This philosophy of life may for euphony be called the pig-trough philosophy, and the manners and morals of the pig-trough will dominate the activities of the people who possess it. On the other hand, we have what may in contrast be called the workbench philosophy of life, which regards action and not possession, production and not consumption, as the prime object. They who possess this philosophy will appraise everything according to its relation to action and productivity. That only is hateful which interferes with productive action. That only is lovely which promotes productive action. If I possess this philosophy, my enemy is not the man who plays against me in a game, but the man who refuses to allow me to play at all. Likewise in business my enemy is not the man who tries to win in industrial competition, but who tries to keep me from working or competing at all.

Thus it will be seen that the fundamental question which must be settled before anything else can be settled is the question of the philosophy of life which dominates the competitive process. If the world is dominated by the pig-trough philosophy, competition is not only inevitable, but it will invariably take on the morals of the pig-trough and become unethical and unchristian. But it would be futile to attempt to correct this by doing away with industrial competition so long as the same philosophy of life dominated individuals. So long as we had learned books written on the "economy of happiness" and the "efficiency of consumption," in which everything is expressed in terms of consumers' satisfactions, so long as it was conceived to be the chief end of industry and human effort to enable men to fill their bellies with the husks of material wealth, the rivalry would be unethical and unchristian no matter what form it took, whether it were political rivalry, military rivalry, or economic rivalry. Merely changing the machinery of government, or the methods of holding property, or of conducting industry, would in no way alleviate the grim and deadly character of that rivalry.

To put Carver's point in the frame of reference of this book, professionalization does not obviate either the need to maintain a favorable self-image or the relationship between the individual's evaluation by others and his self-image. What professionalization does accomplish is to shift the emphasis of assessments from success in obtaining rewards to success in making contributions. This is most clear in the extreme case: the dedicated scientist appears more interested in what he can contribute to the advancement of knowledge than in what he gets by way of rewards from his society. This change in emphasis has consequences for each of the governing principles of American society:

1. Most obviously, it reduces the emphasis on material things. A former teacher of one of the authors would concentrate so on whatever research he happened to be doing at the time that he would forget to eat. (His family and friends watched him carefully to prevent malnutrition.) This same professor would become so engrossed in the problem he was discussing that he would not notice that the ash of his cigarette was growing perilously long. His students watched in horrified fascination until the ash finally fell on his suit and was ineffectually brushed. Clearly, he was not trying to be the nattiest sociologist in the University, and his colleagues and students respected him more rather than less because he was oblivious of clothes and food and physical comforts.

2. The institutionalization of self-reliance becomes unnecessary. In the world of commerce, self-reliance is supposed to motivate the businessman to exert himself. In a university, the chemist expects that facilities will be provided so that he can channel all his exertions into his research. If the chemist were given nothing by the university and had to wangle somehow his equipment, laboratory, reagents, and library privileges, it might be quite a test of his self-reliance to conduct research under these conditions, but most Americans would consider such self-reliance a little ridiculous and probably wasteful. Of course, for historical reasons Americans are so attached to self-reliance that the suggestion that it is no longer necessary is somewhat shocking. The self-reliant frontiersman, trusting only to his squirrel rifle, is part of America's self-image. But, in point of fact, Americans no longer live on the frontier. Self-reliance and the division of labor work at cross-purposes. To be able to do without others is impossible; and to attempt to deny one's dependence on others is to be a Dan Marner. (See pp. 194 to 201.) Perhaps Dan Marner would have been a hero of the wild frontier; in New York City, he is antisocial.

Put another way, the self-reliance principle fosters the freedom of those individuals who are prepared to be ruthlessly exploitative at the expense of those who recognize the interdependence inherent in the division of labor. From the point of view of these latter persons, the self-reliance of a Dan Marner reduces considerably *their* range of choice. On the other hand, a society which accepts the obligation of providing opportunities to its members enhances the individual's freedom to realize his full potentialities. The State Employment Service, for example, reduces the necessity for self-reliance on the part of the unemployed. Free public education obviates the necessity for a self-reliant struggle to read and write. Only by frontier standards are the school and the State Employment Service a threat to initiative.

3. Competition tends to change its emphasis. Of course, competition remains a method of allocating people to roles. Thus, scientists compete for grants from foundations; and professors compete for academic promotions. The biologist whose colleague publishes first the theory *he* is working on may feel as worthless and inadequate as the business executive whose colleague is promoted to the vice-presidency he hoped to get.[5] However, competition among scientists is *less likely* to produce such feelings of inadequacy and worthlessness. This is because the scientist, in his devotion to the advancement of knowledge, tends to be more concerned with "truth" and less concerned with the differential rewards which *he* receives from the successful pursuit of truth. Competitors for a role do not necessarily have an intense emotional investment in playing the role themselves. For example, it is conceivable that a Rutgers freshman tries out for the Varsity football team and, when he fails to make the team because of the availability of better players, is not too disappointed. He may be more interested in seeing *Rutgers* have a strong football team than in *his* playing on the team. In precisely the same way, the scientist may care less about the honor of being the discoverer of a new principle than in seeing the principle discovered. Thus, for the socialized member of the scientific community, self-assessment does not depend on competitive success to the same extent that a businessman's self-assessment depends on *his* competitive success.

4. Finally, the principle of negotiated exchange, like that of competition, tends to operate differently under conditions of professionalization. Consider the notoriously weak relationship between scientific importance and commercial value. A university physicist with a world-wide reputation may earn one-third the salary of his former student now employed by an industrial research laboratory. Under these conditions the rewards

[5] See Robert K. Merton, "Priorities in Scientific Discovery: a chapter in the Sociology of Science," *American Sociological Review,* Vol. 22 (December, 1957), pp. 635–663.

obtainable as a result of the process of negotiated exchange are less a basis for self-assessment than the data for social accounting. Poorly rewarded roles are less critical to the society.[6]

Of course, professionalization is a matter of degree. Just as athletic rivals vary in motivation from those who play only to win to those who play for the fun of playing, so there are degrees of dedication to one's occupational role. Moreover, this variation in dedication is not confined to what are ordinarily thought of as professions. As Nelson Foote, an industrial sociologist, points out, there are strong elements of professionalization even in the labor role.[7]

The concept of the professionalization of management . . . is familiar and goes back at least as far in social thought as the book by another profound nonacademic sociologist, Mr. Justice Brandeis' *Business—a Profession.* The concept of the professionalization of labor, however, is so novel as to require clarification. . . . Professionalization generally implies the transformation of some nonprofessional occupation into a vocation with the attributes of a profession, and the specification of these could be indefinitely detaining. As a modicum, the possession (1) of a specialized technique supported by a body of theory, (2) of a career supported by an association of colleagues, and (3) of a status supported by community recognition may be mentioned as constituting an occupation as a profession.

Now the sons of laboring men may become professionals by the university route, as multitudes in Detroit do. And the proportion of engineers and other professionals in the working force may increase at the expense of what is normally meant by labor in that city. This, too, is happening; technical schools are turning out graduates at a forced pace and are still falling far short of demand. But, strictly speaking, to speak of the professionalization of labor in Detroit is to describe what is happening to the laboring men themselves. By every criterion of professionalism

[6] Of course, financial rewards are not the only type of reward to be taken into account. The physicist may consider himself compensated in prestige for his (relatively) low university salary.

[7] Reprinted from "The Professionalization of Labor in Detroit," by Nelson N. Foote, which was published in the *American Journal of Sociology,* Vol. 58 (January, 1953), pp. 371–379, by permission of The University of Chicago Press, Chicago, Illinois. Copyright 1953, by The University of Chicago Press.

which sociologists would take as valid, they are becoming professionalized.

To consider only the three minimum attributes.

1. Save for the unskilled jobs not directly in the sequence of production, like sweeping, each operation in Detroit manufacturing utilizes more and more general theory—mathematical, physical, chemical, even physiological and social-psychological —as improvements in product and process are evolved. The skilled and the semiskilled worker are being replaced by engineers; the unskilled, by complex automatic machinery under the tutelage of dial-watchers who are engineers also. Many such operations, to perform which wins more or less freely the designation of engineer, are done by men who did not go to an engineering college but were retrained on the job and upgraded. It has already become reasonable to imagine a point very few decades off when almost every employee in the plants of Detroit will be an engineer of one kind or another.

The basic conditions which make this outcome possible are that it corresponds not only with popular aspirations, which could be unavailing, but with a development in the nature of manufacturing itself. That development calls for a new concept, which we shall term "the generalization of processes." . . . some students of industry are still struggling with the conception of mass-production methods as necessarily requiring the breaking-down of formerly complex and skilled manual operations. Yet the division now found everywhere in advanced manufacturing industries between the development of product and of process has made nearly obsolete the dilemma caused by the degradation of skills. As soon as imaginative attention is reoriented from the final product to the processes by which it is formed, a resynthesis commences, proceeding along the axis of theory and not by the putting-together again in their old combinations . . . operations which had been broken down—a procedure proposed by the romantics. The movement toward fractionation is countered, and the trend is inevitably toward professionalization as an intrinsic feature of further industrialization.

What happens is this: once attention is focused upon process, it immediately becomes plain that there is an expanding repertoire of processes which develops independently of the identity of the products made. Operations like metal-finishing, for instance, become the same throughout industry. Likenesses in processes are recognized, published, standardized, and elaborated around the world; the single industry ceases to be distinguished by the peculiar skills of its workmen and retains its identity only through its product and market. Improvements in product depend upon invention of the sort symbolized by Thomas Edison, but improvements in process depend upon research and experiment requiring basic scientific theory. Here is the reason for the recent geometric expansion of industrial research; here, also, for the marvelous efficiency and massive growth of subcontracting. Once freed from bondage to particular products, the possibilities for analyzing and generalizing processes are illimitable.

The exploration of the implications of this fundamental reorganization of manufacturing perspective is a painfully unfilled gap in the literature of industrial sociology. That it transforms industrial operations into technique guided by theory is its obvious relevance here. Second, the explosive force of the unceasing technological changes so unleashed is an obvious instance of a diligently pursued activity which, as said above, makes return to a static and stratified order more and more incredible. One example only, taken from General Motors: the steam-locomotive industry, thanks to the development of diesel electrics, is being rapidly wiped out; but, while the particular skills of the old-fashioned boilermakers are thus made obsolete, the general techniques of the one industry's engineers are readily transferable to the other. If there is to be security for personnel, it will come not through trying to freeze the status quo, as in the building trades, but through acquiring generally transferable techniques guided by theory: not to cling to dry land, as it were, but to float.

2. The second essential of professionalism is that careers be supported and regulated by the association of colleagues. It is repeatedly asserted that the unions during the past half-generation have sought security for their members. While this observa-

tion cannot be denied, it is unduly simple. If attention is focused upon the industrial unions—both CIO and AF of L—and consideration given to the succession of changes they have forced upon industry, we must agree . . . that the philosophies neither of class struggle nor of business unionism suffice to explain their actions, however well they may fit selected manifestations. A few of their policies and practices, to be sure, can be validly understood as expressions of those inherited definitions of the situation. In the symposium sponsored two years ago by the Industrial Relations Research Association, for example, several critics made a plausible case for interpreting the latest demands of the United Auto Workers under Walter Reuther as nothing more than the old familiar cry for more. Likewise, no one living among the steel strikers of South Chicago while they were out [in the summer of 1952] could fail to recognize that a bitter and painful class struggle was going on. . . .

What the industrial unions are trying to do, above, beyond, and often in spite of the things unions have done traditionally, is so to reconstruct industry as to assure to every man in it a career. And a career, nowadays, is far more than a status and a function. Perhaps the difference could be sketched by saying that a career is a procession of statuses and functions which unfold in a more or less orderly though undetermined sequence in the pursuit of values which themselves emerge in the course of experience.

The history of the successive major achievements of the United Auto Workers of Detroit may suffice to illustrate this interpretation. To demonstrate its validity and adequacy depends of course upon its success, relative to other interpretations, as the basis for predicting what is to come. The union contract can be viewed as a log of past achievements. In Detroit guessing what clauses will be added is a great game known in union circles as "What next?" and in management circles as "Now what?" It is a game the sociologist can learn to play and learn from playing.

Recognition of the union as bargaining agent was necessarily the first step and remains the first clause of every contract. In Detroit that decisive step was taken in 1937 only after challenge and struggle over the previous conceptions of property—which definitely did not include property in a job. In the usual second clause, which delimits the bargaining unit, how carefully "employeeship" is defined! Every contract we know disputes the assertion that everyone in the corporation is an employee. And it is the union which wants ever to widen the definition; it is the management which is unwilling. The third clause, usually devoted to union security—and still in process of development, as in the recent steel dispute—is largely an extension of the first and second. Thereafter, in no standard order, come the major clauses which represent the successive achievements in reorganizing the social structure of industry.

The right of representation—the whole theory of representative government, by implication—is written into the representation clause, just as the common-law philosophy of right to counsel and fair trial is written into the clause on grievance procedure. Each man stands not as an individual alone but as a member of a body governed by public law and the principle of equality before the law, in the writing of which he has had the opportunity to participate through representatives. Within the bargaining unit, these provisions create a society of political equals, and, while political equality alone does not make a society of equals, it is a precondition.

The seniority clause might seem pre-eminently to justify the interpretation that what the worker wants is secure status and function. Its almost universal inclusion in contracts answers an almost universal demand for recognition of a continuous and deepening obligation to the employee by the corporation which employs him, as shown further by the fact that seniority provisions often extend far beyond the ranks covered in formal bargaining units. As a protection against arbitrary termination of this relationship, seniority seems permanently established as a just institution. It insures that any man can hold the place he has gained, short of justifiable discharge or company collapse. But it is, in its more dynamic aspects, especially in connection with promotion and transfer, that seniority most conspicuously contributes to making possible a predictable, developing career. And it is here that the union typically presses for extension of

the principle; management, for its containment. Superficial observation suggests that seniority operates to hamper and restrict
the efficiency of a growing firm, because newer employees cannot be promoted over older. But in actual practice, however, no
one gets promoted by seniority to a job he cannot handle. The
gain in morale, in the stability of the working force, in the elimination of nepotism and favoritism—all are credits to be set
against the lesser gains derived from management's free-handed
control of promotion. By making everyone wait his turn, everyone is assured eventually of reaching a job which matches his
highest powers, which is one object of a career. The really
genuine impediment to the function of seniority in making fullest
use of the talents of every employee is due to the restrictions
upon transfer horizontally within the system, not to the orderly
scheduling of promotions upward. Management has not welcomed extensions of the seniority unit, and in most cases it
remains only department-wide. In some cases, it is plant-wide,
but rarely is it company-wide, and never industry-wide. Generally when a worker changes jobs outside his department or
plant, regardless of cause, he loses all the ground he has gained
in length of service. Ultimately the pressure for labor mobility
will come even from management for the merging of seniority
jurisdictions so as to expedite transfers. . . .

Most contracts in industry carry provisions closely associated
with the seniority clause which govern procedure on layoffs and
rehiring when employment is discontinuous. But what is involved here comes out most fully and uniquely in a demand as
yet embodied in very few contracts—the demand for continuous
income. The annual wage is but another name for the salary and,
in the view set forth here, is one of the most convincing evi-
dences of the movement toward professionalization of labor. For
the salary has become standard for the professional; even the
older professions, which during the liberal era subsisted on fees,
are moving steadily toward salaried status. The two largest professions, engineering and teaching, are almost completely salaried: the steady unionization of these two groups in Detroit is
replete with ambiguities which dramatize the transformation of
professionalism itself. At the moment, the coming of the annual

wage seems as far off as the coming of worker pensions seemed just before it happened. When it comes, we can expect a loosening of current contract clauses dealing with hours of work and overtime pay—except for regulation of numbers of apprentices, perhaps the most traditional clause in the contract. Standards as to services required will remain, of course, but the precise calculation of hours given in a week is derived from the old conception that the relation of worker to employer is that of seller and buyer. Professionals on salary do not count their hours so strictly or measure their obligation primarily by this unit. The annual wage or salary offers not merely steady income but dignity and responsibility to the job and to its holder; these too are aspects of a career.

In the case of the 1948–49 contest over pensions, the resolution of labor was strengthened, and the resistance of management was weakened, by the argument that management was unjust in taking pensions for itself while denying them to labor. The demand for the annual wage is fortified by the same emphasis upon equality and will be no easier to withstand as it gathers force. It is now labor's next item on the agenda, as publicly announced.

The silent revolution by which American industry took responsibility for its aged workers would surely have baffled the revolutionaries of 1848—especially the authors who that year wrote the *Communist Manifesto*. Subsidized retirement plans are neither socialist nor liberal, and, despite their expression of fraternal obligation, it is as absurd to compare them with feudal guilds as to condemn them as handouts. Not only is the high proportion of aged workers strictly a modern phenomenon but the gigantic trust funds now administered jointly by union and management for the welfare of workers were hardly conceivable prior to the unique conditions of latter days. With regard to health insurance, another welfare clause in recent contracts, interpretation is somewhat confused by the fact that the industrial unions seem to regard it as a stop-gap on their way to making free access to the means of health a function of government, like free public education, rather than a function of the corporation. Even if so, the union may still have to be the guardian as it is of workmen's compensation and unemployment insurance. The more advanced health clauses, except of course for sick leave with pay, cover the whole family rather than the employee alone, as is also true, in a sense, of life insurance plans. These complications tend to hide the career implications of welfare provisions from a first glance across their widening range. But, while we have concentrated upon contract clauses, it makes little difference if union achievements in establishing welfare mechanisms are written into contracts or into social legislation, as long as their purpose remains the same. When a man and his family are pressed too closely by the hazards of existence—age, injury, sickness, death, loss of income—his attention must be concentrated upon short-time survival. If this can be more or less guaranteed by mutual aid, the sense of security gained is not only seen as a good thing in itself but opens up opportunities for self-development, a longer view of personal planning, and an elaboration of self-consciousness, which are basic to a career. The degree to which workers consciously foresaw what could follow, once their life histories were no longer a succession of emergencies, could be debated. There is undebatable evidence of many kinds—in home-building, recreation, community activity —that achievement of insurance against disasters has led not to torpor and loss of moral fiber, as hostile persons charge, but to self-development. . . .

By this point it may seem more reasonable than when first suggested above to assert that the best oracle from which to derive predictions is to ascertain in what directions the unions are pressing and the companies are resisting. Thus there are several other standard clauses which constitute legal recognition of major changes wrought, or still being wrought, in the social organization of industry. Only a few more need mentioning to complete the case for professionalization as embodied in career.

Thus we come to the steady pressure, not only against long hours of work, but for holidays and vacations, by which the leisure time of the mass of Detroiters has already been multiplied several-fold, with all this means for personal development. Consider likewise the stabilization of employment effected through the introduction of arbitration clauses and the umpire system as a means of reducing sporadic stoppages—a development which became almost universal at the end of the war, following War Labor Board experience, but for which the initiative came primarily from the union. Finally, unimagined new demands lie ahead, instrumental to making careers open to all.

3. Following the standard divisions of culture into technology, social organization, and ideology, we come finally to the evidence for professionalization in the third respect. It is common for anthropologists to include under ideology not only such patterns as religion, values, and ethics but also language and knowledge in general.

It is important to recall technology here, because the professionalization of labor presents a challenge to certain commercial attitudes toward the possession of technology, construed as nonmaterial knowledge. In establishing the Republic, a desire to secure to the inventor the just fruits of his genius led to laws of patent and copyright. As these have worked out since, however, a steady process of commercialization has tended to use the patent system to fasten various kinds and degrees of monopoly upon technology, as if it were private property. As long as invention was construed as applying to specific products, that commercial view was perhaps permissible, though much could be said in condemnation of certain of its consequences. As recognized in patent law itself, however, when referring to basic processes, the claim to private property in technology contradicts the concept of science as a joint stock of generalizations to which all men have contributed and to which all men should have free right of access and use. The generalization of industrial processes mentioned above is going to make progressively harder the task of those who seek to utilize the patent system as a device for monopolizing technology and extracting thereby a stream of unearned income for themselves. That is, one of the conspicuous ethical principles of organized science is the obligation to publish findings freely, to keep no secrets for commercial (or national) advantage. Fortunately, certain leaders in industrial research, like Mr. Kettering of General Motors, have long cautioned against any opposition by business to this principle, and perhaps for this reason no contest seems imminent.

Meanwhile the body of generalized know-how continues to grow mightily and will grow even faster as corporations give stronger support to basic research.

Now there is only one way, apart from enjoying its products, that a citizen may come to employ his claim to that vast body of socialized knowledge. That way, of course, is education and, in particular, higher education. One of the most impressive findings made in Detroit was the unwillingness of youngsters there to enter vocational high schools; whether they achieve college or not, they prefer college entrance courses, to the exasperation of firms seeking able apprentices. As everyone knows, the transfer of general knowledge is a more arduous process—for both giver and receiver—than of any other kind of property known. Simple inheritance from one's parent is minimal; each must acquire for himself. Yet acquisition of a share of this knowledge has come to be a more effective and persistent means of claiming an income from the community, and having it honored, than almost any other. The Jeffersonian idea held that free public education was necessary so that each citizen might cast his weight in democratic government. As exhibited in hundreds of beautiful temples of learning around Detroit, this ideal pulses more strongly than ever, but it has received a new infusion of meaning through the professionalization of labor. Increasingly free public higher education is becoming the evident and required means whereby each man can claim his full patrimony in the industrial system. The recent G. I. Bill for Korea veterans is only the second of many measures which are sure to follow. Regardless of their immediate financial difficulties, faculty members of the colleges and universities can count on multiplying demand. In particular there is bound to be a tremendous growth of refresher and re-training courses for previous graduates, as the rate of innovation climbs further in every field of knowledge. The time is not far off when three or four weeks of a worker's year may be spent in a "workshop"—college style.

Certain consequences of this trend seem predictable by inference. One of these is that the man who does not keep growing on his job will find his position increasingly insecure, as his qualifications for the job grow obsolete in relation to those of

others. The permanent maintenance of an advantageous status
position, as if the position itself were his property, may become
more difficult. On the other hand, the positive incentive for the
refreshing of competence may come more from interest in the
progress of one's career, viewed retrospectively and prospec-
tively, and less from simple status comparisons, viewed competitively. There are many ways by which an order of aspiration
and development like this might be embodied organizationally,
so that it would be futile to predict which forms will be tried.
But this much can be assayed in advance: *where emphasis is put
upon the development of personal careers rather than upon
preferment in a hierarchical system of status relatively unrelated
to actual contribution, the sense of incessant striving for a
security which is never attained will diminish in American industry.*[8] The present psychological state of affairs, especially in
management ranks, is hardly a tribute to our ingenuity in organizing structures in a way to achieve purposes. In the revolutionary productivity clause of the General Motors contract, the
way has been opened to make economic development a social
value shared by all the personnel of industry, as against the invidious and vain pursuit of local competitive advantage. The
rate of circulation of individuals up and down between the
layers of a hierarchy is a very puny dynamic for economic
development as against the sharing by appropriate organization
of a common interest in economic development. . . .

It was said above that a profession is characterized by a
code of ethics supported by public trust. Multitudinous though
subtle harbingers of this outcome may perhaps be summarized
by pointing to the image of the responsible worker acting competently and conscientiously within a framework of rules and
accepted tasks. The evolution in Detroit has been realizing this
ideal so fast during the last fifteen years that the old order has
almost been lost from memory. Those who knew the old shop
department in Detroit and the way it was dominated by the
foreman can testify, however, to the scope of the transformation
which has been worked. The foreman has been nearly super-

[8] Emphasis supplied by Bredemeier and Toby.

seded, remaining primarily as a trainer of new workers, a fixer of "bugs," and a scheduler and reporter of work and materials flow, often holding his job subject to informal veto by his men. The standard grievance system—which many observers agree is the most important day-to-day influence of the union upon the worker, coupled with institutions like last-step arbitration and the umpire system—have steadily indoctrinated both labor and management in the understanding and observance of an objective and fair set of work rules and standards, supported by all. In the sense in which the term means most to Detroit workers, "bosses" are being replaced by impersonal rules which they help to make and enforce.

In some respects, it is not easy to identify the client public of the worker in industry. If it is taken to be the consumer of the industry's product or service, however, it must be noted that professional standards of quality and dependability have steadily triumphed over commercial short-cutting. The credit here probably goes more to the engineering societies than to the unions, but it nonetheless constitutes the professionalization of which we speak. In the gestating philosophy of Detroit's union leaders there are already many concrete declarations testifying to their widening sense of responsibility toward the consumer, as to prices. This evolution has been several times arrested, but again there is evidence on which to predict further movement along these lines, as the logic of professionalization would suggest.

Industrial union leaders are leaders not merely of their unions but of the citizenry of the entire industrial community, outside the plant as much as inside, as much now as during any of the previous fifteen years. This is pre-eminently true in politics but extends into the voluntary associations, into race relations, and even into the formation of public opinion on world affairs. Indeed, while by no means does it appear justifiable to describe them cynically as a new elite, it is illuminating to recognize that the union proper is only one of the several vehicles this group of leaders employs to carry forward a program which embraces fundamental changes in the social structure of the entire industrial community. . . .

SUMMARY

To summarize, the prospect of a society in which everyone becomes a professional—the equal of colleagues in his own, and the equivalent of members of other professions, despite unlimited qualitative differentiation—is that toward which advanced industrial communities seem to be moving.

We believe that professionalization tends to develop in most occupational roles and also in roles that are not occupational at all. For example, aspects of professionalization seem to be infiltrating the housewife role. The drudge has turned into a combination dietician-child psychologist-interior decorator-accountant-purchasing agent. Of course, this is not to say that professionalization is a panacea. We believe, it is true, that the frustrations generated by the materialistic orientation of American society will decrease if the trend toward professionalization goes much further. On the other hand, American society is proverbially complex; there are so many directions in which it is moving simultaneously; only the foolhardy would attempt to predict the course of American casualties and costs.

ANNOTATED BIBLIOGRAPHY

Addams, Jane, *Twenty Years at Hull House* (New York: The Macmillan Company, 1910). ⟮ An autobiographical account of a well-educated woman who dedicated her life to bringing hope into the lives of the residents of a Chicago slum. The settlement house movement which Jane Addams helped to launch is now an institutionalized feature of the American scene.

Carr-Saunders, A. M., and Wilson, P. A., *The Professions* (Oxford: Clarendon Press, 1933). ⟮ A scholarly account of the history of the professions in Great Britain. Although this pioneering book does not concern itself exclusively with those aspects of professionalization which are discussed in Chapter 17, it provides valuable background for understanding professionalization in all its aspects.

Drucker, Peter, *Landmarks of Tomorrow* (New York: Harper & Brothers, 1959). ⟮ A stimulating discussion of the need for and probabilities of developing changed attitudes toward work, in the light of the modern scientific and organizational revolution.

Finer, Herman, *Road to Reaction* (Boston: Little, Brown & Company, 1945). ⟮ A rebuttal of Hayek's *The Road to Serfdom* by a leading political scientist. Finer warns that Hayek's position is a road to authoritarian reaction.

Hayek, Friedrich A., *The Road to Serfdom* (Chicago: University of Chicago Press, 1944). ⟮ The argument for self-reliance, bargaining, and competition by an economist. Hayek warns that efforts similar to those suggested by the present authors lead to "serfdom."

Jung, Carl, *Modern Man in Search of a Soul* (New York: Harcourt, Brace and Company, Inc., 1933). ⟨ An analysis of the psychological problems of modern man in spiritual terms. Jung, a famous psychoanalyst, summarizes his clinical experience as follows: "Among all my patients in the second half of life—that is to say, over thirty-five—there has not been one whose problem in the last resort was not that of finding a religious outlook on life."

Merton, Robert K., *Social Theory and Social Structure* (Glencoe, Illinois: The Free Press, revised edition, 1957). ⟨ Chapters 11 and 12 (15 and 16 in the revised edition), entitled "Science and the Social Order" and "Science and Democratic Social Structure," illuminate the ethos of science in a way that makes clear its contrast to "self-reliant materialism."

Schweitzer, Albert, *Out of my Life and Thought* (New York: Henry Holt and Company, Inc., 1949). ⟨ The autobiography of a man often called "one of the world's truly great men." Musician, philosopher, theologian, physician, and medical missionary, Schweitzer in many ways illustrates a world view which could obviate the social problems described in this textbook.

Tumin, Melvin M., "Rewards and Task Orientation," *American Sociological Review,* Vol. 20 (1955), pp. 419–423. ⟨ A clear analysis of the difference between competition for rewards and competition for productive task performance. We have modified the title of Dr. Tumin's paper for the subtitle of one section of this chapter.

Wootton, Barbara, *Freedom Under Planning* (Chapel Hill, North Carolina: University of North Carolina Press, 1945). ⟨ An economist's analysis, in nontechnical terms, of the possibilities of combining freedom with a planned economy. In general, the author argues that freedom and planning are compatible.

Index of contributors and annotated authors

Subject index